Betrayed

Betrayed
Promoting Inclusive Development in Fragile States

Seth D. Kaplan

First published in hardcover in 2013 by PALGRAVE MACMILLAN® in the United States—a division of St. Martin's Press LLC, 175 Fifth Avenue, New York, NY 10010.

Where this book is distributed in the UK, Europe, and the rest of the world, this is by Palgrave Macmillan, a division of Macmillan Publishers Limited, registered in England, company number 785998, of Houndmills, Basingstoke, Hampshire RG21 6XS.

Palgrave Macmillan is the global academic imprint of the above companies and has companies and representatives throughout the world.

Palgrave® and Macmillan® are registered trademarks in the United States, the United Kingdom, Europe and other countries.

ISBN: 978-1-137-51842-2

The Library of Congress has cataloged the hardcover edition as follows:

Kaplan, Seth D.
    Betrayed : politics, power, and prosperity / Seth D. Kaplan.
        pages cm
    ISBN 978-1-137-35303-0
        1. Poverty—Developing countries. 2. Economic development—Political aspects—Developing countries. 3. Equality—Developing countries. I. Title.
HC59.72.P6K365 2013
339.4'6091724—dc23   2013020508

A catalogue record of the book is available from the British Library.

Design by Amnet.

First Palgrave Macmillan paperback edition: January 2016

10 9 8 7 6 5 4 3 2 1

For Esther

Contents

List of Tables and Figures

Foreword

By Jerry Rawlings, Former President of the Republic of Ghana

To be an African today is to be both an optimist and a pessimist. In some ways, Africa is doing better than a generation ago. There are fewer wars, and conflicts, although just as we congratulate ourselves on this, another erupts as it has recently done in Mali. There is (a little) less poverty, elections are more common, and economic growth rates are up. All this is encouraging. But the 1990s were a very tough time in much of Africa; so, while the recent improvements are welcome, they are long overdue. They have made a bad situation a little better. They have not transformed Africa's situation. Numerous severe problems remain, and they have very deep roots.

Chief among those problems is the failure to share economic growth equitably. Weak governments and political regimes dominated by selfish elites are letting powerful cliques, clans, and classes grab the lion's share of the benefits of progress. Those at the bottom of society get the scraps, if they get anything at all.

At first glance, many countries look as if they are making solid progress, the kind of progress that many assume must surely trickle down. Nigeria, for instance, has enjoyed over a decade of democracy and strong growth spurred by high oil prices. But Nigeria's poverty levels have not dropped—they have risen.

Across the developing world, the same pattern repeats itself: There *is* economic growth, and a few people are doing extraordinarily well while a small middle class is making healthy gains; but most people are seeing only modest increases in their incomes, if at all. Pervasive forms of exclusion and discrimination ensure that most people cannot escape their poverty. A similar phenomenon is evident in the global North, but it is much less extreme than in the South.

Better access to education, to new technology, and to ideas and information from around the world has increased popular expectations—but they are rarely being met. The resulting frustration has been driving millions into the streets to demand the chance to better their lives. The Arab Spring is often interpreted as a demand for political democracy, but it is really the product of anger over unequal access to opportunity. A vast underclass of people want to be treated as equals—with equal access to public services, infrastructure, good schools, business licenses, and courts. Cries for change are really cries for admittance to economic, political, social, and legal systems that work equally well for everyone.

One in every two people in the world lives in a country that does not provide access to opportunity, largely because of failures in how elites and governments act. The door is firmly closed to everyone except those with the wealth, the power, or the connections to take advantage of weak institutions and bribe corrupt officials.

This situation can be addressed only when elites and leaders stop betraying their responsibility to govern for the benefit of *all* citizens. Power is not something to be taken lightly. The powerful bear a heavy responsibility to those they govern. Traditional societies understood this very well. Their leaders—whether tribal chiefs in Africa or clan chiefs in Central Asia—knew that by fulfilling the moral obligation to govern wisely and fairly they would enhance not only their own prestige but also their communities' well-being. But colonialism weakened these ancient bonds, and many postcolonial states are still struggling to find a way to bind governments to peoples.

In the absence of equitable government ministries, impartial court systems, and all the other well-run institutions that enable states to work for the benefit of entire societies, the developing world needs political, business, nongovernmental, and community leaders who have the public interest at heart, who are fundamentally *inclusive*. What should such leaders seek to accomplish? They should strengthen national institutions so that they function efficiently and equitably, and this strengthening is not merely a matter of providing more funding and resources, but of morality. They should work hard to ensure that no group or region is left behind. They should bridge divisions while challenging self-centered political cultures. They should ensure that everyone has the chance to share in the benefits of economic growth.

This is what my government tried to achieve when I was president of Ghana. We worked hard to strengthen the sense of common identity, decentralized power to enable many more citizens to become part of the decision-making process, increased spending in less developed parts of the country, introduced a long series of economic reforms to jumpstart the ailing economy, and built up new institutions that would foster a new political culture in the country. None of this was easy: we had to overcome many obstacles, face down many opponents, adapt to changing circumstances, create new coalitions, and challenge many assumptions along the way. We made significant progress, but inevitably there is much still to do. Change comes slowly to a country, and so a country needs leaders with the determination and perseverance to see it through. Indeed, painfully achieved gains can quickly slip away if subsequent leaders either take them for granted or are seduced by opportunities for self-aggrandizement.

Seth Kaplan makes a compelling and eloquent argument for empowering all citizens, especially the poor. He explains how hard-working individuals are shackled to their poverty, how discrimination stifles the entrepreneurial hopes of entire groups of people, and how political and economic exclusion conspire to keep elites rich at everyone else's expense. Having revealed the systemic mechanisms that keep so many people poor, Kaplan then presents a very different kind of apparatus, one that can empower, enrich, and uplift. It is, he says, up to the elites and leaders of the developing world to start building and operating this machinery. To be sure, the international community has a role to play, but it is a supportive role. In this drama of empowerment, it will be the men and women of the developing world who take center stage.

Acknowledgments

First of all, I want to thank Esther, who provided not only support and patience throughout the writing of this book but also love.

This book could not have been written without the generous assistance and wise advice of many people over the years.

In particular, I want to thank all the people who made a special effort to review the book and provide comments: Frauke de Weijer of the European Centre for Development Policy Management (ECDPM); Consul General Stephen Engelken, recently retired from the State Department; Mark Freeman, the Executive Director of Institute for Integrated Transitions (IFIT); Duncan Green, Oxfam's Senior Strategic Adviser; Kate Almquist Knopf of the Center for Global Development; Judith Manelis, independent consultant; Marco Mezzera of the Norwegian Peacebuilding Resource Centre (NOREF); Gary Milante of the World Bank; and Andrew Natsios, former Administrator of the U.S. Agency for International Development (USAID) and currently Executive Professor at Texas A&M University. Others at the Overseas Development Institute and Princeton University have contributed many ideas to the book over the years. I am especially grateful to editor Nigel Quinney for his guidance in shaping the book and excellent line editing.

At Johns Hopkins University, Peter Lewis, Paul Lubeck, Melissa Thomas, Julie Micek, and their colleagues were not only very supportive as I prepared the final draft but also helped make my transition to a new school and city much easier than I thought possible.

I am also indebted to all the unnamed scholars, policymakers, development experts, on-the-ground development workers, government officials, business executives, entrepreneurs, and other professionals from across the world who have helped me understand the dynamics of developing countries over the years.

I owe a heavy debt of gratitude to the people of the developing world I have met during my research for this book. Some I have worked with; others have kindly hosted me on my travels or given graciously of their time to share their experiences and insights. Thousands, indeed millions, of the people I have seen in the poorer parts of the world have inspired me with their endeavor and enterprise in circumstances that would daunt and dispirit many of us from richer countries.

This book belongs to all of these people no less than it belongs to me. Except, of course, for the mistakes: they are all mine.

ACKNOWLEDGEMENTS

PART I

An Old Problem

CHAPTER 1

The Same Species, the Same Dreams

Over the past twenty-five years, I have traveled in some of the world's poorest countries, such as Somalia and Bolivia, and worked alongside some of the poorest citizens in developing countries, such as Nigeria and China. Working as an investor and manager in the developing world, I have had to deal with the rich and the powerful. But I have also had to recruit local employees and research what products local people need and desire. And I have had to confront at least a few of the same challenges—bureaucratic mazes that lead nowhere, officials who will do nothing without a bribe, shortages of everything from fresh water to electricity—that the locals endure in spades. I have also spent weeks and months as a guest in the homes of everyday families from Rada in Yemen to Coroico in Bolivia, from Multan in Pakistan to Mombasa in Kenya, in each place seeking to learn about the local culture and society.

Some of the poor people I have met had become resigned to their fate, had grown passive because of past failure, or had tired of trying to overcome resistance to change within their family or community. Others were fearful of losing the little they did possess by investing in business ventures, or they lacked the skills, savings, or contacts to believe they could get far. Yet the vast majority was brimming with energy and initiative.

During the seven years I lived in China, for instance, I witnessed millions of poor people help transform global supply chains and geopolitical relationships. Employees, colleagues, and friends rarely lacked for determination. Their grandparents and parents often had been illiterate and desperately poor, and the younger generation has been more than happy to take risks and work tirelessly to escape the same fate.

The Chinese have been able to build themselves a better future because they have been fortunate to have both of the two key ingredients for robust economic growth: First, they live in a country whose people are linked together through extensive social networks and who share a common identity. Thus, there are few societal barriers preventing the great majority of people from seeking their fortune on a relatively level playing field. Second, their government finally adopted a set of policies to capitalize on China's enormous pool of human and social capital—an emphasis on inclusive, export-led growth and on investing in infrastructure and education.

This winning combination has helped China make great strides forward over the past three decades. It's hardly perfect, of course. China still suffers from the widespread corruption and malfeasance typical of struggling states and still lacks the mechanisms to hold officials accountable, typical of democratic regimes. But it's on the right track. A friend, Zou Qifang, like many across the country, struggled to acquire an education when he was young (before the government started its development drive) but has over the past decade built the country's largest chain of dental clinics. Bit by bit, he learned the management skills he has needed to grow his business. Similar tales could be told of nearly all of the country's most successful entrepreneurs.

What I have seen not only in East Asia but also in West Africa, the Middle East, South America, and other poorer or downright impoverished corners of the globe has dramatically changed my picture of the world's poor. My unique perspective has fostered an appreciation for the talents and ambitions—and the obstacles—that are typically ignored or airbrushed out of the portraits of the poor to be found in media reports and aid appeals.

The poor are not a different species from us. Nor are they culturally unrecognizable. Like us, they have dreams for themselves and their families, and they are willing to take risks when they see something worth achieving. They display resourcefulness, sometimes getting ahead and sometimes suffering setbacks. And just like us, there are great differences among individuals in their attitudes, skills, and experiences.

If anything, the world's poor must work harder and show more initiative than we do because the challenges they face are so great. Difficult circumstances beget resourcefulness and creativity beyond what we can imagine, because we have grown up in predictable environments. We know precisely what we need to do to graduate from high school, to get into college, to build a career. We know—or can easily discover—what we need to do to set up and run a business. We assume that if our legal rights are abused, we will get our day in court. We expect when we turn on a faucet, we will get water, when we flick a switch, we will see light. The poor in the developing world have no such luxuries. Their education is typically brief and irregular. To grow a business they have to pay bribes they cannot afford and jump dozens of bureaucratic hurdles they cannot see. The courts, perhaps the entire legal system, may be closed to them or weighted against them. If they have a faucet to turn or a switch to flick, it may work, but it may not—not today, and maybe not tomorrow, next week, or next month.

But what the poor lack most of all is opportunity.

*   *   *

The poor are poor because they are excluded, deliberately or not, from opportunity—from the opportunity to go to school, to get funding to grow their businesses, to get a fair hearing in a court of law. The elites who control corrupt governments and divided societies don't just keep prosperity out of reach; they don't let the poor even see the glimmer of a brighter future.

Instead of working to build inclusive societies with growing prosperity for all, most of those with power and money prefer to serve their own narrow self-interests—even if it means that many of their compatriots will go without proper schooling, remain stuck in shantytowns for life, or even starve. The Nigerian novelist Chinua Achebe points an accusing finger at his own country's leaders, but what he says is true about the elites in many corners of the developing world:

> The trouble with Nigeria is simply and squarely a failure of leadership. There is nothing basically wrong with the Nigerian character. There is nothing wrong with the Nigerian land or climate or water or air or anything else. The Nigerian problem is the unwillingness or inability of its leaders to rise to the responsibility, to the challenge of personal example which are the hallmarks of true leadership. . . . Does it ever worry us that history which neither personal wealth nor power can pre-empt will pass terrible judgment on us, pronounce anathema on our names when we have accomplished our betrayal and passed on? We have lost the twentieth century; are we bent on seeing that our children also lose the twenty-first? God forbid![1]

The anger palpable during the Arab Spring can be felt in slums, cities, and farms across the developing world, where hundreds of millions of people feel betrayed by those who control the levers of power and wealth in their countries and use that power for their own benefit. As Paulo Silva, who lives in a slum in Luanda, Angola's capital, angrily states, "Angola is a rich country, but we don't get any of it. The people in power are eating all the money."[2] Or as one member of a discussion group in Kagera, Tanzania, explains, "When you have no power, stop dreaming; you will have no freedom, no equality, and democracy will remain a story to you."[3]

If the poor are given opportunity—if they are allowed to see the chance of a brighter future and to reach for it—they can transform their own lives. Policies that offer a better chance of participating as equals in marketplaces and governments can unleash the power of hundreds of millions. Equal access to schooling, financial services, information, transportation, courts, and other drivers of empowerment will transform the lives not just of individuals and families but also of businesses, communities, and entire countries. But much has to change first.

A number of other books published in the past few years have focused on the world's poor, but none has focused on the poor as the instruments of their own salvation. Authors such as William Easterly (*The White Man's Burden*), Paul Collier (*The Bottom Billion*), and Jeffrey Sachs (*The End of Poverty*) have instead tended to concentrate on the role of outsiders, especially Western governments and aid agencies.[4] Other writers, such as Dambisa Moyo (*Dead Aid*), have sought somewhat simplistic solutions in the better use of international financial markets.[5] Hernando de Soto (*The Other Path* and *The Mystery of Capital*) looks for ways to empower the poor in his writing but then settles on a narrow set of prescriptions related to property rights and legal reform.[6] Daron Acemoglu and James Robinson's *Why Nations Fail*, published in 2012, emphasizes the importance of inclusive institutions to economic success but defines these narrowly, failing to take into account the diverse ways in which inclusiveness has been achieved in various places. As a consequence, *Why Nations Fail* has a hard time explaining why many countries, especially outside the West, have succeeded.[7] Other authors, including Jared Diamond (*Guns, Germs, and Steel*), Max Weber (*The Protestant Ethic and the Spirit of Capitalism*), Niall Ferguson (*Civilization*), and David Landes (*The Wealth and Poverty of Nations*), have sought to explain the prosperity or poverty of countries by looking at things like the environment, culture, institutions, competition, rule of law, and religion.[8]

What Is an "Inclusive Society"?

This book lays great stress on the extent to which poverty is related to social and economic *exclusion* and on the critical role that *inclusive* societies play in tackling poverty. But what exactly is an "inclusive society"?

In inclusive societies, elites feel a sense of moral, psychological, or social obligation to other people in their countries, especially the poor. This sense is strong enough to inspire elites to introduce or support government policies that give the poor the opportunity to improve their lives. The roots of this readiness among elites to extend opportunity to all members of a society can usually be found in a shared sense of identity, whether national, cultural, ideological, religious, or ethnic, or in some other form of intellectual, spiritual, or physical kinship. Effective institutions that serve people equitably can intensify this sense of attachment or compensate for its absence.

In exclusionary societies (discussed in chapter 4), elites have little affinity for the poor and instead see them as significantly or even fundamentally different. This attitude enables elites to justify their continued subjugation of or indifference toward the poor. Exclusionary societies are most likely to be found in countries with deep social fissures based on ethnicity, religion, caste, or clan and a long history of elite-dominated political and economic systems. Exclusionary tendencies are reinforced in countries with ineffective governments that cannot hold leaders accountable or prevent the rich and powerful from corrupting the state. In such environments, elites have little or no incentive to act inclusively.

Such exclusionary attitudes, it should be noted, have little to do with how market-oriented a country's economic policies are. A country could adopt the most pro-market reforms yet still leave most of its population disadvantaged, unable to access the economic opportunities created by those reforms because those in power favor their cronies or systematically underinvest in certain parts of the country. In such an environment, a handful of people would get rich, but most would stay poor—Africa and the Middle East offer many examples of this phenomenon.

The World Bank's *Voices of the Poor* and *Moving Out of Poverty* series come closest to looking for ways to empower the poor; indeed, they helped inspire this book with their unflinching portraits of the hardships the poor must confront at every turn. But while these series deliver in terms of letting the world hear the "voices of the poor," their solutions for "moving out of poverty" do not take into account some of the most important aspects of their own research. They do look at poverty through the eyes of the poor, but they do not integrate what they see about power relationships into their prescriptions for a better world.

This sort of problem is all too common. Many academics and practitioners have long recognized the crucial role that strong institutions and "good" politics play in promoting development, but few experts took this understanding and used it as the foundation for practicable policy recommendations until recently. The ideology that frames debates on poverty has too often downplayed the political causes of poverty by focusing on very specific factors, such as the poor's lack of access to technology. The poor themselves would not make that mistake. They know all too well how the economic and political system work to deny them opportunity while preserving the status quo. Elites take advantage of the poor without feeling any obligation to ensure governments work equally for everyone. "Money, money, money!" complained one Cambodian villager. "There is no responsibility or accountability from authorities and government officials."[9]

In recent years, a number of European development think tanks and research programs have conducted multiyear studies on the politics of development, bringing much needed attention to the subject. By seeking to understand the incentives that drive political behavior and the power dynamics that determine how countries and economic sectors evolve, these studies have broken new ground in our understanding of development, state building, and poverty.[10] In the United States, Douglass North, John Joseph Wallis, Steven Webb, and Barry Weingast—the editors of *In the Shadow of Violence*—have similarly blazed a new analytical trail, developing a completely new framework for understanding how the politics of developing countries work.[11]

Betrayed is indebted to the pioneering work of these recent works, and draws on them in a number of places in the following chapters. In other places, however, such as when I discuss strategic urbanization or the role of leadership, I draw chiefly on my personal experiences and observations in China and elsewhere in Asia.

Betrayed is not another work focused on Western aid and how it might work better. Instead, it is a book aimed squarely at the lives of the poor and what it might take to give them the chance to make better use of their own hard work and resourcefulness. It concentrates on the billions of impoverished people in less-developed countries—making up roughly one-half of the developing world's population—who are disadvantaged because of how their states and economies fail them. *Betrayed* is about how to foster the political change and economic opportunity that will produce more inclusive societies and empower the poor so that they can prosper on their own.

The power to bring about that change lies chiefly with leaders and elites of the developing countries, and for that reason most of the suggestions in this book for creating inclusive societies are addressed, explicitly or implicitly, to those leaders and elites. But the international community also has a significant, if fundamentally supportive, role to play in this transformation, and thus this book is also aimed at *everyone* who is interested in making the developing world a much more inclusive place: not just Western government policymakers, those who work for official development agencies, and academics, but also the NGOs who are fighting for the world's poor and the millions of people in Western societies who care about that fight.

The audience for this book is thus very broad, as is the cast of actors who appear in its pages. But throughout the book it is the poor and their leaders who take center stage.

CHAPTER 2

The Blame Game

Confronted by perennial poverty in Africa, Asia, and Latin America, Westerners have an old habit of pointing an accusing finger at the poor themselves.

In the nineteenth century, for instance, an American traveling to Mexico declared the inhabitants to be the most "lazy indolent poor Starved set of people as ever the Sun Shined upon." Another visitor remarked that the Mexicans are "too ignorant and indolent for enterprises and too poor and dependent were they otherwise capacitated."[1]

In the early twentieth century, a British school textbook, cowritten by Rudyard Kipling, the Nobel Prize–winning author of such children's classics as *The Jungle Book*, explained that the Caribbean contains

> a large population, mainly black, descended from slaves imported in previous centuries, or of mixed black and white race; lazy, vicious, and incapable of any serious improvement, or of work except under compulsion. In such a climate a few bananas will sustain the life of a negro quite sufficiently; why should he work to get more than this? He is quite happy and quite useless, and spends any extra wages he may earn upon finery.[2]

Such blatant racism has largely disappeared from public view in the past hundred years, but many people still equate poverty with laziness. One American (whose own industriousness has produced a resume that runs from professor of economics to financial planner to talk show host) concluded after visiting a "spectacularly verdant" region of the Andes in 2000 that "there is reason to believe that many Altiplano people are lazy. How else could it be that a non oppressed people, living in a relatively free society, would perpetually remain in abject poverty?" The local Indians' "lethargic, even indolent" behavior was due to their lack of a Protestant work ethic.[3]

A lot of people in the rich world pin the blame on culture. "Underdevelopment is a state of mind," as the title of a book by Tufts professor Lawrence Harrison puts it.[4] Oscar Lewis, an influential anthropologist who died in 1970, created the concept of "the culture of poverty." Poor people, said Lewis, feel a sense of "helplessness, of dependency, of not belonging. . . . Along with this feeling of powerlessness is a widespread feeling of inferiority, of personal unworthiness."[5]

The late Harvard professor Samuel Huntington made a name for himself by portraying the world as a seething cauldron of sharply distinctive and competing cultures. In Huntington's world, culture is destiny. Why, for instance, has South Korea prospered while Ghana has not? Because, says Huntington, "South Koreans valued thrift, investment, hard work, education, organization, and discipline. Ghanaians had different values. In short, cultures count."[6] A contributor to *Culture Matters,* a book coedited by Huntington and Harrison, echoes the point: "Work is not highly valued in progress-resistant societies . . . the entrepreneur is suspect . . . a job well done, tidiness, courtesy, punctuality . . . are unimportant in a resistant culture."[7] Such attitudes are deeply ingrained, dating back at least to biblical times. After all, Proverbs cautions: "How long will you recline, O sluggard? When will you arise from your sleep? A little sleep, a little slumber, a little folding of the hands to recline, and your poverty will come like a traveler, and your lacking like an armed man."[8]

For most well-off people in the rich world—as well as in developing countries— the poor are to blame for their troubles. This holds true whether the poor are in Africa, Latin America, and Asia, or much closer to home. Bill O'Reilly, the popular (if controversial) American television host, declares that poor people are "irresponsible and lazy . . . because that's what poverty is."[9] More than six out of every ten Americans believe that poor people are at least partly to blame for their own poverty.[10] Even many people within poor countries believe that the poor only have themselves to blame for their situation. Community members and local government officials in Tanzania, for example, dismiss the poor as "these people" (*hawa watu*), hapless individuals responsible for their own plight.[11]

What often goes unsaid in these perceptions is an underlying prejudice, an assumption that there is some fundamental difference between the poor and "ourselves." Whether racial, ethnic, religious, geographical, gender, caste, or class in origin, such attitudes can quickly become a rationale for exclusion on account of "otherness." And billions suffer from exclusion, from "otherness." If we count all the people trying to scrape by on less than $1.25 a day (which, as the following chapter explains, is one internationally accepted standard of poverty), we arrive at a total of something like 1.3 billion people, one-fifth of the world's total population. If we use a figure of $2.50 a day (another standard), we arrive at roughly 3 billion people, roughly one-half of the developing world's population. We arrive at much the same range of figures if we add up all the people structurally excluded from economic and political power across the world (a phenomenon discussed in chapter 4).

As far as Huntington and fellow moralizers are concerned, dividing humankind into two groups—and assuming that the poor are not "one of us"—makes perfect sense: one part of the world consists of people like them—hardworking souls who have earned the wealth they enjoy; the other consists of billions of idlers whose poverty is exactly what they deserve.

* * *

Not everyone plays this blame game, however. Or, to be more accurate, some people play the game differently. While Huntington and O'Reilly lob insults in the direction of the lazy, untidy, unhygienic poor, others take aim at cruel capitalism, at a free market system that not only breeds but actually demands billions of the destitute.

There is, of course, a long historical tradition (from Robin Hood to the French Revolution) of blaming poverty on an oppressive political and economic system and the tyrants who run that system. The modern version of this tradition took shape in Victorian times. As the Industrial Revolution steamed across Western Europe and North America, chugging from London to Berlin, New York to Chicago, a variety of political groups, most of them on the left, saw armies of ragged children in the streets of grimy cites and concluded that merciless capitalism was responsible.

Marxists took the argument a step further and blamed capitalism for extending a new form of poverty across the world via imperialism. Shortly before he wrested control of a revolution in Russia and set the country on its totalitarian course, Vladimir Lenin declared that imperialism has "emerged as the development and direct continuation of the fundamental characteristics of capitalism in general . . . imperialism is the monopoly stage of capitalism."[12]

Lenin may now reside in a mausoleum in Red Square, but the association between capitalism and poverty in the colonial and postcolonial world lives on. Today, many people blame globalization and international business for poverty. For instance, according to John Mohan Razu, a professor of social ethics,

> Poverty and globalization are an intimately linked process and thus breed on one another. . . . Capitalism under the guise and in the form and process of globalization has excluded a vast majority of people. It lives and grows through exclusion and escalation of poverty . . . its manifestations are poverty and hunger, migration, homelessness, illiteracy, unemployment, ill-health and a host of other inequities.[13]

Such thinking is especially pervasive among antiglobalization protesters, whose noisy demonstrations often dominate the news emanating from meetings of international leaders. For activists such as David Korten, author of *When Corporations Rule the World*, business competition necessitates "hiring child labor, cheating workers on overtime pay, imposing merciless quotas, and operating unsafe facilities. . . . In many Southern countries, to say that conditions verge on slavery is scarcely an exaggeration."[14]

Such accusations fly thick and fast in the battle between right and left over where to place the blame for global poverty. Yet, for all their differences of opinion, the two sides have one thing very much in common. Both treat the poor as victims—victims either of their own inherent failings or of the flaws inherent in capitalism. Neither side gives much credence to the notion that poor people might in fact be able to help themselves. Indeed, like a punching bag between two boxers who decide to throw punches at each other instead, the poor often seem to be forgotten.

As a result, debates over what to do about global poverty are generally reduced to exchanges involving two simplistic, antagonistic points of view. One school of thought believes that the poor deserve their miserable fate and should either be left alone or given just enough charity to survive. The other camp believes that it is up to governments (or international donors) to intervene on the poor's behalf because the economic system is to blame for their parlous condition. In portraying poverty as a permanent condition that is difficult to change, one version suggests that the poor are beyond assistance, and the other suggests that only we can save them.

But neither side sees the poor as they really are. Both, in fact, grossly distort reality.

*   *   *

Anyone who has spent a good amount of time in poor countries can probably tell a lot of stories about the would-be entrepreneurs on the lowest rungs of society.

During my time in the developing world, I have seen these micro-entrepreneurs at what seems to be every street corner, in every alley, at every bus stop, and in the hundreds in markets and along roads. They appear in the largest of cities, the smallest of towns, and everywhere in between where people gather. When a bus stops in the middle of the night for a brief pit stop—along the road from Recife to Salvador de Bahia in northeast Brazil, for example—out of nowhere appear a few ragged but determined individuals selling everything from bags of water to morsels of fruit to candies for the kids. Similarly, small markets dot the landscape of almost any decent-sized metropolis from Turkey to Somalia to India, vendors hawking everything from soap, milk, and vegetables to bricks, brooms, and cooked meals. In rural areas, many laborers painstakingly beat out a living from the earth for half a day and then try to sell some surplus goods (or their labor) to earn a few extra rupees or francs or shillings.

The desperation of some of these small peddlers shows in their faces and actions at times. They lunge to reach the bus or car window as we sprint by. They jostle one another in their anxiety to make a sale. They grimace when nobody buys.

But where one scene shows desperation, another shows a hunger to get ahead—and the confidence that it is possible given enough work and determination. In some cases, starting with nothing more than a few products to sell or working from a small stall or shop, these tiny entrepreneurs slowly build up their assets, graduating to more permanent spaces, taking on workers, and growing their businesses and skills. In places such as Hargeisa, the capital of the unrecognized state of Somaliland, streets hum with activity. Shoppers look for deals in the markets, business people negotiate contracts in the offices, families plot strategies for getting ahead in their homes. Everywhere there is the energy of expectation for a better future. In such countries, belief in the powers of the market would surprise many who campaign against capitalism. As Milward, a man in chronic poverty from Malawi, explained, "What restricts me is just the amount of money I get. But I am not confined inside. I think big." Abdus Salam, a mover from

Bangladesh, similarly believes, "I couldn't have come to this position if I hadn't labored, dealing in rice and paddy. . . . Doing both, I have been able to get my children educated. That's the best achievement in my life."[15]

Of course, in some other countries optimism can be difficult to sustain. In Nigeria, for instance, a great many people suffer despondency because of their miseries. But even in Lagos, millions of families are energetically trying to better their lives. People take on multiple jobs to earn extra cash, start businesses with the hope of exploiting an unrecognized niche, and work hard to upgrade their skills.

A series of recent books tell a similar story. In fact, they tell thousands of similar stories. Based on the personal histories of poor people in the developing world, they offer a treasure trove of tales of struggle against hardship. This is not light reading, however. As Angel's story in the accompanying feature box makes all too clear, our heroes and heroines don't usually get the luxury of a Hollywood ending. But not all stories of the poor are destined to have unhappy endings, as Arvinda's attests.

The World Bank's three-volume series *Voices of the Poor* (2000–2002) and its four-volume collection *Moving Out of Poverty* (2007–2009) offer an unprecedented depth and breadth of perspective. The database on which these books draw includes more than 60,000 interviews with poor or formerly poor people from over 500 communities across 15 countries, providing a diverse and compelling picture that stands in stark contrast to what most in the West have been led to believe.

Portfolios of the Poor (2009), coauthored by four people working in microfinance, interviewed far fewer people but in greater detail in order to understand how they manage their money. Yearlong financial diaries demonstrate how people living in Bangladesh, India, and South Africa on less than $2.00 a day employ various financial tools, many linked to informal networks and family relations, to stretch their earnings to meet their needs. The *Chronic Poverty Report* (2009), produced by the Chronic Poverty Research Centre in the United Kingdom, summarizes much of the latest research on what holds back the poor.[16] *Poor Economics* (2011), by Abhijit Banerjee and Esther Duflo, offers rich detail about how the poor actually live, demolishing a number of widely held misconceptions along the way. Other books spotlight particular communities. Diane Singerman's *Avenues of Participation* (1995) explores how Cairo's urban underclass work together to achieve common goals. *Ordinary Families, Extraordinary Lives* (2009) by Caroline Moser shows how households in a Guayaquil slum in Ecuador have had to struggle over three decades to build assets and escape poverty.

Angel's Story

Angel, from Zimbabwe, left secondary school after just two years because her family could no longer afford the school fees from its meager income from farming. Aged 14, she was forced to move to town in search of work.

But her job working as a "house girl" for a middle-class family turned out badly when they refused to pay her and she had no legal recourse to recover the money owed her.

In 2002, she moved to Plot Shumba, a nearby settlement of small, fragile, temporary structures for migrants who had nowhere else to go. Many residents had lost their commercial farming or mining jobs and could not afford the rent for an urban apartment. But in February 2003, the army demolished all 50 homes in the plot as part of a drive against squatter settlements. Angel was severely beaten and forced to sleep for a month in a bus shelter. After the landowner obtained a court order enabling residents to return, she rebuilt her shack.

Angel's fortunes improved a bit over the next two years. In February 2004, Angel's cousin helped her get a job selling beer in a bar near a small goldmine, where she fell in love with a gold panner. But the owner of the goldmine went bankrupt a few months later, and both lost their jobs. Angel then moved into informal trading, buying and selling vegetables. Her boyfriend found work in another mine, but one that was unpermitted and unsafe.

In March 2005, she gave birth to their son, only to see her boyfriend die the same month in a pit collapse. In 2006, the state again moved in, razing Plot Shumba to the ground. She again rebuilt her shack, but she was then diagnosed with HIV and her health began to fail. Gaunt, her skin dry, her hair falling out, Angel came to depend on neighbors and food aid from a local nongovernment organization.

The chances of Angel and her baby surviving were extremely low.[17]

Arvinda's Story

Arvinda, born into a relatively cohesive and well-led isolated rural community in Uttar Pradesh (UP), India, has managed to build a more comfortable life for himself over the past decade.

The son of a poor farmer, he was able to attend a secondary school close to his home—until poverty forced him to drop out after the tenth grade. Marrying at 15, he started doing odd jobs to support his family and trying different things to make ends meet. A grocery store venture failed when he could not repay the debt taken to finance it. Eventually, he accumulated some savings and used the money to purchase some farmland.

A series of development projects changed Arvinda's fortune. A new irrigation canal in 2001 increased the yields from his farm, which became a prosperous business. A new road linking the village to the main throughway, access to farmer credit cards, and the building of a dam and 50 wells benefited everyone in the area, increasing what his local customers could afford to spend and helping him gain access to outside markets.

He now acts as a grain contractor in the market near his village and has managed to educate one of his two sons. He has even been able to give financial aid to relatives and purchase a life insurance policy.[18]

What emerges from these collective voices is a remarkable record of "resilience, hard work, and grit" across all countries and contexts, as the World Bank studies conclude.[19] Different countries have different cultures, but none has a monopoly on hard work, thrift, or enterprise. The poor everywhere are actively seeking to better their futures in ways we would easily recognize if the contexts and tools resembled our own. "People do not recognize any exhaustion. Never let go of any chances. If fishermen still have time after seafaring, they will use the time to do other things," explained a member of a men's discussion group in Kramrrak, Indonesia. "If you fall 10 times, you have to stand up 10 times, no matter what happens," Graciela, a 53-year-old from El Mirador in Colombia said.[20] "From agriculture I bought ten used bicycles and a sewing machine. I then repaired them myself and sold them. Then I bought a radio, fifteen goats and pigs. I also bought a car, though an old one, to make my life better, but my ambition is not fulfilled," declared Odwin Severin Lupogo, a middle-aged man from Nyoni in Tanzania.[21]

*   *   *

Within developing countries, the World Bank studies show that there are few distinctions between the poor and the non-poor in their ambitions for their families, in their work ethics, and in their ability to take initiative. But great differences in opportunity separate the two groups. Whereas the middle and upper echelons of society may invest in factories, chain stores, and mechanized farms, the lower echelons end up in backbreaking work, assembling brooms, manning a food stall, or plowing land. As Nasreen, a 62-year-old woman from a shoe repairer caste in Sanghar, Pakistan, explains: "Our entire caste does this work. We have never got a job nor have taken up one. Even if we study, we do not get a job. My son has passed eight classes but he has never got a job. Even those who are educated are polishing shoes."[22]

Capitalism and globalization are not the cause of this divergence. After all, millions climb out of poverty every year across the globe by using the power that markets and trade give them to advance their lives. Many of these people now enjoy a middle-class lifestyle; some have even earned great wealth. Even those who remain poor are able to adapt to various opportunities using the flexibility markets provide to take care of themselves. Moreover, entire countries—such as China and Chile—have used the power of markets to enable vast numbers of people to better themselves within the space of a single generation.

As Sarah Kiwili, a 52-year-old woman from Nyoni, Tanzania, explains:

> My main activity is farming but . . . I [also] make and sell local brew known as *Ngelenge*. I learned the skills . . . from my mother and in 1974 I started my own business. I was able to get a profit of between TZS 500 to TZS 600 a day in 1974. . . . Now I am making a profit of between TZS 10,000 to TZS 15,000 a day. Through local brewing I have been able to send one of my children to secondary school, support myself, care for my children and my ailing mother, and save a small amount of money in case of sudden illness or other adverse shock.[23]

But capitalism does not operate in a vacuum. As this book argues, where markets do not work equitably, where they disenfranchise the poor because of various forms of discrimination and exclusion, the poor are likely to stay poor. Such market failures—often caused by the failures of government—do not empower anyone. In cases such as Angel's, the state acts unfairly, helping the strong at the expense of the weak, and making the poor work much harder than they should to achieve any improvement in their lives. The fault, therefore, is not with capitalism per se, but with how it is often implemented in countries whose governments work for only a subset of the population.

Such failures are rooted in the divisions that plague societies—and that produce political systems that deliberately exclude entire sections of the populace. Governments run by and for a subset of a population naturally disadvantage large numbers of people, aggravating social frictions, undermining the legitimacy of the state, and increasing the difficulties facing the poor. In such environments, markets that should be empowering the hardest-working and the most inventive end up rewarding those with the most connections and the greatest ability to hijack the rulemaking process.

* * *

Betrayed shows how these divisions hold back the poor—and what might be done to overcome them.

The rest of this first part of the book explains who the poor are, why they are poor, and how poverty holds back entire societies. Chapter 3 gives an idea of the number and types of people in the developing world who are submerged in poverty. Chapter 4 describes how their societies are structured in ways that stifle their ability to improve their lives. Unless the poor have equal access to such things as schooling, roads, and information on prices for their farm goods and on work opportunities, they cannot participate as equals in their economies and societies. Chapter 5 explains how poverty hurts everyone within a state, not just the poor. The poor's lack of opportunity means that many developing countries can do little to reduce poverty—and risk falling into a vicious trap of high poverty and low growth.

Part II of the book looks at what might be done to escape this trap—at how those who have been betrayed by their elite compatriots can better access opportunity and gain an equal footing in their own societies. Why do some governments make poverty alleviation a national priority and others do not? What are the best ways to enable the poor to overcome their exclusion and compete with others on a more level playing field? How can the elites who control governments be convinced to act in ways that are more likely to empower the poor? How can economies be energized to create the jobs and opportunities that will enable the poor to enrich themselves and their communities? What combination of national and local policies, of political and economic steps, of measures both big and small can unlock the potential of those who are not deemed to be "one of us"?

Part III, the final section of the book, examines the role of social entrepreneurs and the international community. It starts by asking what individuals, NGOs, and companies within countries can do to empower the poor. These are the players best positioned to promote change when governments are unable to. Later, it examines foreign aid, asking what have donors done well and what have they not. Although foreign aid has helped improve the lives of the poor in many ways, it has rarely improved how poor countries work. Far too often, Western governments and international aid agencies have tried to come up with economic solutions to what are in fact political problems. At times, aid has even contributed to social exclusion, funding policies and programs that have disadvantaged the poor. Although a few development agencies have accomplished miraculous work, most have mixed or downright dismal records when it comes to changing the power and institutional dynamics that hold back the poor. Instead, more effort should be put into doing things that help the poor help themselves.

CHAPTER 3

Who Are the Poor?

The poor are an immensely varied group.

In Lagos, Nigeria's steaming capital of some 15 million souls, where I lived for a while in the late 1980s, the overwhelming majority of people are poor. Except for those lucky enough to live in the city's few wealthy districts, almost everyone struggles to stay afloat, even government workers with steady jobs. The desperation is obvious on the streets. Downtown overflows with beggars, markets teem with ragged hawkers, and in every alley a middle-aged woman is working over a small fire cooking cheap food to sell to passersby. Many poor people live on the streets: some are old, many are crippled, others are orphans as young as five. Recent migrants from across the country crowd into filthy, unsafe slums. Life is not for the fainthearted; survival is a serious business, to be fought for every day.

In the rural highlands of Bolivia, everyone is poor, from the farmer to the teacher to the small business owner. The local population, mainly Aymara who trace their roots back almost a millennium to before the rise of the Inca, live in small villages on the Altiplano in the central Andes. As I discovered when I visited the area doing research for my last book, life is far more tolerable than in Lagos, as food is rarely scarce and social bonds are strong. But families have few possessions and very little opportunity to make money. Schools are poor, and few children stay in them for long. Until recently, the schools used a language—Spanish—that most people did not even speak. Jobs are scarce. Work on farms is backbreaking. Work in the old mines is dangerous. Valley towns such as Chulumani, where I spent a few days in 2006, have more fertile land and a couple of restaurants and shops, but little else. The home where I stayed, like many homes in the area, had no refrigerator, and cooking was done outdoors in a cement basin over a fire. Rain quickly washed out the roads and made movement of any kind treacherous.

In a remote coal-mining town in the mountains of Kyrgyzstan, six out of every ten people are unemployed. Many families face hardships like those endured by 11-year-old Bakyt and his family. The boy and his two brothers are the main breadwinners, because his mother is disabled and divorced from his father, who provides no financial support. The brothers work in the local coal mines, lugging sacks through narrow tunnels. The family's house is rundown—the windows are broken, and it is very cold in the wintertime; they cannot afford to fix anything or even to buy wood to heat the place. Like Bakyt, his sister skips school, for as long as a month at a time, to take care of her mother and sick grandmother. His family cannot afford butter or sugar, let alone meat. Bakyt has bread for breakfast and fried potatoes or fried macaroni and bread with tea for dinner. The family reuses the same teabags over and over again to save money.[1]

In Gitega province, Burundi, which is often hard-hit by floods, Véronique Begimana lives with her six children in a house her husband built out of metal. He has since died of AIDS (with which Veronique, too, is infected), and the roof now has holes. She and her children eat nothing in the morning. "When times were better," she says, "we used to cultivate the hills and the swamp areas and this would feed me and my family every day. Now there is very little to eat. Sometimes we eat cassava leaves that are diseased and these give us diarrhea. . . . I felt safer when my husband was alive, but now I am head of the household, life is very difficult. I dream of finding a job that gives me enough food to feed us every day. . . . But without food or money it's difficult to have hope for the future. Things don't change very much for us. Life isn't beautiful."[2]

* * *

Despite these differences, the poor have at least two things in common. One is obvious: they have very little or no money. The other is less so, but it is just as much a part of their poverty: they don't just lack for money; instead, they are trapped in a web of deprivation. The next chapter explains how the strands of this web are woven—how everything from corrupt politicians and weak courts to poor education and even bad weather can conspire to chain hardworking people to poverty. First, however, this chapter explains roughly how many poor people there are in the world, where in the world they are, and which kinds of people are most likely to be poor.

One in Two

The numbers of poor people vary a lot depending on how they are defined and counted. The simplest—and most commonly used—method of tallying the poor is to add up all the people below a certain income level. A complementary approach is to look at health, education, and living standards, which together provide a keener sense of the many different ways in which, as the Nobel Prize–winner Amartya Sen puts it, "human lives are battered and diminished."[3] This latter approach is the basis for figure 3.1, which divides the world into four tiers of human development: the countries in darkest gray are in the top tier of the Human Development Index for 2011; the countries in the lightest gray are in the bottom tier. There is, of course, a strong correlation between human development and income.

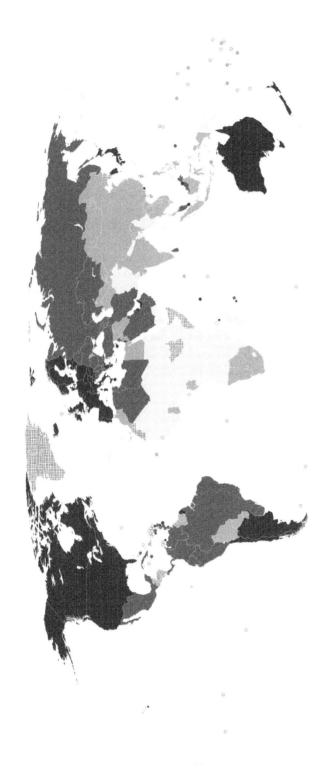

Figure 3.1 The World According to the Human Development Index, 2011

Source: United Nations Development Programme, *Human Development Report 2011—Sustainability and Equity: A Better Future for All* (New York: UNDP, 2011), table 1, 127–30, http://hdr.undp.org/en/reports/global/hdr2011/download/.

The World Bank, whose figures are often cited, employs the income method. It currently uses an international poverty line of $1.25 a day per person to calculate *extreme* poverty, an average of the national poverty lines of the world's 15 poorest countries.[4] According to the World Bank, 1.3 billion people, more than one in five of those living in the developing world, were below this line in 2008. That is a dreadfully large number of people, but the good news is that the proportion of the world's population living on less than $1.25 per day has fallen by half since 1990. In other words, thanks not least to China's extraordinary economic growth in recent decades, the level of extreme poverty in the world has been dramatically reduced. (A number of researchers are extremely optimistic about continuing declines in extreme poverty. Two based at the Brookings Institution in Washington DC calculated in 2011 that extreme poverty is falling much faster than the World Bank thinks. They believe that the world had only 900 million extreme poor in 2010, and that this number could fall to as low as 600 million by 2015.)[5]

The news, however, is not all good. If we raise the poverty bar just another $1.25 per day, to $2.50 per day (the median poverty line of all developing countries *except* the poorest 15),[6] then, as noted in chapter 2, about 3 billion people qualify as poor. In other words, one in every two people in the developing world lives in poverty.[7] That proportion is dropping, but more slowly; the total number is higher than it was in 1981, but lower than it was in the late 1990s.

Figure 3.2 shows the progress made between 1981 and 2008 in tackling different levels of poverty.

Life on $2.50 per day is easier than on $1.25, but it hardly means that one is living in the lap of luxury. Most of that money must be spent on food, leaving little available to invest in "productive" (i.e., time-saving) assets such as bicycles, sewing machines, phones, or anything but the most basic farming tools. In a survey taken in 2004 in Udaipur, Rajasthan, one of the poorest districts in India, with a large tribal population and an unusually high level of female illiteracy, only 1 out of 6 people who lives on less than $2.50 has a radio, only 1 in every 10 families has a chair or a stool, only 1 in 20 has a table, and only 1 in 50 has a television. Fewer than 1 in 100 has an electric fan, a sewing machine, a bullock cart, a motorized cycle of any kind, or a tractor. No one has a regular phone.[8]

Of course, different countries yield vastly different circumstances for the poor. Whereas almost everyone has access to electricity in Mexico and Indonesia, in rural Nicaragua and Guatemala, only one in three people are on the grid. In large parts of the countryside in northwestern India and Timor-Leste, it's fewer than one in eight. In rural Tanzania and Papua New Guinea, almost no one has access to electricity.[9]

Amazingly, 3 billion actually underestimates the number of people around the world who experience poverty at one time or another. Indeed, it is misleading to divide a population into two segments, one poor and one non-poor. Many people move in and out of poverty on a regular basis.

How many more people are "sometimes poor" than are "always poor"? Twice as many, at least. In Zimbabwe, the ratio of "always poor" to "sometimes poor"

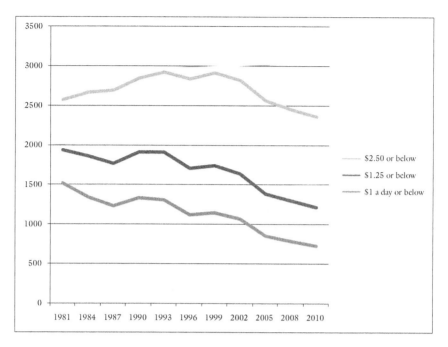

Figure 3.2 Number of People in Poverty, 1981–2008

Source: World Bank's Development Research Group, PovcalNet: the online tool for poverty measurement, http://iresearch.worldbank.org/PovcalNet/index.htm.

in the first half of the 1990s was one to six. For China in the second half of the 1980s, it was one to eight. In Bangladesh, while one-half of the people in the countryside were poor in 2000, three-quarters had experienced poverty during the previous dozen years. Clearly, the great majority of people in impoverished countries live either in poverty itself or in its shadow all the time.[10]

People who live on or very close to the poverty line are vulnerable to any sort of change, either in their own lives or in the world around them. The time of the year, for instance, can drive lots of people into destitution simply because their incomes are seasonal. Without access to banks, the poor are often hamstrung in their ability to save for a bad season, a funeral, or even a child's education.

A family illness can be disastrous. "Those who are poor," said Bakyt, the boy from Kyrgyzstan, "they should not get sick. If you are not healthy and do not have money, nobody needs you. This is the case with our mother—nobody needs her except us. We do not have relatives who would help us if we fall sick."[11]

Political instability or an economic downturn can have equally devastating effects on the poor. Indeed, in these days of worldwide industries and markets, a ripple in international markets can become a large wave by the time it reaches the poor. And a major shift in global demand can hit the poor like a tsunami. A spike in food prices in the mid-2000s hurt tens of millions of the world's poor, especially in urban areas.

A Global Picture

Poverty is spread out unevenly across the globe. As maps 2 and 3 show, countries in North America, Europe, the southern half of South America, Australasia, parts of the Middle East, and a few places in East Asia have relatively few people living in extreme poverty; countries in Central and South America and much of Asia have a significant percentage of extremely poor citizens; India and Sub-Saharan Africa have a very large percentage.

In the developed world, poverty is confined to small pockets. In the countries classified by the World Bank as "middle-income" (countries in which the average income per person is between about $1,000 and $12,000)[12], poverty is much more prevalent but typically concentrated in disadvantaged groups and regions, the underclass, and areas with depressed economies. In "low-income" countries (countries where the average income per person is below $1,000 per year), poverty is found almost everywhere apart from a few privileged enclaves.

Rich states such as the United States, Japan, and the countries of Western Europe have grown richer in recent years. The gap between rich and poor has widened considerably in many places, but, for the most part, the poorest citizens in these states have nonetheless seen their living conditions improve.[13] A handful of East Asian states (South Korea, Taiwan, and Singapore) have joined them in the high-income group. Yet even in these seas of prosperity, the legacy of social exclusion can keep a few groups disadvantaged. Poverty levels are still much higher for people who have suffered from some form of discrimination, such as African Americans in the United States, and Roma and Muslims in Europe.

The largest numbers of poor people two generations ago were found in the heavily populated countries of Asia. Today, however, rapid growth in East Asia—especially in China—and changing demographics means that poverty, globally speaking, is increasingly concentrated in Africa and South Asia. Throughout the world, the countries (or regions within countries) that are plagued by a combination of deep social divides and bad government (often called "fragile states") have made the least progress of all in reducing poverty.[14]

One would expect that most poor people would live in the poorest countries. That was true in the past, but not today. Low-income countries are indeed full of poor people, but most poor people in today's world live in lower-middle-income countries with very large populations. These states were originally in the bottom category but have grown rapidly enough that they have climbed up a notch in recent years. In terms of *average* income, these countries are doing relatively well; their wealth, however, is very unequally distributed. Countries such as China, India, Indonesia, Nigeria, and Pakistan have made substantial economic gains over the past two decades, lifting their average annual incomes above $1,000—but hundreds of millions of their citizens have been left behind, still mired in poverty.[15]

Other middle-income states (for instance, in Latin America and the Middle East) have recovered from a long period of stagnation and grown at a fairly rapid

Figure 3.3 Percentage of Population Living on Less than $1.25 a Day, 2007–2008

Source: UNDP, *Human Development Report 2009—Overcoming Barriers: Human Mobility and Development* (New York: UNDP, 2009), table 1, 176–78, http://hdr.undp.org/en/reports/global/hdr2009/.

Under 2%
2% - 5%
6% - 20%
21% - 40%
41% - 60%
61% - 80%
No Data

clip over the past decade. Again, however, these economic gains have more often than not been concentrated among elites, with disadvantaged groups and regions remaining disadvantaged. This is especially true in countries such as Angola, Sudan, and Nigeria, which have graduated to middle-income status solely on the basis of growth produced by their mineral wealth. But even places such as Brazil and China, which have tried hard to combat poverty by building inclusive states, still contain vast armies of impoverished and disadvantaged people. Many of the countries that emerged from the ruins of the Soviet Union—termed "countries in transition"—suffered large rises in their poverty levels throughout the 1990s but have fared much better since.

Low-income countries have experienced mixed fortunes in recent years. Although some—such as Bangladesh, Ghana, and Ethiopia—have grown over the past decade or so in ways that let the poor share in some of the benefits of that growth, most have not. Many low-income countries suffered through a long period of stagnation starting in the 1970s, and, although most have returned to growth in recent years, the benefits have not been widely shared with the poor. Almost all remain highly inequitable. Life in conflict-prone places (including Afghanistan, Somalia, and the Congo) is the hardest. That is not to say that life is completely unbearable—new technologies and medicines have reached most parts of these countries and improved many lives in some way—but poverty is grinding and all but inescapable.

Relative levels of poverty vary a lot depending on the region and country. In terms of extreme poverty, almost one in every two people (386 million) in Africa lived on less than $1.25 a day in 2008.[16] In some African countries, the situation is much worse: in Liberia, Burundi, Madagascar, and the Democratic Republic of the Congo, more than three-quarters of the population have to try to survive on less than $1.25 per day.[17] In 2008, Sub-Saharan Africa was home to 30 percent of the world's poor, up from 11 percent in 1981.

Another part of the world unlucky enough to have seen its share of global extreme poverty rise is South Asia. In 1981, it had 29 percent of the world's poorest people; in 2008, it had 44 percent. All told, 570 million people in South Asia, more than one out of every three, fall below the $1.25 per day line.[18]

China cut the proportion of its population living in extreme poverty from over five-sixths in 1981 to less than one-seventh in 2008—a decline of over 650 million people! Yet the country still has over 170 million poor living on less than $1.25 a day.[19]

The rest of the world has a lot fewer poor in absolute numbers, mainly because of a combination of smaller overall populations and higher average incomes. Some states have proportions of poor similar to Africa: in Haiti, Timor-Leste, and Uzbekistan, for instance, one out of every two people earn less than $1.25 a day. Other countries, usually with higher average incomes, have ratios similar to China's: in Yemen and Georgia, roughly one out of every six people earns less than $1.25.[20] Figures 3.4 and 3.5 show how extreme poverty is divided up by region around the world.

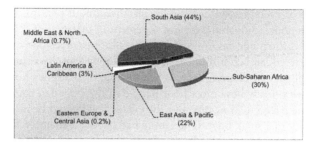

Figure 3.4 Number of Poor on $1.25 per day, 2008

Source of Data: Shaohua Chen and Martin Ravallion, "An Update to the World Bank's Estimates of Consumption Poverty in the Developing World," February 29, 2012, http://siteresources.worldbank.org/INTPOVCALNET/ Resources/Global_Poverty_Update_2012_02-29-12.pdf.

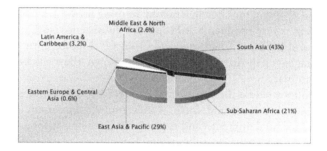

Figure 3.5 Number of Poor on $2.50 per day, 2008

Source of Data: World Bank's Development Research Group, PovcalNet: the on-line tool for poverty measurement, http://iresearch.worldbank.org/PovcalNet/index.htm.

Which Kinds of People Are Most Affected by Poverty?

Not all poor are equally impoverished. At the national level, variations in economic conditions, physical assets, education levels, and the inclusiveness of governments can dramatically affect the chances to better one's lot. Even within a country, variations between regions in investment, infrastructure, and schooling produce great difference. *Moving Out of Poverty*, in fact, finds that three-quarters of the variation in poverty reduction depends on the village or area, not the state, in which the poor live.[21] A person's ethnicity, gender, and social status also have a big impact on whether they are poor and just how poor they are.

Although migration has increased the incidence of urban poverty in recent years, it still remains disproportionately a rural phenomenon, with three out of every four of the most destitute (surviving on less than $1 a day) living in the countryside.[22] Life may be hard for many in the cities, but it is even worse outside: the poverty rate in the countryside is twice as high. In some countries, the difference is even greater: in Peru, for instance, about two-thirds of the rural population is poor, compared with just 4 percent in urban areas.[23]

Life in the countryside has some advantages—for instance, food can be cheaper or can be bartered, and communities are often closely knit. Even so, it is easy for villages to fall prey to despondency. When visiting a colleague's home village in the Niger Delta, I saw how most poor people in the Nigerian countryside live. There was one paved road nearby, but the village itself could be reached only by crossing a river in a small boat. One family had its own generator, but otherwise the village had no power at all. The local school did not have enough chairs and chalk, never mind books for the students. Homes were for the most part small and dilapidated. The church was well attended, but decades of wear and tear had taken a heavy toll. Everything seemed worn down by the tropical climate. Mosquitoes were everywhere. Anyone with high hopes for their futures had to look elsewhere to achieve them.

In the most impoverished places, the poor eke out an existence on tiny farms. The soil is usually poor, the climate semiarid, farming methods are old-fashioned, and equipment is very rudimentary. People sow subsistence crops mainly—such as sorghum and millet in Chad; rice and cassava in Liberia; corn, cassava, and wheat in Paraguay; and rice in Bangladesh—and own a few chickens, goats, or other small animals.

Many families straddle the urban-rural divide, with one or more members—mostly men—going back and forth. Cities provide important employment opportunities for rural migrants, and remittances can help pay for daily expenses, dealing with emergencies such as illness, and launching a relative into some small business. This trend has led to a remarkable increase in the number of households in the countryside headed by women. Husbands return once every year or so as they struggle to earn some money in the cities to send home.

Households headed by women who have lost their husbands—through death, divorce, or abandonment—are in especially dire straits, both because they must make do without the husband's income and because women are easy targets of discrimination. On average, such families have only half as much to live off compared to other female-headed households.[24]

The Survival Strategies of the Rural Poor

Worsening conditions in some places have made the poor adopt more desperate measures to survive than in the past. Certain wild foods that were formerly gathered only in an especially difficult year are now regularly consumed, particularly in areas where populations have experienced immense growth in recent decades (such as in many parts of Africa) or hardship is worsening (such as in parts of Central Asia). Meanwhile, some traditional coping strategies—such as depending on assistance from kin or neighbors—are under increasing threat from changes in society, urbanization, and growing poverty.

Rural dwellers have diverse survival strategies. Off-farm incomes such as hawking goods, load carrying, wood collecting, weaving, and hairdressing activities are extremely important to the most impoverished. Better-off farmers may be able to focus on repair work, tailoring, and various forms of trade and commerce. Some may be forced to migrate in search of jobs, to sell possessions, and even to reduce consumption of food.

Based on a study published in 2001 by the World Bank, the following table shows the strategies used by Zambian farmers to cope with periods of hardship.

Strategy Farmers	Who Use This Strategy (%)
Reducing food intake/meals	67
Substituting ordinary meals with poorer food	54
Reducing other household consumption	51
Piecework on other farms	40
Food for work	39
Begging from friends	34
Other piecework	25
Substitution of wild food	19
Informal borrowing	16
Sales of assets	12
Relief food	11
Petty selling	9
Taking children out of school	5

Source: This is drawn from Howard White and Tony Killick, *African Poverty at the Millennium: Causes, Complexities, and Challenges* (Washington DC: World Bank, 2001), 22.

Palmira from rural Mozambique typifies many. "I can no longer cope with hunger," she says. "There are times when I suffer and I can't work, and I can no longer cope with this great suffering. This is my way of life. It is only me, my granddaughter and my daughter, who is suffering from this mental disorder. . . . Finding money for clothes and food is difficult, and we suffer when I cannot go to the field because of some disease."[25] Deborah, a Maasai from Kenya, faces similar hardships: "I have eight children. . . . Sometimes there is no money for school fees . . . my husband died a while ago and all the household problems are mine. . . . My *shamba* [farm] is only one acre . . . sometimes the maize crop dies due to lack of rainfall, and access to seedlings is very difficult. . . . The road linking Oloitokitok [her home] and other major towns . . . is in a very bad condition. . . . People are selling their produce at throwaway prices."[26]

Women as a whole are at a great disadvantage. They tend to get a smaller share than men of the family's budget for everything, including food; they have less access to education and medical treatment; and they are frequent targets of domestic violence (something exacerbated by poverty). In Africa, women do two-thirds of the work and produce 70 percent of the food, but earn only 10 percent of the income and own only 1 percent of the land. They are twice as likely to miss school. Girls aged 15 to 18 are four times as likely to contract AIDS as boys of the same age. Fewer than two out of five women in Africa survive to reach the age of 65.[27]

Whether man or woman, the chief breadwinner of a poor rural household is likely to be illiterate or have only a few years of education. Their children (especially the girls) will attend school irregularly or not at all, because their families need them to work at home or look after younger siblings or sick or aged relatives. In many countries, children from the poorest one-fifth of households receive only half as much schooling as the children of the richest. In some countries, the ratio is even worse: in India, the richest children go to school for eleven years, whereas the poorest get just over four years of education. In Guatemala, the equivalent figures are eight and two years, respectively. In Mali, the poorest children, on average, get less than half a year of schooling in their entire lives.[28]

According to Basran, one of 20 family members sharing a small, rickety home on the edge of Manchar Lake in Pakistan, "The basic reason for [the poor getting poorer and the rich getting richer] is education. Rich people find jobs after completing their education. Some of them have agricultural land. We are just fishermen. We are surrounded by misery all the time. The people with jobs and the landlords, they all live in the city. They earn there. What are we, *Meer Bahar* (fisherfolk)?"[29]

Large households are more likely to be impoverished, but this is partly because the poor often have more children. Young children either cannot earn a wage or, if they do work, earn much less than an adult. Yet they must eat as much as their parents, and if they go to school will typically have to buy pens and books. To feed a family with many young children, parents have to take on extra jobs; older children have to leave school earlier to work; and, in the worse cases, someone— usually a mother or older sister—has to go hungry.

Infrastructure and public services in the countryside tends to be patchy at best. In regions with little political clout, the government may deliberately withhold funds necessary to provide medical care, build schools, or construct and repair roads. With limited or no access to good transportation, poor households will be unable to get any surplus crops they might grow to market or to commute to jobs elsewhere; they will be forced to buy many goods at inflated prices; and they will benefit little from any growth taking place elsewhere in the country.

Location, in fact, is a crucial component of poverty. Poverty is almost always more heavily concentrated in one or more geographical regions of a country, such as India's east-central "poverty square," much of north and west China, northeast Thailand, northern Brazil, and the areas farthest from the capital in most African states. The more remote the area from economic activity and infrastructure, the more likely it is to be disadvantaged. For instance, households in Tanzania living within 100 meters of a gravel road on which a bus service runs all 12 months of the year earn 30 percent more than the rural average.[30] Residents in Kinshasa, the capital of the Democratic Republic of the Congo, live as much as 13 years longer than citizens in some other parts of the country.[31]

The poor tend to be better off in cities, but not much better off. And they face their own set of difficulties. Housing and transportation, for instance, tend not to be big expense items in the countryside, but they are in towns. Yet, with little schooling and few skills to offer, the urban poor find it almost impossible to get a steady job that pays them enough to cover their rent and bus fare as well as to buy food. So they must supplement their income in whatever ways they can. Some take on informal work, getting paid under the table, to work on construction sites and in restaurant kitchens. Their job status means less income— sometimes a lot less—than a formal worker being paid above board, but they have no choice. Others try low-level self-employment, trading in small-time consumer goods such as cigarettes, shoes, and pocketbooks or even working through garbage piles to recycle things such as plastics and paper.

Many of the urban poor are recent migrants from the countryside. These migrants tend to be young men and come in search of work. But cities are rarely hospitable to these new arrivals. The unfamiliar surroundings are much less secure, the work much more arduous, and the neighbors much less friendly. Existing residents and governments are often relentlessly hostile, resulting in discrimination and exclusion.

But life may be equally difficult even for those who have lived their whole lives in the city. Many junior-level civil servants and public enterprise workers have lost their jobs in recent years and been unable to find similar work. Even when they have kept their jobs or found one for the first time, expanding labor forces and low skill levels have meant lower salaries, forcing people to work a second job, typically a low-paid, under-the-counter job.

Living conditions can be appalling, especially in large metropolises, such as Rio de Janeiro, Lagos, and Kolkata. Many poor live in vast slums—tightly packed concentrations of flimsy shacks and shanties that rural migrants have built on the outskirts of cities. Water, sanitation, and other utilities are usually lacking, making the incredible overcrowding even harder to bear. UN official Naison Mutizwa-Mangiza recalls his first trip to Nairobi's Kibera, Africa's largest slum, which is home to 700,000:

> There is the poor physical quality of the environment, overcrowding, houses so close together, tin-roofed, walls often of mud, with just a very small window. But it is the smell from lack of sanitation that hits you in the face. You have to jump over numerous small trickling drains, filthy and filled with smelly water mixed with other types of waste, including feces. There are no toilets; people use plastic bags in the night for defecation and then throw these out in surrounding dumps and streams.[32]

Wherever they live, the handicapped, abandoned, aged, and orphaned are extremely vulnerable to falling into poverty. In fact, in many African languages, the word for *poor* literally means "lack of support": *umphawi* in the Chewa language of Malawi means "one without kin or friends."[33] Conditions for these groups have deteriorated in recent years because of the breakdown of traditional social structures. Urbanization, AIDS, and violent conflict have all dispersed what were once closely knit people. Increases in the number of poor have made it harder for communities to help their own people even when they have not gone to the cities in search of work. The safety nets provided by family, community, and ethnic or religious group now have many holes. Yet those nets are still usually the only protection poor people have. Outside of emergency relief and immunization programs, the assistance provided by foreign aid and nongovernmental organizations (NGOs) is too distant, irregular, and piecemeal to help most people.

Illness is much more prevalent among the poor—and much more likely to devastate lives of the sick and their families. The poor can rarely afford to visit a doctor or buy medicine. Minor, treatable ailments become major, untreatable ones. Epidemics sweep entire regions, countries, even continents. AIDS has been especially devastating in Africa, killing off millions of breadwinners, breaking up families, and creating armies of orphans. No one escapes its impact. As Warren from Zambia explains: "If someone has it, it affects us as well. . . . [But] the most affected are those who actually look after orphans—the old people. [A]n old woman who cannot even . . . hold a hoe is looking after grandchildren."[34]

Child poverty is especially serious because it bodes ill for the future of both the people affected as well as the countries where they live. Yet hundreds of millions of children—including far more than one out of every two in many places—are poor.[35] Orphans are the worst off. "No one would know the difference between a slave and a poor relative," commented a man from Zambia (where "poor relative" is commonly used to describe someone abandoned to a relative).[36] Half of all children under five in South Asia and one-third of those in Sub-Saharan Africa are malnourished.[37] Such children are ill-prepared to learn much from whatever schooling they get; in some cases, they can be permanently disabled by malnutrition.

Being born into a particular social group can also consign a person to lifelong poverty. Groups that are discriminated against, whether by the government or in more informal ways, are more likely to be poor and to have even less chance of escaping poverty than the rest of society. Discrimination may target ethnic groups (such as the minority groups in the Vietnamese highlands), religious groups (such as non-Muslims in Sudan), castes (such as the Dalits in India), indigenous peoples (such as the Maya in Central America), the disabled (everywhere), or even livelihoods (such as pastoralists like the Maasai in Kenya). All are likely to be denied equal access to schools, equal treatment in courts, and equal opportunity in the job market. They are also likely to be the least prepared to gain from any economic opportunity, because they lack not only skills but also social connections and role models on how to act in a modern economy.

Violence and the Poor

Wide social divisions are likely to produce highly unstable political regimes and generate violence, even war. Plenty of research testifies to the fact that discrimination and inequality, especially when they permeate the economic, social, political, and cultural spheres simultaneously, make conflicts more likely.[38]

Armed conflict and poverty are highly correlated. Nearly 40 percent of low human development states (which have relatively low levels of life expectancy, literacy, education, and standards of living) were affected by armed conflict between 1997 and 2006, compared with less than 2 percent of high human development states.[39] According to the 2011 World Development Report,

> People in fragile and conflict-affected states are more likely to be impoverished, to miss out on schooling, and to lack access to basic health services. Children born in a fragile or conflict-affected state are twice as likely to be undernourished and nearly twice as likely to lack access to improved water; those of primary-school age are three times as likely not to be enrolled in school; and they are nearly twice as likely to die before their fifth birthday.[40]

Some 1.5 billion people—more than a fifth of the world's population—live in countries grievously affected by political and criminal violence.[41] Africa, where two-fifths of the world's conflicts in 2006 took place, is the most affected.

The poor suffer more than anyone else from violence and conflict. In the short term, because they often live in the areas where fighting takes place, they risk death and injury and the destruction of their homes. In the long term, they have to cope with the destruction of public infrastructure, disruption of livelihoods, the undermining of law and order, and the erosion of social stability and culture.[42] Many spend years as refugees. Child soldiers are likely to experience trauma that will endure far into their adult lives. As Vasco, who was forced to join a militia for eight months in Timor-Leste when he was just 14, says painfully, "They ordered us to rape. . . . They beat me with a piece of wood every day. . . . I wake up still from bad dreams. I am still constantly afraid."[43]

Even where violence does not erupt, the insecurity that social conflict brings is itself a major cause of poverty. People refrain from making all sorts of investments, worry about the safety of their property, and refrain from taking any step that will not pay off immediately. Emigration increases. Prices rise. Governments often react by becoming more repressive and more exclusionary, and officials may become more corrupt as they worry more about their own futures.

The fate of the over 42 million refugees and internally displaced people (IDPs) is often even worse, especially if they are from minority groups.[44] With few belongings, and often suffering from hunger and the trauma of their dislocation, refugees are vulnerable to exploitation and abuse. Forced into unfamiliar surroundings, often without any family or communal support system to alleviate their misery, they are vulnerable to mistreatment by officials, local populations, and even peacekeeping troops at times. In many refugee camps in Sierra Leone, Guinea, and Liberia, for instance, young girls between the ages of 13 and 18 were forced to exchange sex for money, a handful of fruit, or even a bar of soap. Parents tended to turn a blind eye to this "mechanism of survival" even though the sexual exploitation produced a slew of pregnancies.[45]

Rebeka Dz'da Buma, a 51-year-old widow who was displaced when militia attacked her village in the Democratic Republic of Congo (DRC), bemoans:

> What is difficult is to have to go out everyday in search of food. If we don't go out, we don't eat. . . . I am very unhappy with the kind of life we have as displaced people. It brings back bad memories, I am disappointed with life. I am scared that my children will become street children and then bandits. I am also scared for their health. We have problems such as malaria and diarrhea. . . . I have hyper tension— I didn't have that before. I would like us to go home and start our life again.

Anasthasie Bodha, a 60-year-old IDP also from the DRC, laments: "The question I am asking myself all day long is: 'How am I going to do to find food tomorrow?' When I think about my life, my stomach hurts."[46]

*   *   *

If you are poor in the developing world, trouble doesn't come at you from just one direction. It flies at you from all corners, and it hits very hard. Children are more likely to die young or be physically or mentally impaired by malnutrition. Families are unable to afford goods—fertilizer for farms, books for schools, time-saving conveniences for homes—that could enhance their living standards. Illnesses that might be adequately addressed if properly treated end up leaving people permanently disabled, chronically ill, or worse. The net result is that poverty becomes self-perpetuating, extending not just from father to son and mother to daughter but over countless generations.

In some parts of the developing world, such as China, the numbers of the poor are diminishing. But for those in the developing world who are still mired in poverty, a difficult life is becoming even harder in some respects. The poor have always had to cope with the hardships caused by an uncertain climate, changes in season, political conflicts, and sickness; but their challenges are multiplying in some important ways because of rising populations, worsening ecological conditions, and, especially, the breakdown of traditional social support systems. Where these are accompanied by breakdowns in the rule of law—governments flattening homes and grabbing businesses, heightened ethnic tensions, state services collapsing, destruction of infrastructures, and the spiraling cost of some basic commodities—the poor are as vulnerable as ever.

The next chapter explores in depth the reasons, old and new, why the poor are poor and why they cannot climb out of poverty. As chapter 4 explains, the single most important reason is that states—and the markets they regulate—too often end up working for only a small minority of a country's population. As a consequence, the poor are excluded, often deliberately, from the chance to participate on an even footing in economies and in government.

CHAPTER 4

Why Are They Poor?

"Big people seldom understand the issues of the poor," says Kishore, who used to polish shoes for a living but now owns a small shop in Pakistan. "Poor people only can imagine the issues of the poor."[1]

For a rich person—whether from the West or from the developing world itself—it is indeed hard to imagine the struggles the poor face each day. Only if you have lived among the impoverished—whether in India or Bolivia or Yemen—can you have some idea of the range of problems they face, some understanding that poverty is about much more than a lack of money.

The many different causes and characteristics of poverty can be grouped together in many different ways. One simple but revealing arrangement is to divide them between "macro" features—those things that affect entire societies or parts of a society—and "micro" elements—those things that affect specific communities, families, and individuals. As shown in figure 4.1, macro features form the roots that sustain many micro features. The stronger the roots and the richer the soil in which they take hold, the more likely it is that communities, families, and individuals will thrive.

On the macro level, poverty is strongly influenced by a combination of economic policies, the quality of government, and how power is exercised. When a state adopts measures that reduce or eliminate growth—by, for instance, reducing macroeconomic stability, the competitiveness of markets, and the construction of important infrastructure—it is the poor who suffer the most. Equally, when the government can't or won't provide education, apply the law equally, build roads throughout a country, discourage discrimination, or distribute public spending equitably, the poor have the most to lose. The macro level includes all public goods, such as security, the rule of law, national infrastructure, and the government's capacity to get things done.

On a micro level, poverty is all about having too little of almost everything. Poor people are likely to have limited skills, no access to reliable health care, few work opportunities, few hard assets, and no ties to those with money or power. Some, but not all, micro characteristics are dependent on macro

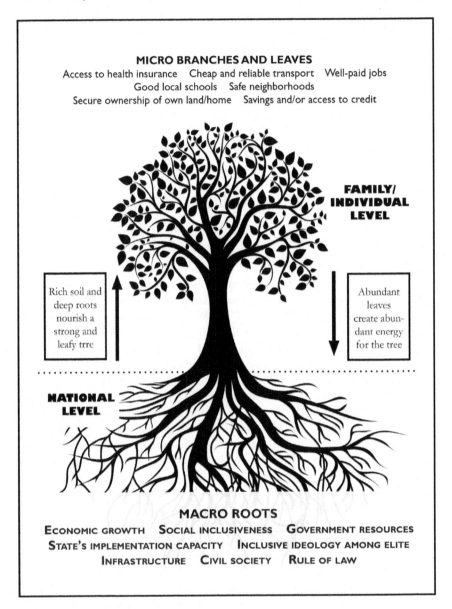

MICRO BRANCHES AND LEAVES

Access to health insurance   Cheap and reliable transport   Well-paid jobs
Good local schools   Safe neighborhoods
Secure ownership of own land/home   Savings and/or access to credit

**FAMILY/
INDIVIDUAL
LEVEL**

Rich soil and deep roots nourish a strong and leafy trre

Abundant leaves create abundant energy for the tree

**NATIONAL
LEVEL**

MACRO ROOTS

ECONOMIC GROWTH   SOCIAL INCLUSIVENESS   GOVERNMENT RESOURCES
STATE'S IMPLEMENTATION CAPACITY   INCLUSIVE IDEOLOGY AMONG ELITE
INFRASTRUCTURE   CIVIL SOCIETY   RULE OF LAW

Figure 4.1   The Empowering Tree

characteristics—and this relationship is amplified if a person is poor. For instance, a poor person's access to justice and good transportation links is strongly influenced by a state's ability to provide an efficient and uncorrupt justice system and an extensive and well-maintained road and rail network.

When the state cannot provide good services, the richer sectors of society may be able to buy alternatives (such as houses in gated and guarded communities when security is bad or the attention and support of a high-level official when the rule of law is bad); the poor cannot.

Table 4.1 summarizes the macro and micro characteristics of poverty and indicates the kinds of practical problems they create. Although both the macro and micro deficiencies are important, it is the macro that matter the most, as will be discussed in chapter 6. But, whereas most books on the macro aspects of poverty focus on economics (or social development spending), this book puts politics front and center because it has been underemphasized elsewhere—and remains the most intractable aspect of the overall equation. Instead of looking at such macro *economic* issues as tax and spending policies, trade, and investment, or asking whether governments should be spending more on education and health care, this book examines such macro *political* questions as why elites betray the poor, why governments don't work better, and why the poor are not being empowered by the growth that many developing countries are currently experiencing. Although it focuses on national-level issues, the political problems the book addresses are very similar to those at the local level.

The multidimensional and reinforcing nature of these deficiencies make it extremely difficult for the poor to escape the poverty trap by investing in their own skills and improving their lot on their own. Few poor people suffer from all the disadvantages listed in table 4.1, but most suffer from many of them. Furthermore, because the poor are so exposed and vulnerable to sudden jolts of all kinds, a problem in just one area of their lives can tip the balance and send them plummeting into disaster.

*   *   *

It's hard to generalize about a group that includes up to one in every two people on the planet. But, as the table shows, almost all poor people in the developing world face one thing in common: little or no access to opportunity.

This chapter explains how this lack of opportunity prevents the poor in the developing world from bettering their lives. It begins by looking at the role of social divisions in this tragedy and then goes on to discuss how the poor's own governments—deliberately in many cases—deny them the opportunity to escape poverty.

First, however, it presents a story—Maymana and Mofizul's story—that offers a window into the lives of the poor across the less developed world. Although their government and the more powerful players in their community have to a large extent failed them, the two have persevered to eke out a meager existence. But hard work and resourcefulness are not enough to overcome the ways in which their society disadvantages and discriminates against them.

Table 4.1 Macro and Micro Characteristics of Poverty

	Disadvantage the Poor Face	Practical Consequences
At the Macro Level		
State	Poor quality and/or level of public services	Little schooling; biased courts; weak property rights
Market	Bureaucratic procedures and/or corruption; unequal infrastructure spending	Higher prices; unable to register business; imbalanced competition
Social Structure	Exclusion from schools, land, and jobs because of gender, caste, ethnicity, or religion	Unequal implementation of the law; unequal rights to land; disadvantaged access to business/government
Economic Conditions	Growth concentrated in a few sectors/regions	Few job opportunities
Geography	Remoteness	Limited access to markets, jobs, and schools
Climate	Semiarid climate, infertile soil	Lower incomes, higher risk of poor harvest
At the Micro Level		
Physical Assets	Little land; property not recognized by government; few or no assets of value	Highly vulnerable to exploitation; no assets to fall back upon in crisis
Education	Fewer marketable skills when searching for jobs; less knowledge of rights; less ready to innovate	Less secure and lower paid employment; less able to challenge government for rights
Family	Weak family support network	More vulnerable to shocks
Social Networks	Limited access to powerful officials and patrons	Less access to jobs, licenses, public services
Health Care	Limited access to health care	More likely to suffer from ailments; more likely to become disabled
Access to Transport	Less access to good transportation	Harder and costlier to travel in search of work and other opportunities; harder to sell goods
Access to Financial Instruments	Limited access to formal banks/insurance	No safe instruments for saving; high borrowing costs; no insurance for health/death
Income Opportunities	Fewer, lower-quality, and less secure jobs; less access to protections of formal job market	Lower incomes; greater vulnerability to income reduction

40

Maymana and Mofizul's Story

Maymana and Mofizul live in a fertile and densely populated area of central Bangladesh. Their village is near to a main road, which ensures that trade with surrounding areas is brisk. The location also gives villagers access to important government services and major NGOs that provide training, health care, and loans.

In the early 1990s, their household had five members: Maymana, her husband Hafeez, and their three children. Hafeez had three rickshaws that he hired out and an acre of land that he farmed. They were poor but had a reasonably stable life, some assets, and did not lack for basic needs. However, two of the children—the daughters—required dowries, and the son, Mofizul, had a growth on his back and was often sick. He was excluded from school because of his disability.

At this time, Hafeez started coughing a lot. An untrained pharmacist in the bazaar sold him some medicine, which had no effect. The staff at the government-run health-care center asked for bribes. When he visited another doctor, twenty miles away, it cost so much he had to sell a rickshaw. To pay for special tests, he had to sell a second rickshaw. Weekly income plunged, forcing the family to cut back on food.

The two daughters, worried that the family could not provide for their dowries, took the matter into their own hands. They bought young goats, fattened and sold them, and then repeated the process a few times to raise money. Male members of the wider family, with some help from Hafeez, arranged marriages for both.

Hafeez lost a lot of weight and was confined to the house. His last rickshaw was sold off, and his wife and son (the daughters now having left home) had to depend on whatever rice could be produced from the land they owned. Maymana earned some extra money doing domestic work.

In 1998 Hafeez died, probably from throat cancer. His father promptly repossessed the land, forcing Maymana to borrow and even beg for money. Fortunately, the wider family, neighbors, and the local mosque helped out. Mofizul, now 12 years old and often sick, found some casual work at a timber mill, but for very low wages.

Maymana sued her father-in-law, but, despite the fact that the formal law would probably have awarded her the rights to her husband's land, the local village court ruled against her in December 1999. Such a judgment is typical in a country where informal custom discriminates against women and often triumphs formal law.

An uncle let the now-homeless mother and son live on a scrap of his own land. There, on a patch of dirt the size of a tennis court, they lived in two small mud huts, one roofed with rusty iron and the other with plastic sheeting. They had no furniture, equipment, or livestock, nothing except a few old cooking utensils. But they persevered.

Maymana patched together a meager livelihood from casual work, borrowing, begging, and charity. But her illiteracy (she had only two years of schooling), age (she was in her late forties), poor hearing (she was almost deaf), and unpredictable health all limited her opportunities to get a job. She gleaned rice wherever and whenever possible. Mofizul, now 13, started receiving half the pay of an adult, but the work was irregular. Locally, there are too many unskilled workers for too few jobs, so he will probably always be poorly paid and have no job security.

The state issued Maymana a Vulnerable Groups Development (VGD) card, entitling her to 30 kilograms of wheat every month—but because the local government councilor who approved her participation was a political rival to her uncle, the latter forced her to return the card.

Three of Bangladesh's major NGOs operated in the village at the time, providing services such as microloans. But they avoided Maymana, possibly because both the staff of the NGOs and the members of local microcredit groups saw an aging, deaf widow with no secure income as a dangerous investment. She herself was worried about meeting their requirements for weekly payments and was therefore reluctant to approach them.

The future for Maymana and Mofizul looks bleak, but at least they have their own resilience, the support of a robust social network, the small homestead with its two huts, and some semi-regular earnings with which to avoid destitution. Many families in Bangladesh are much worse off.[2]

The Root of the Problem: Social Exclusion

Lack of opportunity is so widespread and its impact so powerful in less developed countries because of the nature of their societies. Weak government and divided populations combine to create a governing system that inevitably produces inequitable social relationships and self-interested politics that work against the interests of the weak and deprived. And the two factors reinforce each other in a poisonous mix that has long-term effects on how countries are governed and how the poor live. As a consequence, hard work alone cannot help those at the bottom of society build more comfortable and secure lives.

In the case of Maymana and Mofizul, for instance, courts, schools, healthcare providers, local government officials, insurance providers, and even family members are all too ready to discriminate against them if it serves their interests and no custom or law blocks their way. Such conditions are not unique to Bangladesh. Indeed, the great majority of lesser developed countries suffer from the same ailments—and produce the same pattern of disadvantages for the poor.

The countries most likely to stifle the hard work of the poor in this way are those that suffer from a combination of deep social fissures and a lack of effective government. In contrast to more cohesive countries, where elites feel that the poor are "one of them" (and that they therefore have an obligation to act on their behalf), or in countries with more effective institutions, where elites are held accountable for their actions (and therefore have an incentive to act more inclusively), elites in these places have little reason to care about the poor. They feel like they have little or nothing in common with their poorer countrymen and see little point in helping the poor participate as full citizens in the social, economic, and political life of the country. And the elites aren't usually just indifferent to the fate of the poor. Often, they deliberately exclude them by manipulating weak governments in ways that work against the interests of the poor. Once established, these attitudes and practices can become ingrained in the political culture—perpetuating themselves over generations.

Many of these divisions go back at least to colonial times (and even further in some cases, such as India, Ethiopia, and Nepal), when European powers redrew the maps of Africa, Latin America, and parts of Asia, carving out states with borders that simply ignored local political groupings and geographies. The result is a large number of countries that are a patchwork of distinct racial, ethnic, religious, and clan groups—most of which had no historical experience of working together.

The European imperialists tended to favor particular groups and regions—largely because this helped the Europeans exploit their territories in the easiest and least expensive way possible. They disbursed power, wealth, social services, and infrastructure in ways that created major economic and political disparities between different groups and different areas within the same country. When the colonialists left, the favored groups were in privileged positions—and ever since they have naturally fought to maintain their status.[3] Meanwhile, those less favored have naturally fought to reverse their positions.

Weak government, which is easy to exploit, and a dearth of alternative opportunities to make money have accentuated these tendencies and produced a zero-sum game in which various groups compete against each other for power in order to acquire the resources controlled by the state. As a result, rule by exclusion has so permeated society in much of the developing world that it affects how each group views the others. Even a sudden change in a country's governing regime does not change the pattern. Until the American invasion of Iraq in 2003, the Sunni population dominated the state at the expense of everyone else. Since Saddam Hussein's overthrow, Shiites have naturally sought to replicate the model, with themselves in charge. In Kenya, political parties compete at election time based on ethnic affiliation, not political platform. When the competition gets out of hand, as it did in 2008, violence can erupt. Groups such as the Kikuyu seek to maintain their central position in society, while others fight because they believe it is "our turn to eat."[4] In Syria, the minority Alawites, who constitute about one-eighth of the population, monopolized power for four decades, despite much opposition from the majority Sunnis at times.

Officials in these postcolonial states often find that their own standing and well-being is better served by taking care of people from their own "identity group" or ruling clique—even if it means hurting everyone else. The lack of solidarity across groups, which often has deep roots and is based on different histories and beliefs, means that no one—and especially not the people who pull the levers of power—works for the good of the country as a whole.

Where cooperation does extend across ethnic and religious lines within a ruling elite—as in Nigeria—it is usually only a cynical alliance of opportunity among different factions within a narrow ruling elite. In all these weakly governed states, various cliques compete to take advantage of the general lawlessness in society to siphon off money from everything from state construction projects to gold mines to warfare. In such cases, identity divisions may be manipulated for short-term personal or political gain, widening the gulf between groups and further extending the hold of the wealthy over everyone else. In states with a weak sense of national community, the ruling regime is more likely to grab control of wealth-producing assets, restrict markets, disenfranchise portions of the electorate, and even dupe foreigners into providing more aid than to try to formulate policy that might encourage growth.[5]

This political and economic exclusion naturally produces a social exclusion (or high degree of "adverse incorporation" in society) that limits access to all kinds of public services and business opportunities. The overall effect has severe consequences for its victims. In Brazil, for instance, nearly three times as many black women die from complications of pregnancy and childbirth as white women. In Bolivia, the poverty rate among the non-white population is more than double—37 to 17 percent—that of the white population. In Vietnam, the government estimates that 90 percent of the poverty in the country will be concentrated within ethnic minorities by 2010. In the Indian states of Uttar Pradesh and Bihar, primary school enrollment for lower caste and tribal girls is 37 percent, compared with 60 percent for girls from higher castes (and compared to 70 percent among boys from higher castes).[6] As one villager in Assam, India, explained, "In our village, we see inequality among the people. The villagers are divided into rich and poor, literate and illiterate, high and low."[7]

Tens of millions of people across the globe are impoverished and uprooted by the armed conflict, communal violence, and terrible human rights violations these social divisions cause. Francis Deng, who has served as the UN Secretary-General's representative on internally displaced persons (and had earlier been Sudan's foreign minister), explains that his

> thirty-three in-depth missions around the world revealed that the conditions of the victims of these internal wars had much in common, nearly always characterized by an acute crisis of national identity that privileges some to enjoy the full rights of citizenship and marginalizes others on the basis of race, ethnicity, culture, and religion to the extent that citizenship becomes only of paper value.[8]

Of course social divisions by themselves do not cause inequities. Every market economy has them. But where societies are weakly integrated, such inequities are likely to be far greater because the mechanisms for spreading wealth—markets and governments—break down (see below). As Lemaron, a 29-year-old who runs a hair and beauty salon in Kenya, reports, "What makes us live in this cycle of poverty is a lack of good foundations in life. Those people who are rich in Kenya—the biggest percentage—are those whose great grandparents left wealth and riches for them."[9]

The combination of inequality and exclusion both creates poverty and perpetuates it. Starting with little income and meager assets, the poor are excluded from the resources, opportunities, information, and social networks necessary to improve their condition. Imbalanced distributions of public spending, unfair laws that privilege one group over another, and officials beholden to powerful interests all play their role. Discrimination in land and water rights, access to schools and financial institutions, and job markets all work to reduce the scope for the poor to use their own initiative to improve their circumstances. Referring to a powerful few in her Bangladeshi village, Rahima describes: "The canal belongs to them. No one can fish there or bathe cattle."[10] Table 4.2 provides examples of the most important resources that are typically denied to the poor and the mechanisms by which they are denied.

As described in the previous chapter, the poor are trapped in a vortex of low capabilities and meager assets that spins from generation to generation.[11] A 45-year-old man from a lower caste in Uttar Pradesh complained, "There is no freedom, sir. Only the Thakurs [upper caste] are free. Neither can we do any work, drink water, nor can we do anything else."[12]

Of course, discrimination is practiced not just by elites and governments but at all levels within society. Ethnic groups discriminate against other ethnic groups, castes against other castes, clans against other clans. Even the poor discriminate against the poor at times if it serves their interests. In India, for example, a hierarchical social structure oppresses the poor. As one Indian observes, "It was the calculus that governed life: Am I his sahib, or is he mine? Who should shout at whom? Whose body must apologize for its presence, and whose must swagger? Whose eyes must stay down?"[13] When national and community leaders repeatedly and all too obviously act in unfair ways, many in a population will take the cue to act similarly. Such behavior spreads when government officials are incapable of fighting bias within their ranks, when most of the population is struggling daily just to survive, and when a society is divided into dissimilar groups forced to compete for scarce resources.

The deck is stacked especially heavily against poor women such as Maymana, who face discrimination not only at the societal level, but also within their own communities and families. Beholden to men by custom, law, and the power structures of many impoverished societies, they receive unequal treatment in how money is allocated for education and health care. Even their freedom to wear what they want and travel where and how they wish is often severely curtailed. As a 55-year-old woman in Tanzania remarked:

> If a Yao woman tells her husband: Please let's us build a better/modern house, the normal reply is: "Are you more intelligent than me? Are you another man in this household so that we are two men? I am feeding you, do you want to rule me?" Once he utters such words, and at the same time he has a good sum of money, it is evident that he has got a secret woman he may marry anytime, even without informing his wife.[14]

Seventy percent of the people living in extreme poverty are women. Women also bear the physical brunt of the anger and frustration that poverty generates: globally, between 16 and 50 percent of women in steady relationships are assaulted

Table 4.2 Social Exclusion Processes

Resource	Potential Benefits	Mechanism of Exclusion
Agricultural Land	Source of stable income and a secure shelter	Land tenure laws
Urban Land and Home	Permanent, secure shelter; access to loans (through mortgages); reduction of risk from income loss	Discriminatory or corrupt registration schemes; restrictions that limit housing construction
Public Infrastructure	Better access to public services, education, and health care; longer lives; higher incomes	Little or no public provision of roads, electricity, water, and sanitation
Education	Better job prospects; more able to demand rights from governments; less vulnerable to exploitation	Unequal public provision; no road or transport links to public schools; disproportionate spending on higher education
Transportation	Links to markets and jobs; access to information on wider world, technology, social change	Unequal provision of roads or bus service
Employment	Stable income, chances to upgrade skills, access to insurance	Discriminatory job markets
Information	Knowledge about jobs, education, political rights, and prices in markets	No road links; poor schooling; discriminatory language policies
Security	Safer homes and communities; higher incomes from the confidence to invest in farms and businesses; higher prices for property; more likely to invest in upgrading housing	Discriminatory laws, courts, and police
Social Networks	Access to licenses, jobs, loans, political favor	Influential social groups (often based on ethnicity, religion, caste, gender, etc.) exclude outsiders

Gendercide: The Ultimate Form of Discrimination[17]

How bad is discrimination against girls and women? Some societies have gone so far as to declare war against baby girls. Distorted sex ratios in parts of East and South Asia suggest that tens of millions of female fetuses and babies have been eliminated in one way or another over the past two decades.

The historically strong preference for boys was bluntly stated by an older woman in Shandong province, China, after the killing of a newborn girl: "Doing a baby girl is not a big thing around here. . . . It's not a child. It's a girl baby, and we can't keep it. Around these parts, you can't get by without a son. Girl babies don't count."

Not all traditional societies show a marked preference for boys over girls. But in those societies where the family line passes through the son and in which he is supposed to look after his parents in old age, a son is worth a lot more to the parents than a daughter. In such places, a girl is deemed to have joined her husband's family when she marries. In India, the dowry that a girl's family must pay to her husband's family can be enormous. No wonder that a Hindu saying declares, "Raising a daughter is like watering your neighbors' garden." No wonder, too, that doctors in India advertise ultrasound scans with the slogan "Pay 5,000 rupees [$110] today and save 50,000 rupees tomorrow."

The fateful collision between ancient prejudice, rapidly spreading technology that can determine the prenatal sex of children, and declining fertility has resulted in as many as one-quarter of all female babies being eliminated in some parts of China and India. Other East Asia countries—including South Korea, Singapore, and Taiwan—similarly have peculiarly high numbers of male births. The same is true in the Caucasus (Armenia, Azerbaijan, and Georgia), and parts of the Western Balkans (Serbia and Macedonia).

Such discrepancies produce more crime and violence caused by frustrated single men and rising levels of bride abduction, trafficking of women, rape, and prostitution. It may also contribute to the high rate of female suicides in China and South Korea; women find it hard to live knowing that they have aborted or killed their baby daughters.

by their partners.[15] The conditions are even worse in war zones: one-third of the women in the conflict-ridden Congolese province of Kivu have been raped. Tens of thousands have been molested, mutilated, and sexually abused in Sudan through its long history of warfare without a single person being held accountable by either national or international justice.[16]

The disabled such as Mofizul—and their families—also suffer great misfortunes from the inabilities of their states to prevent discrimination. In Tanzania, for instance, households with disabled members are 20 percent more likely than other households to be living in poverty.[18]

Making the Problem Worse: Government

While governments in most countries generally strive to moderate such divisions—by, at the very least, offering equal protection before the law to everyone—in deeply divided societies they often exacerbate them. Beholden to a segment of the population, politicians, bureaucrats, and judges end up directly and deliberately perpetuating social exclusion. (In many cases, groups of people are not actually entirely excluded but are included on terms that make it all but impossible for them to compete economically and politically with other groups. For instance, many poor people must take low-paying jobs in bad conditions and on uncertain terms because their lack of education and desperate need to earn money puts them in a highly disadvantageous position. This phenomenon is known as "adverse incorporation.") The vicious cycle—of social exclusion producing unfair governments, which in turn produce social exclusion—feeds off of itself.

Indeed, according to scholars Douglass North, John Joseph Wallis, Steven Webb, and Barry Weingast, elite domination of political institutions and economic returns are really two sides of the same coin. They are part of a grand bargain among powerful interests that helps maintain stability (by providing an incentive to support an existing governance arrangement) in countries where governments are too weak to do so on their own.[19]

In the Philippines, for instance, a small number of families have used their huge landholdings and wealth to dominate politics for generations. The country has millions of families, but just 170 of those families have produced 7 presidents, 2 vice presidents, 42 senators, and 147 representatives since the 1900s.[20] In the 2007–2010 Congress, more than three-quarters of the lawmakers were members of powerful political families. It is no surprise that these families have used their power to grab most of the economic gains that the Philippines has made since becoming independent. In Pakistan, powerful clans exploit their almost feudal positions in society to dominate government in ways that perpetuate their positions. Bureaucrats defer to elites. Courts and police are beholden to powerful interests. State enterprises are managed for the benefit of the rich and well-connected. In Bahrain, the ruling Sunni royal family has systemically excluded Shiites from important positions in government and the security services and ensured that they have less access to public services and wealth (most of which is controlled by the state in the petroleum-rich country). In Côte d'Ivoire, southern politicians amended the national constitution to deny millions of northerners the right to identity cards, disenfranchising them in the process and ensuring the south's continued control of government.

"I always think about why our area is lagging behind other parts of the country? Why are our rights not extended to us? Why we are given this contaminated water?" asks Pakistan's Karim Bux, who has lived his life near Manchar Lake, which is slowly dying because of environmental degradation. "Sometimes we think that Pakistan does not consider us Pakistani. The government does not pay any attention to our area. . . . All people living here are human beings but why they are not giving us our rights?"[21]

Spending time with the world's poorest people quickly demolishes any conception that their governments might possibly offer a cure for their impoverishment. On the contrary, more often than not, it is their governments that are a major cause of their predicaments!

The villages in countries such as Pakistan, Bolivia, and Sudan and the slums of cities such as Recife, Nairobi, and Mumbai offer depressing testimony to the powerlessness of the poor. Government indifference is seen everywhere. Roads are often unpaved, schools are undersupplied, and streets are insecure. Government, if present at all, is seen as a predator to be avoided. The police ask for bribes, and officials act only if pressured by influential interests. "If the powerful speak, people abide by it without any judgment," describes a man in Assam, India. But "no one cares for a poor person in society. The people with the money consider a poor man no more than a pest," laments someone from Uttar Pradesh, also in India.[22]

Most people in developing countries believe that their governments serve only a select few, whether the rich and the powerful in a distant capital (or district) or simply the more advantaged and well-connected close to home. According to various surveys, 93 percent of Bolivians, 75 percent of Brazilians, 74 percent of Salvadorians, 66 percent of Indians, and 60 percent of Indonesians believe that their governments are run for the benefits of a few big interests.[23]

Corrupt politicians and officials grow rich at the expense of the weak. As one poor person in Cambodia complained:

> It is easy to buy power here since the pockets of all high officials are open. . . . Those with power just make a few trips to the forest and cut trees; then they can earn enough money to cover their expenses for a position. . . . It would be fortunate for us if they didn't use their power to reap profits from us . . . but that is not the case. Normally they threaten other villagers for money. . . . How can the poor survive? . . . The poor are normally the victims and the powerful people are those who benefit.

Another Cambodian from a different village echoed these concerns: "If we don't have connections or money [for bribes], it is hard for us to claim our rights. Nowadays, right or wrong is just on the lips of powerful people."[24] Similar stories can be heard throughout the developing world. In a village in Uttar Pradesh, India, for example, a woman said, "For farming, the big officers close the deals. They don't do any work without taking money. How will we pay money when we can't even fill our stomachs?" A man concurred, "You need a license to start a business. It may be anything—opening a meat shop, rearing hens—all need a license. The licenses are distributed at the district level, and the middlemen make money for giving them. People usually pay up to save themselves from trouble."[25] Connections can mean the difference between life and death. As Mircho from Sindh, Pakistan, declares: "An influential person or an important officer gets the right medicines and treatment at the government hospital but those who are poor are given 'No 2' (sub-standard) medicines, due to which most of the patients die. They survive only by luck."[26]

The picture is the same throughout most of the developing world. In Nigeria, few public officials are driven by a keen sense of public service; most have only a vague notion of serving the public, coupled with a far sharper sense of serving their private interests. Colleagues at my company spent more hours strategizing how to obtain licenses and deal with bureaucrats than how to win a greater share of the market. Relationships based on blood—or at least a long association—easily trump all others, making it almost impossible for outsiders and newcomers to win the ear of officials. In Bolivia, the indigenous people I met railed endlessly about how they had been excluded from power for centuries. In Somaliland, person after person recounted to me how their own government (when it was a part of Somalia) had bombed the capital, Hargeisa, to bits when the local people had protested about how it treated them.

Part of the problem is that institutions—including government agencies, courts, city administrations, and police forces—in these countries are too feeble to play the vital roles they perform in other countries. They don't formulate policies and laws that will benefit the country as a whole. They don't implement those policies and laws in an evenhanded fashion. They don't referee between competing interests and groups. And they don't, in many cases, because they can't. The colonial powers that established the governments in these countries never bothered to ascertain whether the institutions they introduced actually met the needs of their inhabitants. To make matters worse, the colonialists either trained only a select, small group of locals to help them run these institutions or—as in the case of the Belgian Congo—trained no one at all and ran everything entirely by themselves. Of course, when the Europeans eventually upped and left, the institutions they left behind were unloved or actively despised, and few if any locals had the knowledge and experience to operate them. The great social divisions that the colonialists created by the way in which they carved up their territories (discussed in the previous section) spawned political elites with little desire or capacity to try to bridge these divides.

The resulting dysfunction has proved hard to overcome. Many governments simply lack the tools, the competence, or the desire to restrain a continual, frantic competition for the spoils of power. Short-term, selfish opportunism always trumps long-term investments that might help everyone. Nigeria has earned well over $400 billion from oil exports since independence, but gross mismanagement and corruption has allowed highways and universities to crumble and kept 76 percent of the people in poverty.[27] A class of rich ex-generals monopolizes political and economic power, erects palatial villas, and represses any grassroots association that threatens to challenge the status quo. The best ways to get ahead in Nigeria are to join the army, go into politics, open a business with a corrupt ex-general, bribe a government official, or emigrate.

In socially fractured countries with weak institutions, a sharp dichotomy exists between public and private morality. Behavior that is seen by society as unethical when conducted in the private sphere raises few eyebrows when conducted in the public sphere. A man who misuses the money of a family member or a clan association will be ostracized; a man who takes advantage of his position as a public official to enrich himself will not. Corruption in public office may not necessarily be condoned, but it is widely expected. An official with a reputation for taking bribes provokes less disdain or anger than an official who refuses to use his position to help a classmate get a job. The consequences for the quality of governance are severe. Public funds are misused, the rule of law is weakened, wealthy interests gain unfair advantage, and state policies go astray.

As Peter Ekeh explained in a landmark 1975 article,

> Most educated Africans are citizens of two publics in the same society. On the one hand, they belong to a civic public [i.e., to institutions such as the military, the civil service, the police, etc.] from which they gain materially but to which they give only grudgingly. On the other hand they belong to a primordial public [i.e., to clan, ethnic, religious, or other groups] from which they derive little or no material benefits but to which they are expected to give generously and do give

materially. To make matters more complicated, their relationship to the primordial public is moral, while that to the civic public is amoral. The dialectical tensions and confrontations between these two publics constitute the uniqueness of modern African politics. . . . The unwritten law of the dialectics is that it is legitimate to rob the civic public in order to strengthen the primordial public. . . . Of course, "morality" has an old-fashioned ring about it; but any politics without morality is destructive. And the destructive results of African politics in the post-colonial era owes something to the amorality of the civic public.[28]

The tribalism inherent in these countries' political cultures engulfs the countries' already weak governing bodies, tribalizing them in the process, and preventing any apolitical bureaucratic structure emerging that could gain some allegiance from their populations. Similarly, the weakness of the state makes people fall back upon their traditional loyalties and personal relationships, because these are the only forms of protection and support available. As development economist William Easterly explains, "Ethnic diversity [and other forms of diversity—SK] has a more adverse effect on economic policy and growth when institutions are poor. To put it another way, poor institutions have an even more adverse effect on growth and policy when ethnic diversity is high. Conversely, in countries with sufficiently good institutions, ethnic diversity does not lower growth or worsen economic policies."[29]

The weakness of such governments put the poor at a severe disadvantage. The inability of the Bangladeshi authorities to police courts and markets or even to provide the most basic public services hurt the country's weakest members far more than its strongest. Mofizul entered the workforce with fewer skills than his neighbors. Hafeez repeatedly paid too much for ineffective health care. The village court discriminated against Maymana in awarding her father-in-law the land. And the VGD supplement was blocked because of a local political rivalry. The government's weakness even indirectly contributed to the family's dearth of insurance: scant regulation encouraged the embezzlement by employees of the premiums paid by other poor people in the same district to the largest local life insurance provider, and families of deceased policyholders were not being paid. Those who had been cheated out of their premiums could not even afford to bring a lawsuit against a company of this size to reclaim their losses.

In such places, the law is of little help. Key components of the justice system— including the police and the judiciary—typically work not for the benefit of justice but for the rich and the powerful. Those who are supposed to maintain law and order often use their authority to line their own pockets—most perniciously at the expense of those who can least afford it. In many places, the poor have more to fear from the police than from criminals. Twenty-nine percent of Kenyans surveyed in 2006 said that they had to make "extraordinary efforts" to avoid problems with the police in the past year. The poor who are the victims of or witnesses to a crime often see no point in reporting it to the authorities, especially if the perpetrator is wealthy or belongs to a politically or socially influential group. The rule of law is not just hard to find—a 2008 United Nations' report estimated that four billion people live outside the protection of the rule of law—[30]it is hard for most people to define, because they have never seen anything like it.

These institutional weaknesses play into the hands of sectarian and elite interests, producing governments staffed by officials with much to gain by encouraging social exclusion and disenfranchisement. Regimes of this type do not act for the general interest, only for the narrow interest of the groups that support them. Many of Pakistan's problems can be traced to the feudal nature of its politics and the stark concentration of power in a tiny elite that has dominated the state for decades. Some scholars estimate that Pakistan's elite includes fewer than a thousand people—fewer than a thousand in a country with a population of over 180 million![31] In Nepal, divisions generated by ethnicity and caste yielded a narrow ruling class concentrated in the capital and great poverty across the countryside. This inspired a long Maoist insurgency, which deposed the king. Many of Africa's internal wars since independence—a depressingly long list that includes wars involving Sudan and South Sudan, the Democratic Republic of Congo (DRC), Chad, Angola, Nigeria, Côte d'Ivoire, Senegal, Rwanda, Burundi, Mozambique, and Ethiopia-Eritrea—are rooted in ethnic exclusion.

The Difficulties of Creating Free Markets

Capitalism has shown itself to have the power to transform the lives of poor people in the developing world. In one form or another, that odd combination of free markets, self-interested individuals, and government regulation that we call modern capitalism has enabled some poor countries to make remarkable strides toward prosperity. China, which mixes a strong role for both private and public enterprise, has grown faster than any state in history by how it has used markets, competition, and government investment to unleash the creative drive of its huge population. India, Turkey, Chile, Costa Rica, Botswana, and the Gulf Emirate states have also progressed rapidly in recent decades using their own flavor of capitalism. Although these countries still contain a lot of poor people, at least there is a steady stream of them graduating to a better life—and hope that the rest will also do so within a reasonable timeframe.

In all these cases, properly functioning markets are empowering because they give everyone a relatively equal chance to turn their inventiveness and perseverance into a better life. Although differences in backgrounds, skills, and contacts do yield different levels of opportunity, these should not deter capitalism's ability to offer everyone the ability to trade their own hard work for greater comfort and security. For Hafeez and his daughters, markets did indeed bring greater wealth when they were able to take full advantage of its chances. Similarly, hundreds of millions across the globe have gained from globalization's dynamism in recent decades by working at new factories, migrating to booming cities, and opening their own businesses.

But the great majority of the world's poor live in countries where such opportunity is either fleeting or simply nonexistent because of how society and government work to prevent these forces from empowering ordinary people.

The narrow elites that "capture" government also "capture" the benefits from increases in trade and economic activity. Instead of empowering the poor, as it has in countries such as China and Vietnam, globalization ends up hurting the poor by further isolating them from the dynamic changes occurring in prosperous enclaves within their own states and elsewhere in more robust countries. Instead of Adam Smith's "invisible hand" working to improve the lot of the great majority of society, the all too visible hands of self-serving officials work to exclude most people from even participating in the most promising economic activities.

This is unfortunate because globalization—the immense growth in international cultural and commercial exchange spouted by the enormous reductions in the cost of transport, communication, technology, and cooperation across borders—touches all countries around the world, whether its benefits are widely shared or used to further cement a small group's hold on the levers of power.

Where governments have actively sought to spread its benefits far and wide, globalization has been a great boon to the poor. China in particular has excelled at this—in fact, much of its economic miracle is firmly rooted in it. Heavy investments in education and infrastructure; a wide set of policies to encourage labor-intensive manufacturing, foreign investment, exports, and technology transfer; and a consistent, if imperfect, drive over many years to upgrade the regulatory and judicial institutions related to business have all paid off handsomely. As a result, the country sustained average economic growth of over 9 percent for the three decades after its reforms started in 1979, while attracting far more foreign investment—over $80 billion in 2007 alone—than any other developing country.[32] Exports rose one-hundredfold from $14 billion in 1979 to $1.429 trillion in 2008.[33] Meanwhile, the infant mortality rate and maternal mortality rate both fell by 40 percent between 1990 and 2005.[34] Access to telephones during this period rose almost one-hundredfold.[35] As mentioned earlier, some 650 million Chinese have escaped poverty since the beginning of the reform period. During the seven years I lived in Shanghai, there was so much building going on that it almost seemed like new highways, rail lines, universities, museums, and investment zones were appearing on a daily basis.

China is hardly a model state. Corruption and government malfeasance are widespread. Officials often side with businesspeople and sometimes even criminal gangs at the expense of the poor. But China has got far more things right than not, especially when compared to its counterparts in many less developed countries. Although some get rich by using their contacts to gain a government contract, for most people the best ways to get ahead are to work for a foreign company, open a factory exporting goods to the United States, or sell some product into the burgeoning domestic consumer market.

In most developing countries, these other avenues are closed. Privileged groups can breezily manipulate rules and regulations to their advantage. Favored firms win contracts in smoky offices; favored regions are given better roads and access to electricity; and favored investors can call ministers at home to get an immediate response to their needs. This type of crony capitalism infects regimes across the world—including Russia, Malaysia, Iran, Egypt, and Kenya—producing far different results than what proponents of free markets have in mind. Privatizing Telmex, Mexico's dominant telecom company, has yielded almost two decades of monopoly profits for its owner, possibly the richest man in the world, but higher prices, fewer phones, and lower service for Mexico's people. The Revolutionary Guards have come to dominate Iran's economy since the overthrow of the shah because no other business group can match their political influence and ability to intimidate officials and competitors into backing down.

Such market distortions often have little to do with regulations or the law. When the Egyptian government carried out a radical restructuring of its economy at the behest of the International Monetary Fund, for instance, it created a predominantly free market system on paper. But, in practice, politically connected families who supported the government gained special access to loans, were able to buy state-owned companies at low prices, and had the connections that helped them form lucrative joint ventures with foreign investors. In contrast, many businesspeople who lacked the right pedigree were denied loans by state-controlled banks. Crony capitalism ensured that a few people dominated the economy because markets were being allocated politically. While the country's gross domestic product grew rapidly over many years, the percentage of the population in poverty rose.[36] The resulting anger fed into the Arab Spring.

In such environments, international trade and investment may end up benefiting far fewer people than they should. After all, only those with the means and education can jet off to Miami, Dubai, and Hong Kong to check out products and snag trade deals. Foreign investment offers jobs to those best trained and most assimilated to international business norms.

Meanwhile, the socially excluded poor are so disadvantaged that they are unable to even participate in the more dynamic parts of the economy. Roads do not reach many villages. Banks do not serve most of the population. Large numbers of people have neither legal title to their land nor access to formal registries for their businesses. Limited education and isolation leaves many without the qualifications, social skills, or network of contacts necessary to take advantage of any economic opportunity that might come their way.

Geographical, cultural, and educational gaps with the dominant business class prevent the poor in northern and northeastern Brazil from benefiting from the impressive developments taking place in the south and southeast parts of the country, even when they migrate there. Those trapped in lower castes in the more backward parts of northern India gain little from the country's blossoming information technology industries and the dynamic changes occurring along its coasts. As a group of women from Assam, India, declared: "There is no problem in doing business. All can do it. But where there is no light, no bridge, and no roads, what business will you do?"[37]

When economic expansion occurs in ways that exclude the poor from most of its benefits, it might be called "anti-poor growth." Anti-poor growth is especially common in divided societies with abundant natural resources, such as in Nigeria, Angola, and Sudan. In these states, those who control the government amass great personal wealth at the expense of everyone else. Although the cities of Lagos and Abuja are studded with a few pockets of sparkling wealth, the Niger Delta, where Nigeria's land-based oil is located, is among the country's poorest and most polluted regions.

Whereas free and fair markets could catalyze initiative and inventiveness, inaccessible and unfair markets discourage initiative while disenfranchising large numbers of people. As a result, many poor people oppose the very instruments that should be their saviors. Indigenous peoples in Latin America, for example, are at the forefront of opposition to globalization because they have benefited little from it in the past. When visiting Bolivia, I heard many diatribes about the evils of foreign investment. And the country's nationalization of its hydrocarbon sector by Latin America's first indigenous president—Evo Morales—brought great pride to many of its disenfranchised peoples. But the lack of domestic technical and management expertise holds back Bolivia's ability to profit from these resources without outside investment.[38]

*   *   *

The real tragedy of the poor is not a dearth of enterprise, but how social exclusion causes markets and governments to fail them. It's all but impossible to build a business for yourself and a better life for your family when your village has no roads, your government officials are beholden to a local elite, and you have limited access to competitive markets for agricultural products, labor, and consumer goods. The fault lies not with capitalism—but with how it is suffocated and deformed in these countries.

Exclusion and discrimination have dire consequences for whole countries, as we shall see in the next chapter. States that greatly limit the ability of large sections of their own populations to fully participate in society end up with stunted growth prospects. Although many developing countries are currently enjoying a growth spurt, they will not sustain it if they do not do a better job of harnessing the capabilities of their own peoples.

CHAPTER 5

Breaking Out

The contrast between how the rich and the poor live can shock anyone not used to it.

In the wealthy enclaves of many developing countries, lifestyles may differ tremendously, but the overall scene is familiar to a Western visitor. Living rooms have couches and tables, photographs and artwork, and often carpets and bookcases full of books. Kitchens vary a lot but are filled with many things I instantly recognize: refrigerators, sinks, cooking utensils, and so forth. Computers are not in every home, but in many, especially if there are children or if someone works at home. A maid or nanny may come and go. Apartment blocks are modern; houses are large. In short, when I visit a wealthy family in Sao Paulo, Nairobi, or New Delhi, I enter an environment that would not be out of place in London, Berlin, or New York.

But when I leave one of these affluent neighborhoods with their well-paved streets full of well-dressed children carrying books and knapsacks to and from school and wander just a little way, I see scenes with no comparison in any developed country. A few blocks away, or even sometimes just around the corner, everything is different: the sounds, the smells, the sights. Although a few spots— such as the open-air markets—can be exhilarating, most places are shocking and depressing. Throngs of people are trying to eke out a living on the street in any way they can, peddling everything from shirts to sunglasses, shoeshines to sweet potatoes. Most appear to earn too little to feed themselves. Some areas stink from piles of uncollected garbage and streams of overflowing sewage. Others ache under the crowds trying to get a bus home. Nowhere is quiet: in public areas, hawkers are selling from morning to night; in private areas, the noise from homes packed so close together echoes through the grimy lanes that divide them. Streets are never empty. Long lines of silent, resigned people snake from government offices, where officials work at their own glacial pace, indifferent to their supposed constituents.

Invitations to Westerners to visit poor homes are rarer, simply because Westerners are more likely to meet or work with wealthy and well-educated locals than with illiterate farmers or slum dwellers. But by talking with people on trains, at market stalls, or even just on the street, a connection can be made and an invitation extended.

The poor homes I have visited in the rolling hills of the Caucasus Mountains in Azerbaijan, on the windswept plateau outside Ulan Bator in Mongolia, in the slums of Recife in Brazil, in a small dusty village in Yemen, or in the green countryside of southern Punjab in Pakistan look and feel nothing like a Western home. The diversity of fabrics, foods, and folk customs across these countries astonish. The warmth and hospitality amaze, often surpassing what much wealthier people offer. But lives are difficult, homes meager, possessions few.

Homes are often hovels made of the cheapest materials, sometimes even just rocks collected from nearby, a few sheets of metal, and the poorest quality cement. In Mongolia, my hosts lived as their ancestors have lived for centuries, in a yurt— a portable structure made of wood and covered inside in felt made from the wool of their sheep; but for a thermos and a radio on the yurt's messy floor, I could have forgotten that we were in the twenty-first century. No electricity or running water alleviated the hard work of daily life. In Yemen, my hosts had almost no furniture and cooked in a circular clay oven heated by wood. Their modest house, which the husband and a few friends had built with their own hands, was lit by oil lamps. In some better-off countries—such as Brazil—stoves and refrigerators are more common, but they are old and poorly made. Things like microwaves are unheard of. Radios are ubiquitous, but televisions are often shared or watched outside on the street or in a shop. Computers are nowhere to be seen.

In the poorer parts of cities, jumbles of homemade—and illegal—connections stretch above streets and across districts until they reach the main electricity lines. Cars are outnumbered by bicycles. In very poor areas, the only vehicles one is likely to see are a small truck or two delivering goods to local shops and occasional, rundown automobiles acting as taxis and vans used as buses. In the countryside, donkeys and horses often easily outnumber everything but people. The dirt roads are full of poorly clothed—and sometimes poorly fed—children on their way to work, not school, or offering to shine my shoes for a few coins, or simply begging. The nonchalant attitude of youth that is so familiar in developed countries has no equivalent among the grim and anxious looks of adolescents often found in poor places.

These snapshots of life in the developing world only hint at the depth of the divide between rich and poor. Although living within the same cities—or even across the same streets as in some Latin American metropolises—the population inhabits two different worlds. Whether because of education, ethnicity, or history, society is cleft in two. One group, much smaller than the other, is tied into the larger world by education, infrastructure, and ambition; it is generally doing well from globalization. The other group, encompassing in many places the great mass of people, is hemmed in by its poverty, isolated from the opportunities that globalization presents, its ambition seemingly limited to the hunt for daily survival.

*   *   *

Countries segregated like this naturally have economies divided in the same way. Whereas a small segment of the population has the education, experience, and contacts to fully participate in the economy, most people have only enough to join at the margins or not enough to join at all. A lack of skills, unfamiliarity with modern methods, the misfortune to be born into a caste or social group traditionally consigned to menial work: the great majority of people are excluded from economic opportunity by such disadvantages. For an individual, the result is a personal tragedy. For the country as a whole, the result is a national disaster: by limiting the number of people able to directly contribute to—and benefit from—development, the country can never hope to prosper.[1]

In such places, any growth that economies generate ends up resembling a building being erected on a very narrow foundation. The building may rise higher and higher for a while, but the slender base makes progress harder and harder to achieve and more and more prone to collapse. One strong wind or storm, and it could all come tumbling down.

Countries that grow their economies using the resources of only a small proportion of their populations greatly limit their own potential. Instead of tens of millions of people endeavoring to create wealth, start new businesses, and boost exports, only a few million do so. Instead of states taking advantage of all their human capital—and all the financial, social, and physical resources each person might be able to invest in improving their own lots—they leave most of these assets to rot.

Restricting the size of the pool of people who can participate in and gain from progress affects how businesses, families, and individuals think about their own prospects. Limited opportunity and high risk generate little optimism, which in turn discourages investment. Thousands and thousands of individual decisions cascade across a whole economy, eventually hurting everyone. Companies are reluctant to invest because there are few qualified employees to hire; workers may work hard but are not very productive; and markets are small and stay small. Innovation lags because low education levels prevent the adoption of new technologies. Lack of access to financial markets and the lack of a legal system able to enforce business contracts stifle risk taking by everyone but the few who can confidently control the decisions made by judges and high officials.

States such as Nigeria, Pakistan, and the Philippines may be able to grow rapidly when they first start developing, because they are starting from a very low base. But their growth inevitably slows down over time. Countries caught in this low-growth or no-growth trap fail to reach anywhere near the wealth of rich countries nor the steady growth rates of more inclusive East Asian states such as Korea and Singapore. There is simply not enough fuel feeding their economic engines for them to keep their motors running at anything but a snail's pace.

Mineral-rich economies that depend on one or a few natural resources for all their wealth are similarly deprived of the investment needed to grow beyond their unstable foundations. They may deliver growth for a time, but they, too, will be held back if their populations are not engaged in wealth creation. Only a tiny portion of society participates in or contributes to growth in Angola, Libya, and Venezuela—all of which depend almost exclusively on oil for their wealth. If prices stay high, growth continues—though few share in the affluence it brings. However, if prices drop for an extended period of time, state budgets become tight, wealthy districts become quiet, and the poor have even fewer crumbs to nimble at. Venezuela has seen rising inflation, weaker growth, and growing poverty as its oil production has fallen. Many banks and factories in Russia are forced into bankruptcy every time energy prices drop.

In many mineral-rich countries, elites auction off the natural resources to foreign bidders, widening the gap between the increasingly rich and powerful group at the top of society and the dispossessed rest. The elites, of course, don't care about this divide. They know that their wealth does not depend on the masses, so they have even less reason to share their political power or prosperity with the rest of society.

Social exclusion, by denying large numbers of people the chance to participate in the more dynamic sectors of the economy, is thus a major drag on growth. By their indifference or even hostility to the idea of giving poor people a better education, better roads, and better access to banks, political and social elites keep their countries—albeit not themselves—poor.

When someone cannot even read—as over four of every ten people cannot in places such as Pakistan, Morocco, Côte d'Ivoire, Yemen, Haiti, and Chad—they are unlikely to have the skills and know-how necessary for many jobs.[2] Figure 5.1 charts global literacy rates. When the cost of obtaining the licenses needed to start a business is higher than average annual incomes—as it is in Zimbabwe, the Democratic Republic of the Congo, Angola, and Nicaragua—few people can afford to join the ranks of lawful business owners.[3] When public or private credit registries (which list the credit histories of individuals and companies) cover few people—as is the case in most of the world's poorest countries—only

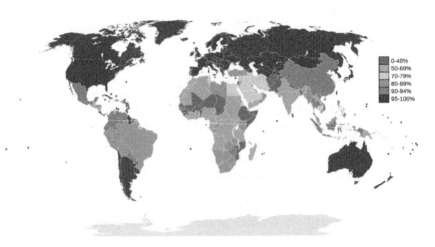

	0-49%
	50-69%
	70-79%
	80-89%
	90-94%
	95-100%

Figure 5.1 World Literacy Map, 2007–2008

Source: Central Intelligence Agency, *The World Factbook 2009* (Washington DC: CIA, 2009).

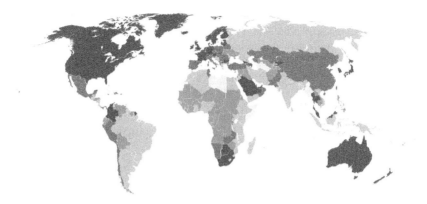

Figure 5.2 Ease of Doing Business Index 2009

Key: Dark gray nations rank higher on the Ease of Doing Business Index, lighter gray nations lower. (The lightest gray indicates a lack of data.)

Source: Based on World Bank Data; see http://www.doingbusiness.org/EconomyRankings/.

those with close ties to banks or substantial physical assets to mortgage can get loans.[4] Figure 5.2 uses an index produced annually by the World Bank to show the ease of doing business worldwide. Higher rankings indicate better, usually simpler, regulations for businesses and stronger protections of property rights. It is noteworthy that the two maps have much in common and are similar to the one in chapter 3 that charted the percentage of populations living on less than $1.25 a day.

Almost all developing countries face the challenge in one form or another of overcoming the social divisions that limit their economic potential. Without a reduction in poverty—without a reduction in the deprivations that prevent the poor from fully participating in economic and social life—they eventually become trapped in self-reinforcing, low-growth dead ends. Or, as one World Bank publication explains, "Countries do not grow fast because they are too poor to grow . . . poverty and growth interact in a vicious circle where high poverty leads to low growth and low growth in turns leads to high poverty."[5] Without substantially upgrading their people's skills and increasing their poorer classes' access to opportunity, developing countries are unable to sustain growth over a long period.

"The country's miserable infrastructure (lack of roads, sewer systems, electric power, water, etc.) does not allow my investment to flourish," remarked one Ethiopian, now living in the United States. His explanation of why other members of the Ethiopian diaspora were unwilling to invest back home cited several key factors.

The country lacks the necessary skilled manpower. . . . The country is divided into ethnic enclaves and there is limited freedom of movement of both people and assets. As a result, my investments will be restricted to a limited ethnic enclave thereby adding more constraints and inhibiting growth. . . . Because of these restrictions, the market size is also rather small, thereby limiting the prospect of the growth of my investment and business in the future. . . . The financial sector is controlled by the TPLF [the country's leading political party] and its cadre-controlled businesses. As a result, my investment may face challenges in case I needed some more financial support. It has been reported that the government-controlled banks are bent to extend loans mainly to the government controlled businesses.[6]

Families in exclusionary societies invest less because the return on education is lower, their property is less secure, and the cost of borrowing money is higher than in inclusive societies that provide ready opportunity for all their citizens. Fewer students stay in school, and those who do attend are held back by their bad health and the meager quality of their programs. As Alberto, a displaced person living on the outskirts of Pasto in Nariño, Colombia, said, "The one who that has the economic power, is the one going to study even without have talent . . . but the poor person with talent and intelligence, does not have opportunity, because he does not have enough money."[7] Similarly, Nafas Dil, a 40-year-old woman who works as a tailor in Nangarhar in east Afghanistan commented, "In our community, girls stop their education very early, not only because there is no female teacher but also because they have to help their families working as tailors. Families are very poor and they need their help."[8]

Fewer people invest in business because inferior infrastructure reduces gains from trade. And fewer people take risks—such as changing jobs or starting a business—because the risks of failure are greater. Dorothea Mapunda, a 45-year-old woman from Luhindo, an isolated village in Tanzania, explained how poor transportation impacts risk taking:

Farmers fail to market/trade in Mbinga town because of lack of reliable transport. One trip to Mbinga per person is TZS 6,000 and TZS 2,000 per bag of maize of 90–100kg, so farmers fear the expenses involved and the unreliability and uncertainty of the market. If you take your maize to Mbinga and find the selling price is low or there were no customers, what would you do?[9]

The fact that the courts in many of these countries are too susceptible to influence peddling or corruption to protect the rights of the masses to their property also makes the poor risk-averse.

China is one of relatively few developing states to have recognized the wisdom of bridging the divisions—geographic as well as social—within the country, at least partly because it sees almost all of its people as integral to its national identity (see chapter 7). It builds new train lines to its remotest regions, makes the development of its poorer Western half a national priority, and experiments with policies to address its growing urban-rural income divide. As a result of China's inclusive policies, hundreds of millions of Chinese people and tens of thousands of Chinese firms have vigorously invested in anything that might give them advantage in their opportunity rich environment.

In much of the rest of the developing world, this lesson has yet to be learned. Despite its promotion to a club of elite developing countries, Brazil continues to grow much slower than its East Asian counterparts because it has historically ignored its disadvantaged, especially when they were black, Indian, or mixed race. Only 44 percent of Brazil's 19-year-olds have finished high school.[10] The country's poorest municipality has income levels barely one-tenth of its richest.[11] The underclass in its cities is far more obvious than in any of the much faster growing Chinese and Vietnamese metropolises. (Brazil has, however, belatedly recognized at least some of these mistakes over the past decade or so.) India is likely to face similar problems in time if it does not resolve its own social divisions. One-third of its people—and almost one-half of its women—still cannot read. Mumbai, its commercial capital, has tens of thousands of people living on its streets and millions in its slums. Large sections of its north and east regions— containing hundreds of millions of people—are falling further behind its more dynamic regions because of exclusionary caste practices.

Pakistan needs to find jobs for tens of millions of its young people. But it won't generate enough growth to create those jobs unless it abandons what the Council on Foreign Relations describes as a "feudal system of land distribution" and unless it stops denying the vast majority of its people the most basic of social services. The latter stifle the "labor market efficiency" and "technological readiness" necessary to encourage investment in many sectors.[12]

For the average country, a 10 percentage-point increase in the number of people in poverty reduces investment as a share of GDP by 6 to 8 percent and the growth rate by about 1 percent a year. Such differences may seem small, but their cumulative impact over years and decades is enormous. And in many countries, the poor account for a much larger proportion of the population than 10 percent.

Empowering the poor is thus not about whether more growth or more redistribution is needed—the place where debates on how to end poverty usually begin and end. Strategies that do not focus on growth forswear perhaps the most potent weapon for improving human well-being ever discovered. (Before capitalism helped usher in the industrialized age, most people lived stunted lives with short life spans, little education, and little chance to fulfill their full potential.) Yet failing to take account of the constraints preventing the poor from participating in and contributing to growth undermines its very generation.

* * *

Growth matters a great deal to the poor. It produces jobs, entrepreneurial opportunities, and rising incomes. It provides more money for the government to spend on schools and roads. And, in the long-term, it can produce social change that weakens the forces holding the poor back.

Countries that have been able to generate the most sustained periods of economic expansion have experienced the largest reductions in poverty. East Asia has shown the most dramatic fall because many of the region's countries have topped the global growth tables. Vietnam, for instance, cut its poverty rate in half—from 58 percent to 29 percent—between 1993 and 2002 by growing 6 percent a year. Chile, the country in Latin America with the longest history of economic success, has reduced poverty from 43 percent of the population to 13 percent over the past two decades.[13]

Indonesia's remarkable national growth over the past few decades has benefited people across most of its long archipelago. "The number of carpenters and brick-layers could still be counted on the fingers [ten years ago]," commented a man in a coastal village on the outskirts of an urbanizing area in North Maluku in 2005, "but since then a lot of villagers have become tradesmen."[14] In Kegalle, Sri Lanka, a worker observes, "Factory development was a main reason [for better earnings]. Along with continuous orders we got continuous work. Laborers got good returns; a profit sharing scheme was introduced."[15]

Growth can have an especially large impact if it is spread among a population emerging from conflict. Reza Gul, a 55-year-old female farmer from Parwan, Afghanistan, recalls that "in the past there weren't any buyers of raisin, but now there are. Our men go to Charikar and Qara Bagh and they know about the price of raisin. During the time of the Taliban, raisins were cheap, because Taliban blocked the ways and people could not export raisins to foreign countries. But now raisins generate a good income."[16]

Not all growth helps the poor in the short term. Improvements in the produc-tivity of agriculture have a clear, significant positive effect on farmers' incomes (see chapter 11), but gains in productivity in manufacturing, construction, and most services tend to boost workers' wages only moderately in the short term. And greater productivity in capital-intensive industries such as mining and utilities may not help the poor at all.

Some types of growth may even be detrimental to the poor for a period of time. Growth generated by lowering tariffs and boosting trade, for example, can displace laborers, encourage companies to hire high-skilled employees at the expense of those with less education, and reduce the money available for public services. Deregulation of financial markets may spur productivity gains at the expense of the poor, especially when few of the latter have access to banks and insurance companies. When growth is accompanied by high unemployment, statistics may suggest that the poor are doing better even though they are actu-ally increasing in number. For instance, when economic gains are substantial but divided among few people, statistics will show that average incomes are rising even though the proportion of poor is in fact growing.

But, over the long term, growth is unquestionably beneficial—indeed, it is essential if the poor are to be empowered. Growth, after all, is the only way to create wealth, without which no one can hope to better their lives. One World Bank study, by the economist Aart Kraay, even estimated that 95 percent of the variation in poverty over the long term depended on growth.[17] In other words, even if growth brings some disadvantages for the poor in the short term, it will eventually bring many more benefits.

This is not to say that short-term considerations are unimportant. Losing one's job or being rejected for a job because of a lack of qualifications does not feel good. It is especially painful when there are no other jobs to be had and when one's family has no assets to fall back on.

Policies that help the poor cope with change must always be a part of strategies to reform economies and accelerate growth. But, as will be discussed in the next part of the book, nothing is more important to reducing poverty than enabling the poor to take full advantage of economic opportunities in the first place. For instance, while welfare may soften the blows inflicted on farmers when lower trade barriers allow in cheaper agricultural goods, the rural poor will get richer only if they have access to things such as new roads, better storage facilities for the harvest, and cheaper and more reliable sources of credit and insurance.

Removing the constraints that hold back the poor will accomplish much more than trying to make growth "pro-poor" (i.e., beneficial to the poor). After all, the more the poor have the skills and resources to be the drivers of growth, the more likely they will be its beneficiaries. The poor should be seen not as passively waiting for help but as how they actually are: eager to make the most of their lives. "My desire to improve my situation is the biggest desire I have," said Humberto, a poor man in the El Gorrión barrio in Colombia. "I set a goal for myself every day. When I got here, I thought how difficult it would be for me to move on. Before, I used to ride a bicycle, but I had the hope and goal of having a motorcycle and now I have one. The idea is setting goals." The developing world is full of Humbertos. If development agencies were to recognize this, they would treat the poor as partners, not as victims or patients.

Breaking the vicious cycle of high poverty and low growth requires enabling far more people to participate in job markets and to exploit entrepreneurial opportunities as equals. The aim should be to transform the vicious circle into a virtuous circle—a virtuous circle in which greater inclusion of the poor within societies and economies leads to higher growth, which leads to greater inclusion, and so on. The result will be larger pools of educated workers, larger markets, and larger inputs of creativity and capital. Families will have more incentive to keep their children in school longer, invest in productivity-enhancing goods, and take business risks. Economies and political systems will become more resilient. Growth and democratic accountability will increase. The whole cycle will, in turn, encourage another wave of participation that produces more growth.

One of the greatest challenges facing most developing countries today is to become more inclusive. But how can they dismantle the political and social barriers that exclude, disenfranchise, and demoralize? Answering that question is the task of the next part of this book.

PART II

A New Agenda

CHAPTER 6

Self-Belief and Power

As we have seen in the first part of this book, social exclusion—and the forces that create and sustain it—is a major cause of poverty. As this second part explains, the solution to that problem is empowerment.

The first step toward empowerment is belief—belief that one has the ability to control one's life. Belief by itself cannot empower the poor, but without belief the poor will not try to break free of the social, political, and institutional forces that hold them back.

Individuals who feel in control of their destinies—who have a strong sense of what psychologists call "personal agency" or "self-efficacy"—are far more likely to set goals and pursue them energetically, in the process spurring wealth creation, social change, and development. But how can one boost self-efficacy?

Broadly speaking, there are two ways. It can be done on an individual basis, by addressing the "micro" conditions that affect individuals and their families. Poor micro conditions—for instance, dirt roads with too many ruts and schools with too few qualified teachers—deter people from believing they can improve their lives. Why work hard to grow crops if you can't get them to market because the roads are impassable? Why let your children stay on at school instead of becoming a breadwinner for the family if the schools provide only the most basic education? Positive micro steps such as paving local roads and hiring local secondary school teachers would make individuals readier to invest their time, effort, and hopes in activities that can build a better future.

The second way to boost self-efficacy is to tackle the "macro" conditions that affect entire societies or parts of a society. Improving the macro environment doesn't directly involve building better roads or schools for poor individuals or families; it means creating an environment in which leaders, elites, and governments are more willing and more able to build them and do in fact build them. Positive macro steps include, for instance, promoting social cohesion, creating a more robust government apparatus, and strengthening the rule of law.

Both of these approaches can be effective, but the second one—tackling macro factors—is especially powerful.

The good news for the poor in the developing world is that the macro environment *can* be changed. The bad news is that those who are in the best position to change it—namely, the governments and elites of developing countries—often don't want to change it. Either they are simply too selfish to use their influence for the benefit of the poor, or they see social exclusion as either unfortunate but inevitable or as acceptable and even desirable. Not everyone thinks this way, and every country's elite contains individuals who want to encourage their states to become more inclusive and development-oriented. But if these forward-looking individuals are to make a difference, they need to promote a combination of two things: a mechanism for prodding other members of the elite to support inclusive state-building measures (to be discussed in chapter 7), and a state apparatus strong enough to implement those measures (discussed in chapter 8). The more potent this combination is, the more likely a society is to integrate the poor socially and economically into the life of the country.

In this chapter we explain how all this fits together. We look at the importance of self-efficacy to empowerment, then at the importance of the macro environment to self-efficacy, and finally at the need for elites to take on the challenge of building inclusive states that can empower all their citizens. Put differently, this chapter explains why the elites in the developing world play an outsized role in determining the fate of the world's poor. The other chapters in this second part of the book describe in greater detail what the elites might do if they were ready to embrace an agenda for change.

The Power of Belief

One of the most important lessons I have learned from my many years in the world of business is the extent to which performance depends on motivation. Employees who feel empowered by the corporate mission or personal incentives are far more likely to work hard and creatively than those who see their jobs as an obligation to be fulfilled. As numerous books on business management underline, if workers believe that what they are doing matters, they will try to accomplish more—both for themselves and for the company.

Similarly, one of most striking impressions I get when traveling among the poor is the extent to which environments influence internal belief—and thus external action. The people with the most confidence in their own ability to change their lives take the most risks, demonstrate the most initiative, and are most willing to face down, tear down, or climb over obstacles.

I encounter the same thing whether I am in Senegal or Somaliland, Bolivia or India. But how many of these people I meet and how self-confident they are varies from country to country or region to region. People everywhere seem to share the same hunger for a better life for themselves and their children, but only in some countries or part of those countries do people believe that they have a realistic chance of achieving a better life. Elsewhere, most people tend to be skeptical that they can change their lives, pessimistic that investing in the future will be rewarded, or fearful that challenging the status quo will get them into trouble. They may work hard, but more out of necessity than because of a drive to succeed.

Self-belief matters a lot. Whether someone faces the future with confidence or not impacts every big decision they make: whether to keep their children in school or send them out to work, whether to stay where they were born or to migrate in search of a better life, whether to invest their spare cash to set up a small business or to bury their money underground in fear of some coming calamity. When taken together, these individual decisions have immense consequences for whole societies, as discussed in the last chapter.

In Shanghai these days, it seems that almost every young person has confidence in the future and faith in their own power to improve their lot. Conversations are full of energy and optimism. Most people talk about doing something to take advantage of all the opportunities they see around them. Owners of small businesses work late into the night, and few hesitate to buy and refurbish an apartment or house if they have the extra cash to do so.

One gets the sense that Shanghai must always have been abuzz with entrepreneurial activity. In fact, however, these attitudes are relatively new. Visitors to China a century ago often complained that the population was lethargic and uninventive. China's culture, they said, was to blame. Max Weber, widely regarded as the founder of modern sociology, famously explained that the country's backwardness was due to its adherence to Confucianism. Confucians focused on achieving "a cultured status position"; in China, Weber declared, "The 'superior' man coveted . . . a position, not a profit." As a result, few Chinese devoted themselves to business and other money-making endeavors.[1] As recently as one generation ago, visitors to China still commented on how risk-averse and unimaginative the Chinese were. Communist ideology, they said, had reinforced the conservatism of Confucian culture and stifled ambition. What would these visitors make of Shanghai today!

Another country that has undergone a dramatic transformation is India. Today, India is fast becoming a nation of entrepreneurs constantly looking for new opportunities. It is almost as if "growth itself is now the driver of change and is begetting more growth," as one Indian economist explained.[2] This is astonishing given that before 1991, when it launched major reforms, most people inside and outside of India assumed the country could grow only slowly because its people seemed wedded to a fatalistic outlook rooted in their Hindu culture. Indian economist Raj Krishna coined the disparaging phrase "Hindu rate of growth" to contrast his country's performance with the much faster growth rates of its East Asian neighbors.[3]

What explains these recent changes among people in China and India? Not culture. Not, anyway, that amorphous thing known as "national culture," which is certainly real and recognizable but is also hard to define and easy to mistake. The culture of a nation, of a people, typically evolves gradually, over centuries. It does not transform itself within a generation. What past visitors to India and China mistook for national culture was something that can reshape itself far more readily, something that can respond to concrete changes in the political, economic, and social environment. What it was, essentially, was the presence—or, more accurately, the absence—of a sense of personal agency, of self-efficacy. Environments that once discouraged initiative, risk taking, and hard work now encourage them.

Although all people have goals they want to accomplish and things they want to change, those with a strong sense of self-efficacy are far more likely to view challenging problems as tasks to be mastered and to recover quickly from setbacks and disappointments. They see failure as informational, not demoralizing, and have a deep belief that persistent effort will allow them to succeed. Self-efficacy is therefore different from self-esteem. Whereas the latter measures a person's feelings about themselves, the former reflects that person's confidence in their ability to achieve a desired outcome.

Albert Bandura, the psychologist who introduced the concept in the 1970s, explains that "perceived self-efficacy operates as a central self-regulatory mechanism of human agency. People's beliefs that they can produce desired effects by their actions influence the choices they make, their aspirations, level of effort and perseverance, resilience to adversity, and vulnerability to stress and depression."[4]

The strength of self-efficacy varies from individual to individual. But it also varies from society to society because self-efficacy is heavily shaped by one's external environment. Those societies that provide positive feedback for taking risks and tackling difficult problems enhance their population's self-efficacy. Those that repeatedly provide negative feedback dilute, undermine, or otherwise weaken self-efficacy.

Although self-efficacy is important everywhere, it is especially important to the poor in poor countries. In the developed world, where discrimination is usually less extensive, the rules for getting a loan or getting into a school are more predictable, and most people have enough education to get a decent job, major decisions carry limited risk. Failure may hurt one's ego but is unlikely to damage one's health or threaten one's life. By contrast, in many societies in the developing world discrimination is rife, economic rules are unpredictable, and good education and decent jobs are scarce commodities. It is no wonder that personal agency is also in short supply. Vulnerable to volatile economic conditions and insecure property rights, with few if any savings or assets to fall back upon, the poor are understandably reluctant to take extra risks. Their day-to-day lives are already remarkably risky.

The Power of Belief: The Example of Oy

Oy, a 39-year-old mother of two young children from a small farming village in Thailand, has made incredible strides in a few short years, both because opportunity is plentiful in her rapidly growing country and because of her hard work and willingness to take risks.

Born into a family of laborers, Oy worked in harsh conditions from a young age, even migrating to another village at one point to work on a ginger farm. When she and her husband, a craftsman, were married, they started out in a small shack made from woven bamboo and grass on a piece of land owned by relatives. "When we were still poor, when we living in a shack, people looked down at us. They would not talk to us at all. They would talk badly of us to other people." But at least her husband had a steady job and was hardworking and supportive.

Things began to change in 1991 when she started selling vegetables at a market that was near Bangkok. Starting with the Thai melon that her uncle cultivated, Oy slowly expanded her business to include many other fruits and vegetables, learning and experimenting as she proceeded. She gathered the vegetables from various people in her village, sold them in the market, and split the proceeds with the producers. "I was the only person who would buy the vegetables and sell them outside. I would get up at 2 or 3 am each morning. Wholesale trade started in the market around 2 or 3 am with retail trade at 4 am. I had to be there until 8 am each day."

Thailand was growing rapidly during most of this period, producing growing markets for many goods. Saving a little bit every year, Oy's family bought land, a pickup truck to transport the vegetables, and eventually a car and extra land for their children. She started to cultivate corn, cassavas, bananas, and other fruit. They built a proper home for the family. "Our house was a shack earlier. This gave me more willpower. I would wake up very early. I was committed to building a permanent home like other people." Her husband's fortunes also improved when he landed a government job in the highway department.

None of this was easy for either of them, and cooperation was important. "My husband had to get up early to take the vegetables and me to the market, and later in the day he would pick me up and take me home. I had to leave my children with my relatives. I was sleep deprived and tired each day. Truthfully speaking, I felt ashamed selling in the market. But when things were difficult, the shame just disappeared."

"All we had was perseverance and physical labor. Being poor gave us the perseverance to better ourselves. . . . From having nothing at all, we were able to have everything that we wanted. This was possible because of our commitment, ability to economize, and knowing how to save. . . . It is we who cause change."[5] Oy's personal qualities have been crucial to her success. But her environment has also mattered a lot. Despite having made some political and economic mistakes in the past few decades, Thailand has gotten enough things right to give the poor the chance to improve their lot. It has had relatively little political violence and a fairly cohesive elite (though that may be changing), relatively stable economic conditions, a decently functioning (if corrupt at times) government apparatus, a secure environment for risk taking, growing (if uneven) opportunity, few barriers to advancement, and steady (if uneven) increases in education, infrastructure, and financial services.

Many development practitioners have argued that enhancing self-efficacy is critical to efforts to help the poor take advantage of their "psychological, informational, material, social, financial and human capital."[6] The World Bank's *Moving Out of Poverty* study, for instance, documents that "this sense of personal agency appears to precede the acquisition of other valuable assets, such as education, money, or a house. People see these as reinforcing their internal efficacy, which has to come first."

The World Bank even went so far in 2000 as to declare that empowerment is one of "the three pillars of poverty reduction."[7] The bank's president at the time, James Wolfensohn, declared that the poor should not be seen as being passive recipients of aid but rather as "agents of change" who need to be empowered.[8] Nobel Prize winner Amartya Sen has gone one step beyond this in arguing that personal agency is itself intrinsically valuable; and therefore the expansion of poor people's capabilities ought to be the centerpiece of all development efforts.[9]

Many poor people would agree with these sentiments. Jainer, a 29-year-old man from Colombia, reflects that "I never say, 'I can't.' I say, 'I can, but I just don't know how.'"[10] Amit, a young man from Uttar Pradesh in India, believes that "a strong breeze can break branches. A whirlpool in the ocean waters can sink boats. But a strong willpower can give courage, and even if your destination is a thousand miles away, you can be successful."[11] Loida, a manual worker from the Philippines, says, "I think I can face anything; it is just a matter of self-discipline."[12]

When Such Belief Is Not Possible

Poor men and women know all too well when their personal agency is shackled, when their initiative and determination will not yield results. "Poor people have a deep and immediate understanding of power and power relationships," notes the World Bank study. "They know their own powerlessness in the context of deep-seated inequalities in economic, social, and political structures."[13]

Environments that do not reward initiative and determination can easily dull the energies and diminish the capabilities that people have. This is why reduced access to opportunity is so devastating. In the same way that a teacher who expects little from his or her students tends to get what he or she expects, societies that have low expectations for entire sections of their populations demoralize them. Excluded socially and economically from opportunity, vast swathes of the population set their goals correspondingly low. Without any role models or information suggesting that they can do more, the poor adapt to their meager prospects by making choices that leave them even more deeply mired in poverty. Less eager to invest in education, less willing to challenge an unfair status quo, and less convinced of their own self-worth and abilities, they fall further behind the rich and the powerful within their own countries.

Too few people in most African states and in many Middle Eastern, Latin American, and Asian countries believe that hard work alone will substantially raise one's standard of living unless one belongs to the elite, has a good connection to an important official, or emigrates. In Thailand, Vietnam, and Korea, the poor can afford ambition, but in countries such as Nigeria, Bolivia, Pakistan, and the Congo, most poor people see little hope of ever becoming less poor.

In some, perhaps most countries, expectations can vary a lot from region to region. Even in Thailand, where Oy has seized the opportunities available to her, geography can be fate. Oy lives near Bangkok, the economic engine and political capital of the country and rich, relatively speaking, in opportunities and government resources. If Oy lived in Thailand's far north (which is much poorer and historically has received much less government investment) or Muslim south (which has a violent secessionist movement), it is unlikely she would have achieved as much or would have even considered taking the risks she did.

"People here have lost hope of getting out of poverty," says Lemaron, the 29-year-old owner of a hair and beauty salon in Kenya, who has had to walk on crutches since catching polio when he was three.

> They believe that being poor is God-given. Every day they wake up, they admit that they are poor and there is nothing they can do. People have written themselves off. . . . It is not just [Maasai] traditional beliefs or customs [which cause this] because among other tribes—Kikuyu, Kamba, Luo and many others—there are people who have lost hope in life . . . [and] believe poverty is their way of life and nothing can change. . . .
>
> My disability has not stopped me from doing anything! And you should take good note of this! . . . I don't believe disability is inability. I can declare to the whole community that I am capable of doing anything a normal person can do. . . . I have been fighting against discrimination so much that it has become part and parcel of my life . . . my greatest enemy is not my disability but poverty. . . . What makes us live in this cycle of poverty is a lack of good foundations in life. Those people who are rich in Kenya—the biggest percentage—are those whose great grandparents left wealth and riches for them.

Despite his accomplishments, Lemaron remains poor because he lives in a poor neighborhood where "very few people here can afford a meal and [still] have an extra coin left for beauty."[14]

Hopelessness can spread from one generation to another until it becomes an enduring trait. The original theory of the "culture of poverty," posited by anthropologist Oscar Lewis in the mid-twentieth century, argued that that poverty is "an adaptation to a set of objective conditions of the larger society, [but] once it comes into existence, it tends to perpetuate itself generation to generation because of its effect on children."[15]

Reversing the Tide

Fatalism may become an enduring trait of a family or a community or even a society, but it need not become an immutable trait. The external macro environment—in the form of pervasive economic, political, and social exclusion—can undermine self-efficacy and generate a self-limiting sense of hopelessness. But if the macro environment changes, then what happens?

For an answer we can look to the Middle East and North Africa. For decades, authoritarian regimes dominated the region. The vast majority of people were systematically excluded from political opportunity. The legal systems in these states severely restricted rights of expression and association; anyone who dared speak out was reminded by security forces, riot police, jailers, and executioners that dissent was not an option. Many outsiders looked at Arab society and concluded that it was simply inhospitable to democracy; cultural determinists claimed that Islamic culture was fundamentally incompatible with democracy.

In reality, however, their populations had low expectations for themselves and were too afraid to act. The result was the political passivity that the region's regimes encouraged and enforced. Over the course of a generation, however, much more education and more exposure to international norms through satellite television dramatically changed people's expectations for themselves and for their countries. Bit by bit, fear eroded and anger grew. Then, in 2011, emboldened by the example of their neighbors' taking to the streets to protest, large numbers of people rose up and challenged their governments in state after state.

If a population's attitudes toward politics can change, why not their attitudes about their own prospects? If the poor had better skills sets, better access to opportunity, and better mechanisms for working together to advance their own interests, wouldn't they also have different expectations for themselves and act differently?

Why Macro Matters More to the Poor than Micro

As discussed in chapter 4, empowering the poor requires action at both the micro (the individual) and the macro (the societal) level. At the micro level, the poor need better access to schooling, job opportunities, doctors, social networks, and property rights. At the macro level, empowerment depends on energizing the economy, enhancing the effectiveness of government, improving the national infrastructure, strengthening the political forces pressing for pro-poor reforms, and reducing the disadvantages produced by discrimination and inequitable access to the law, to public services, and to markets. Both micro and macro factors can play important roles in locking people into poverty or enabling them to escape from it, but macro factors are the more powerful. Macro factors:

- affect a much larger number of people than specific micro factors
- directly influence some micro factors (for instance, the capacity of the education ministry directly affects how well individual schools are run)
- indirectly influence many micro factors (such as access to finance and health care)
- can dramatically affect investment—especially in the type of labor-intensive and skills-building projects most likely to help the poor
- can enhance the self-efficacy of entire populations

- can accelerate the pace at which a population learns new skills and imports new technologies and determine whether it gains or loses from globalization
- can affect the ability of a population to gain from and contribute to growth, with large repercussions for the economic potential of whole countries

Given that poverty is multidimensional and that a number of the deficiencies that hold people back depend on macro factors, it is extremely hard to empower the poor without tackling them.

Macro causes of poverty, however, tend to be amorphous, hard to classify, and hard to target. That is not to say that they are unassailable. They can be tackled, but they must be tackled from two sides simultaneously: the economic and the political. A combination of economic policies that promote growth—including measures that ensure stable macroeconomic conditions, competitive markets, and the construction of important infrastructure—and political policies that enable all segments of a population to participate in and contribute to that growth can be profoundly empowering. These policies, though, tend to take a long time to have an effect; for many years, their impact is hard to gauge and even hard to see.

The micro causes of poverty are much easier to identify, target, and monitor. After all, it is much simpler to count the number of children receiving vaccinations or graduating from high school than it is to determine whether a government is acting equitably. For this reason, micro factors are often more attractive to anyone who wants to make a difference to the lives of the poor and who wants to be seen to be making a difference.

Measures that target individual micro steps are not to be disparaged. Each one can improve the quality of life of many people. A program to improve access to small, low-interest loans, for instance, can help to launch, sustain, and grow numerous family businesses. And the collective impact of many micro steps can, *incrementally and over a long period,* empower the poor to the point that they will be able to compete with the elites who control governments and markets. However, such steps must work in conjunction with each other to really be effective—and too often they are introduced in isolation without regard for the larger picture. After all, how useful is a microloan if there are no roads available to get produce to market? And where roads are built and how they are maintained typically depends on the attitudes of elites—a macro factor.

In other words, while action on individual deficiencies can improve lives, it can only work to rebalance inequitable power relationships very slowly. Generations of people will live and die in poverty before their descendants finally achieve equal opportunity. Many indigenous people in Latin America, for instance, are still fighting for equitable treatment at the hands of their government centuries after independence.

Moreover, if prospects at home are so bad, many of the more fortunate among the poor who do gain access to better education and health care are unlikely to stay at home unless their countries offer them opportunities that match their improved capacities. As Bassem, a Christian from Egypt who moved to Beijing, explained, "Seriously, there are many reasons [I left]: a lousy economy, lousy discrimination, a lousy political situation, a lousy working environment and [poor] salaries. . . . Religious discrimination is [also] a major thing. But the social one and the 'wasta [nepotistic string-pulling] culture' are surely causing a lot of desperation."[16] The brain drain of the best and the brightest prevents improvements at the individual level from filtering into changes in government ministries, universities, courts, and health clinics—the very institutions that must change for society to be more welcoming to the poor.

This is why steps to improve the macro conditions are so important to empowering the poor. Micro steps operate within a macro environment. The details are important, but the big picture is more so.

The Choice Facing Elites

In most developing countries, the best way to empower the poor is to change the macro conditions in which they live. The power to make such changes, however, is concentrated in the hands of a small number of elites, most of whom usually

---

Inspiring the Poor's Belief in Themselves

Government and societal action to create more equitable access to opportunity may be the most effective way to enhance the self-efficacy of the poor, but it is not the only way.

Religion, for instance, can play an important role in imparting greater (or lesser, depending on the religion, time, and place) self-confidence, keener awareness of the right to social equality, and sharper leadership and work skills. The combined effect is to make the poor more willing and more able to challenge their low status. Much as Protestantism has been said by many historians to have contributed to economic development and political reform in Europe between the 1500s and 1800s, today some Latin American Pentecostal and African charismatic churches are contributing to change by transforming the poor's ability to overcome their disadvantaged positions in society. These churches create an independent social space within which "people may participate in the creation of a different kind of sub-society . . . those who count for little or nothing in the wider world find themselves addressed as persons able to display initiative and to be of consequence," writes David Martin, a sociologist of religion. "The initial impact of Evangelical conversion occurs . . . as a major mutation of culture: restoration of the family, the rejection of *machismo*, the adoption of economic and work disciplines and new priorities."[17] In countries such as Brazil and Nigeria, these voluntary religious associations compete for members among the poor and then provide them a unique platform to develop self-efficacy and leadership skills that can then be put to use in the wider society.

display little concern for the wider society. Ordinary citizens typically have little or no control over the state, and the state itself is usually limited in its ability to make or implement policy.[18]

If empowering change is going to come, it has to come via those political leaders or other members of the elite who not only are in a position to change the macro conditions but also have a strong incentive to do so. They need a strong incentive because there are powerful *dis*incentives at work.

In the first place, they may believe that they have an obligation—both a practical and an ethical obligation—to prioritize the interests of their own constituents over the interest of the state as a whole. This attitude is hardly uncommon among elected officials who run government departments in developed countries. The chief difference between the developed and the developing world in this respect is that in the former "constituencies" typically refer to the voters in electoral districts whereas in the developing world, officials are more likely to see their "constituencies" in terms of ethnic groups, religious denominations, clans, and other groups with which they are strongly associated.

In the second place, members of the elite may know no other way of exercising authority. In a socially divided country with weak institutions, personal relationships typically predominate over any state-mandated laws.

In such environments, leaders may feel completely justified in using state resources to reward their own constituency at the expense of everyone else, no matter how corrupt and self-serving they may look. Governments in many parts of Sub-Saharan Africa, for instance, build more schools and hospitals in areas where the local population belongs to the same ethnic group as the government's leadership.[19] Even Félix Houphouët-Boigny, who was generally considered an inclusive leader during his three decades in power in Côte d'Ivoire, acted this way. From early in his reign, he invested substantial state resources in turning the village from which he came, Yamoussoukro, into a major urban center. Eventually, in 1983, he moved the country's capital there, building a six-lane highway, a five-star hotel, a convention center, and an international airport with one of the longest runways in Africa—all at the expense of the state.

Many officials feel justified in taking bribes, not because of their allegiance to a particular constituency, but because they feel unjustly underpaid, because their work environments are especially trying, or simply because everyone else takes bribes. As a public-sector employee in Kaolack, Senegal, explained, "I believe corruption at the town hall can be tolerated up to a certain level. Because it is [perpetrated by] officials who are badly paid and are the victims of social problems."[20] A young examining magistrate in Niamey, Niger, said that "my experience of nine to ten months has taught me the bitter lesson that, in the mind of the people, justice can be bought. . . . There is not a single case where the family of a prisoner has not approached us and made us some kind of offer. . . . Everyone is tempted, including the defendant, because if you have no money, you cannot obtain justice in this country."[21]

Such officials face a political and economic calculus very different from that encountered by their peers in the rich world. The presence of a weak government

incapable of enforcing the rule of law and easily co-opted by wealthy and powerful forces creates a difficult environment for progressive-minded individuals,
forcing them to make uncomfortable choices. Let us imagine, for instance, that
a senior government official wants to promote inclusiveness and decides to start
hiring and promoting people in his ministry based purely upon talent, not upon
family ties and bribes. Nepotism and corruption in human resource policies are
macro problems because they affect how governments perform. And they are
a self-propagating problem, because people who are hired or promoted based
on personal connections or bribes are themselves likely to disregard merit when
it comes to making their own decisions. They will routinely refuse to use their
authority for the benefit of people who may have talent or justice on their side
but who lack connections or money.

Government officials who break the law in wealthy countries typically risk a
great deal for relatively little reward. Besides getting fired and put in jail, most
convicted white-collar criminals are also ostracized by their friends and family.
In many developing countries, however, the reverse is true. Officials who break
the law can reap considerable rewards without facing significant risks. Corruption is so ubiquitous that an individual who refuses to participate in it may be
abiding by the letter of the law but is certainly flouting convention. That person
may even end up antagonizing relatives, friends, superiors—everyone, indeed,
who stands to benefit from the corrupt status quo. A government official in India
pointed an accusing finger at politicians: "Frankly we [in our department] are
subjected to a lot of pressures from politicians."[22] A Senegalese official saw the
problem as pervasive within society:

> [I get a lot of] pressure from the boss or pressure from these people or those
> people. . . . And, for me, the only way to stop the pressure is to say no. That means
> accepting that you are unpopular. . . . Our problem [is that] the check on public-
> spiritedness is emotion, it is the pressure, and that is Senegalese.[23]

Even powerful individuals risk being ostracized, fired, or worse if they seek to
replace a corrupt system with a meritocracy.

John Githongo, for instance, tried to fight corruption in the highest levels
of the Kenyan government as the country's permanent secretary for governance
and ethics but ended up resigning in despair and fleeing the country in fear for
his life. He later identified the country's vice president, energy minister, finance
minister, and former transport minister as part of a $600 million scam, in which
the president himself was supposedly complicit. Carlos Castresana, the Spanish
judge at the helm of the UN International Commission against Impunity and
Corruption in Guatemala (CICIG), resigned after the government launched a
smear campaign against him for opposing its choice of attorney-general, a person
he identified as having links to organized criminals. Only 2 percent of crimes are
ever solved in Guatemala, which is the reason the special commission was initially established.[24] Few dare confront even the lower ranks of the army or police
when they abuse their authority in places such as Pakistan, Egypt, Algeria, and

Iran, knowing full well that those who protest abusive behavior risk bringing it down on their own heads.

Our government official who wants to promote inclusiveness may thus think twice before taking on nepotism and corruption. He may well decide that a safer option is to donate money to a school in a poor district or to throw his weight behind a vaccination campaign. Either of these micro steps will produce concrete benefits for many individuals, but their impact on society overall will be less than if the official had persisted with his efforts to turn his ministry into a meritocracy.

What, then, might persuade our official to tackle macro problems, even though he knows that micro steps provoke less opposition, provide more photo ops, and produce faster and more visible results?

Fortunately, as the next three chapters describe in detail, there are a variety of options. One way is to focus on projects that have a macro impact but are of relatively modest dimensions or that do not directly threaten anyone in power. For instance, our official could help to reduce discrimination by hiring some (appropriately qualified) people from disadvantaged backgrounds. Or he could support a school that brings together people from different ethnic and religious groups. He could also set up a new think tank to research more inclusive policy options. A second way is to work on initiatives that provide plenty of good publicity for senior officials but that also impact macro factors. For example, our official could work with the media to highlight how some of his colleagues in the government are wisely investing money in poor areas, coverage that will boost both awareness of the government program and the public profile of the colleagues involved. A third way would be to set a personal example while not trying to shame or expose others. Our official might, for instance, refuse all bribes himself but not insist others do so. Or, in a bolder move, he might demand meritocratic hiring practices within the most critical area of his department or ministry but not expect other areas to follow suit. Forming a reform club with other members of the elite who share a common ideology and quietly lobbying for some changes behind the scenes or supporting collective action by the poor themselves may also be possible.

A crisis can offer enlightened elites a rare window of opportunity to enact change. Often produced by an economic or political shock—such as a sudden rise in the cost of food, a collapse in the price of an important export commodity, a war in a neighboring country, or the death of an important political actor— these windows of opportunity can give elites the chance to overcome the inertia that normally prevails in the political and economic systems. Very occasionally, these windows can be exploited to entirely transform the macro environment. For instance, in Eastern Europe, the overthrow of the Communist regimes in 1989 ushered in a completely different way of governing and overturned decades of economic stagnation. More often, they enable more incremental reforms to be introduced or accelerated.

Every country, region, and village offers a different set of circumstances, challenges, and opportunities. The objective for every enlightened person should be to take whatever forward steps are feasible, given his or her situation. He or she might be a government official, a businessperson, an academic scholar, a politician, an activist, a tribal elder, a sheikh: whatever his or her position within the elite, opportunities will present themselves. The more steps one person takes, the more likely he or she is to inspire other members of the elite to do something themselves. The power of a virtuous circle of change should not be overestimated. And the rich as well as the poor can need some help in boosting their self-efficacy—boosting, in this case, their belief that they can, individually and collectively, build a more inclusive society.

As the next chapter explains, leaders who want to empower the poor will face less opposition in countries or regions that are already reasonably cohesive and inclusive-minded. Elsewhere, leaders must strive to foster unity and promote an inclusive ideology among both the elite and the public. They must also develop a set of incentives that can nudge other members of the elite to support measures geared toward inclusive state building. At the same time, as chapter 8 will explain, it is one thing to adopt progressive policies but another to realize them. If these policies are to be moved beyond plans and rhetoric, leaders and elites must strengthen their governments' implementation capacity.

CHAPTER 7

Building Support for an Inclusive Agenda

When Ghana became independent in 1957, its citizens had high hopes for the new country's future. So, too, did Africans across the continent. Ghana had been one of Africa's wealthiest and most socially advanced colonies, with schools, railways, and hospitals. It was the world's top exporter of cocoa and a leading producer of gold. And it was led by one of Africa's most enlightened and best educated leaders.

Yet the country went backward for the next quarter of a century. It suffered from successive military coups d'état, political repression, and years of economic stagnation. Incomes grew smaller every year; poverty soared.[1] Millions moved abroad in search of a better life. When I visited in the mid-1980s, I could see plenty of evidence of this decline: electricity cables lay broken beside half-fallen poles; roads were poorly maintained; the University of Ghana, once one of the best in Africa, was full of dilapidated buildings and overgrown yards; people in the streets seemed resigned to a dismal future.

Today, in contrast, Ghana is one of the continent's most successful states. Its economy has grown by a robust 5 percent per year over the past 25 years, raising the income of the average Ghanaian by more than 70 percent. One in two people used to live below the poverty line; today, only one in four people do. Investment has quadrupled. Exports have soared. Many more children go to school. People live longer. And Ghana has become a vibrant democracy, with competitive elections, a vocal press, better protection of basic rights, and stronger governance. The country is far from perfect, but it is one of Africa's strongest countries politically, economically, and institutionally.[2]

What changed?

When Jerry Rawlings came to power on December 31, 1981, little was expected of him. A junior officer with limited military training, he was the latest in a long line of leaders who had come to power by way of a coup (the country had eight heads of state between 1966 and 1981). But he transformed the country during his 19 years in power, reforming almost every aspect of government policy.

Although best known for his economic reforms, the steps Rawlings took to make the state more socially inclusive and more institutionally robust may be his most important legacies. Embracing an ideology focused on improving the quality of life for all Ghanaians, Rawlings reversed a history of widening ethnic tensions and narrow self-interested government.[3] He introduced a constitution that required the state to actively promote national integration by prohibiting discrimination and prejudice based on birthplace, origin, ethnicity, and religion. He also decentralized government; extended public services to the less developed north; expanded health care; and made sure Ghana was able to absorb over one million migrants expelled by Nigeria in 1983. And by strengthening the capacity of government to make and implement policy, introducing a democratic constitution and fair elections, and then stepping down after winning the mandated limit of two presidential terms—at the age of only 54—he established institutions that enabled his achievements to outlast him.

The contrast with neighboring Côte d'Ivoire could not be greater. Once West Africa's brightest economic star, Côte d'Ivoire has been mired in conflict between its southern and northern halves since the demise of its charismatic first president, Félix Houphouët-Boigny, in 1993. Laurent Gbagbo, president from 2000 until he was violently ousted in 2011, manipulated his country's ethnic, religious, and regional divisions to stay in power, wrecking his country's institutions, economy, and whatever sense of unity had been built up in its early years. As always seems to be the case, the poor suffered the most from the country's political chaos and economic decline.

A similar situation exists in nearby Nigeria. The country has few political leaders who act on behalf of the country, only strongmen who do not differentiate between their own interests and those of the government. People may talk proudly about being Nigerian, but their loyalty is not to the country but to their community, to their benefactors in power, and to themselves. Patronage dominates relationships between the elite and everyone else. Powerful leaders live in palaces while most citizens must get by as best they can in a country where millions of people do not attend school or have access to electricity.

What can be done to encourage Nigeria's and Côte d'Ivoire's leaders to behave more like Jerry Rawlings? As this chapter explains, part of the answer lies in reshaping the forces—including ideas, relationships, and incentives—that in turn shape the attitudes and behaviors of the elites who run these countries.

Attitudes Can Matter More Than Democracy

What members of the elite think and do in developing countries affects the poor profoundly because the rich and powerful in these places can largely do what they want. Ordinary citizens have very few ways to hold their leaders accountable.

In poor countries where elections are held regularly, democracy should act as a mechanism to promote accountability and encourage leaders to introduce policies that benefit everyone, poor as well as rich. That, anyway, is the theory. In practice, while democracy does nurture accountability in the long run, in states and regions suffering from the type of social divisions and inequities outlined in chapter 4, democracy rarely accomplishes this in the short run.

What Nuhu Ribadu, former chairman of the Economic and Financial Crimes Commission in Nigeria, says about his country can be said about many poor countries around the world:

> The political culture of Nigeria masquerades as a democracy, but in reality is no more than an exclusive club for a tiny elite accountable not to the millions of citizens they, in theory, represent but to an even smaller clique of power brokers, barons, and what we now inelegantly call godfathers. . . . Imagine a system where everything that is supposed to help to strengthen the state and uphold the rule of law is instead compromised and undermines it. This is true in Nigeria, but also in Cameroon, Sudan, the Democratic Republic of the Congo (DRC), and most African nations.[4]

In many places, elections are held but are not fair. Victories are often achieved by the kind of massive margins that are never seen in full democracies. In 2007, for example, Gurbanguly Berdymukhammedov won Turkmenistan's presidential election with nearly 90 percent of the vote. In 2010, Pierre Nkurunziza received 92 percent of the vote in Burundi. Omar al-Bashir, who has been in power in Sudan since 1989, won the presidency in 2010 with 68 percent of the vote, a feat accomplished by manipulating every stage of the electoral process, from miscounting a census in 2008 to denying his opponents television time just before the vote.[5]

In other places polls are fairer, but campaigns revolve around vote buying rather than debates about policy and government performance. Changes in administrations do not change the dynamic of elite-dominated politics, as in Pakistan. As a result, the ruling elites in much of the developing world—including large parts of Africa and Central Asia—have little worry that they will be voted out of power anytime soon.

Politics is not for the weak and impoverished in these places. As a young woman from Uttar Pradesh in India explained, "Only those who have money and goons with them are in politics. They eat other people's money and don't even belch."[6]

Even in countries where the elite do not monopolize political office, democracy by itself cannot empower the poor. Why not? In part because elected representatives are likely to become corrupted and co-opted by the system. "After being elected," complained Piara, a farmer and mover from Digbari in Bangladesh, "the chairman and members become blind; they eat up all the aid received from the government."[7] Elections, no matter how free and fair, also may simply entrench ethnic and other divisions within a country, the majority dominating the minority and perpetuating traditions of social, economic, and political exclusion. For all these reasons, when it comes to empowering the poor, a democratic system is less powerful than an inclusive ideology.

Democracy, it should be stressed, can make a difference in some instances. In Bihar, India, for instance, Nitish Kumar overturned decades of narrow caste politics (which had rewarded leaders based on caste loyalty no matter how badly they governed) to enact a sweeping reform agenda that emphasized the shared benefits of development. He jailed criminals who had operated with impunity, constructed roads and bridges in a state in dire need of better infrastructure, expanded the number of seats reserved for women on village councils, loosened bureaucratic rules to encourage investment, and greatly expanded education and health-care facilities. The economy in India's poorest and once most ungovernable state responded, growing by 11 percent annually for five years, the second-fastest rate in the country. He was reelected in a landslide in 2010.

Jayant Sinha, a political strategist, nicely summarized the change: "Distributional politics have been set aside for performance politics. The communities have tried this game of voting into government their caste-based candidates and their brothers for a share of the pie. But people have realized that doesn't work as well as the grow-the-pie approach."[8]

Unfortunately, however, the kind of success that Kumar has enjoyed is rare in the developing world. Moreover, even when progress is made through the democratic process, it can be quickly reversed. The underlying caste divisions in Bihar will take generations to erase, and in the meantime everyone—from Kumar himself to the investors who continue to shy away from Bihar, fearful that its recent spurt in growth may be fleeting if caste-based politics reassert themselves—knows that the progress made is vulnerable to rapid reversal.

The countries in the developing world with the best record of empowering the poor—by adopting policies that generate growth, promote inclusiveness, and strengthen the capacity of the state—are those whose elites are united behind an inclusive approach toward nation building. They are not, it should be emphasized, necessarily inclusive in terms of seeking to share their political power with their impoverished compatriots. To the contrary, in many cases they share the exclusionary inclinations of elites throughout the developing world when it comes to deciding who gets to be a minister or president. They are inclusive, however, in terms of seeking, through their policy choices, to make sure government functions for the well-being of all or at least most of the country's citizens.

In this sense, their rule is based on an implicit "social contract," on an unspoken agreement between the ruling clique and the rest of the citizenry that allows the elite to remain in power as long as it continues to improve the standard of living of the citizens. Although the Chinese Communist Party (CCP), for instance, has never faced an election, it enjoys substantial popular legitimacy because of the tremendous economic results it has produced. An amazing 87 percent of the Chinese population says it is satisfied with the direction the country is taking.[9] Comparable percentages for other countries don't come close. The Botswana Democratic Party has won every election since the country's independence by delivering decades of rapid growth while promoting an inclusive, non-ethnic citizenship and democracy. Oman's Sultan Qaboos is an autocrat, just as former Egyptian president Mubarak was, but Qaboos has much more legitimacy than Mubarak ever had. Why? Because the sultan has governed with an inclusive vision that has lifted his society out of poverty, improved the status of women, and built roads and schools throughout the country's rural interior.[10]

Of course, such social contracts can only go so far without democracy. Once people escape crushing poverty, their expectations change. A poverty-stricken peasant may well enthusiastically support an autocrat who wants to give the poor greater economic opportunity. But by the time that peasant has become a relatively prosperous farmer or merchant, he or she may well see that same autocrat as an outmoded obstacle to the development of a political system in which the former peasant can actively participate. Autocracies in South Korea, Taiwan, Indonesia, and Chile all adopted pro-growth policies that gave their citizens excellent opportunities to improve their lives, but all were eventually forced out of power by very unhappy populations who had acquired an appetite for political power after they grew richer and their expectations regarding their leaders changed.

Three Tools with Which to Build Support for an Inclusive Agenda

Unfortunately, the elites in most poor countries have no such inclusive ambitions. Their vision is restricted to a narrow tunnel of self-interest. Or, rather, the vision of *most* of the elite is blinkered in this fashion. But elites are not monolithic; they are made up of disparate actors and subgroups, each with their own worldviews and interests. In the great majority of countries, at least some members of the wealthier, better educated, and more powerful sectors of a population have a broader view, a forward-looking vision of a state that can provide opportunity to all its members.

Although far from paragons of political virtue, people such as Paul Kagame of Rwanda, Fernando Henrique Cardoso of Brazil, Meles Zenawi of Ethiopia, and Mahathir bin Mohamad of Malaysia have all piloted their countries through tumultuous times and into periods of sustained and rapid growth that were accompanied by substantial improvements in the lives of the poor.

And one doesn't have to be in charge of a country to make a difference. Less prominent and less politically powerful members of elites can also have a significant impact. As we shall see in chapter 12, people like Dr. Agnes Binagwaho from Rwanda, Wangari Maathai from Kenya, Sir Fazle Hasan Abed from Bangladesh, and Roshaneh Zafar from Pakistan are making substantial contributions to building an inclusive, development-oriented state. Sometimes, these enlightened individuals seek to magnify their influence by creating organizations. Sri Lanka's Sarvodaya Shramadana Movement, Bangladesh's Grameen Bank, and Brazil's Todos Pela Educação were all started by members of their countries' elites; and all are working in one way or another to empower the poor.

As discussed in the previous chapter, these enlightened individuals face many obstacles when they try to promote an inclusive state-building agenda: some petty, some substantial. Corrupt bureaucrats, self-serving politicians, regional powerbrokers, ethnic and religious leaders preaching gospels of prejudice and exclusivity: individually and collectively, they will try to disarm or destroy anyone working to foster change.

But enlightened individuals are not without their own weapons. They have a trio of tools at their disposal with which they can try to advance their agenda. One tool is *social cohesion*—that is, the social, cultural, and psychological bonds tying all members of a society together.[11] The more socially cohesive a state is, the more likely its leadership will act inclusively, see growth-inducing policies as in its interests, and invest in strengthening the capacity of the state. The second tool is an *inclusive pro-development ideology*, a worldview that explicitly calls upon its adherents both to help all other members of a given society, including the poor, and to promote pro-growth policies. The third tool consists of steps that can shape the *incentives* influencing members of the ruling clique, encouraging them to come together behind an inclusive pro-development agenda.

Social Cohesion: The Glue That Binds

The countries most likely to prioritize inclusive development are nation-states.[12] A nation-state is naturally cohesive, its people sharing a common history, language, culture, and social system. Every day, these ties strengthen the sense of a common identity and group allegiance. The attitudes that this sense of a common destiny produces translate into governments both more oriented toward development and more concerned for the welfare of the poor.

Nation-states, it should be pointed out, have rarely emerged peacefully and painlessly. To the contrary, most have evolved through long processes marked by bloody wars, savage power politics, forced assimilation, and conspicuous greed and egotism.[13] Such tumultuous births, however, can yield remarkably stable and prosperous countries. Examples of nation-states include France, Germany, Japan, and Turkey.

Not all nations are states, and not all states are nations. The Kurds are a nation without a state. The Iraqis have a state but not a nation. Although very diverse ethnically and religiously, the United States has many similarities with a nation-state because most people who have immigrated into the country have adopted a common creed and culture.

In the developed world, nation-states are common. In the developing world, they are relatively rare (because the borders of states were created by colonial mapmakers, not by the local people), but where they exist they tend to be far more cohesive and unified than their neighbors. By virtue of being based on a common identity, nation-states contain fewer identity-driven rivalries than are found in the rest of the developing world. They are also more resilient, better able to unite in the face of adversity rather than breakdown into competing factions. They are thus also less prone to conflict.[14]

Some nation-states, such as Turkey and Vietnam, organized themselves around a common cultural heritage. Others, such as Botswana and Costa Rica, had colonial borders that luckily left them relatively homogeneous. The citizens of these places view outside countries as their true competitors, rather than other groups within the state, and are thus highly motivated to pull together to build up the power and standing of their homeland. Helping the poor improve their condition is considered crucial to helping the state advance and is therefore assigned a high priority by policymakers.[15]

Fewer fissures also mean that fewer people are likely to be denied public services and equitable treatment at the hands of the state. Elites who see the poor as "one of us" are far more likely to ensure that they have access to schooling, employment, infrastructure, security, and opportunity.

China is one of the best examples of this process in action on a large scale. At least 90 percent of its population shares a strong national identity based on thousands of years of common social, economic, and political evolution. Despite some internal divisions and a huge population, it is among the more cohesive states in the developing world. As a result, it has been able to call upon deep reserves of group affinity to make modernization a national mission in recent decades. The contrast with a place such as Nigeria—which has more than two hundred different ethnic groups, conflicts over religion, and a very short history—could not be greater.

Most nation-states in the developing world have similar track records to China in tackling poverty and empowering the poor. As mentioned in chapter 5, Vietnam (another East Asian nation-state that brings together people with a common history, language, and culture dating back over a millennium) and Chile (one of the most homogeneous countries in Latin America) have stellar records both in promoting growth and in reducing poverty over the past two decades.

But even nation-states can't afford to take social cohesion for granted. They need to take steps to reaffirm and bolster it. And states that aren't nation-states must, of course, do far more. They must create what does not exist or what exists only weakly, and then nurture and strengthen it. Singapore has relentlessly and systematically labored to construct a cohesive unity from three ethnic groups (Chinese, Malay, and Indian), who found themselves at odds in the wake of independence in 1965. The new country's leadership wisely opted to focus on equity in public services, education, inclusive growth, and other policies that both raised living standards and promoted social integration. As a consequence, Singapore is today a model of stability and prosperity. The country's founding father, Lee Kuan Yew, is confident that his country's success is due to building "social cohesion through sharing the benefits of progress, equal opportunities for all and meritocracy, with the best man or woman for the job, especially as leaders in government."[16]

Leaders in some Latin American countries have come to recognize the importance of social cohesion to stability and growth in recent years, belatedly reversing centuries of exclusion and neglect of their mainly nonwhite poor. According to a UN booklet on the region:

In Latin America and the Caribbean, the idea of social cohesion has emerged as a response to persistent problems which, despite certain achievements over the past few years, continue to exist: high indices of poverty and indigence, the extreme inequality that characterizes our region and various forms of discrimination and social exclusion dating back to the distant past. . . . While there are usually many reasons for these gaps, the frail material foundation of social cohesion is a stand-out factor.[17]

As we will see in chapter 10, Latin America has pioneered some of the most innovative programs aimed at boosting opportunity for the poor.

One of the most demanding efforts to foster social cohesion is taking place in Rwanda, which was torn apart by genocide in 1994, when 800,000 members of the country's Tutsi population were slaughtered by their Hutu neighbors. Rwanda's president, Paul Kagame, is trying to cultivate a national identity to serve as a foundation for social cohesion:

> Nation-building is a long and challenging political process, but one that leaders, together with the citizenry, must undertake with seriousness. We must understand that most nations have their unique circumstances and each one, throughout history, has built and developed itself around certain distinguishing core features. The first of these has always been the conscious cultivation of a national identity, the sense of belonging, based on shared values, tradition, history and aspirations. National identity is the foundation of social cohesion . . . to correct a historical wrong and institute inclusive politics. The Rwandan people learned the hard way the danger of politics of exclusion where the winner takes all, and have opted for a model that builds on inclusive politics of power sharing and consensus building.[18]

National leaders have tried to use a variety of unifying forces to overcome the problems posed by ethnic and religious diversity within their country's borders. Tanzania has adopted Swahili as its national language; Senegal has celebrated its unique Islamic and African cultural heritages; Pakistan has attempted to forge an Islamic identity.

These efforts to build a common identity can succeed only if they are multigenerational and multidimensional. The young must be educated from an early age in languages, symbols, and ideas that everyone within the country can accept. The media must cultivate a shared self-image and show a population how it differs from its neighbors. Political parties representing sectarian or sectional interests must be banned. Government officials must consistently display no favoritism toward any group. Steps must be taken to institutionalize cooperation between the country's different ethnic and religious groups, such as making agreements to share the profits from a country's natural resources equitably throughout the country, and drawing up constitutions that mandate that all groups be represented in cabinets, civil services, legislatures, and militaries.[19]

None of this is likely to be achieved easily or without opposition. In states that lack a sense of national identity, the ties that bind individuals to their own groups are powerful. "Spoilers"—those who seek to wreck efforts at reform—will try to undermine unity by appealing to ethnic, religious, tribal, or clan divisions. But each enlightened member of the elite can resist spoilers and promote cohesion in his or her own sphere of influence. A television producer can create programs that promote a common culture. A leader of a political, economic, or social group can make its activities and membership more inclusive. A teacher can work to eliminate prejudice among his or her students. A public official can try to ensure that schools are funded equitably throughout the country. A judge offered a bribe to rule against a disadvantaged group can refuse to accept it.

Inclusive Ideologies

While the process of building social cohesion takes generations, inclusive ideologies can impact the thinking and behavior of elites within decades, even years. Both political and religious ideologies can, if they extol inclusiveness and are embraced by elites, inspire concrete action to help the poor.

Political Ideology

One of the best historical examples of an ideological impulse to help the poor can be found in the Communist states of the twentieth century. They based their legitimacy partly on their avowed intention to improve the lives of society's most disadvantaged groups, and they made it a priority to demonstrate that they were better than capitalist countries at combating poverty. Although many people suffered under Communist rule (especially during politically engineered catastrophes such as Mao's Great Leap Forward and Stalin's purges, to say nothing of the devastating famines that Communist mismanagement and ruthlessness created), the most destitute were almost always better off economically—at least in the short term—than they had been under the regimes that the Communists displaced. Education and health indicators, for instance, dramatically improved for Russian workers and Chinese peasants in the years after their revolutions. Cuba's economy has performed miserably for decades, but its literacy rates are the highest in Latin America and poverty rates among the lowest. Communism's emphasis on building up the capacity to govern also helped strengthen the organs of the state, something essential to inclusive development.

The problem for the poor in twentieth-century Communist states, however, was that the stultifying economic systems limited personal agency and eventually produced stagnant economies that hurt everyone. This problem has been avoided in those countries that have embraced the "developmental state" ideology pioneered by Germany and Japan in the nineteenth century and since adopted and adapted by countries as diverse as China, Singapore, and Rwanda. This ideology centers on a national modernizing mission driven by inclusive growth and the building up of the state in ways thought to quicken economic transformation. It has proven to be the ideology that brings the greatest benefits to the poor over time—even though it does not directly focus on them at all.

By emphasizing the need for unity in the face of external threats and promising faster growth that will enrich both elites and the masses, the leaders of these countries have been able to put together broad coalitions and push through major reforms that some powerful interests might otherwise have been able to obstruct. Although the developmental state ideology has often led to some unsavory practices (such as the repression of opponents), it has also consistently yielded governments that see great value in education, basic health care, infrastructure, entrepreneurship, wealth creation, and a robust government apparatus—all of which benefit the poor tremendously. It also extols the value of social cohesion, which is why many of the same states that embrace the developmental state approach also actively promote social cohesion.

In recent decades, this developmental state ideology has proven so successful that it has spread widely in East Asia. South Korea, Singapore, Malaysia, Indonesia, and Taiwan have all used various aspects of it.

Developmental state ideology has had an impact on Africa, too. Ethiopia's prime minister, Meles Zenawi, frequently urged African states to shift to a new development paradigm centered on the developmental state. "It is the establishment of developmental states which transformed the political economy of Asian countries and paved the way for sustained and accelerated growth and transformation of their economies," Zenawi remarked in 2011.[20] Rwanda has become well-known for the efficient and effective implementation of a strongly pro-development and economically inclusive agenda in recent years and has achieved annual growth rates exceeding 10 percent.[21] President Yoweri Museveni of Uganda adopted a similar model when he took office, building a reputation for his commitment to the economic transformation of his state (which has waned considerably in recent years). Museveni's Uganda and Zenawi's Ethiopia drew praise for their poverty-fighting credentials in the *Chronic Poverty Report (CPR) 2008–09* and have made more progress toward the Millennium Development Goals (MDGs) than have the great majority of African countries.[22] (The MDGs are a series of development targets established at a UN conference in 2000.) Even though these three countries generally have had inclusive policies, they have nonetheless been marked by some regional differences in terms of improvements. Conflict zones, such as northern Uganda and southeastern Ethiopia, have done less well than more peaceful areas of those countries.

Mahathir bin Mohamad laid out his interpretation of the developmental state model in 1990, when he outlined an agenda for Malaysia he called "Vision 2020":

> We must be fully developed in terms of national unity and social cohesion, in terms of our economy, in terms of social justice, political stability, system of government, quality of life, social and spiritual values, national pride and confidence. . . . [This requires] establishing a united Malaysian nation with a sense of common and shared destiny . . . a prosperous society, with an economy that is fully competitive, dynamic, robust and resilient . . . the eradication of absolute poverty regardless of race, and irrespective of geographical location . . . the narrowing of the ethnic income gap, through the legitimate provision of opportunities. . . . [Our] economy must be able to sustain itself over the longer term, must be dynamic, robust and resilient. The Government will be proactive to . . . escalate the development of the necessary physical infrastructure and the most conducive business environment— consistent with its other social priorities.[23]

By providing ample benefits in exchange for loyalty to the state and model, the developmental state ideology has helped defuse potentially divisive ethnic, religious, and geographical divisions. It has also reduced the incentive for anyone to develop and disseminate an alternative ideology, one likely to produce division, exclusion, and destabilization. Growth begets growth, itself becoming a driver of change. The greater the opportunity to make money legitimately, the readier people will be to turn away from exclusionary politics and corrupt practices.

Religious Ideology

Religion and some traditional value systems can also inspire a devotion to inclusiveness and encourage behavior that promotes growth. Islam, for instance, has pushed autocratic governments in the Middle East to improve the living conditions of their poor citizens. Islam requires believers to give a fixed portion of their income to the poor and needy, and it calls on society as a whole to develop charitable foundations to care for a community's most vulnerable members.[24]

Of course, Islam—like any ideology—is neither static nor monolithic. Different groups of believers emphasize different strands within the faith, and different historical currents and circumstances bring out different elements. Although the rituals practiced by people in, say, Saudi Arabia, Indonesia, Turkey, and Iran may be broadly similar, the role of religion in how those countries govern themselves and how their societies function varies enormously. Even so, Islamic states have a remarkably good record of helping their poorer citizens. Of the 11 countries that qualify as "Across-the-Board Consistent Improvers" in the *2008–2009* CPR, 9 are Muslim, and 7 are Arab.[25] What makes this all the more remarkable is that many of these countries (Syria, for instance) have deep, internal sociopolitical divisions. Moreover, many (such as Egypt and Morocco) are not at all wealthy and have very limited resources with which to help the poor. All told, of the 16 countries in the Middle East and North Africa covered by the CPR, 12 are in the top two categories.[26] (In comparison, only 19 of the other 115 countries covered in the report qualify for the top two categories.)[27]

Like Islam, Christianity, Hinduism, and other faiths have tenets and practices within their faith that could be interpreted as supportive of inclusive development. The Fathers of the Second Vatican Council declared in a "Message to Humanity" in 1962 that the church's focus should fall "first of all on those who are especially lowly, poor, and weak. . . . We want to fix a steady gaze on those who still lack the opportune help to achieve a way of life worthy of human beings."[28] The Catholic Church has made social justice, equity, and social inclusion worldwide higher priorities in recent decades. Evangelicals have expanded rapidly across the developing world, partly because they often create a community that helps to empower the poor by providing them with a variety of practical services and opportunities to play leadership roles. Churches of all stripes provide a range of social services to the poor in developing countries where the state cannot or will not do so.

Other traditional value systems can play these roles, too. As Francis Deng, a noted Sudanese legal scholar and a former UN diplomat, and others have recognized, many African cultures have long embraced "governance forms based on community participation and consensual decision making. . . . For all concerned, the system was set up for *participation* in power, not its *appropriation*. The underlying philosophy was one of cooperation, not confrontation." Ghana's Rawlings has emphasized how local cultural norms influenced his style of rule while he was in power, encouraging him to devolve power downward, closer to the people.[29] Just five days after seizing power on New Year's Eve in 1981, Rawlings declared that he "wanted a chance for the people, farmers, workers, soldiers, the rich and the poor, to be part of the decision-making process."[30]

Harnessing Ideology

The power of political, religious, or cultural precepts can be harnessed in numerous ways. For instance, members of the elite who want to nurture more inclusive and development-oriented states could take some of the following steps:

- Work together with other prominent members of the elite to develop a national vision of unity and progress, as Mahathir did in Malaysia.
- Urge opinion leaders who have the ear of the top members of the elite to emphasize that promoting inclusive development is the duty of any responsible leader. Muslim and Christian clerics, for example, could be encouraged to take a hard line against any individual who repeatedly acts in ways that harm the poor or the development of society.
- Establish a governance academy where both current and future leaders can be not only educated in public administration but also imbued with a sense of duty to adopt and implement inclusive pro-development policies.
- Institute a financially attractive "governance prize" that can be awarded with much fanfare to a number of public servants every year for their work on behalf of the poor and good government.
- Establish a national think tank tasked with developing an inclusive ideology based on homegrown values and norms.
- Partner with leaders of neighboring countries or regional organizations to espouse a more inclusive development model. Peer pressure can be very powerful—which is one reason why in 2007 tycoon Mo Ibrahim created the Ibrahim Index of African Governance, which measures the quality of government on the continent and aims to pressure leaders to raise performance.
- Point out the ways in which inclusive policies can bolster the nation's sense of identity and mission. For instance, members of Pakistan's elite could develop a developmental state ideology and argue that its adoption is a necessity to compete better in the country's geopolitical battle with India.

Incentives

Even the most inspirational and eloquent of leaders can do only so much to persuade members of the elite to embrace inclusive development as an idea. Especially in societies that are deeply divided, administered by highly corrupt governments, and have very narrow ruling cliques, inclusive leaders will have to find creative ways to reconfigure the incentives that currently make many members of the elite hostile toward development and social inclusion.

Depending on the circumstances, everyone from warlords to corrupt businessmen and ethnic and religious leaders may stand in the way of leaders hoping to forge a national, regional, or local consensus behind an inclusive, development-oriented state building agenda. Some will have legitimate concerns, while many will just worry about their own positions, interests, and profits.

Overcoming these spoilers is not easy and may not always be possible in the short term. Even in the long term, it may require Machiavellian strategizing and maneuvering to co-opt, isolate, circumscribe, or overthrow them. Champions of reform will have to win over powerful individuals and societal groups that have previously pursued narrow private interests and persuade them to join a broad coalition working to nurture growth and spread its benefits more widely.

Different circumstances will call for different strategies to tackle opponents of reform. Where a state is relatively robust, the pro-reform coalition may be able to negotiate with opponents to accept a pro-growth deal. Offering compensation, whether financial or in some other form, may help to bring potential spoilers on board. Various forms of popular pressure—from taxpayer protests to campaigns by religious coalitions (see below)—may also overcome elite resistance to change. But where the state is weak and society is fragmented into a series of patronage networks, the pro-reform group may have to be much more creative if they are to co-opt powerful forces. As Alex de Waal and David Booth, British analysts of African issues, have argued, the least worst option in some cases might be to integrate these powerful actors and their support networks into some form of governing arrangement. Key individuals could be given high-status positions and a share of the gains produced from greater investment in return for their willingness to curb their disruptive behavior.[31] A deal to buy the support of an important power broker may initially limit the scope of reform. But if that deal increases economic opportunity (by decreasing political uncertainty), it will gradually lead to a more equitable and inclusive environment.

No matter whether the state is robust or weak, local businesspeople (or businesspeople from neighboring states or diasporas) will have an important role to play, because their investment capital will be crucial to igniting growth. Before they invest their capital, they will want guarantees from whoever controls the government that their property and anticipated profits will be secure.

Whatever the mechanism adopted and whatever the deals concocted, the key is to build momentum. As the coalition in favor of inclusive development grows stronger, it will be better positioned to actually implement pro-development policies, which will in turn further strengthen the coalition. Just reaching agreement—even if only narrowly focused on promoting economic growth—will be helpful in the short term and provide momentum that would eventually yield more far-reaching social and political change. Of course, the more divided a society is—whether from civil war, ethnic or sectarian rivalry, or a long history of oppression or discrimination—the harder it will be to forge stable pacts.[32]

Latin American countries such as Brazil, Argentina, Chile, and Mexico offer concrete examples of how reform coalitions can be constructed in relatively robust states. Each was able to make politically difficult market-oriented reforms (such as trade liberalization, privatization, and the reduction of subsidies) in the late 1990s. The advent of economic crisis—brought on by the Asian financial crisis—spurred events, but significantly changing the regulatory environment of the previous 40 years would not have been possible without the development of a broad consensus among important actors. A substantial shift in both elite preferences and the opinions of ordinary voters—important as the countries democratized—helped forge a consensus in favor of policy reform. In the end, enough influential members of the elite—including politicians, union leaders, and well-placed businesspeople—became convinced of the need for the reforms and had enough backing within their constituencies to support them.[33] The net result was both a surge in growth and a marked reduction in poverty in the countries that sustained their reforms over time. Brazil became one of the most important economies worldwide, enjoying a boom in foreign investment. Growth substantially enlarged the middle class and was accompanied by increasingly aggressive government efforts to help the poor benefit.

Indonesia under Suharto shows how reform coalitions can be constructed in less robust states. The role of local businesses was extremely important. A highly diverse country ethnically, religiously, and geographically, Indonesia was on the verge of anarchy when he took over in 1967 after an extended period of chaotic misrule and economic mismanagement. Suharto was able to fashion a stable, fast-growing regime based on an alliance committed to inclusive development between himself, the military, and business within a relatively short period. Corruption was widespread, but major investment projects were protected by a system of centralized bribe collecting that protected property rights, reduced uncertainty about costs, and even ensured a degree of predictability concerning returns. A firm opening a factory, for instance, could be confident that the requisite bribe would secure their rights and limit future kickbacks.[34] Simultaneously, the regime sought to court the rural masses (who had supported the previous government) and introduced policies that helped the poor. The technocrats that were brought in to run much policymaking were ordered to deliver what came to be known in Indonesia as the "development trilogy"—growth, equity, and stability.[35]

Although the model was extremely wasteful, politically repressive, and environmentally destructive, it brought rapid development and delivered many benefits to the poor. Between 1966 and 1997, Indonesia was one of the fastest-expanding economies in the world, creating millions of manufacturing jobs, becoming self-sufficient in rice, and achieving major advances in education and literacy. Incomes grew at 4.5 percent a year between 1965 and 1990, while the proportion of Indonesians living in poverty fell from almost two-thirds in 1975 to just over one-tenth in 1995.[36] Although the Suharto model eventually disintegrated—as he grew old, corruption spiraled out of control and economic management become less inclusive and more wasteful—the country's current stability and democratization would not have been possible without all the gains achieved during his rule.

Other leaders have tried to form inclusive development coalitions of various flavors, though with mixed results in some cases. Leaders in Malaysia and Vietnam, for instance, have sought to build cohesive and prosperous nations by combining an ideological commitment to development, a system of payoffs to important players for their support, ample protection for investors, and programs that provide all citizens with greater education and health care and opportunities to raise incomes. In Africa, Mozambique has enjoyed almost two decades of rapid growth, democratic elections, and rising incomes after a war that left over a million dead because the two protagonists forged a lasting pact that produced enough spoils to satisfy each side yet did not prevent reforms that jumpstarted the economy.

In the least developed states that were able to co-opt important players behind a pro-growth agenda, elite self-interest and corruption have not been eliminated but channeled in ways that have promoted a series of publicly useful outcomes, such as state modernization. Corruption has been used to buy support for modernization among important members of the elite and to reduce business risk (the payoffs are linked to better protection of corporate assets) in countries badly in need of investment. The poor benefit as long as the result creates lots of jobs and generates resources that the government spends on public goods—such as schools, health care clinics, and roads—that matter to the poor.

Of course, this process is anything but ideal, but given the situation in many countries—and the miserable track record of alternative approaches to jumpstarting development over the past half-century—it might be the best that can be hoped for in some places. Working within existing political constraints while trying to loosen them; rewarding existing elites while trying to convince them of the need for more inclusive policies; accepting corruption and other evils in the name of a handful of greater goals: these are the tradeoffs that inclusive-minded leaders must accept if they want to make a difference. Avoiding the pitfalls of crony capitalism requires ensuring both that investment increases growth and jobs in the short term and that efforts are simultaneously made to transition to a more law-based system of economic governance in the medium term.[37]

* * *

How can business, community, and religious leaders convince political leaders to act more inclusively? How can pro-reform forces grow larger, stronger, and more cohesive? How can they use their power to change the incentives shaping those who control power?[38] Many options present themselves:[39]

- Encouraging leaders to create a legacy that future generations both at home and abroad will applaud.
- Creating partnerships between business associations, political parties, and trade unions to promote a pro-growth agenda that benefit a wide range of people, as occurred in several Latin American countries in the late 1990s.
- Sponsoring activities that bring together political and economic leaders from disparate factions to discuss national problems and build personal trust. Somaliland's transition to stable government and democracy was initiated by a series of interclan conferences financed by local businesspeople and community leaders.[40]
- Building up organizations that enhance the ability of the poor to work together to advance their political interests (see chapter 12).
- Working with leading businesses to formulate a series of government reforms (such as the establishment of an industrial zone, the introduction of streamlined dispute-resolution arrangements, or the construction of key infrastructure), which, if enacted, will trigger an agreed-upon level of investment and job creation.
- Creating a coalition of major taxpayers to lobby for legislation to better protect private property and strengthen the rule of law.
- Developing a network of reform advocates from across the political spectrum to share ideas, forge new relationships, and work together toward common goals.
- Reaching across ethnic and religious divides to tackle national problems in a way that creates a more permanent alliance for a development agenda. By uniting disparate religious groups to fight against poverty and disease, the Nigerian Inter-Faith Action Association (NIFAA) reduces interreligious conflict and promotes a common perspective on some of the country's larger challenges. The coalition could be expanded to push for more spending on the poor or a greater emphasis on social inclusion from political leaders.
- Uniting dispersed, disaggregated, and therefore weak political forces into a stronger, consolidated movement that can press for policies that benefit the poor, such as better schooling and more rural roads. Indigenous groups have banded together in the Andes countries to create large political parties (and other groupings) with enough clout to force governments to introduce inclusive policies.
- Reorienting a political party, business association, or activist group currently structured around patronage, ethnic, or regional bases toward an issue- or interest-based agenda that encompasses a broader grouping of peoples. The reelection of Nitish Kumar in Bihar, India, may spur other politicians in northern India to focus on issues related to public services and development rather than caste.
- Strengthening mechanisms that hold leaders accountable for their actions. Establishing nongovernmental organizations that monitor public policy,

spending, corruption, and inequities in public expenditures can increase transparency and give the public greater ability to influence their leaders. So can strengthening independent media and the skills of investigative journalists.

Many of these steps will be easier to take during a window of opportunity, when the obstacles that usually stand in the way of reform can be more easily pushed aside.

Combining the Three Tools

These three tools for persuading elites to adopt an inclusive state-building agenda—fostering social cohesion, encouraging inclusive ideologies, and forging reform coalitions to reconfigure the incentives of elites—can be used separately but have much more effect when they are combined. After all, they are mutually reinforcing: The more cohesive a population is, the more inclusive its attitudes will be, and the more likely that its leaders will see state building as in their own interests. The more ideologically committed to inclusive development elites are, the more likely it is that a population will become cohesive over time. The more that elites see broad-based growth as in their own interests, the more likely they will promote national cohesion and a state-building ideology.

Of these three, social cohesion is probably the most powerful tool over the long term, but an inclusive ideology can be very potent in the short to midterm, and incentives can greatly accelerate progress along the path of positive change. In developing states, reform-minded elites are unlikely to have the luxury of deciding which of three tools to focus on: any and all of them will have to be used whenever and wherever there is a chance to promote inclusiveness and growth.

Reform champions need to determine what tools they have available and how best to use them. They can do this by asking questions about the people whose support they need: What interests do key members of the elite share with the poor? How can the elite be encouraged to act more inclusively and to adopt a long-term development-oriented perspective? What is shaping the relationship between politicians and investors, and how might their common interests be funneled toward productive investment? What ideology might be used to help spur action toward more inclusive and development-oriented behavior? What common elements (language, history, etc.) might be used to strengthen national cohesion? What are the elites' major sources of income and prestige, and how might these be better used to encourage more inclusive publicly minded action?[41]

Answers to these questions should be factored into the development of a practical plan that promises not only to spur inclusive development but also to reward the elite. By explaining how the elite will benefit from such a plan—for instance, by reducing crime and by increasing the security of existing wealth—leaders can slowly encourage more productive activity, a more equitable use of resources, and more inclusion of the poor. The more robust and widespread the growth that results, the more likely it is to start a virtuous circle that brings in more members of the elite and produces a more sustainable process that can benefit more people.

At the same time, enlightened members of the elite should be doing everything they can to strengthen the government apparatus, the topic of the next chapter. The effectiveness of each of the three tools depends to some extent on the ability of the state to perform its core functions—delivering public services, enforcing the rule of law, and acting as the arbitrator between various parties and factions. Where it cannot, elites are far less likely to see or feel the need to act on behalf of anyone but themselves.

CHAPTER 8

Constructing a More Effective State

At around 6:30 p.m. we were stopped by a group of policemen manning a checkpoint under a bridge. There were 10 of us passengers. One of the police entered and told the bus driver to "do his duty." When the driver asked him what this meant, the policeman said, "You should know . . . give us ₦500 [500 naira was equivalent to about $4]." The driver offered $50 instead. Angered by this, the policeman ordered everyone out. We told him he had no right to do what he was doing. He said, "You can't talk to a policeman like that . . . it's an offense!" We responded, "No, what you're doing is an offense!"

One lady passenger had a large amount of money—about ₦50,000 ($417). When they found it, they interrogated her about where she got it, saying it was an offense to carry this kind of money. The other passengers gasped and said, "What kind of an offense is that?" The woman started crying, pleading. She got down on her knees and begged them not to take her money. They threatened to take her to the station and we yelled at them saying she had done nothing wrong. The police told her to give them $20,000. When we heard this we screamed, saying, "Why should she do that?" Then one of them said if any of us said anything we would be handcuffed.

The woman sobbed and vowed to lay a curse on the policemen so they wouldn't see any good things in life. Hearing this, the policemen aimed their guns at her and threatened to shoot her if she did so. Then she fell on the ground shaking. They kept us there for one hour. When the woman got back on the bus we tried to comfort her. We felt so sorry—she was a very poor woman who made her living selling used clothes. She said she'd borrowed the money from her boss because of a problem she had at home and that she had no one else to help her—she said her husband was dead. But the police don't care about any of this.[1]

C ountless ordinary Nigerians could tell similar stories. Taxi drivers, market traders, and shopkeepers routinely encounter armed police officers demanding bribes. Victims who report a crime to the police discover that the police refuse to investigate unless the victim pays for the privilege. Meanwhile, criminals with thick wallets bribe the police to avoid arrest or prosecution, to influence the outcome of a criminal investigation, or even to turn the

Source: Cartoon by "Basati" [E. B. Asukwo]. Originally published by Human Rights Watch as part of their report *"Everyone's in on the Game": Corruption and Human Rights Abuses by the Nigeria Police Force* (New York: HRW, August 2010), 57.

investigation against the victim. Senior police officers take a cut from the money extorted by junior officers.[2] The same pattern of pervasive corruption and of governments unable to tackle it extends across much of the developing world.

Almost all the world's poor live in countries where the state is too weak or too dysfunctional to provide the kinds of basic services that both citizens and businesses need if they are to thrive. What kinds of services are these? A police force that protects rather than preys upon society. A court system that decides cases on their merits, not according to the size of bribes. A road network that extends across the entire country, not just around the capital. A health-care system that is accessible to everyone, not just the wealthy.

Some states in the developing world cannot provide such services because they lack the required resources. They have little or no money to spend on services and too few well-qualified officials to deliver them. Legal systems are hampered by shortages of trained judges, prosecutors, attorneys, and public defenders. Pakistan's state judicial system, for instance, is starved of every imaginable resource. The 17 million people living in Karachi had just 110 judges to try the more than 100,000 cases pending as of May 2009. Some of the courts are supposed to handle more than 100 cases a day. In the whole of the Khyber Pakhtunkhwa, a province of some 20 million people, there was exactly one fingerprinting machine available to the police as of mid-2008—and this is the area where the government faces the largest threat of unrest from the Pakistan Taliban.[3]

The number of poor children attending schools across the developing world has risen in recent years, but few of these children are learning much, because their governments lack the capacity and the human resources to give a good education to the children once they get to school. In Bangladesh, for instance, over one-half of 11-year-olds are unable to write basic letters or numerals, despite a gross enrollment rate over 100 percent.[4] Similar underperformance is common in health-care systems, legal systems, regulatory systems, transportation systems, administrative systems—indeed, in all the systems that depend on good government to work well.

Other states fail to implement their own laws, programs, and policies, not because they lack the required resources but because they are badly organized and chronically corrupt. In spite of having a big and relatively competent state apparatus compared to most poor countries, India is daily held back by the dysfunction that plagues much of its government. Despite having the world's largest public food-distribution system, 42 percent of all children in India are underweight because the system is riddled with corruption and inefficiency. Ration booklets are often used as collateral for short-term loans, even though this is illegal, and allows moneylenders to purchase grain at subsidized rates and resell it at six times the cost in the open market. Clerks often refuse to issue the cards and then use them for their own families and friends. Government inspectors extort monthly payments from the clerks who sell the subsidized grain; the clerks in turn bribe local officials to get or keep their jobs; moneylenders slip money to clerks who let them use the ration cards to collect subsidized grain, sugar, and fuel. Some 70 percent of the roughly $12 billion annual budget is wasted.[5] "In India, it is not because of the government" that things get done, explains Vidya Srinivasan, who oversees logistics for a big outsourcing company. "It is in spite of the government."[6]

Everyone who has worked in poor countries for any length of time can relate a series of similar horror stories. Sometimes the villain is corruption, other times incompetence or mindless regulation. Policies that might be enacted to help the poor are not; when they are, governments are unable to ensure that they deliver the results intended.

If the poor are to be empowered, they need their states to be stronger, more efficient, more effective, and more impartial. They need states that can deliver basic services and protect basic rights. They need states in which both citizens and businesses feel secure enough to take risks. Building these kinds of states is no easy task: it demands patience, persistence, and action on numerous fronts simultaneously and over a long-time horizon. But it can be done if leaders have the commitment, the creativity, and the discipline to make maximum use of their assets and to use growth as an incentive to spur change.

Good Intentions Are Not Enough

Those leaders must also recognize, however, that wanting to transform their states is not enough. Adopting an inclusive state-building agenda (as outlined in the last chapter) is an essential first step, but implementing that agenda is very likely to encounter all kinds of obstacles. Good intentions alone cannot create lasting change in the conditions in which the poor live and work. To do that, a state also needs to have effective administrative, security, and legal systems that stretch across all its territory.

Tony Blair, former British prime minister and current adviser to numerous African governments, explains, "Good leadership is . . . not merely a function of good intentions but of the capacity of the institutions that support leaders to turn those intentions into practical results." Unfortunately, "That capacity is often under-developed . . . effective governance requires the presence of capacity."[7]

Poor countries struggle under the burdens of shoddy infrastructure, limited administrative skills, pervasive patronage networks, scant financial resources, and rampant corruption. These, in turn, accentuate whatever tendencies officials might have (as they do everywhere) to interpret decisions in ways beneficial to themselves.[8] The net result is governments that have very limited "implementation capacity"— very little faculty to put into practice the decisions made by their leaders.

In such countries, ideas that look good on paper often end up looking irrelevant—or worse—by the time they have struggled through multiple layers of bureaucracy and start impacting society. Reforms meant to improve economic and social conditions can do the opposite if policymakers do not take into account how the reforms will be implemented by ineffectual and corrupt officials, judges, and lower-level administrators. The implementation capacity of government typically drops the farther one gets from wherever decisions are made and money is managed, which in poor countries is typically only in the capital.

As Atul Punj, the chairman of one of India's largest infrastructure building companies, comments:

> Policies are all in place. It is the implementation in which we are lacking. It is the ability or the governance issue that needs attention. It is the systems that allow these programs to get rolled out that need attention. . . . What we need really do is make the bureaucracy at the lower levels much more efficient. It is a systemic fix that we need.[9]

A Nigerian lawyer similarly notes, "Nigeria boasts a government unable to deliver basic social services. It is plagued by corruption so endemic and monumental it is hard to separate it from state policy. It lacks the capability or discipline to prevent threats to public safety and national integrity and is assailed by active challenges to its legitimacy."[10]

Government capacity varies tremendously by district and region. Even in countries with relatively robust central governments, such as Brazil and China, regional and local affairs in areas where the poor live may be managed so haphazardly and corruptly that the local population encounters the kinds of situations found in countries with very feeble governments.

The poor depend more than anyone else on how well government works—and are the most likely to suffer when it does not work well. They cannot afford to send their children to private schools, to visit a private clinic when ill, or to pay off a policeman. If they are to escape poverty, they need a government that is robust enough to implement its policies competently, regulate private business honestly, and ensure the law is carried out evenhandedly.

The development of robust administrative, judicial, and security systems is also crucial if reforms are to be sustainable. A ministry of justice that is able and willing to prosecute corrupt judges, for example, will make other judges think twice about accepting bribes; as corrupt judges become fewer, the authority of the ministry will grow, which in turn will further reduce the number of judges willing to risk taking a bribe. But the reverse is true, too. A ministry of finance that demands bribes from businesspeople looking for government loans will encourage even honest-minded entrepreneurs to pay up; soon, those who abstain from corruption will be forced out of the marketplace, and the business world will have become as thoroughly corrupt as the ministry of finance. The functioning of the state is thus at the center of either a virtuous or vicious cycle that affects how everyone—from elites to businesspeople to the poor—acts and is acted upon.

Corruption: A Necessary Evil?

As the examples offered in this chapter make abundantly clear, corruption hurts the poor and impedes the development of a more capable state. And yet, in some instance, corruption can actually help the poor, at least in the short term, by spurring growth. In such cases, it may be better seen as a necessary evil, something unavoidable in the early stages of the development of a modern state.

Corruption is a broad term that encompasses many diverse activities, only some of which are completely negative. In China, for instance, although corruption is deeply rooted and widespread, it does not necessarily determine the allocation of key resources in most cases. While it serves to reduce efficiency, increase costs, and can produce egregious results at times, given the low overall level of development in the country, it does not have a large effect on growth (though this will change as the country grows richer). On the contrary, it may actually act as a lubricant to circumvent stifling regulations and smooth the establishment of the trust necessary for businesspeople to have enough confidence in officials to want to invest at times.

The same situation has existed in various forms across much of East Asia—including in Korea, Indonesia, and Thailand—at similar stages in their development. Cambodia, which ranked 154 out of 178 countries worldwide on Transparency International's 2010 Corruption Perceptions Index,[11] has seen rapid growth for two decades.[12]

In many countries, corruption actually is not viewed negatively but is seen as a positive force and reflects a value system that prioritizes loyalty to family and clan over loyalty to an impersonal institution. In such places, it may be so important to maintaining stability and reinforcing the glue that holds together a state that eliminating it—which would be impossible in any case—would have dire consequences. As one writer on Pakistan commented, "Western language about 'corruption' in Pakistan suggests that it can and should be cut out of the political system; but in so far as the political system runs on patronage and kinship, and corruption is intertwined with patronage and kinship, to cut it out would mean gutting Pakistan's society like a fish."[13]

Countries would be far better off without corruption (and associated practices such as rent-seeking and neopatrimonialism) in the long term. But they should not always be seen as the primary barrier to progress at early stages of development. Instead, other problems—such as weak social cohesion or the lack of security for investments—are probably at work. Corruption is typically a symptom of a deeper malaise, not the cause of that malaise. A better understanding of the phenomenon as it exists in a specific country is essential for that country to judge whether efforts to tackle corruption should be high on its reform agenda. In some places and at some times, it may not be nearly as important as other reforms.

Top-Level Change Is Not Enough

Creating a robust government apparatus able to implement policy can take generations, because it involves changing the professional culture and improving the skills of an army of mid- and lower-level government officials.[14] In most poor countries, few officials have any idea how to build organizations, professionally manage people, and coordinate operations across geographic regions and economic sectors. Few judges have been to law school, few policymakers have attended professional workshops, and few police have been adequately trained for their jobs. Pay and motivation are both low. Organizations work at cross purposes, without clear goals, and without clear divisions of responsibility. Change is hard because dysfunction in one policymaking body, courthouse, or police station reinforces it in another. If some progress is made in one area, corruption elsewhere can quickly undermine it.

Faced with the scale of the challenge, some reform-minded leaders and elites have sought to promote far more rapid reform by appointing technocrats to top-level government positions. And quick results can be achieved. In the field of macroeconomic management, for instance, just a handful of capable finance professionals working in a few offices can ensure that the currency is stable, inflation is low, and the budget deficit does not get too far out of control. Indeed, the one area where almost all poor countries have seen large improvements in recent years has been macroeconomic management. Many African countries, for instance, have introduced profound macroeconomic reforms since 1995, taming inflation and opening up their economies to international trade in the process. They could do this because their states had much stronger professional and technical capacity for policymaking in these areas than they did a generation before.[15]

The reforms have generated much needed growth, but the poor have rarely benefitted significantly, because governments still lack the capacity to enforce the rule of law, improve infrastructure, and distribute the fruits of growth through improved public services.

Small countries, such as those that dot West Africa, may suffer from severe shortages of qualified people, especially if they have just emerged from years of conflict or stagnation. Oversized states, such as the DRC, face the Sisyphean task of building sufficient capacity to expand their authority across their great land masses, especially given that weak infrastructure sharply reduces their ability to project authority across distances. All poor countries struggle under the burden of far too few professional managers, civic-minded public servants, and well-trained lower level officials.

The State-Building Continuum

States can be grouped along a long continuum from unconsolidated and ineffective to fully consolidated and highly effective. State building is the process whereby a country moves along this continuum, integrating its people and parts, and growing its capacity and resources to undertake a growing number of increasingly demanding tasks.

Robust states are forged in fits and starts over long periods. The institutions that govern them similarly must evolve over time to reflect changing capacities, societies, and needs. Although governments in rich countries today work through highly developed administrative and legal systems that deal with a seemingly countless number of issues, most of what they do constitutes a recent addition to a modest portfolio.

Many of the tasks that central governments work on nowadays either did not exist in the past or were handled by leaders and institutions much closer—geographically and socially—to the people they served. In many countries that now belong among the ranks of the world's most developed states, national governments had little role in local security, infrastructure, and schooling, for instance, before the nineteenth century. Environmental issues, to take another instance, did not become part of a government's portfolio until the second half of the twentieth century.

Part of the reason for this is that state builders historically have had to amalgamate many diverse fiefdoms into a greater whole. They have been obliged to balance the drive toward bureaucratic centralization with the need to co-opt local power brokers (from village elders to the rulers of tiny states) by allowing them to retain some control over their own affairs. The United States was originally an amalgamation of independent states that were reluctant to see a strong federal government develop; except during the Civil War, the federal government did not play a large domestic role before the twentieth century.

Although situations vary tremendously, most developing countries today are only partly through the state-consolidation process that more developed countries completed decades or even centuries ago. In fact, where they are simply the products of European colonialism, developing countries may have no more than a few decades of state-building history behind them and are trying to overcome much greater diversity—in terms of ethnicity, religion, language, history, and customs—than anything attempted by richer, more developed states in the West and in East Asia.

Most Arab states, for instance, never existed in their current form before World War I. When they did achieve independence after World War II, their governments were staffed by officials with no experience running countries. (Before World War I, most were part of the larger, Turkish-run Ottoman Empire.) Many—including Syria, Iraq, Lebanon, Yemen, and Libya—are but amalgamations of tribes, clans, and various religious and ethnic groups whose loyalties are more likely to be to their identity grouping than to their countries. The mixture of autocracy and political instability that holds back the region is both cause and effect of the shallowness of the states' consolidation processes so far. In many ways, the region mirrors the problems experienced by Latin America earlier in its postcolonial history, and by parts of Africa and Central Asia today. Most Arab countries are still decades away from creating the cohesion and robust institutions that developed countries take for granted.

Places such as Afghanistan, Somalia, and the Democratic Republic of Congo (DRC) retain central governments with such little capacity to govern effectively that nonstate actors often play major roles in maintaining security, making and enforcing laws, and promoting local enterprises.[16] The Catholic Church is the biggest provider of education and health care in the DRC. In Afghanistan, local communities and governments have often proved more effective than the central government at meeting the needs of citizens.[17] In such places, consolidation has barely begun.

Elsewhere, countries may have completely integrated their parts but still lack the capacity to perform many of their basic tasks well. Even Brazil and Mexico, states much further along the state-building continuum than most developing countries (and with centuries of history behind them), must contend with severe corruption and government agencies incapable of meeting citizens' expectations. Their implementation capacities are still far behind those of developed countries in some important areas.

All countries go through this process of state consolidation, though each does so in its own way, confronting unique challenges and experiencing unpredictable spurts and setbacks. Developing a strong national identity, which helps to integrate diverse peoples in a way that strengthens the legitimacy of national institutions, can accelerate the process.

Pyramid of Governance Priorities

States should prioritize where they invest their limited governance and financial resources based on where they are situated along the state-building continuum, what governance assets they have (see next section), and what might help them best progress. The process of advancement can be depicted in terms of a series of levels on a pyramid of governance priorities.[18] Figure 8.1 shows this pyramid, which is meant to be descriptive rather than prescriptive. Each country will progress at different rates in different areas and will have to determine its priorities and sequencing depending on its unique circumstances. Of course, some areas, such as security and the rule of law, will always have a higher priority than others.

Prioritization is especially important to instill confidence in a reform program, as it helps signal that a leadership has a clear strategy and is willing to make difficult choices. Overcoming intractable problems that have prevented the end of conflict or that have discouraged investment depends on setting realistic goals that clarify what compromises must be made to move forward.

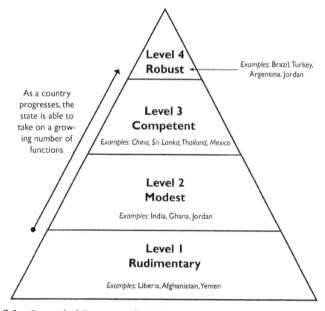

Figure 8.1   Pyramid of Governance Priorities

Characteristics of Each Level of the Pyramid

Level 1: basic security established for most of country; major ethnic and religious groups accept legitimacy of government; stable currency; limited public services (such as policing and some schooling) provided in the capital and possibly other major cities.

Level 2: modest system of justice in place; constitution adopted and widely accepted (if not always followed); roads and electricity available in parts of major cities and to ports; government can provide basic services (e.g., education and health) to significant numbers of people; simple business regulatory framework established; government has established a robust macroeconomic framework.

Level 3: competent courts established to settle corporate disputes; reasonably comprehensive business regulatory framework established; rule of law widely accepted; relatively efficient customs processing; stable electricity supplies; traversable road network throughout country; adequate property rights protections; basic network of universities and technical training schools; most citizens literate; corruption reduced to manageable levels; judicial system works reasonably well if not always effectively; rules for changing power widely accepted.

Level 4: robust government administration; efficient and predictable courts; roads extend throughout the country; public services provided to all citizens; limited corruption; advanced research capabilities; dense road network; all citizens have access to electricity; elaborate higher education system; well-managed education system; democratization of key institutions; large set of proactive social groups to hold governments accountable.

Building on What Works[19]

A country's place on the state-building continuum will help determine the challenges its leaders face in fostering a virtuous cycle of better governance, more state capacity, faster growth, and higher investment. For weak countries on the bottom end of the state-building continuum, the foremost challenge may be trying to put in place just enough security and basic infrastructure to spur investment and growth. For countries further up the continuum, the leadership's priorities may be focusing on reforms that enhance the ability of government to deliver public services and regulate markets.

But even among countries at much the same place in the continuum, challenges and priorities will also be shaped by each country's unique circumstances. And unique challenges demand customized solutions. A particular weak state will face many of the same challenges as other weak states, but how it responds to those challenges should be determined by assessing the country's particular strengths and weaknesses. No country should seek to precisely duplicate what has been done elsewhere—especially not what has been done in Western countries, which have confronted very different circumstances.

Indeed, instead of comparing themselves with developed countries and inevitably seeing only deficits and liabilities, the leaders of developing states should think more like a businessperson and start by assessing what strengths they already possess.[20] Then, much as a business executive tries to glean profits from the company's assets, government leaders should seek to boost the return on their existing governance resources (say, for example, a reasonably good educational system). The greater the return (in the form of, to continue the example, a well-educated workforce that starts more companies and attracts more foreign investment), the more resources will be available to be reinvested (such as increased taxes that can be spent on improving schools and infrastructure in poorer areas).

Those who perform these assessments should take an open-minded approach to what might qualify as a governance asset (see the feature box below). A country's governing capacities, for instance, could include not only the government's own apparatus but also a wide variety of nongovernmental organizations and social institutions, from traditional systems of justice to religious schools to parliamentarians' relations with their constituencies. An assessment will likely produce an inventory of rather messy and unorthodox assets, but many may be more effective at delivering one or more public services than approaches that focus only on the central government.

Governance Assets Can Take Many Forms

Governance assets can take very distinctive forms, depending on a country's history and sociopolitical dynamics. In some countries, such as Somalia and Yemen, tribal or clan structures with a long history might be leveraged to improve the delivery of social services by giving local community councils direct grants and letting them decide how to use the money (as the National Solidarity Program in Afghanistan has done). In other countries, multinational companies with a significant in-country presence, such as oil and mining companies, might be persuaded to build infrastructure and invest in schools to meet public needs. Sometimes, NGOs or community organizations are best placed to implement central government policies locally. On the other hand, where the central part of a country is much more developed than outlying areas, such as in Brazil, the central government may have to play a more proactive role at the local level. Islands of effectiveness can appear almost anywhere: in South Africa, the national Revenue Service stands out; in Nigeria, the government of Lagos State stands out; in Bangladesh, NGOs working to improve the lives of the poor stand out. In places recovering from conflict that has devastated the state, the only governance assets available are typically a combination of traditional social networks, religious groups, and ad hoc institutions developed in response to the absence of government.

In many countries, traditional institutions that predate the modern state may have far greater relevance than the central government for the general population. Traditional property rights, for instance, affect 90 percent of land transactions in Ghana and Mozambique. In Sierra Leone, 85 percent of the population use customary law.[21] In Somaliland, the Isaaq clan and their partners have built a successful hybrid governance model that combines both the traditional and the modern and that leans heavily on the capacity of the clans to police their members.

"Working with the grain" (a phrase that has become popular among some political scientists working on African development and which refers to working with existing indigenous community-level institutions rather than seeking to impose new models) gives poorer segments of a population a chance to feel part of the government. Whereas many aspects of the modern state are alien and even incomprehensible to indigenous peoples, making use of existing governance implementation capacity (which is usually a hybrid of old and new) can give the least Westernized parts of a local population real "ownership" over the rules governing them. Making wide use of the knowledge and experiences that people already possess—instead of forcing them to learn foreign ideas about how states ought to work—also helps empower people who have previously been on the social or political margins. Importing foreign ideas about governance and the law can, in fact, disenfranchise large numbers of people who depend on and prefer indigenous systems of justice, land tenure, and dispute resolution.

Making traditional institutions part of the governing apparatus is not without its dangers. Such institutions can be just as inequitable and dysfunctional as modern state institutions, if not more so, and incorporating them into the state can thus entrench discrimination and incompetence within government. The key criterion for judging any and all governance assets is the extent to which they deliver better public services, including the management of property rights, the rule of law, and the arbitration of disputes.[22] Creativity and a careful understanding of how local institutions actually work are essential to success. Somaliland, Malaysia, and Botswana have all found ways to successfully integrate traditional leaders into a modern parliamentary system.

Many Asian countries have, in fact, grown rapidly despite—or, more probably, because—they did not try to emulate the institutions, norms, and practices of developed countries. Indonesia, Thailand, and China have been able to foster rapid growth and increase public services by basing their governing regimes on historically and culturally familiar forms—even if these often fell short of international standards. Thailand, for example, gave the king a special role. At the same time, they have not forgotten to enhance their legal and administrative systems as new needs arose.

Crucially, countries should not try to do too much when they have only enough capacity to do a few things. Reforms aimed at improving how government work should focus on a handful of the most useful and the most feasible interventions. The success of a few projects can strengthen the capacity to take on other projects in the future. Rwanda's Strategic Capacity Building Initiative, for instance, aims to concentrate the state's capacity development resources on areas most important to achieving its policy priorities.[23] Just as private companies must specialize and learn to make the best use of limited resources, governments will have to do the same if they are to be a positive force in very difficult environments.

Promoting Evolutionary Change

Once some building blocks of decent governance have been identified or established across a country, the key becomes how to allocate resources to the entities most likely to deliver results and then how to accelerate the development and synthesis of these entities into a more coherent, capable, and cooperative whole. The division between central and local (to be discussed in chapter 9), public and private, modern and traditional will vary greatly depending on the circumstances. Given that money, time, knowledge, and human and organizational capacity will almost always be in short supply, leaders will have to depend in the short term on what already works well or has the promise of working well, while looking for gradual, incremental progress over the long term. A technically sophisticated and administratively competent bureaucracy will be necessary at some point (as discussed in chapter 11), but certainly not at the beginning of the development process.

Nudging reform of the government apparatus forward requires searching, experimenting, learning, and adapting, again much like a business executive who consistently seeks to restructure his or her operation in order to improve the way it works. This may include trying out various methods of sharing power and resources and various incentives for encouraging officials and important actors to support an inclusive development agenda. Changes in one part of the system will prompt changes in other parts; over time, a series of small improvements can be expected to accumulate and evolve into an interdependent, dynamic process.

This evolutionary process will take a very long time given how complex and deeply rooted bad governance can be in the developing world. Six decades after independence, India still has not brought security—and government—to all its territory. The Naxalite–Maoist insurgency affects a third of the country's districts and effectively controls huge areas of the countryside. Even after three decades of aggressive reform and restructuring, drawing on a wealth of resources and skills, China's government apparatus is still dysfunctional in many ways, particularly outside of the capital and a few relatively wealthy areas.

Progress toward a more capable state will be slow, fitful, and subject to many setbacks and retreats. But many rich countries have followed a similar course for centuries. Indeed, some, such as Italy and Belgium, do not seem to work all that well at times even today—yet their people live quite comfortably. Portugal, Spain, and Greece all lived under dictators but a generation ago. France is now in its Fifth Republic—having experienced a variety of bloody revolutions, chaotic uprisings, foreign occupations, and collapses of democratic rule in the past two centuries.

Indonesia has had a chaotic history since the beginning of World War II—experiencing occupation, revolution, autocracy, two highly disruptive changes in power, secession, war, financial crisis, and even a period of mass killings when hundreds of thousands were slaughtered—yet today it is considered one of the rising stars of the developing world. Indonesia's first president, Sukarno, helped unite the highly diverse archipelago. Sukarno's successor, Suharto, brought broad-based development that lifted millions out of poverty. Since 1998, a series of leaders have helped consolidate democracy. Each phase has brought its own troubles, but with marked progress in some key areas along the way that helped set the stage for what followed. Democracy, for instance, might not have turned out as well as it has without the many reforms passed by Suharto during his reign. The country's great diversity and size make it essential to accommodate a spectrum of local needs, experiment with different forms of government, and negotiate reform with different interest groups.

Incremental reform in the developing world could take numerous forms, many of which could directly benefit the poor: Export processing zones that provide streamlined customs administration could produce new businesses and more jobs, both of which will create pressure for add-on changes. Strengthening the central banks could improve the financial discipline of banks, something that would lead to a stronger private sector and create momentum for reforms elsewhere in government. Public health campaigns that limit the spread of infectious diseases could lead to increases in tourism and inward investment, which would in turn spur demands for further change. Better arrangements for resolving disputes between private parties could increase property rights and expand business dealings, both of which would increase growth and help create a virtuous cycle leading to more reform.[24]

The Importance of Security and the Rule of Law

Although all areas of government are likely to need reform, measures that strengthen security and the rule of law typically have the largest consequences, as change in these areas filter through to all others. Many improvements, such as to the investment climate, the efficiency of government operations, or the delivery of public services, will depend on improvements in security and the rule of law.

The poor stand to benefit more than any other social group from better security and closer adherence to the rule of law. After all, the poor are usually most exposed to violence, crime, and expropriation. They are also most likely to be denied access to justice because they cannot afford to bribe a policeman to investigate their case, pay a judge to hear it, or to hire a lawyer to defend it. Such problems are made worse by the dearth of any possible legal assistance. In many developing countries, the problem is not so much paying a lawyer as finding one: In Zambia, for instance, there is only one lawyer for every 25,667 people. In Cambodia, there is one for every 22,402 people. (In contrast, in the United States, there is one lawyer for every 749 people.)

In the least developed places, putting into place a robust legal system will require integrating various elements of traditional, or "customary," systems of justice into more modern systems. Imported models have little relevance when as much as 90 percent of a population depends on some form of customary law, as is the case in much of Africa.[25] A hybrid approach that builds on what already works and integrates diverse local traditions with modern legal codes and a centralized judiciary will be most effective. Establishing clear and enforceable state-level rules that can be used to help mediate and oversee these different traditions and resolve incompatibilities is essential. Eritrea's community court system, established in 2003, brings the state legal system both physically and psychologically closer to the people while integrating and formalizing customary dispute-resolution processes into its lowest tier of courts.[26] Customary courts, it may be noted, are particularly capable at dealing with many of the issues that are of great concern to the poor, among them disputes within families and protection of land, property, and livestock.

Building in-country organizations dedicated to researching and proposing new ways of implementing the rule of law given the social context and various norms and capabilities already in existence would empower local peoples to find solutions to problems that they know best. Better documenting the customary laws that guide much behavior and formulating ways to link and synthesize these with state laws could offer many opportunities. The Justice for the Poor program in Indonesia, which assesses community-level dispute resolution mechanisms and seeks out useful strategies for better integrating these with state legal systems, offers one example of what could be attempted in many places.[27]

Improvements in security and the rule of law also matter immensely to companies, which will not invest their funds if they have little confidence in a state's ability to protect private assets and rights. Few would invest in China during the first few years of its reform era because investors remembered their bad experience with the Communist regime decades earlier—when it had expelled all foreign businesses from the country. Bolivia under Evo Morales has struggled to attract investment to exploit the country's plentiful natural resources because his government has nationalized foreign assets and rewritten many laws in ways disadvantageous to private investors.

The more a state can ensure the security of all persons and property and equitably enforce the law for all its citizens and companies, the more likely it will empower the poor and encourage its population to invest in the future.

The Importance of Growth as a Springboard

Wherever on the state-consolidation continuum a state may be, taking steps to jumpstart economic growth is vital. Whereas stagnant countries force elites to fight over the spoils of power, expanding economies create incentives for businesspeople and politicians to seek profit from emerging opportunities—and to address the governance problems that prevent more such opportunities from appearing.

"Just-enough governance" (or "good-enough governance") is an approach geared toward enabling states to do just enough to generate growth. Just-enough governance is a much more realistic goal for developing countries early in the state-building process than "good governance." The latter, typically advocated by international development agencies, assumes that such countries have the capacity to advance on all fronts simultaneously, and that such an advance is a prerequisite for growth to start. But this ignores the historical record, as mentioned above. In fact, as noted by the economist Ha-Joon Chang:

> The developed countries in earlier times were institutionally *less* advanced compared to today's developing countries at similar stages of development. . . . Despite this, the developed countries . . . grew much faster than the developing countries . . . This suggests that, contrary to what is assumed in the "good governance" discourse, many institutions follow, rather than lead, economic development. . . . It took the developed countries a long time to develop institutions in their earlier days of development . . . decades, and sometimes generations. . . . Thus seen, the currently popular demand that developing countries should adopt "global standard" institutions right away, or after very short transition periods, is unrealistic.[28]

As Dani Rodrik and others have pointed out, an emphasis on just-enough governance allows reformers to prioritize the most important binding constraints—in areas such as regulation, infrastructure, and state capacity—and thus make the best use of their scarce political capital.[29]

Setting growth in motion can begin a virtuous cycle whereby the forward momentum feeds upon itself, encouraging more investors to enter the market and pressuring governments to remove bottlenecks that are slowing progress. The process is not pretty and will likely consist of ugly tradeoffs, appalling corruption, massive government failures, and gross market distortions of one form or another. But it will also generate substantial results over an extended period as growth encourages reform, and reform encourages growth. Institutions gradually improve; more and more people become willing to take risks; elite expectations and calculations shift; and the political and economic regimes slowly become more institutionalized and sophisticated to satisfy the rising demands of investors.

Bangladesh offers a vivid example of how this works in practice. Although well-known for the dysfunctionality of its government and its widespread corruption, a series of just-enough reforms—to macroeconomic management, trade policy, and a number of industries—have combined with an unusually strong nongovernmental role in the delivery of public services to feed growth and reduce poverty. In the three decades following the country's independence in 1971, per capita income more than doubled, the poverty rate fell from 70 percent to 40 percent, and life expectancy at birth rose from 45 years to 63 years. Countries such as Albania, India, Thailand, and Zambia have similarly grown rapidly, despite the overall weaknesses of their governments.[30]

The risk is that at some point growth will stall or the momentum for change will dissipate, undermining the cycle. As Brian Levy of the World Bank explains:

> As growth proceeds . . . one or another institutional constraint may threaten to short-circuit expansion—perhaps weaknesses in the delivery of infrastructure or key public services, perhaps a rise in corruption as public officials seek their share of the growing economic pie, perhaps rising social alienation with a growing sense on the part of citizens that government doesn't care about their everyday problems, perhaps the need for more sophisticated laws and institutions to underpin an increasingly sophisticated economy. . . . Sustaining growth thus becomes something of a "highwire act"—continually managing crises and putting out fires in an environment that the casual observer would consider quite dysfunctional, but one that nonetheless defies the odds by sustaining continuing dynamism.[31]

Fortunately, just-enough governance creates substantial incentives for most of the elite to prevent this from happening. They have a vested interest in sustaining growth, for the opportunities it creates. The longer this process continues, the more likely it will lead to institutions that can underpin the rule of law, support a more sophisticated economy, and are geared toward servicing a greater share of the population.

Greater Connectivity Improves the Ability to Reform

All these efforts to improve government will yield better results if leaders also take steps to accelerate the psychological and physical integration of their states—in other words, to create a stronger sense of "togetherness" among the entire population and to give citizens and institutions the ability to connect with one another more easily and more quickly.

Improving connectivity can be achieved in numerous ways: for instance, investing in more and better roads and telephones, developing public and commercial transportation systems, broadcasting television programs that reach the entire country and that promote a sense of nationhood, promoting trade and the spread of information. These kinds of steps are not usually directly associated (at least not among those working on development issues) with enhancing the implementation capacity of the state. Yet such measures will dramatically strengthen the centripetal forces bringing people together[32] (including their sense of a common identity) while reducing many bottlenecks and roadblocks that prevent the projection of government authority across distances.

As discussed in chapter 4, governments in developing countries provide starkly uneven levels of public service—including even basic security—across their territories. Great geographical disparities typically exist in the quantity and quality of schools, health care, policing, courts, and so on—with grave consequences for those who live in the less well-served places. In the DRC, for instance, Kinshasa's residents live as much as 13 years longer than citizens in some other parts of the country; and whereas 89 percent of Kinshasa's population has access to healthy drinking water, the average countrywide is only 46 percent—and in some provinces it is a low as a quarter.[33] In Ghana, which is considered one of Africa's best-governed states, a 2003 survey showed that while over three-fourths of adults living in and around the capital, Accra, could read, the rate for those in the northern parts of the country was less than one-fourth.[34] Similar differences exist to some degree even in states further along the state-building continuum, such as Russia, India, and Brazil.

While some of these inequities are rooted in prejudice and differences in political power, many are simply the product of meager organizational capacity and weak connectivity. Places that are hard to reach and to communicate with are naturally more expensive to service, less likely to be visited by top officials, and more likely to be low on administrators' lists of priorities. Better qualified teachers, judges, and doctors may not want to work there. As explained in chapters 10 and 11, lower connectivity also reduces the ability of the poor to help themselves while lessening the incentives for companies to invest in the areas where the poor live.

Connectivity has always been a tool for promoting cohesion and better government. The Roman and Chinese empires relied on transportation networks to control their territories, mainly to collect taxes and move commodities and military forces. In the nineteenth century, the extension of railways into the American hinterland helped the United States organize its territory, extend settlements, distribute resources to new markets, and foster a sense of common identity across its massive territory. Railroads helped a newly unified Germany integrate, expand its economy, and better defend its territory. In the twentieth century, road and highways systems (such as the interstate system in the United States and the autobahn network in Germany) were built to reinforce these goals.[35]

Similarly, East Asian states all made the expansion of infrastructure a major priority early in their state-building periods. China had few highways before 1993, but by 2011 its intercity expressway system exceeded the length of the U.S. interstate highway system.[36] The country has also poured money into trains, airports, telecommunications, the Internet (despite its highly authoritarian regime), and national media, seeing all these as instruments for integration, as well as economic advancement.

In contrast, most less developed states continue to be held back by weak infrastructure that reinforces their divisions and weak governance. Africa, for instance, has proportionally far fewer expressways than any other part of the world. Only 16 percent of the continent's roads are paved. Transport costs are the highest in the world.[37] South Asia is also notorious for its bad road links. Perhaps not coincidentally, these two areas have the largest number of poor people worldwide. Yet roads have been one of the least emphasized elements in development, with severe consequences for the consolidation of states and poor people worldwide.

Increase the Supply and Demand of Qualified Officials

One of the most important keys to strengthening government institutions is increasing the number of highly qualified people who work for the state (or in jobs that can enhance the quality of governance). This involves two dynamics: enhancing the ability of government to make use of a country's existing human resources (the demand for "good employees"); and increasing the ability of a country to produce high-quality human resources (the supply of "good employees"). Unfortunately, today most poor countries fall far short on both fronts.

Although state organs work best when they operate as meritocracies, they rarely do so in the developing world. To remedy this situation, countries need to make it a priority to hire the best people available, train them thoroughly, and promote them on merit.

As Singapore's first president Lee Kuan Yew wrote in his autobiography, "The single decisive factor that made for Singapore's development was the ability of its ministers and the high quality of the civil servants who supported them. . . . We scouted for able, dynamic, dependable, and hard-driving people wherever they were to be found . . . we fielded several Ph.D.s, bright minds, teachers at the universities, professionals including lawyers, doctors, and even top administrators as candidates."[38] Such policies were implemented throughout government bodies, making the state one of the best managed worldwide.

Professionalizing a civil service will usually require moving from a patronage-based regime that officials on all levels will be reluctant to part with. Changing institutional culture and deeply entrenched habits will take forceful and consistent action over a long period. Increasing pay and linking incentives to performance and heavily investing in training can help, but there is really no easy answer to overcoming entrenched cultures that reward corruption, patronage, and kinship ties. This is why simplifying and reducing the tasks of government and making use of a wide range of governance assets are so important.

The supply side matters, too, especially in the long term. As discussed in the introduction, most developing countries suffer from severe shortages of every conceivable type of qualified official. Only much greater investment in the knowledge networks that create the qualified human resources—administrators, policymakers, independent analysts, budget consultants, and so on—to feed into all sectors related to governance can eventually solve the problems of governance. Enlarging and increasing the quality of governance training will augment the capacity of both the public and the private sector. Resources should be poured into academies, public administration institutions, universities, law programs, think tanks, and management schools—the key "nodes" that provide multiplier effects to the human resources across all institutions within a state. Although such efforts may be too expensive for smaller countries with limited resources, larger states such as Nigeria and India have adequate funds and people to manage such projects—what they lack is the political commitment to either invest in governance training or make maximum use of the human resources that result. Poorer countries have much to gain by working together through regional organizations (see next chapter) and with international donors on such initiatives.

Various African governments and institutions, for instance, have established regional entities such as the New Partnership for Africa's Development (NEPAD), the African Governance Institute, the Council for the Development of Social Science Research in Africa (CODESRIA), and the Pan-African Institute of University Governance in an attempt to upgrade the human resources and quality of governance on the continent. Rwanda created the Mobile School of Governance to work with local districts throughout the country. Ethiopia has established a civil service college to upgrade the capacity of the public sector. Think tanks have sprung up across the developing world in recent years from Kenya to Bolivia to Pakistan, though most are small and understaffed. Much more can and should be done in all these areas.

Good Leadership Is Key

Strong and clear-sighted leadership in the struggle to build a more effective state can sometimes deliver immediate and substantial gains. Nitish Kumar, the chief minister of Bihar in India (whom we met in the last chapter), has revolutionized perceptions about his poor and backward state by tackling crime, by streamlining procedures for opening a business (one study ranked the capital as the least expensive place in India to start a company), by investing heavily in infrastructure (spending tripled from 2005–2006 to 2008–2009), by increasing transparency, and by reforming schools and hospitals (the number of school-age children not attending classes has dropped by two-thirds by 2010).

But Bihar was in a very poor condition when Kumar first came to power (Bihar has historically been known for a toxic mix of crime, corruption, and caste politics that stifles all progress), and so he was able to achieve vast improvements relatively easily. Sustaining and building upon these will require much harder work if caste politics and corruption are not to undo the progress that has been made. "Bihar has historically been a non-functioning state," says Shaibal Gupta, an economist at the Asian Development Research Institute. "The main challenge before the state government was to build a functioning state structure, where [economic] inclusion is inbuilt. This is not possible without banishing the last vestiges of feudalism." Yet "identity politics is strong," he also says. "We hope that voters choose development over caste. But in Bihar one never knows."[39]

Institutionalizing change is hard—but it is the greatest legacy a leader can leave to his or her people. And the further a state advances along the state-building continuum, the more it will need robust institutions to sustain its progress.

Leaders cannot do this alone, however. They need the support of other elites and their people. They also need proactive citizens to monitor what officials do and thus create a sense of accountability within government. Traditional social groups, NGOs, community organizations, unions, think tanks, the media, and coalitions of citizens all have a role to play in making sure that officials at all levels of the state (from chief ministers to judges, petty officials to police officers) work to improve how their governments function. And, as we shall see in the final chapter, combining all these efforts to promote political development is ultimately the best way to ensure that progress is sustained.

CHAPTER 9

Getting to a Workable Scale

Hunched beneath the blasting sun in a deep red gash near the base of a mountain [in Bisie, a mining town in the middle of the jungle in the Democratic Republic of the Congo], a 15-year-old named Imani Mulumeo Derwa sifted through ochre-colored earth this summer with his slender fingers.

In a small plastic bag, he stowed tiny rocks he hoped were tin ore. If the day went well, he might find enough ore to buy a plate of rice and beans. If not, he would fall asleep hungry on a dirt floor.

Every Thursday, he must hand over a day's wages to Col. Samy Matumo's men, who control the mountain and illegally extract taxes from every enterprise here. Imani arrived in July [2008], hoping to save enough money to return to school at the end of September. But by early August, he found himself trapped in a web of debt and despair.

"I am stuck here," he said, his weary, almond-shaped eyes betraying traces of a war-tossed childhood otherwise invisible on his smooth, boyish face. "I want to go home but I can't." . . .

Workers sometimes toil in 48-hour shifts in narrow, airless tunnels, with no safety gear beyond their dim headlamps. Because there is no industrial equipment or electricity here, the tunnels are built by hand and lined with wood. Cave-ins are common, and toxic gases fill the tunnels at times, sickening workers. It is impossible to say how many workers have been injured or killed because there are no authorities here to keep track. . . .

"I am full of debt," he said. . . .

The worst is Thursday, when the soldiers come. For boys like Imani, the tax [to stay there] is 500 francs, about a dollar. But that is a whole day's wages. When he does not have the money, he runs into the forest to hide.

"If you don't pay, they will kill you," he said.

Although Imani wants to leave, he has no money to pay the taxes along the road. And his creditors would send soldiers to arrest him if he tried to escape.

"I can't go home," he said.[1]

Imani's troubles reflect his country's troubles. He lives in an area far from the seat of government—and well beyond the reach of the state's limited implementation capacity. Government in Bisie barely exists, and what does exist is completely subservient to private interests. There is no rule of law. Power is in the hands of whoever has the deadliest weapons or the largest militia. Anyone trying to earn an honest living is exploited and terrorized.

Such circumstances don't just hurt the poor. They hurt anyone who might consider investing in legitimate moneymaking activities. Even large corporations cannot confront the power of private armies or overcome the chaos of ungoverned spaces.

Despite owning the exploration rights to the tin mine where Imani works, a company called Mining and Processing Congo cannot get near it because the government is unable or unwilling to force out a rebel militia that controls the mine. The militia fighters are supposed to have been integrated into the national army, and they do wear government army uniforms and collect government paychecks, but they operate like a mafia, preying upon the population. They collect $300,000 to $600,000 a month in illegal taxation alone and have skimmed millions of dollars from the mine. When Mining and Processing Congo tried to start work on a road to the mine, local officials blocked the route. When the company tried to begin work on a campsite for workers, soldiers opened fire on the workers, injuring several. "We have all our documents and permits in order," says the weary managing director. "We have written to the head of the military, the minister of mines, and even the president. But there are no rules in Congo, just the rule of the gun."[2]

The central government has no more control over what happens in Bisie than does Mining and Processing Congo. For instance, even though the government in Kinshasa has repeatedly asked the soldiers to leave the mine, the fighters have simply refused. And Bisie is not an isolated example. The central government has little control over vast areas of the Democratic Republic of Congo (DRC)—in part because the DRC is simply so big. Its enormous size creates a host of problems—such as weak cohesion, meager infrastructure, and a treasure trove of natural resources that are difficult to secure (which makes it easy for warlords to grab and exploit those resources)[3]—that even a competent and uncorrupt government would be hard pressed to deal with. And the DRC's government is neither of those things.

The below two maps help explain how little any set of leaders could hope to accomplish given the DRC's immense governance challenges. One shows how divided the country is linguistically (and ethnically), with four different major languages spoken, each in a different region of the country. The state has over two hundred languages in all. The second shows how the population is dispersed, with concentrated pockets of people separated by great distances.

The dynamics these conditions create give national leaders little capacity to rule distant lands and regional leaders few incentives to work with rulers in the capital, who are often thousands of miles away. Extremely limited transportation and communications infrastructure exacerbates geographical and demographic divisions and ensures the futility of any attempt by central government to impose authority in distant parts of the realm. The DRC is roughly the size of Western Europe, but it has only a few hundred kilometers of paved roads outside its cities.[4]

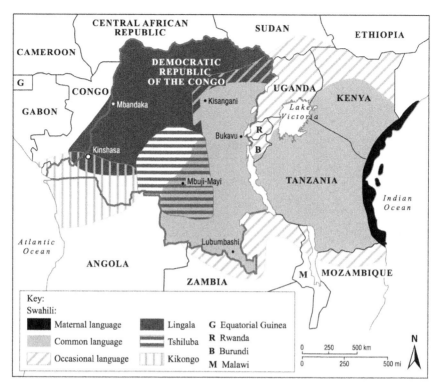

Figure 9.1 Democratic Republic of the Congo, National Languages

Source: Seth Kaplan, *Fixing Fragile States: A New Paradigm for Development* (Westport, CT: Praeger Security International, 2008), map 6.3, 87.

Attempts to strengthen government, extend authority across territory, establish an inclusive ruling coalition, or even secure borders are all beaten back by the centrifugal forces that repeatedly threaten to pull the country apart. Local elites establish their own forms of authority; local businesspeople pay no heed to borders or customs regulations when they trade with businesses in neighboring states; young men, for whom a good job is a fantasy, join militias to rape the country's wealth (and people). Sections of the government are in league with traffickers who trade in illicit minerals and weapons. Corruption is so rife that the state collects scant royalties from its vast natural resources.

The despairing population is among the most disadvantaged in the world, often forced to fend for themselves within a Hobbesian nightmare of chaos and violence. Millions have died from war, malnutrition is widespread, and incomes are far below what they were decades ago.[5] Women are brutalized on a scale unimaginable elsewhere; hundreds of thousands have been sexually attacked with virtual impunity. "They kill, they rape, burn houses, and take people's belongings," said 34-year-old Jeanne Birengenyi of one of the armed militias running wild in Eastern DRC. "When they come with their guns, it's as if they

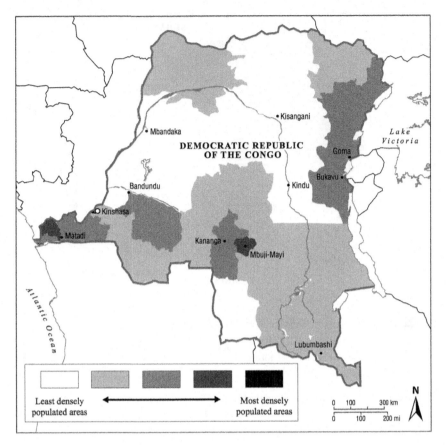

Figure 9.2 Democratic Republic of the Congo, Population Distribution

Source: Jeffrey Herbst, *State and Power in Africa: Comparative Lessons in Authority and Control* (Princeton, NJ: Princeton University Press, 2000), 148.

have a project to eliminate the local population." Jeanne and her 9-year-old niece, Chance Tombola, both contracted sexually transmitted diseases from their assaults. Chance's parents were killed, and her two sisters, aged 6 and 12, were carried away into the forest to be "wives" of members of the militia. No one has seen them since.[6]

Promoting Inclusive Development: The Spatial Dimension

Space, or scale, is a problem for many poor countries. Actually, it presents three different problems. Some countries are too big to be governed effectively. Some are too small to have economic markets large enough to stimulate prosperity. And some—indeed, most—are blighted by uncontrolled urbanization that overwhelms the capacity of governments to manage their cities. In all these circumstances, existing institutional arrangements severely limit the ability of officials, elites, and entrepreneurs to nourish a more inclusive development-oriented state and increase the implementation capacity of government.

A country's "political geography" (i.e., the way in which its population distribution and makeup affect its political processes) can have a very powerful impact on the kind of state that develops in that country and on the ambitions of the people who run the state. Most Western (and East Asian) nation-states have evolved slowly and organically, gradually assuming a size and shape that is governable and economically self-reliant, and that embraces a population united by a shared ethnicity, ideology, or some other cohesive force. Few poor countries, however, are the result of a natural process of evolution. The great majority are colonial inventions, with borders decided by policymakers and bureaucrats in London, Berlin, Brussels, Madrid, and Paris, who had little knowledge and less respect for the interests of the indigenous peoples in Africa, Latin America, the Middle East, and Asia.

Many states across the poor world are chained by the political geographies history has bequeathed them. Places such as Iraq, Sudan, Angola, Libya, Bolivia, and Kyrgyzstan have political geographies that make their elites far more likely to prefer ruling narrowly than broadly—and far more willing to oppose or eject anyone who comes to power thinking differently. At the same time, tiny countries such as Guinea-Bissau and Gambia have such small populations and economies that they are highly prone to government weakness, conflict, and dependence on foreign aid—especially because their neighbors all face more or less the same problems.

* * *

Leaders who wish to create environments conducive to empowering the poor need to take into account how spatial forces affect the incentives for individuals— including politicians, officials, and entrepreneurs—to act in ways that promote, rather than undercut, societal cohesion, good governance, and economic strength. Once the impact of spatial factors is understood, appropriate reforms can be introduced. There are three main avenues for reform. One is to decentralize governments to a level at which the distribution of authority, resources, and incentives creates the maximum chance that the state will work for the benefit of its people. A second approach is to reallocate authority in international regional organizations, enabling small countries to combine markets and resources to attract investment, build robust regulatory regimes, and confront regional problems. The third avenue is to promote strategic urbanization, creating, enlarging, and empowering cities to better absorb and manage migration from rural areas and to be better positioned to improve their own governance.

Decentralizing Governments

Given the toxic political cultures and weak institutions that exist at the national level in many poor countries, building states vertically, with highly centralized top-down governments, may be misguided in some places. This is certainly true for vast countries such as the DRC, which have far too few competent administrative staff to overcome the state's great distances and fractured nature. But it is also true for countries whose ethnic and tribal diversity make any centralized model unworkable as long as the national security, administrative, and judicial apparatus remains extremely feeble, as in Somalia, Iraq, and Afghanistan.

In both these situations, the structure of the state can play a large role in preventing the emergence of a cohesive elite dedicated to inclusive development. National leaders have little incentive to serve distant areas populated by disparate groups because the leaders view these groups more as competitors for state power than as compatriots. Regional elites, in turn, see little incentive to cooperate with governments who little serve them—and can little discipline them. In any case, thin road networks, limited administrative resources, and weak nationwide societal bonds severely limit central governments' ability to serve populations outside the capital.[7] In turn, those distant populations—especially their poorer members—have few mechanisms at their disposal to pressure national leaders to act more inclusively (see the text box "Maximizing the Pressure on Local Officials to Perform").

Although such problems are most obvious in humongous countries such as the DRC, Sudan, and Angola, they also exist in many other poor countries that are similarly divided and have weak governments with limited capacity to govern effectively across distance.

Afghanistan may not be nearly as large as any of these three countries, but it suffers from some of the same ailments. The country's government has few people qualified to administer central agencies and ministries and has difficulty controlling territory far from the capital. Yet, the national government is given a dominant role in state affairs under the current constitution. Meanwhile, ethnic and kinship solidarity—including ties that cross national borders—trumps any loyalty to the state. Village councils may be good at overseeing local issues, but they have few opportunities to reduce the abuse of power and corruption in Kabul.

Somalia has gone two decades without a national government robust enough to counter the centrifugal forces pulling the country apart. Its numerous clans have little interest in working together, each resisting the imposition of a centralized state it will not control exclusively. The state's strongest governing institutions are rooted in these groups' traditional social structures and relationships—but these institutions undermine any authority imposed from outside individual clan areas.

Despite many years of rapid growth, Mozambique's highly centralized development model has produced growing social exclusion and rising social tensions. Poverty is spreading, malnutrition is increasing, and crime is rife. Few people benefit from policies that ignore rural areas, that focus on a handful of mega-projects while ignoring the mass of unemployed, and that enrich a narrow urban elite at the expense of everyone else.[8] The state seems irrelevant—or nonexistent—in large parts of the country, and citizens have few mechanisms to change this. Pedro, a farmer in Mozambique, reflects, "They say that of the 18 million inhabitants here in Mozambique, 80 or 90 per cent live in the rural areas—and those are the absolute poor. . . . The majority of poor people do not have access to a means of expressing what they feel; they are not heard."[9]

Rebalancing Government

In all these cases, elites who want to promote inclusive development should be trying to create a much better balance between the central government, on the one hand, and regional or local governments, on the other hand. Although the ideal mix would vary tremendously according to each country's circumstances, a more horizontal form of government would help promote inclusive development almost everywhere. If poor states were to distribute many important governing functions to their cities and regions, while reducing the central administration's powers and responsibilities, they would give their leaders greater incentives to act in their peoples' interests and make full use of the implementation capacity that already exists on the local level.

This is not to say the central government is unimportant, just that its role should be more oriented toward large-scale planning, setting a clear and logical national policy, establishing guidelines for how policies and projects are implemented and resources are distributed, and developing tools to reward and penalize regional and local governments based on performance (see the box "Maximizing the Pressure on Local Officials to Perform"). The key is to balance the ability of the central government to provide overall guidance with the local or regional authorities' stronger capacity to deliver the services that affect people the most (education, health care, local infrastructure, and the rule of law). Spreading resources out more horizontally may also promote a more equitable distribution of resources across a state.

Such a strategy complements attempts to make better use of various forms of implementation capacity, as discussed in the previous chapter. Success depends on many factors, but one of the most important is the extent to which local officials can be made accountable both to the constituents they serve and to higher levels of government.[10]

Decentralization has helped government deliver better services to the poor in a wide range of settings. In Ethiopia, decentralization to successively lower levels of governance has contributed to significant improvements in access to education. Although policymaking is still relatively centralized, 11 regional governments have some latitude in implementation, including the option to use regional languages as the medium of instruction. A second stage of decentralization to the district level has led to greater administrative efficiency and accountability, while also addressing inequities in school attendance across the country. Block grants have been structured so that those areas that were furthest behind receive more on a per capita basis. Initial problems of capacity at the lower levels of government have slowly been overcome. Primary and secondary school enrollment rose fivefold between 1994–1995 and 2008–2009.[11]

Uganda has built stronger local institutions since the late 1990s, and one notable consequence has been improved access to water. Local districts and town councils were empowered through a system of grants that included provisions to support the recruitment of qualified staff. The Ministry of Water and the Environment shifted its focus from implementing projects to supporting local governments and established regional units to enhance the financial, technical, and human capacity of districts. Whereas only two out of five rural inhabitants had access to an "improved" (i.e., safer) water source in 1990, by 2008 two out of three did.[12]

Decentralization does not work in all settings. In some places, decentralization has created strong incentives for local elites to capture new powers and sources of patronage. In India, for instance, local elites often prevent the delivery of public services to people from lower castes. Brazil has done better at reducing poverty when its central government—which has stronger implementation capacity and is more inclusively minded than other levels of administration—has bypassed local governments controlled by self-interested elites.

Ways to Share Power

There are many different ways to share power. Various forms of federalism, decentralization, and even confederation (often combined with some form of power sharing at the national level) have all helped to stabilize countries such as Sierra Leone, Iraq, Lebanon, and Timor-Leste. Distributing power across society has built broader support for both governments and peace agreements. Powers—such as the right to use traditional justice systems, draft and enact budgets, elect or approve high-ranking officials, regulate local resources, and collect some taxes—have been transferred to regional or local units under such arrangements.[13]

Increasing local autonomy makes it easier to win over locals who distrust their central governments. In fact, as political scientists Alfred Stepan and Juan Linz have argued, all developed countries with more than one large cohesive sociocultural group (including Canada, Switzerland, Spain, and Belgium) are federalist in some form.[14] One of the reasons India has held together as well as it has since independence has been a constitution that pushes power downward to states that correspond to various language groups.

In some countries, preexisting social institutions could be harnessed to boost public service delivery and accountability. In places such as Afghanistan, some substantial form of power sharing may be the only way both to garner support for a central government and to take advantage of the country's robust communal structures. In more strongly divided (or weakly united) places, some form of mixed sovereignty—in which the powers of local entities severely circumscribe those of the national government—might be the best way to enhance the quality of public services and increase the overall cohesion of the state going forward.[15]

Any form of power sharing, however, needs to be carefully calculated if it is not to create more problems than it solves. Too much decentralization can sometimes whet the appetite for secessionism, as may be occurring in Kurdistan in northern Iraq. This can fuel violent conflict with central authorities. But so can too little decentralization, as witnessed in 1971, when East Pakistan fought a bloody war to break away from the oppressive rule of West Pakistan and become Bangladesh.

In the case of the DRC, the best chance for the country to develop robust institutions may lie in some form of weak confederation. Secession for the eastern provinces may end up being the only way to create a coherent government focused on promoting inclusive development in that region.

Some leaders have already recognized the advantages—for themselves and their countries—of relinquishing some authority. Sudan's Omar al-Bashir acceded to demands from Southern rebels for independence in exchange for an end to the country's long-running civil war. The very Kenyan leaders who fought for power in the aftermath of the 2007 election worked together to build support for the new constitution even though it weakens the power of whoever wins future elections. Pakistan managed to pass a landmark agreement in 2009–2010 to rebalance revenue allocation in favor of the poorer provinces, giving them more resources and power in the process.[16] Indonesia increased its national cohesion when it gave local authorities more power and resources in the late 1990s, helping to curtail secessionist tendencies in a number of areas in the process.

Maximizing the Pressure on Local Officials to Perform

For decentralization to work, leaders must find ways to maximize the performance of local officials. After all, government employees working far from capitals manage the great majority of public services, including the provision of education and health care, the regulation of local businesses, and the maintenance of the rule of law.

Besides investing heavily in human resource development (through education and training), leaders should consider how to enhance the two forces most likely to spur improved performance by local officials: top-down pressure from the central government and bottom-up pressure from local societies.

Giving Local Officials a Broad Vision and Top-Down Incentives

Few poor countries have a well-resourced national-level bureaucracy, but fortunately that kind of bureaucracy is not essential to applying pressure on local officials. What is essential is a coherent and realistic vision of what officials should be striving to achieve. Resources can then be allocated and incentives structured in accordance with that vision. For instance, governments can reward (or punish) local officials and local governments by giving them more (or less) pay or revenue in return for working to translate that vision into reality.

One of the least appreciated sources of Chinese economic success is the Chinese Communist Party's (CCP) ability to incentivize the country's officials to foster economic growth. By strongly emphasizing growth, giving local governments substantial power to manage local assets, and then basing promotions within the party partly on economic performance, the CCP has provided its cadres across the country with both a coherent vision and an effective system of rewards (and penalties).

Although few, if any, other developing countries possess China's elaborate administrative system, each country can nonetheless better exploit the bureaucratic resources it does possess by deploying incentives strategically. Rwanda, for instance, has made great strides in improving its system of health care by reforming administrative boundaries and mandates across the whole country and all sectors of activity and by providing consistent incentives to workers and citizens in the form of affordable health insurance and encouragement to use it.

In contrast, in Malawi, the boundaries of environmental planning areas, health departments, and educational districts do not coincide, and the jurisdictions and mandates of state-run organizations, elected politicians, chiefs, and city authorities overlap in ways that produce confused responsibilities and weak coordination.[17] Many poor states that lack the strong central leadership of Rwanda see various politicians and donors promote contradictory visions for improving how government works, yielding little coherence in human resource–driven incentives.

Promoting Greater Bottom-Up Accountability

Leaders looking to improve the performance of local officials must also simultaneously seek to maximize the ability of local people to generate collective action to pressure officials. This bottom-up pressure can be exerted through elections, civil society activities, or long-standing social relationships and norms. In Uganda, for instance, the publication in local media and schools of budget data allowed local populations to monitor expenditure for corruption and waste; the result was a more than fourfold increase in the proportion of funds reaching schools.[18]

While Western-style nongovernmental organizations (NGOs) may have a role to play in pressuring leaders in more developed countries (such as in Latin America), in less developed states NGOs may have more difficulty gaining traction. In such states, populations may be more divided (by ethnicity, clan, etc.) and less confident in their ability to confront powerful actors with the kinds of pressure tactics favored by NGOs. But there are other ways to apply bottom-up pressure—most notably, through kinship or community relationships.

A sense of moral obligation and interpersonal accountability embedded in existing social identities can exert considerable pressure on individuals to perform in the best interests of their communities, especially where traditional ethnic and clan groups are still intact, as they are to varying degrees in Afghanistan, Yemen, Somalia, Bolivia, parts of Southeast Asia, and large parts of Africa. Tim Kelsall, a British social scientist, explains that

> the most robust forms of accountability and public goods provision in Africa today can be found at the local level. . . . [C]onflicts in the extended family, over land, marriage, personal injury, inheritance and so forth, are typically resolved not by state agencies, but by immediate or extended family elders. . . . Within this sphere people feel obliged to act honestly and fairly—even if they often find this challenging—because of the shared experience of growing up together, the ideology of ancestral solidarity, the threat of social ostracism, and sometimes also by the supernatural sanctions that attach to offices such as clan eldership.[19]

Centralizing Authority, Rightsizing Markets

Artificially tiny countries face a different set of stresses that exacerbate the exclusionary policies produced by weak cohesion and weak government. A combination of limited human resources, bad governance, small domestic markets, and inadequate incentives for private investment can easily produce a vicious cycle that overwhelms any attempts at reform. In such places, a renewed emphasis on international regional structures may be the only way to spur development.

These stresses can be especially acute when a small state inhabits a bad neighborhood where almost all countries share analogous weaknesses. Corruption, lawlessness, drug trafficking, and violence in one country are more likely to spread to smaller neighboring states, rather than larger ones, because the former have less capacity to resist contagion. A small government with limited personnel and resources may be unable to secure its borders, counteract the influx of dirty money, or absorb the shock from political instability or economic downturn next door. Criminal elements may find it easier to exploit weaknesses in administration, law, and policing when a state has little institutional depth.

Economic and political progress toward development is also hard to achieve when many small, weak countries are situated side by side. Were any of these diminutive countries to significantly outpace its neighbors, it would immediately be burdened with an influx of people seeking a better life and of criminal elements tempted by its relative prosperity.

West Africa: A Series of Tiny States Reinforcing Each Other's Weaknesses

West Africa, the 15 countries stretching from Senegal to Nigeria, exemplifies the problems confronting a region made up of small states. Pint-sized, expensive markets keep most states isolated from the dynamic changes globalization is bringing elsewhere. The region's aggregate GDP is roughly the same as Norway's—despite having over 50 times more people.[20] Although Ghana and Senegal have made significant political and economic gains in recent years, most of the other states have been rocked by war, ethnic or religious clashes, political unrest, famine, or serious economic dislocation at various times over the past two decades.

Nine of the 15 countries make *Foreign Policy*'s Failed States Index for 2010. Fourteen have "Low Human Development" levels (i.e., low levels of life expectancy, literacy, education, and standards of living), according to the United Nations Development Programme.[21] In essence, 75 percent of the area's people live under governments that cannot deliver basic services—including, in many cases, security. West Africa contains 8 of the world's 14 most impoverished territories;[22] over one-half of the overall population lives in poverty.[23]

Côte d'Ivoire, once West Africa's economic star, has caused immense suffering throughout the region from its two civil wars and ongoing domestic conflict since the early 2000s. Millions of migrant workers were forced to flee, reversing the flow of remittances; trade relations were disrupted, shrinking markets; and criminal activity increased, disrupting legitimate businesses. Côte d'Ivoire's civil war was rooted in identity group tensions but was itself exacerbated by the destabilizing impact of a macabre and bloody war in neighboring Liberia. More than 25,000 peacekeepers are needed to maintain a fragile peace in the region's simmering war zones.

Although West African prices for electricity and transport are among the highest in the world, the region's power grids and transportation systems are woefully inadequate and unreliable.[24] Regulatory burdens force all but the largest businesses underground. In Niger, for example, it takes 9 steps and costs more than the average annual income just to register a business. It takes 39 steps to enforce a contract, and 8 documents to export goods outside the country.[25] Much of the sparse road network across the region is in poor condition,[26] and frequent checkpoints—one every 14 kilometers on the road between Lagos and Abidjan[27]—shrink markets. The onerous business climate and small market sizes mean that little private capital is invested outside of Nigeria in anything but the natural resource sector.

Such Problems Exist Elsewhere Too

The challenges facing West Africa are seen in other parts of the world. For instance, small Central American countries such as Nicaragua and Guatemala suffer from gang-related violence, a poor investment climate, and the corrupting drug trade, all of which they seem powerless to confront. As Mexico uses its extensive resources to fight back against drug gangs, the traffickers move to Mexico's smaller southern neighbors, because they are less able to fight back.

But many of these problems are not limited to the smallest of countries. In Africa, for instance, even medium-sized states have markets that are simply too small to allow the countries to compete in international markets. Combined with the ramshackle transport infrastructure within and between countries and the high cost of transporting goods both domestically and abroad, these small market sizes scare away private investors. Even Pakistan, by no means a small country, would benefit enormously if it were better integrated with its huge neighbor, India. Their bilateral trade, which currently is worth $2 to $2.5 billion a year, could skyrocket to over $20 billion a year, which would provide a significant boost for Pakistan's economy.[28]

The solution, says Mo Ibrahim, one of Africa's most successful businesspeople, is regional cooperation. "We need to look at bigger markets. . . . We are going to compete and beat the Chinese, Indians, Americans and beat the Europeans? How can we do it? We cannot do it! Economic integration is a must. We need to have freedom of movement of goods, capital and people across our borders." He points to Germany as an example. Despite having an economy more than twice the size of the combined economies of Africa's 50-plus countries, Germany long ago decided it needed the European Union to compete with the United States and China.[29] The scope for increased trade in Africa is immense. In contrast to Asia, where intraregional trade among emerging economies accounts for nearly 50 percent of all commerce, in Africa it accounts for just 9 percent. Ibrahim concludes: "In Africa we have 53 mini-states with bad communication, bad roads, bad markets. That's the road to disaster . . . that's why I put the economic integration of Africa top of the agenda."[30]

In a similar vein, the United Nations' Economic Commission for Africa (ECA) declared in 2004 that "revitalized regional integration offers the most credible strategy for tackling Africa's development challenges, internal and external. Why? Because of the many weaknesses that overwhelm the limited capacities and resources of individual countries. Collective efforts, with dynamic political commitment to integration, can help overcome the daunting challenges."[31] The ECA executive secretary, K. Y. Amoako, elaborated:

> I want to see intra-African integration not because we will garner some utopian share of world commerce, but first and foremost because it will improve our lives here. It will free up the time of African businesspeople to do business here. It will lower costs. It will make the African consumer's plight so much more hopeful. We must build for ourselves. If we do that, others will come.[32]

Many Commitments, Some Progress

Despite growing recognition of the importance of regionalism, national leaders have often made bold commitments to cooperation at international meetings but then failed to honor them. Progress often stalls after some hesitant first steps. Efforts to develop regionwide cooperation are plagued by internal instability within key states, by a general lack of capacity and political will to move forward, by a reluctance to compromise national sovereignty, and by rivalries between states. For instance, Mercosur, a South American economic and political agreement meant to promote a regional free market, has been hobbled by internal conflicts over trade policy, especially between Brazil and Argentina.

Attempts at economic integration have also met with fierce opposition from powerful vested interests. Rent-seeking traders and their government patrons—who cooperate to manipulate rules and access to licenses to their advantage—stand to lose much business if formal and informal barriers to the effective coordination of policy are reduced. Even officials concerned not so much for personal gain as for the well-being of their country as a whole have been unwilling or unable to implement agreements intended to spur integration because of the threat of revenue losses from reduced tariffs and of job losses from diverted trade.

Africa is littered with regional organizations that were created with much fanfare but that yielded little. Too many countries committed themselves to adopt policies that they lacked the capability to implement. Limited resources and limited outside help (as discussed in chapter 13) also hurt. The end result is a tangle of overlapping memberships, fragmented missions, and disappointed hopes.

Yet, despite all these obstacles and disappointments, concrete progress is being achieved in many parts of the world. The East African Community (EAC) is composed of Kenya, Tanzania, Uganda, Burundi, and Rwanda. In 2010, the EAC introduced a common market, which is expected to permit the free movement of labor, capital, goods, and services throughout the region. A machine-readable ID card for every citizen is being introduced in EAC member states, which are also working on developing the mutual recognition and accreditation of their higher education institutions. Future plans include the adoption of a common currency and deeper political ties.

Notwithstanding its myriad problems, West Africa has benefitted from the work of two regional organizations (see figure 9.3). Since its founding in 1994, the West African Economic and Monetary Union (UEMOA, composed of eight countries) has advanced stable macroeconomic management, reduced public sector costs, increased investment, raised government revenue as a ratio to GDP, and lowered the external current account deficit.[33] UEMOA completed a customs union in 2000 and has made significant progress harmonizing business laws. The countries have shared a common currency (the CFA Franc) since 1945.[34] The Economic Community of West African States (ECOWAS), a much looser grouping of the 15 West African states, has played a growing role in security since establishing a peacekeeping force in 1990, helping to promote democratic norms and to mediate and enforce peace agreements in Liberia, Sierra Leone, Guinea-Bissau, and Côte d'Ivoire. West Africa would be even more unstable if ECOWAS and UEMOA did not exist.

Regionalism is expanding, albeit fitfully, in regions as varied as Southeast Asia (where the Association of Southeast Asian Nations, ASEAN, has developed an impressive track record of consultation and cooperation), the Andes (with cooperation among Colombia, Peru, and Chile extending from trade to stock market integration),[35] and the Middle East (where Turkey has been pushing since the early 2000s for economic integration with its neighbors). The tiny states of the Caribbean have a reputation for being highly protective of their national sovereignty and for looking to extraregional actors for help rather than to each other for mutual support. Yet regionalism has nonetheless made some strides

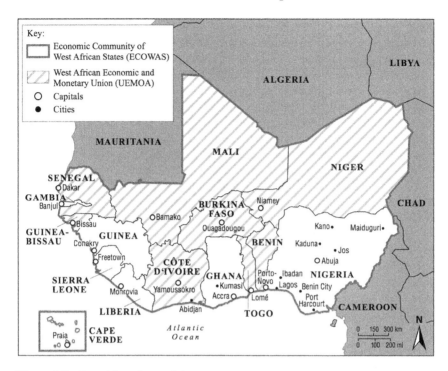

Figure 9.3 West African Regional Organizations

Source: Seth Kaplan, *Fixing Fragile States: A New Paradigm for Development* (Westport, CT: Praeger Security International, 2008), map 5.2, 76.

among these island nations. For instance, the Caribbean Community, created in 1973, promotes economic integration and cooperation among its 15 members; the Caribbean Court of Justice operates as a municipal court of last resort for 12 of these states.

But much more can be done—especially when it comes to transferring to regional organizations the authority and resources they need to better connect countries, improve regulatory regimes, reduce corruption, and promote trade and investment. Although increased trade may cause short-term jobs losses for the poor (as greater competition reorders the allocation of work), it offers the only path to higher growth, greater opportunity for entrepreneurs, and the cross-border cooperation necessary to tackle many security problems.

Strategic Urbanization

Urbanization is one of the most important manifestations—and engines—of industrialization, rapid economic growth, modernization, and state building.[36] It agglomerates economies, providing larger markets and greater services for companies and more opportunities for workers. It is a key source of productivity and income gains, as people shifting from farms to urban manufacturing and services bring huge increases in output per worker.[37] It also provides a major impetus for the changes in values, norms, and expectations that can, over time, play major roles in reforming economic and political systems.

Villages all over the developing world are emptying as people flood into cities in search of opportunity. Whereas only about one-fifth of the people living in the less developed countries in 1950 were in urban areas, today almost one-half are. By the middle of the twenty-first century, over two-thirds will be urbanites. In terms of numbers, the urban population in the developing world was 300 million in 1950 and is projected to exceed 5 billion by 2050.[38]

Yet few countries approach urbanization strategically, instead adopting (whether by default or from a lack of resources) a completely passive approach to how cities form and where people migrate. They thus lose a great opportunity to influence a process that could, through better planning, improve the functioning of markets, the quality of public services, the ability of people to participate in wealth creation, and the effectiveness of governments in a wide range of areas.

In the absence of planning, many of the world's poor are crowded together in slums. The "squatter cities" that rim the metropolises of most developing countries—such as Bombay, Dhaka, Manila, and São Paulo—already hold around a billion people. Conditions inside can be dreadful.

In Lagos, a million people squat in flimsy hovels in almost every part of town. Shina Loremikan, who runs an anticorruption organization and lives in Ajegunle, Lagos's biggest and most dangerous slum, complains that "refuse is everywhere," even in Lagos's two relatively upscale districts. "Black water is everywhere." The drainage ditches of Ajegunle are frequently blocked, and during the rainy season they overflow into houses and across streets, which fill up with sludge, sacks, scraps of clothing, and plastic bags, so that some of Ajegunle's streets seem to be wholly composed of trash.[39]

Yet the numbers living in these horrid conditions keep increasing because cities promise better opportunities to make some money and gain access to modern amenities than do the rural areas. Young people are also drawn to the slums because they are, for all their squalor, livelier and more colorful places than the villages of the developing world. (Intense boredom is an underappreciated yet important driver of behavior among the poor—especially when they are aware of what other, more well-off people may have access to.)

Distributed Urbanization Offers Many Benefits

Every developing state stands to benefit from strategic urbanization—from, that is, strategically distributing urban areas throughout its territory, seeing them as interrelated components of a national development plan to increase growth, promote social change, and create a more inclusive economy and society. Establishing a geographically spread out mixture of large, medium, and small cities and smaller towns—and building a decent road network between these places—would permit more balanced growth and development that will not be overwhelmed by the waves of people moving from rural areas. Governments would be better able to serve a constellation of cities and towns than one chaotic megalopolis. Rural residents could more easily access the services that urban areas provide if those areas were closer to the countryside. Growth would spread out across a country more evenly, benefitting more people more equitably. Urban planning would be easier too.

The states likely to benefit the most from strategic urbanization are large, middle-income countries with lots of poor people—most notably India, but also countries such as Pakistan, Indonesia, Egypt, Nigeria, and even Bangladesh, which is approaching middle-income status. They have the human resources and administrative capacity to conduct large-scale planning, and enough resources (on paper at least) to build out the infrastructure. Moreover, great regional inequities and urban-rural divides call out for just such an approach. Smaller or poorer places that have the necessary administrative and financial resources—including Kenya and Ethiopia—should also be able to adopt it in some form. Even states with very meager governments would benefit from distributing their resources more equitably across major cities and regions.

With appropriate planning and infrastructure development, the poor would benefit whether they move to cities or remain in the villages. Those who migrate would earn more money, have better access to schools and health care, and have more opportunity to improve their lots. Their living conditions would likely be better in every respect. Those who stay behind would gain from the reduced isolation of rural communities and from closer ties to markets and information. Agricultural produce would earn higher prices; new goods and services would be more readily available; and new farming and manufacturing techniques would be learned faster. The rural poor would also have greater leverage in pressing local elites (because the option of leaving or earning income more easily would allow them to resist powerful elites more) to change the inequitable social relations (such as those between men and women or between different castes) that have long held them back.

Strategic urbanization would also contribute substantially to efforts to enhance a state's implementation capacity and inclusiveness by strengthening the presence of government across the entire country and by helping to integrate more people into the country's economic and social life.

Strategic urbanization would improve the quality of government by bringing public services closer to where people are located and by increasing the chances that those services will be well delivered. Local elites generally feel greater pressure to perform competently and fairly than do distant bureaucrats, because the elites are directly affected by the lack of public services and the dissatisfaction it provokes. Less overcrowding also increases the ability of administrators to deliver results. Small and cohesive urban areas present many opportunities to create mechanisms (e.g., elections, oversight committees) that allow local peoples to hold their political leaders accountable.

Despite all its problems, Lagos has actually seen some improvements in government performance in recent years because enhanced powers and elections have enabled the governor, Babatunde Fashola, to work on some of the city's direst problems. Since becoming governor in 2007, he has reduced traffic jams, set up new bus routes, cleaned up streets, increased security, and raised taxes to invest in new expressways, commuter rail lines, and affordable housing. He was reelected in 2011 with 81 percent of the vote.[40] But where urban administrations lack the authority to manage their problems, even good leaders can achieve only so much. Karachi, a megalopolis of some 18 million people, had arguably Pakistan's most dynamic urban administration when Syed Mustafa Kamal, who was but 33 years old when he came to power in 2005. Over the next five years, his administration constructed new roads and overpasses to alleviate the dreadful traffic; improved sewage and drainage to reduce the recurrent flooding; and created new parks and belts of greenery in a city in desperate need of them. But he was held back from undertaking more ambitious schemes by how the country's federal system distributes authority over development and public services. Karachi's mayor, for instance, has no control over the police and does not have the authority to start work on a much needed metro-rail system.[41]

A New Model of Development

Strategic urbanization could be combined with efforts at decentralization to launch a whole new urban-based model of development—in which a substantial portion of a state's resources and responsibilities would be funneled to major cities and their surrounding hinterlands. Greatly empowered mayors—or district governors—would be tasked with larger portfolios than is the case today, handling most facets of government in their areas. Restructuring the state around where people live would remove the difficulties of managing across great distances, produce leaders who focus on the pragmatic concerns of their constituents, and make it easier for citizens to hold their politicians accountable. It would also produce less divisiveness in politics, as local populations would likely be much more cohesive than national ones.

This is already happening in some of the countries that have empowered urban or local governments to act on their own. Local "development states" have even emerged in cities or regions when national governments are struggling. The city of Medellín in Colombia, for instance, has made significant economic and social progress since the late 1990s thanks to local activism that has proven both popular and effective. The poor have especially benefitted from new transport links, publicly funded business support centers, and a locally managed program of cash grants.[42]

Both China and Vietnam have used strategic urbanization and balanced regional development to drive growth, improve the economic potential of poor regions, and alleviate population pressures on major cities. Vietnam, for instance, has sought to evenly distribute growth around three urban poles—Hanoi, Da Nang, and Ho Chi Minh City—and their surrounding provinces.[43] China has systematically distributed growth across its huge territory. The country has 89 urban areas with populations over 1 million. Despite seeing its urban population climb from 77 million in 1953 to close to 650 million in 2007, China has few slums, little urban poverty, and relatively satisfactory (according to surveys of the Chinese public) public services. A big part of this success has been the decentralization of resources and administrative functions to provinces and municipal governments (which together decide 69 percent of all government expenditures, an extremely high figure for a developing country). Somewhat more controversially, both Vietnam and China have used urban registration systems to control migration flows and funnel rural emigrants into smaller and medium-sized cities. Many public services are limited to legal residents in larger cities to encourage migrants to go elsewhere.[44]

In contrast, India has done little to plan for the massive urbanization it is currently undergoing, with stark consequences for its cities and poor people. Only one-fifth of India's urban sewage is treated before disposal, and few cities have sanitary landfills for solid waste. Out of 85 cities with over half a million people, only 20 have local bus service. "Our cities are bursting at their seams with people, but urban services are lacking. We don't have enough trained town planners. Our cities are growing without any plan," observed the urban development minister in New Delhi in 2011.[45]

The kind of plan that New Delhi (and other governments in a similar position) needs is one that sees urban development as part and parcel of a national agenda for wealth creation and state building. Urban planners, and the leaders who appoint them, should look beyond city boundaries to the wider geographic and economic landscape.

Developing detailed national plans for strategic urbanization—including the building of second-tier cities, smaller feeder urban areas, and market towns—would have many benefits for national development. It would also enable the benefits of development to reach as many people as possible. Investing resources in a series of urban areas (instead of just pouring resources into the capital, which is typically the case) and systematically encouraging urbanization within poor regions would create a chain of many moderately sized cities rather than a single congested and squalid megalopolis. Markets would grow in such a geographically fertile configuration. Governments could, for instance, build better transport links both between cities and between urban areas and their rural hinterlands and offer various incentives (such as tax reductions for any business or individual that relocated) to boost the attractiveness of small- and medium-sized cities.

Brazil's government has worked hard to invigorate the economy of its northeast region—historically its poorest area—through improved infrastructure and tax incentives. The Atlantic coastal highway has been widened. A new railway is being built. But the expansion of the port and industrial complex of Suape has been the biggest boon to growth. Lured by tax incentives and what should be excellent transport links, over one hundred firms have moved in—including the car maker Fiat; the southern hemisphere's biggest shipyard; a petrochemical plant; and an oil refinery owned by Petrobras, one of Latin America's largest companies. Workers from across the country are migrating to Suape and other parts of the northeast, and many of those who had left the area in search of better jobs are coming home.[46]

Of course, if these initiatives were implemented in conjunction with the decentralization policies mentioned above, more regional- or local-government-led "development states" would form along the lines of Medellin.

Government and nongovernmental leaders could also make strategic urbanization work better for the poor by protecting, rather than frowning upon, migrants from the countryside. Most governments tend to view migration negatively (because elites see it as contributing to population growth, intensifying pressures on urban areas, and promoting the spread of crime and disease). There are, however, a few exceptions, and their examples may be worth emulating. China, which has at least 150 million migrant workers, has tacitly encouraged migration to provide cheap labor for factories along its coast while relieving social tensions from unemployment inland. Starting in 2006, the central government began to explicitly require local governments to implement national guidelines on equal employment opportunities and rights protection for rural migrant workers.[47] In Africa, Mauritania has tried to create jobs for migrants, while Cape Verde and Senegal have considered strategies to promote remittances and engage migrants in national development. Elsewhere in the developing world, NGOs are working to make the lives of migrant workers easier. The NGO Aajeevika Bureau in India provides support programs (ID cards, skills training, counseling, placement programs) to tens of thousands of rural migrants in southern Rajasthan.[48]

* * *

These last three chapters have all discussed macro issues related to poverty. As mentioned in chapter 6, these have a greater potential to impact the poor because they affect a much larger number of people then specific micro factors, can dramatically affect investment, and can enhance the self-efficacy of entire populations. Macro factors can also shape micro factors. But the poor experience change mainly at the micro level, the level at which they—like everyone else—actually live. We now turn to these micro factors, starting in the next chapter with an examination of how all the various micro factors combine to influence the opportunities, risks, and access to markets that individuals and families face.

CHAPTER 10

Enhancing Opportunity

Kamsoni and Ntogo are two small villages in northwestern Tanzania. Geographically, they are close to each other; economically, they are far apart.

> Located in the northern part of Kagera, Kamsoni is close to the Tanzania–Uganda border and is a major center of trade. A high-quality tarmac road, built in 2003, links the village to the regional capital of Kagera on one side and to the Ugandan border and Kampala on the other. Public transportation is available at least 10 times a day in both directions. Residents of Kamsoni engaged in various businesses, exporting agricultural produce, loading trucks, changing currency, and so on. A woman in the village spoke of the expanded set of choices that her community's location offered her. "During the harvest, I can sell crops to either country. Things like clothes and other assorted goods are cheaper here compared to other areas in Bukoba Rural District. A lot of people are seen coming here to purchase these goods. This gives me the feeling that in other places such goods are expensive, though I have never been there to compare."
>
> As the crow flies, Ntogo is not far away from Kamsoni. It is by Lake Victoria, also close to the Ugandan border. The location offers residents some advantages: a large majority of them depend on fishing as a source of income and also engage in cross-border trade. . . . [But,] unlike the good tarmac road serving Kamsoni, a dirt road leads to Ntogo. It ends abruptly at a swampy area prone to flooding, near the outlet of the Kagera river into Lake Victoria. From there the only way to travel on to Uganda is in small boats. . . . [A member of] the village lamented, "If the road connected us to Uganda directly, say in the absence of the lake, transport and business with Uganda would be easier. Now traveling to Uganda involves engine and rowboats to cross the lake, but crossing the lake in a rowboat is risky."[1]

Better roads lead to greater opportunity. In Kamsoni, it is possible to advance by dint of one's initiative and hard work even if one starts out very poor. "You do not need capital to grow; being trustworthy is more important," commented one person.[2] The influx of money through trade is creating opportunities for new income-generating occupations such as brewing and distilling, running small shops, and changing money, which in turn reduce the dependence on agriculture and initial wealth. Traders also bring in new ideas, exposing people to life outside the village. In contrast, agriculture is the only way out of poverty in Ntogo. Those who have little or no land to farm find it difficult to improve their standard of living; indeed, they often struggle just to survive. Even those who own larger plots or have some money in their family have limited opportunities to increase their wealth.

Markets can be empowering. But, as this book has shown, the poor are often not in a position to take advantage of them. While the preceding three chapters discussed the macro factors that determine whether a person can fully participate in economic opportunity, this chapter examines the *micro* factors. It explains that if a society is to increase access to opportunity, its poorest members must have at least a basic level of schooling, housing, and health care, as well as access to financial institutions and to markets.

The Poverty Vortex

The economy of a developing country is like a deep, turbulent river, with prosperity on the top and destitution at the bottom. Powerful currents churn the water, especially in the river's deeper reaches. Many people are caught in those currents and dragged down into poverty's vortex, but most of those people are eventually released from the downward pull and can climb higher, at least temporarily. Indeed only a fraction—one-quarter to one-third by some estimates— of those who are in poverty at any given point are *always* immersed in poverty. Many more families move in and out of poverty than are perpetually trapped by it. Therefore, reforms that specifically target "the poor" are less likely to help them than are measures to strengthen the upward flows and lessen the pressures pushing people downward.[3]

Policies that increase the pull of upward currents (such as the availability of good jobs) will reinforce the aspirations and reward the initiatives of those trying to swim clear of poverty. Policies that limit the force of downward currents (such as illness) will reduce people's vulnerability, helping them stay clear of dangerous vortexes that can entrap even those who are strong swimmers. The combination enhances self-efficacy, as the poor feel more confident about their futures.

Livelihood Factors

Whether one is sucked into the poverty vortex or remains at a safe distance depends on one's own combination of micro "livelihood factors." Livelihood factors include marketable skills, family support systems, physical assets (such as land and housing), access to reliable health care, and ties to those with money or power. Each factor can be positive or negative, and to differing degrees. For instance, a family or individual may have no marketable skills, some skills, or many skills. Similarly, a family may have no access to health care, limited access, or excellent access. Together, these factors determine how much self-efficacy the poor have and the limits of what they can or cannot do for themselves.

An individual or family with a combination of micro factors in which the positive significantly outweigh the negative has a far greater chance of garnering the income and building the assets necessary to escape poverty permanently then those who do not.

These livelihood factors have strong complementarities—complementary relationships—between them. Improvements in one area can have a major effect on other areas. Better nourished children, for instance, will have higher cognitive abilities and do better at school. Enhanced access to insurance and savings accounts, to take another example, will enable the poor to take greater risks as they strive to achieve higher earnings.

Some livelihood factors are particularly influential. Education can have a particularly powerful "multiplier effect," its positive impact affecting many other factors. But other factors—such as transportation—can be just as powerful. Arvinda, whom we met in chapter 2, was able to prosper only when a new irrigation canal, road, and dam enabled him to make use of his education and entrepreneurial skills to gain access to new markets and credit, while increasing the return and reducing the risk from new investments.

At the same time, however, one or more positive factors can sometimes be outweighed by a single negative factor. The availability of micro loans, for instance, may not lead to higher earnings if the poor have only limited access to public services or transport linkages. A booming city or region cannot help someone if that person does not have enough savings to pay the bus fare to get there.

Social exclusion that disadvantages the members of a particular group (for instance, a lower caste) in one area of their lives can blight their lives as a whole. Discrimination in hiring practices reduces incentives to attend school or to immigrate to a more economically dynamic city. Discrimination in the issuing of licenses or in the allocation of loans weakens the incentives to start a business. As discussed in chapter 5, when discrimination disadvantages a large section of a country's population, it can adversely affect the entire national economy.

An Adequate Collection

The ability of a poor person to generate income and grow assets—the keys to economic and eventually political empowerment—depends on that person having a sufficiently large and varied collection (an "adequate collection") of positive livelihood factors. According to one World Bank report:

> Evidence from country studies underscores the critical importance for poor households of a minimum bundle of asset holdings (chiefly, human capital and rural roads) and risk protection (such as remittances and safety nets) so that they can undertake productive diversification strategies.[4]

Livelihood factors can be grouped into three categories—"opportunity enhancers," "risk reducers," and "connectors"—and an adequate collection must include all three.

Table 10.1 Livelihood Factors: Opportunity Enhancers, Risk Reducers, and Connectors

Livelihood Factor	Opportunity Enhancer	Risk Reducer	Connector
Two-parent household	✓	✓	
Family support network	✓	✓	✓
Health of family		✓	
Socially linked to spheres of political/ economic influence	✓		✓
Access to affordable, reliable health-care providers		✓	
Secure home/land		✓	
Assets (housing, savings, land)	✓	✓	
Security of property rights	✓	✓	
Access to equitable court system	✓	✓	
Education/skills	✓	✓	
Income opportunities	✓	✓	
Secure minimum income		✓	
Transport links to dynamic economic centers			✓
Access to television	✓		✓
Access to cell phone	✓		✓
Tools to manage crop risk		✓	
Tools to manage irregularity of income (e.g., microloans)		✓	
Knowledge about rights	✓	✓	
Access to agricultural inputs/storage	✓	✓	
Access to reliable savings mechanisms	✓	✓	

Opportunity enhancers, as the name suggests, give a person access to opportunity. They include physical, financial, social, and human assets (a *human asset* describes the set of skills or knowledge a person has), as well as access to public and private services. Risk reducers are assets (such as housing) and access to services (such as health care and insurance) that can reduce the risk of being pulled into the poverty vortex. Connectors are low-cost physical and social linkages to markets.

Table 10.1, which lists 20 influential livelihood factors, shows that some fit snugly into one category (transportation into the connector category, for instance), whereas others (such as housing) can fall into two or even all three categories, depending on the circumstances.

Opportunity Enhancers

Expanding access to opportunity requires ensuring that the poor both have the ability to acquire their own assets and have access to a wide range of services. Without these, the poor simply cannot fully participate in markets and compete on an equal footing. After all, without decent nourishment, housing, savings accounts, and schooling, how can the poor be expected to compete with anyone who grew up with all these things and more? How can a poor farmer, for example, hope to sell to markets currently dominated by large and wealthy landowners if he or she can't gain access to fertilizer, improved livestock breeds, credit, and secure property rights?

According to Amartya Sen, who won a Nobel Prize for his work on poverty:

> The ability of the poor to participate in economic growth depends on a variety of enabling social conditions. It is hard to participate in the expansionary process of the market mechanism (especially in a world of globalised trade) if one is illiterate and unschooled, or if one is bothered by undernourishment and ill health, or if social barriers (such as discrimination related to race or gender) excludes substantial parts of humanity from fair economic participation. Similarly, if one has no capital (not even a tiny plot of land in the absence of land reform), and no access to micro-credit (without the security of collateral ownership), it is not easy for a person to show much economic enterprise in the market economy.
>
> The benefits of the market economy can indeed be momentous. . . . But then the . . . sharing of education, epidemiology, land reform, micro-credit facilities, appropriate legal protections, women's rights and other means of empowerment must be seen to be important even as ways of spreading access to the market economy.[5]

Focusing on building a broad range of assets complemented by access to a broad range of complementary services is also important if the poor are to do more than just escape poverty. Most people who do escape poverty do not leave it far behind. As will be discussed in the next chapter, too often people climb out of destitution but then find themselves trapped in dead-end jobs such as pulling a rickshaw, driving a cart, of farming a tiny plot of land.

Risk Reducers

Mechanisms that reduce risk are essential to alleviate what is considered by the poor as the most defining, and most dreaded, feature of "ill-being"—the uncertainty and unpredictability that mark their lives. The chronic vulnerability to unpredictable shocks or a series of negative events explains why so many people face the constant threat—and fear—of descending into poverty. "A single blow can be endured by most people," observed one Indian villager, "but when several blows fall one after the other then it becomes very hard for any individual to cope."[6]

When times are hard, families may have no choice but to take steps that will limit their future access to opportunity. Forgoing health care, selling assets, running up debts, removing children from school, and reducing food intake may all help the poor manage crises but all have severe costs going forward.[7] Assets that families slowly accumulated over many years can disappear in rapid succession. A crisis involving the health of a loved one may force a spouse, parents, or children to sacrifice their own futures to cover the costs of uncertain treatments—or burials. Severe losses can easily damage confidence and lower horizons across generations.

This vulnerability also explains why the poor are often reluctant to take advantage of opportunities to improve their lives or increase their incomes: when so much is at stake, it seems wiser to trust the devil you know than to take a chance on something new. As a result, many perfectly affordable ways for the poor to improve their lives—such as purchasing inexpensive mosquito nets to reduce the risk of catching malaria—are disregarded, especially if the benefits are unclear or won't be seen until sometime in a future they have learned not to trust. A lack of information—all too common among people who often do not read and cannot afford to access most information sources—accentuates such behavior.

Connectors

Increasing opportunity and reducing risk both depend heavily on enhancing the connectivity of the poor. Connectivity can take many forms, all of them important in reducing distances, costs, risks, gaps in knowledge, and gaps in perception (regarding, for instance, legal and political rights). Better roads improve access to education, health care, markets, jobs, consumer products, and ideas. Better telecommunications—usually in the form of cell phones—enhance access to relatives and friends, banking services, customers, and information on markets and opportunities. Better social links help the poor gain access to licenses, loans, employment, and officials who determine the allocation of government funds.

Whether because it is hard to measure or because it is hard to recognize (because few non-poor people understand the depth of the poor's isolation from information, ideas, and markets), connectivity is often given a low priority by organizations that try to help the poor. As discussed below, this needs to change.

Enhancing Key Livelihood Factors

Enlightened actors—whether elites, government officials, or NGOs—who wish to empower the poor must ensure that each of their initiatives has a positive impact on as many livelihood factors as possible, ideally in a way that enhances opportunity, reduces risk, and improves connectivity simultaneously. The combination will maximize the impact on self-efficacy by removing the constraints that hold back people. Turning characteristics that exclude or hamper the poor's ability to take advantage of markets into ingredients that empower them to do so is the key to increasing incomes and assets—and to transforming lives.

Given the sheer number of problems that confront the poor, however, enlightened actors may have no choice but to prioritize among the factors they target. Some factors—such as the size of families—may not be easily amenable to change. Others—such as the quality and extent of roads and public services—may be beyond their immediate control.

Governments, NGOs, and enlightened elites acting on their own will also have to balance between short- and long-term goals. Short-term goals often receive priority, but many cannot be achieved without attention to long-term objectives. For instance, efforts to quickly create new jobs will have very little impact if the investment environment is not attractive to businesses. Improving the supply of electricity, the quality of roads, and the swiftness of customs procedures, however, are typically long-term ventures and usually dependent on a wider effort to strengthen infrastructure.

Governments are undoubtedly the most powerful actors, at least potentially. Some factors—such as the quality of security, the rule of law, and transport links—depend almost exclusively on how well the state operates. And almost all factors are influenced in some degree by the robustness of a country's administrative and judicial systems. Governments are also uniquely positioned to implement broad-ranging programs—as illustrated in the accompanying box, which outlines the Chile Solidario Programme.

The Chile Solidario Programme

The Chile Solidario Programme, introduced in 2002, aims to eradicate extreme poverty nationwide by increasing the ability of the country's poorest people to participate more fully in economic and social life. Unusual for such a program, it sees social exclusion as an important driver of poverty and targets seven different "dimensions of poverty" in an attempt to reduce it. The government-run program aims to both enhance capabilities—through the provision of better education, health care, and child care—and protect against potentially devastating events such as illness or unemployment.[8]

Basic Thresholds is the term the program uses to describe the minimum capabilities that a person or family needs to become fully active members of society. The full list of Basic Thresholds that the program aims to help the poor reach runs to no fewer than 53 items. Below are some representative items in each of the seven dimensions.

Dimension	Basic Threshold
Registration	Recorded in the Civil Registry
	Have identity card
	Disabled are registered as such
Health	Registered with primary health-care unit
	Up-to-date with pregnancy checks
	Children with up-to-date health check-ups
Education	If all adults work, preschool children access child care
	One adult is responsible for education and liaises with school
	Adults can read and write
Household Dynamics	Have effective mechanism for dealing with conflict
	Linked to support programs if violent behavior
	Fair distribution of household work (for all, independent of sex and age)

Housing	Access to energy sources, electricity, gas, etc.
	Adequate sewage
	At least two habitable rooms
Work	At least one adult in regular, paid employment
	No child below 15 not attending school because in work
	If unemployed, registered with labor bureau
Income	Access to family allowance
	Access to noncontributory pension
	Household budget in-line with resources and priorities[9]

The state is more likely to serve the needs of the poor when the poor work together to articulate those needs, engage powerbrokers, use the courts and other state institutions, and press for reforms. Working together through self-help groups, NGOs, and unions increases the bargaining power of the poor. It also encourages the creation of other organizations (everything from utility companies to government agencies) that serve the specific needs of the poor. The net result is better access to a large number of the livelihood factors, including financial tools, housing, and anything that depends directly on public investments, such as education and transport links. Organizations such as India's SEWA (the Self-Employed Women's Association) and Indonesia's Kecamatan Development Project (KDP) help the poor build the trust necessary to work together, coordinate their actions, overcome the divisions that plague society (such as caste, tribe, and religion), and organize politically to press for a bigger share of public funding. These organizations also teach new skills and build self-confidence, enhancing self-efficacy in the process.[10]

Private individuals, private companies, and NGOs can contribute to improving many livelihood factors, such as education, health care, financial tools, and information, and to establishing or strengthening organizations that enhance the ability of the poor to cooperate to advance their own interests. They can also play an important role improving the state, albeit indirectly and over time. Unfortunately, they rarely attempt to work across a broad range of factors in a comprehensive manner, thus limiting their ability to empower the poor. There are some notable exceptions, however, such as Bangladesh's BRAC (an NGO discussed in chapter 12). For most organizations, coordinating their efforts with the state and with other organizations offers the best chance of intensifying the impact of their initiatives.

Comprehensive programs that focus on a relatively small geographical area or group of people will usually have a much greater impact on their targets than programs that focus on a large area or population. The latter may produce some short-term benefits but are unlikely by themselves to overcome the multidimensional nature of poverty. In either case, success depends on enabling individuals, families, and communities to become self-reliant—to be able to start building assets and accessing services without further assistance. The remainder of this chapter discusses the most important livelihood factors and the kinds of policies that can accentuate their positive impact.

Families and Clans

The basic starting point for empowerment is almost always the family, because it plays a major role both in assisting in the accumulation of assets and in providing some degree of risk abatement. It also plays a large role in the social linkages that are the backbone of the only support system most poor people have.

Strong nuclear and extended families play major roles in education and in imparting a wide range of informal training essential to almost every aspect of life. They play key roles in wealth creation: relatives join forces to start new companies or migrate in search of opportunity; family members of all ages assist in running small businesses; kinship groups open up new trading links. Economies of scale reduce expenses, contribute to the building up of assets, and yield a broader set of capabilities to tackle various challenges. As Tomás, a poor man from Mexico says, "What I feel has helped me most is the union of the family. The union is our strength. With unity and agreement, you can do anything." Adriana, a 29-year-old woman from Colombia, echoes this sentiment, "The most important thing is the family union and the desire to keep on living, moving on. Without that, there is nothing."[11]

Families and traditional social groupings such as clans and tribes often assist in taking care of the sick and the elderly, provide insurance against bad times, and reduce the risk that children will be left to fend for themselves. They reduce the chance that young men will resort to violence—a key concern in many countries—by providing them with an incentive to work toward stability and the generation of income. Traditional social groupings have also played major roles in the success and expansion of microfinance ventures by providing the social pressure on borrowers to repay loans.

Different actors can take different steps to encourage the formation and maintenance of families. States can use the tax code to provide incentives to get and stay married; communities can work to reduce the cost of dowries (which can impoverish families and delay marriage); and governments and NGOs can lower the costs of housing and credit for newlyweds.

Empowering Women

Women play an outsized role in building up human capital and reducing poverty because they have the primary responsibility for raising children. Yet they are often far more disadvantaged than men in almost every respect within societies, communities, and households. They receive less than men in terms of public services, have less command over important resources such as land and capital, and have less time to devote to economically productive activities. They are given much less schooling, get a smaller share of food, and have far less access to political and economic opportunities. They are thus more likely to be impoverished—and to be severely impoverished—than men. As a young girl from Andhra Pradesh in India says, "The only wrong thing I did was to be born as a girl in this society."[12]

Few things would do more to help the poor than to educate and empower women. Greater schooling for mothers, for instance, has had almost as great an impact on reducing child mortality in the developing world as vaccines and medicines. Better educated women have a better understanding of how to prevent diseases, when to take their babies to clinics, when to clean water, and when to sanitize their homes.[13]

There are many ways to empower women. Three of the most important are the following:

- Directly investing in basic education and literacy, skills programs, and vocational training that build up women's economic, managerial, technical, and political capabilities.
- Creating networks and associations for women to enhance their ability to defend their interests; giving them practical training in leadership and organizing; and breaking down information barriers that keep them ignorant of their rights and resources.
- Reforming discriminatory laws, policies, practices, and mind-sets. Legislation toward this end can be helpful, but actions taken by community leaders can be much more powerful. The more often and more loudly that political, economic, and cultural leaders speak out about gender inequality and set personal examples of equitable treatment, the more likely it is that such attitudes will percolate down to the poorest sectors of society. Television can also play an important role in imparting such values. The developing world does not lack for role models of powerful women: Liberia, India, and the Philippines, for example, have all had female heads of state in the twenty-first century.

Security and Access to the Rule of Law

The poor are acutely vulnerable to predatory activity in societies with weak governments. Criminals pose a severe and constant danger to their homes, their property, and their personal safety. The government and security forces, too, can threaten the poor's livelihoods and even their lives. As two American human rights lawyers explain,

There is no effective mechanism to prevent those in power from taking away or blocking access to the goods and services. . . . Farming tools are of no use to widows whose land has been stolen, vocational training is not helpful for people who have been thrown in jail for refusing to pay a bribe, local medical clinics cannot treat bonded slaves who are not allowed to leave the factory even when they are sick, and microloans for new sewing machines do not benefit the poor if the profits are stolen by local police.[14]

While improving legislation so that the rights of women, disadvantaged groups, and minorities are better protected is important, enhancing the ability of the state to enforce its own existing body of laws will often do more to help the poor.

Enforcement depends on bolstering the capacity, independence, and ideological commitment to fairness of all government officials, especially national and local police, prosecutors, and judges, who can directly enable or deny access to justice. The kinds of measures that can do this include providing higher salaries (to reduce the temptation of corruption), more robust administrative systems (to encourage positive behavior and root out illicit activities), practical on-the-ground casework training, and legal aid and social services to the poor.

Housing and Land

Housing and land are the most important physical assets the poor can accumulate, both because they are a precondition for the accumulation of other assets[15] and because they are an important form of insurance and can be rented or sold off in times of exceptional hardship. A home contributes to family stability and reduces the physical and socioeconomic vulnerability not only of the household but also of members of its extended family, who may share the home in times of adversity.

Property offers a secure base on which to build up assets—assets that can be used to improve living conditions or increase income-earning potential. Basic physical goods such as lights, toilets, and refrigerators cannot be acquired without a secure home. Some micro enterprises cannot be started without a secure space in which to operate a kitchen or use a sewing machine. A secure plot of land that can reap enough harvest to support a family is essential to the livelihood of anyone living in rural areas.

If a secure home can be found in urban areas, migrants can stay longer and bring their families to settle down instead of returning regularly to their villages. Better jobs, schooling, and health care are typically available in urban areas than in the countryside.

Property transfers made at the time of marriage strongly determine the future wealth of a couple. Women's ownership of land directly improves their welfare, productivity, and empowerment.[16]

Any measure that helps the poor acquire, keep, and improve their own housing or land will have strong multiplier effects on the poor's ability to accumulate assets. Making available more urban space zoned specifically for low-income housing, strengthening the property rights of slum dwellers, and connecting poorer districts to main road arteries and electricity grids would provide a much firmer foundation for the urban poor. More secure land (and water) rights would help the rural poor. More equitable rules on property rights—properly enforced—would help women.

Education

By far the most important opportunity-enhancing factor is education, because it builds human capital and empowers people to solve their own problems. It also has a large multiplier effect across many other components of poverty.

Education is crucial to expanding income-generating options, increasing knowledge about new technologies and opportunities, and changing inequitable relationships. By enhancing expectations and aspirations for the future, it also plays a crucial role in fostering personal ambition and increasing pressure on leaders to perform better. Well-educated parents, especially mothers, are also important to promoting investment in the education and health of children.

But building human capital is about far more than just attending school, especially given the precarious state of most schools in the developing world. Getting more poor children into the classroom—which many countries have done in recent years—does not necessarily mean that they are learning much. In India, for instance, more than 50 million school-going children cannot read a very simple text.[17] In South Africa, only 15 percent of those children who finish grade nine acquire a basic level of competency in math and science skills as measured on internationally comparable tests. The average math ability of Brazilian school students is no better than the abilities of the bottom 2 percent of Danish students.[18]

In many places, including India, parts of Brazil, Africa, and some areas of China, the quality of education is so deficient that even graduates do not have the qualifications companies want. As S. Nagarajan, the founder of call-center company 24/7 Customer Pvt. Ltd., comments, "With India's population size, it should be so much easier to find employees. Instead, we're scouring every nook and cranny." The vast majority of applicants cannot communicate in English and lack a grasp of basic educational skills such as reading comprehension; Nagarajan says that his company can hire only three out of every hundred applicants. Seventy-five percent of technical graduates and more than 85 percent of general graduates are unemployable by India's high-growth industries.[19] Problems can be found in almost every corner of the school system, from textbooks (which often do not use local languages) to exam systems to curricula. Many teachers have an elite bias that encourages low expectations of their poorer students. Educational administrators are similarly inclined to look down on certain castes, social classes, ethnic and religious groups, and on girls in general. As a report on basic education in India concluded:

> Many teachers are anxious to avoid being posted in remote or "backward" villages.
> One practical reason is the inconvenience of commuting, or of living in a remote

village with poor facilities. . . . Another common reason is alienation from the local residents, who are sometimes said to be squandering their money on liquor [whether true or not], to have no potential for education, or simply to "behave like monkeys." Remote or backwards areas are also seen as infertile ground for a teacher's efforts.[20]

What the poor need is not more schools but better teacher training and educational systems that provide the structure and incentives to ensure good classroom outcomes. Building teachers' colleges is rightly a high priority for many Asian countries, because it helps to enhance the quality of education at all levels. Developing the capacity of government to manage education systems—as highlighted in chapter 8—should be one of the highest priorities of reform.

Schooling (and textbooks) in the languages of the poor would substantially expand access to education in places where the language of instruction (often English, French, or Spanish) is mainly spoken by elites—but not by the poor.

Less traditional ways to spread knowledge can substitute for classrooms and textbooks to some extent. Radio and television, for instance, can be highly accessible avenues for instruction, for both parents and children. Soap operas and informational programming are already used in parts of the developing world to spread knowledge about institutions (such as banks and government procedures) and values (such as the rights of women). In Brazil the spread of Rede Globo *telenovelas* (soap operas) has been linked to lower fertility rates.[21] In India, music videos have been used to spread literacy.[22] Cell phones—which are all but ubiquitous even among the poor—could offer a way of teaching subscribers how to read and write.

Mass media could also teach parents about the value of education. Such messages, if broadcast while governments are trying to make higher levels of the educational system more widely accessible, could spur families to keep their children in school longer and to demand improvements in the quality of teaching.

Creating mechanisms to evaluate talent without regard to educational qualifications would open doors for some of those who were disadvantaged by their schools. Before the global recession, Infosys, one of India's IT giants, allowed anyone to walk in and take a test that focused on intelligence and analytical skills rather than textbook learning.[23]

Access to Roads and Transport Links

Better access to transportation links—usually produced by greater state investment in more and better roads, although improved waterways and train networks can also be invaluable—are the most important form of connectivity. Without them, reforms in areas such as schooling and microfinance will have limited impact. When roads improve, almost everything improves: public services improve; food security gets better; access to health care and schooling expands; consumer goods become cheaper; markets for goods grow; business activity increases; urban jobs come within reach; income-generating opportunities multiply; information about just about everything is easier to find; and rigid social structures break down faster with the arrival of new ideas.

Atul Punj, the chairman of one of India's largest infrastructure building companies, explains:

> The development at the rural level is all about connectivity. If you don't have a road—sorry, a rural road—you can't get to a school. You can't get to a hospital. You can't get your produce to market. . . . Seventy percent of India's population is still directly involved with agriculture. When you have 40% of perishables being lost because they cannot be taken to the market or the lack of a cold chain because of the lack of connectivity, that sector has really been hammered consistently. . . . What will change is the ability for children to go to school [faster] rather than in some cases walking 10 km (6.2 miles) a day. Or getting [sooner] to a hospital for medical attention. You will start seeing a lot of economic activity taking place at the rural level rather than pure migration to the urban centers, which has its own problems.[24]

The same is true for roads between urban areas and across borders, and any infrastructure that enhances trading links (such as ports and customs facilities). In fact, many studies show that public investment in roads is one of the most important factors in poverty reduction and productivity growth.[25] As we will see in chapter 11, reducing the cost to move goods is essential to encouraging investment and creating jobs.

Yet roads have been one of the least emphasized elements in development, with severe consequences for the poor in less developed countries worldwide. Nearly two-thirds of African farmers are effectively cut off from national and world markets because of poor market access. Only 16 percent of the continent's roads are paved. Transport costs in Africa are higher than in any other part of the world.[26] South Asia is also notorious for its bad road links. Perhaps not coincidentally, these two areas have the largest number of poor people worldwide.

By contrast, Indonesia helped poor households successfully enter the market economy by consistently investing in roads for three decades. Bangladesh increased the vibrancy of its rural economies through investments in roads, bridges, culverts, and marketplaces.[27]

Health Care

Many of the risks that the poor face relate to the human body, because it is often a poor person's main productive asset—but also potentially his or her greatest vulnerability. It is, in most cases, an uninsurable possession that can, in the wrong circumstances, be transformed from a source of earnings to a great drain on resources. Serious illness or the death of a family member is by far the largest threat to the well-being of poor people. When a breadwinner falls ill or dies, his or her household can easily be sucked into poverty's vortex. "We face a calamity when my husband falls ill," says a poor woman in Zawyet Sultan, Egypt. "Our life comes to a halt until he recovers and goes back to work."[28]

The lack of inexpensive, reliable health care markedly increases these risks. Instead of an accessible health-care system, the poor face "a proliferation of fly-by-night operators, over-prescription, over-charging by private providers, spurious drugs, and other such avoidable social evils," as one academic who used to work in the Indian administrative service explains.[29] Limited numbers of qualified medical personnel, rising expenses, and weak regulation combine to make medical treatment either unattainable, useless, or positively harmful.

Even in many parts of China, the rising cost of medical care has outstripped increases in income to the extent that millions are falling into poverty by exhausting their savings to pay for medical treatment. In India, every year sees 3 percent of the population—more than 30 million people—pushed into poverty by high medical expenses.[30]

Few things can reduce the risks facing the poor more than access to inexpensive, reliable health care. A billion lives would be swiftly transformed by better access to free preventive services such as vaccinations, regular check-ups, nutritional supplements, worming medicines for children, and so forth. Increasing access to health insurance through a government-subsidized scheme (in countries that have the capacity and resources to run it) would enable the poor to concentrate more on building up their assets. The cost of providing these services would be relatively low, especially if resources were shifted from curative care, which is disproportionally consumed by the rich (and which typically receives large portions of overall budgets). And a government that invested in preventive health care would reap considerable economic benefits in the form of a healthier, better educated, and therefore more productive workforce.

But, as in the case of education, improving overall access to and the overall quality of health care requires dealing with larger systemic issues, including increasing the supply and quality of medical personnel; improving the management of the health care system; and improving the quality of information that reaches the poor (see below). These measures in turn depend on improving the implementation capacity of the government so that it can better regulate the health-care sector, better supervise private providers, and better allocate the incentives driving the market.

Level of Income

People with little or no stable income behave very differently from those with a minimum level of guaranteed income. Whereas the former can become so conditioned to their poverty and vulnerability that they shy away from any endeavor that does not have immediate payback, the latter look to the future with some confidence and plan for the longer term.

The best way to create jobs that pay regular wages is to build a robust economy. But even robust growth can bypass disadvantaged families on the margins of society. People who lack basic education and health care and who have few or no social ties to elites are rarely in a position to benefit from growth. If these people are to be brought into the economic and social mainstream, governments (or large NGOs) need to introduce programs that either promise a minimum income stream or give people the ability to acquire an income-producing asset (a cow, say, or a sewing machine), ideally in return for those people making investments in their own futures.

The best known example of this type of program has transformed social policy for the poor in parts of Latin America. Known as conditional cash transfer (CCT) programs, these initiatives provide families with a minimum level of income—a small monthly stipend ranging from $5 to $33 per child—as long as parents keep their children in school and take them for health checks. CCT programs can be remarkably cost-effective in middle-income countries with a state strong enough to target the poor accurately. In the Latin American countries that have adopted them, CCT programs cost are about 0.5 percent of GDP. The returns on this investment have been considerable. Mexico's Oportunidades has reduced poverty by 8 percent; Brazil's Bolsa Família has raised millions out of the depths of extreme poverty.[31]

CCTs have been shown to contribute directly or indirectly to development in a wide range of ways, enhancing health, nutrition, education, gender equality and women's empowerment, and economic inclusion and growth.[32] Where complemented by the spread of mobile telecommunications, roads, and electricity, CCT's have helped transform rural areas economically. Brazil's northeast, traditionally its poorest region, is now its fastest growing, partly because of the cash transfers millions receive there.[33]

Worldwide, 45 developing countries now give over 110 million families some sort of cash transfers, from universal child benefits in Mongolia to pensions in South Africa to family grants in Latin America.[34]

The main drawback of cash transfers is that they depend on a certain minimum level of state capacity that many poor countries do not have. They may also be unaffordable in places where almost every family needs them and governments have few resources. Even so, they may offer a more effective way to use those limited resources than other programs now being funded.

Financial Tools

Increasing the ease with which the poor can save, borrow, insure, and transfer funds can also have a large impact—especially since most poor people have never stepped into a bank and have no more secure place to stash their meager savings than their or their neighbor's home.

Better financial tools reduce insecurity (by reducing incidences of lost or stolen money), unpredictability (by providing savings or insurance that can be used when incomes drop), deprivation (by allowing food to be purchased when needed instead of simply when money is earned), and vulnerability (by providing options when a crisis such as a drought or a family illness strikes). They also expand opportunity in countless ways: it becomes easier to plan and invest for the future, expand businesses, take risks to test out new income ideas, gain access to remittances, and buy goods that are not available locally.

Microcredit—the lending of very small amounts of money to the poor—reached 128 million families in 2009,[35] bringing immense benefits in the process. Access to small loans can help people to smooth out a bumpy pattern of earning, to purchase various consumer durables, and to start small enterprises. By itself, however, microcredit is not the empowering elixir some advocates proclaim, especially when it is not combined with complementary measures that multiply its impact.

Microsavings and microinsurance, which are more recent innovations, can similarly help empower the poor. Ensuring that "no frills" banking accounts are available for a nominal fee encourages the poor to use them. Increasing the supply of products that promote disciplined asset accumulation—such as "commitment products" that force those who sign up to make weekly or monthly deposits (often toward specific goals such as their child's education)—maximize the impact of savings schemes. Various forms of agricultural insurance are being experimented with across the world.[36] Health insurance and life insurance for borrowers (it covers loans if a borrower dies) are being rolled out for the first time by NGOs in countries such as Ghana.[37]

Technology holds vast potential to expand access to financial products by broadening the range of service delivery points. South Africa's Standard Bank and the Togo-based pan-African lender Ecobank Transnational, for instance, are rolling out smaller branches, self-service kiosks, and community lending programs to extend their reach across the continent.

Cell phones may be the best way to expand the reach of some financial services, as has proven the case in Kenya. The popular M-PESA (*M* is for mobile, *pesa* for money in Swahili) program allows people to deposit money through an agent or ATM, transfer money to another mobile user, and redeem it. Entrepreneurs can accept payment this way, reducing the costs and risks of carrying cash. Migrants can send money home hundreds of miles away with a click.[38] Kenyans transferred $7 billion in 2010, 20 percent of GDP. The explosive growth in mobile money will boost savings and investment as new mobile-based services come online. It should also prompt broader productivity gains, as mobile-money agents become conduits for all sorts of commerce and information.[39]

Information

A crucial aspect of poverty is the poverty of information. Unable to read or at least read well, too poor to buy a magazine or newspaper, lacking social ties to people in government or other important institutions, wary of new ideas and unfamiliar faces, and uneducated about how a modern economy works, the poor are severely disadvantaged in many aspects of their lives simply because they do not know enough to make good choices. Many poor people, for instance, may not understand the value of immunizations, how much fertilizer they need to use, how to avoid getting infected with AIDS, or what value their children gain from the first few years of education.[40] In such circumstances, the poor can be easy targets for unscrupulous sellers of everything from pharmaceuticals to consumer goods to land. They are also susceptible to abuse at the hands of elites and officials simply because they do not know their rights or how to work through a government bureaucracy properly.

A dearth of information also explains why the poor aim low at times. If one's friends, family, and neighbors have never had a well-paying job, one is unlikely to strive for such a job oneself. Not knowing how to plan a career, apply to certain types of school, win scholarships, or write a resume and conduct an effective interview will similarly preclude many from reaching for lofty goals—or even believing they are within the reach of someone from a poor background. Many poor people think that no matter how hard they work, they can never become more than a bus conductor, messenger, or typist.

As one software engineer from a less well-off rural family in India replied when asked what he thought was the best way to help young people from backgrounds like his:

> I don't need much money for doing this. I would just give more knowledge to the people. This is what you need: You need to create the balance, the urge in people to become whatever they want to become. You just have to make it visible to them—what are the possibilities, what they can achieve if they take this approach—and confidence that they themselves can do it. That would be enough.[41]

Information thus works like other types of connectivity—including roads and cell phones—in reducing the distance (in this case, the figurative distance) the poor have to travel to improve their lives. It expands their access to health care, higher level schooling, jobs, markets, and all types of public services. It also can be liberating: knowledge about democracy and what kind of government people elsewhere have can dramatically change expectations, and thus increase popular pressure on leaders.

Running information campaigns and building information-providing institutions are among the cheapest ways to increase connectivity—helping the poor both expand opportunity and reduce risk in the process. Employment exchanges, career-counseling services, college guides, health-care information, business advice bureaus, consumer handbooks, informational radio shows, and libraries can all revolutionize the types of information the poor have access to—with great consequences for the choices they make.

Role models on television and other mass media can show the poor that they can advance to better schools and jobs and higher positions in life while providing some guidance on how it can be done. In Bangladesh, BRAC launched the *Medha Bikash* (talent development) program in 2005 to assist capable students from poorer households gain fellowships to attend specialized classes, career counseling, and college.[42] Expanding access to television "exposes people to new ideas and different people. With that will come greater opportunity, growing equality, a better understanding of the world, and a new appreciation for the complexities of life."[43]

The cell phone (and the Internet in places where it is available) can help out with many of these things. It reduces the costs to access information, provides ready data in many areas, connects people great distances apart, and improves coordination. It can fuel the expansion of learning and how the poor understand some of their most basic challenges. But, of course, nothing is better than being socially networked with educated and well-informed people, either through family ties or some other personal connection. These provide the best information and role models of all.

Building Up Assets and Capital[44]

If a poor person is to escape the poverty vortex permanently and to have the chance to rise higher, he or she needs to accumulate four different kinds of resources: physical assets, financial assets, human capital, and social capital. Some representative types of each of these kinds of resources are shown below.

Physical Assets	Housing
	Plot of land large enough to feed family
	Refrigerator
	Sewing machine
	Kitchen
	Television/radio
	Bicycle/motorcycle
	Cell phone
Financial Assets	Permanent job
	Secure savings
	Insurance
	Remittances
	Rental income
	Social welfare (such as CCT)
Human Capital	Health of self and family
	Knowledge/marketable skills
	Good work habits
	Degree/technical certificate
	Interview skills
	Commitment to saving money
	Access to information
Social Capital	Strong family units/extended kinship ties
	Good social network/ties to higher classes
	Attends church/mosque
	Participates in community activities

Building up Assets, Changing Society

A large and well-balanced collection of positive livelihood factors gives a poor person a sense of control over his or her life—a strong sense of self-efficacy. Knowing that their most important basic needs—for housing, food, income, health care, security, and so on—are met or can be met releases people to devote more attention to building up their assets and careers, and doing the most they can to help their children.

The more the poor are able to orient themselves toward the future with a belief in their own powers, the more likely they will be able to accumulate the broad range of human, social, financial, and physical assets[45] (see the box "Building Up Assets and Capital") that allows them to fully participate in markets and societies. As Caroline Moser has shown in her book about hard-pressed families in the slums of Ecuador, *Ordinary Families, Extraordinary Lives*, the poor, like all households, act as strategic managers of the complex asset portfolios they possess and the risks related to its maintenance and growth.[46] They seek to accumulate the economic resources that enable them to improve their well-being, make their lives happier, increase their social position, and reach for their aspirations.

If circumstances are propitious, this process of accumulation should slowly allow the poor to accumulate the power to change the social structures that dictate how communities, regions, and states are governed—and that currently work to exclude them (as discussed in chapter 12). Such change will reduce discrimination, narrow inequities, and eventually ensure that markets and governments act equitably and inclusively.

But none of this will happen fast, especially when many of the ingredients outlined above depend on the robustness of the systems that states run—education systems, health-care systems, regulatory systems, legal systems, transportation systems, and administrative systems. Improvements in these areas are much harder to achieve—yet much more important than any individual intervention.

This does not mean that incremental progress is not feasible. Governments can do many things even with their limited capabilities and resources to help the poor, as indicated above. And there are many initiatives that individuals and organizations can take to help empower the poor at the micro level, even when larger changes are not possible. Those that instigate a larger process of change are especially valuable: well-targeted scholarships can create social linkages that eventually help whole castes, villages, or remote regions gain access to new opportunities; libraries that include large informational components can raise educational horizons, provide access to knowledge about business management and careers, and increase expectations for farmers, job seekers, and students; low-income housing can transform the choices available to individual families and create stronger linkages between urban and rural areas.

Areas typically neglected in the past but potentially having strong multiplier effects because of how they impact other factors are also especially ripe for attention: transport linkages, teacher training colleges, a chain of small multipurpose health clinics, and steps to lower the expenses related to marriage could all have outsized impacts. Such small changes will accumulate over time into large changes. The poor will gradually become empowered, societies will gradually become more equitable, and better macro conditions will gradually feed into faster changes to a broader set of micro factors.

Of course, all these changes require that the poor generate more income, the topic of the next chapter. And this requires reducing the risks, costs, and various barriers to linking up locations and companies such that businesses—small and large—can invest more and grow faster. Improving the functioning of markets—by, among other things, growing their sizes—is the key to creating the income-generating opportunities so essential to the livelihoods of the poor.

CHAPTER 11

Enlarging Markets, Spreading Wealth

Hodat, a woman in her thirties in Garkuno Miani village in Pakistan, struggles to make ends meet because her family can no longer catch enough fish in nearby Manchar Lake. The lake has become severely polluted in recent years, and fish stocks have plummeted. Her sons still go fishing, but the catch is so small that the money they make from selling it isn't enough to keep the family afloat. "We are very poor and no one supports us. The water in this area is filthy and has no fish in it. We have nothing." Yet, despite deep frustration with her powerlessness, she is determined to make the most of the skills and resources she does have.

Hodat survives by doing her best to diversify. She and her daughter-in-law now earn money from sewing and embroidery. Together with her husband, they also run a small shop. "We women do *bharat* [Sindhi embroidery], make *rilli* [traditional patchwork quilts] and *chatai* [mats]. . . . I have a sewing machine and a grocery shop of my own where tea, sugar, potato and onions are sold. . . . I, my daughter-in-law and my husband run the shop in a room of the house. I and my daughter-in-law do stitching [as well]. I charge 50 rupees. I stitch four to five *shalwar kameez* [pajama-like trousers] in a day. In this way we make a good livelihood for ourselves, but other people in this area do not earn well—and that's why we want the contaminated water from the lake to be drained.[1]

Wherever one goes, the poor tend to be entrepreneurial—they have to be, just to survive. Poor families try out many income-generating ideas over time. Often, they juggle a few simultaneously in the hope that they will be able to put together enough money to survive—or perhaps even to start building a better life. They also seek to do what a stockbroker or accountant would call "diversifying." They farm plots in different locations, take jobs in different places, and try out different trades—calculating that when one or more of these mini income streams dries up, they will still have some money trickling in. One survey in West Bengal, India, discovered that the average family had three working members with seven occupations between them. Even Bengali households who owned a piece of land only spent two-fifths of their time farming it in order to limit their exposure to stormy weather, crop failure, and fickle prices.[2] And yet, despite these efforts to stay afloat, all too often they sink. Harvests cannot be easily transported to cities, family members get sick, corrupt officials take away earnings.

Besides running their own farms or small businesses, the other main employment for the poor is casual, unskilled labor, often dirty, dangerous, and semi-legal, and paid by the day. In rural areas, more than half the poor who have jobs work as casual laborers. In urban areas, the proportion is smaller, but not a lot smaller.[3] Work on a construction site or on a farm during harvest season is highly irregular. Many jobs last only a few days or weeks and end on short notice. Casual laborers spend a lot of time doing nothing, waiting around for the next job to come their way. It is hardly surprising that poor people see creating steady jobs for young people as more important than expanding education, reducing maternal mortality, or tackling malaria or tuberculosis.[4]

Part of the reason why the poor can't make a living as casual laborers is the same reason why they can't prosper as micro entrepreneurs or farmers: too many people with few or no skills competing in too narrow a market. There are simply too many workers with limited education chasing too few opportunities for unskilled labor. There are too many hawkers in the streets selling the same set of cheap goods. And the families farming their small plots are surrounded by thousands of other families farming more or less the same thing, all cut off from larger markets by the limitations of their governments, infrastructure, and skills.

The same problem, however, can be tackled by the same solution. And in this case, the solution—or at least part of the solution—is for the governments of developing nations to create bigger and better markets for farmers and businesspeople while giving poor people the chance to acquire the education and the skills that will make them far more capable as business owners and far more attractive to employers.

This chapter starts by discussing the role markets have historically played as a driver of economic development and then explains how markets are today hindered from working efficiently in many poor countries. The second half of the chapter examines the four areas where action is most needed if countries are to create inclusive growth that benefits the poor.

A History of Expanding Markets = A Tale of Prosperity

Countries have traditionally grown rich by enlarging the size of markets and making them easier and cheaper for farms and businesses to access. Better access enables businesses to expand, hire more workers, and specialize.[5]

Agriculture and manufacturing first grew up around seas, rivers, and canals, because these were the best ways to reach large markets inexpensively. Moving goods by what Adam Smith and his eighteenth-century contemporaries called "water-carriage" was considerably cheaper than doing so by "land-carriage." Products could be carried a vast distance by ship or barge more cheaply than they could be hauled a short distance overland. In the Industrial Revolution of the 1700s and 1800s, the cost of transporting goods by land fell sharply, thanks to the construction of railroads and wider, smoother roadways. As a consequence, farmers and manufacturers could reach much larger markets within their own country and neighboring states than ever before.

With larger markets came the need to ensure that contracts would be honored despite large distances between suppliers and buyers and that money could be moved securely. As early as the late Middle Ages, financial and legal instruments such as banks and letters of credit were invented to enable trade to be conducted more easily across distance and time. Over the following centuries—and especially in the nineteenth and twentieth centuries—these and other innovations were woven into an intricate system of security, contracts, laws, courts, banks, and insurance companies that made transactions predictable and inexpensive.

In the 1960s and 1970s, rapidly emerging countries made the expansion of markets—initially for farm goods, later for manufacturing goods—key drivers of their phenomenal growth. Southeast Asian states such as Indonesia, Malaysia, and Vietnam all invested heavily in expanding their agricultural sectors in the early stages of their modern economic development, because the bulk of their populations lived in rural areas. They built road networks, subsidized the introduction of new technologies, and invested in irrigation—all steps that increased the profitability of producers. Later, they took advantage of reductions in the cost of telecommunications and transcontinental shipping and invested in measures—such as efficient customs systems, export promotion agencies, and trade fairs—that reduced how much it cost their companies to reach international markets, especially the United States. Similarly, China invested heavily in infrastructure, opened special economic zones, and entered the World Trade Organization to reduce the costs and uncertainty of accessing important overseas markets.

Higher Costs and Risks = Smaller Markets

In today's poor countries, however, the markets that farmers and factories can inexpensively access are very small. Bad infrastructure, social divisions, petty corruption, weak contract enforcement, and the insecurity of property make it too costly and risky for producers to reach many customers, especially customers in distant cities and countries. Governments typically do not invest in ways that increase productivity and profitability for the mass of small and micro businesses that dominate the local economic landscapes.

Many of the problems businesses face in these places can surprise people from the developed world. When I worked in Nigeria, for instance, I discovered that my company had to have its own generator, its own mailmen, its own commuter vans, and its own security just to operate. And we needed to nurture special relationships with various government departments if we wanted to conduct business. All of these things cost money—money that most small- and medium-sized enterprises and micro businesses do not have.

Most of these problems are different from those typically identified as the biggest hindrances to doing business in less developed countries. While too many or poorly conceptualized regulations—the main target of international surveys of local business conditions—can certainly hold back companies, too high transaction costs is a much bigger problem for the great majority of companies in these places. Moreover, such conditions are by no means unique. For instance, try getting a product through customs in Senegal:

> The customs officers play on our impatience. They know we are in hurry so they do it to make us look for an arrangement. It is rare for a custom officer to request an arrangement explicitly. If they know that your affairs are not in order, they start by making threats to put you under pressure. Then they show that they are willing to help you and this is when you have to understand their game and make a proposition to them. Then you bargain it. If, on the other hand, the custom officer really doesn't find anything having checked, he says: "give me the cola money" [the bribe].[6]

Or try getting a license from a government official in Morocco:

> Authorizations are not distributed fairly, but are based on corruption and clientelism. If you give money, you will receive your permit in two days. If you don't, you'll be sent from one department to another until you give up your project or pay the bribe.[7]

Or try getting a loan to start a business in India:

> In 2002, thinking about doing business, I had applied in the Block Office for a loan of 10,000 rupees. But the people in the Block Office had not given any importance to my application. Actually they want bribes.[8]

Or try transporting a good any distance in Niger:

> When you drive to Zinder or Maradi with a loaded truck, every customs officer on the road, in particular those in the squads, ask us for something even though we have completed the necessary formalities at the outset. You are forced to give them something or they threaten to unload the truck for a so-called check. You see the set-up they create to get at us. Well, imagine them asking you to unload in the bush where there is no help on hand. What's more, the truck owner does not pay you for it. So you understand why we give into their pressure against our better judgment.[9]

The proliferation of checkpoints in regions such as West Africa (see figure 11.1) slow traffic and sharply raise costs. Transport costs in Africa can be as high as 77 percent of the value of exports, a much higher percentage than in any other part of the world. The size of that figure helps explain why Africa finds it so difficult to build a manufacturing sector and reduce its dependence on exports of natural resources.[10]

The lack of security is also a major hindrance. One in every three firms in Latin America, and more than one in four firms in Africa, Eastern Europe, and Central Asia identify crime as the biggest problem their businesses face. And the burden is highest on those least able to bear the cost: firms in Sub-Saharan Africa lose

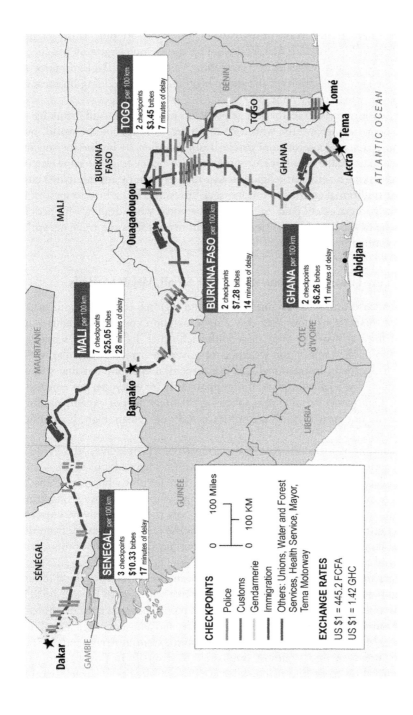

Figure 11.1 Checkpoints on West African Transport Corridors

Source: "Survey Results from the 3rd Quarter 2009," West Africa Trade Hub, November 10, 2009,
http://www.watradehub.com/sites/default/files/resourcefiles/feb10/9th-irrg-report.pdf.

169

a higher percentage of sales to crime and spend a higher percentage of sales on security than do companies in any other region of the globe.[11]

It is also hard trying to do business when the lights are out. Thirty of the 48 countries in Sub-Saharan Africa—including the region's largest oil producer, Nigeria—face regular power cuts.[12] According to the World Bank's Enterprise Surveys, the lack of electricity is the single biggest obstacle to doing business in conflict areas, where many poor live.[13]

Social divisions often exacerbate these problems by dividing—and shrinking—markets. Social ties grease the wheels of commerce throughout the world, but where those ties are loose or nonexistent business suffers. A businessperson in, say, Yemen may be able to enforce a contract with someone from the same clan or mosque by asking an elder or religious leader to intervene, by appealing to a customary or traditional court, or by using social pressure. But a businessperson is far less likely to get a debt paid, or a loss compensated when dealing with people to whom he or she has no social ties. As a result, market sizes and trade networks are often limited by the extent of these ties.

Few Linkages + Weak Linkages = Small, Weak Markets

These extra costs and risks fracture national and regional economies into many small local markets by how they drive up transaction costs. They reduce the ability of firms to work or even trade with each other, reducing the scope for specialization. They reflect the weakness of governments—in particular, their inability to create an institutional and infrastructural environment that stimulates productivity. Such conditions limit opportunity for everyone, but especially the poor. Companies refrain from investing. Planters do not expand production. Jobs are not created. Skills are not learned. Prices remain high. Economies remain anemic.

Such conditions hit rural areas—where most poor people live—the hardest. Urban areas may have many problems but at least they have a lot of people—and high population density means large markets. But farmers who grow crops in areas of low population density far from cities and who have few ways of getting their crops to urban areas have no reason to boost their productivity. Government and infrastructure tend to become thinner the farther one travels from the capital, making it harder for both farmers and businesspeople to ship products to markets and to ensure they get paid when they do.

Linkages are crucial to nurturing clusters of businesses, which help local industry expand and diversify. For instance, a rural area will start to prosper once it boasts not only farms but also canning factories, repair shops for farm machinery, silos and warehouses to store agricultural produce, and a host of other specialized businesses. Many Latin American, Middle Eastern, Central Asian, and African countries, however, find it almost impossible to diversify in this way, in part because their businesses find it too expensive or too risky both to reach sizeable markets, whether overseas or on the other side of their own countries, and to work closely with other firms because of problems with contract enforcement.

As a result, investment in these places is concentrated on exploiting natural resources for export, not on building factories. This lack of investment in manufacturing plants severely affects the poor, because factories are the easiest place for unskilled workers to find employment in the early stages of economic development. While businesses that provide services (such as banks, telemarketers, and software companies) can also absorb new workers—especially women—they depend on better-trained people that many countries may not have.[14]

Middle Eastern countries do not have large industrial sectors despite being closer than Asian economies to Europe's large markets and despite having a potential workforce in the legions of unemployed youth. Why? In large part because (thanks to corruption, weak rule of law, heavy-handed governments, or, more recently, internal political instability) they are simply too expensive and too unpredictable to operate in.[15] India manufactures and exports far fewer products than China does, at least partly because India's poor infrastructure and high levels of corruption make it difficult to produce low-cost goods. Protectionist labor laws, which are meant to help workers, sharply increase the cost of establishing and managing factories in India, thereby reducing the demand for Indian labor.[16] African garment manufacturers cannot compete internationally because of expensive and intermittent power supply, weak transport infrastructure, and corruption.[17]

Such conditions significantly disadvantage microenterprises and household businesses—the leading source of employment outside the agricultural sector in developing countries—as well as small- and medium-sized enterprises (SMEs—companies with between 10 and 250 employees), the crucial driver of home-grown economic dynamism in most developing countries.[18] Unlike larger, richer companies, these companies cannot, for instance, easily buy generators (to deal with power outages), hire their own private police (to compensate for corrupt and inefficient police forces), secure a government minister's help in reducing corruption on roadways, or get ready access to credit from banks.

And, as usual, the poor suffer more than their better-off compatriots. For instance, micro entrepreneurs typically have to pay higher interest rates and larger bribes than SMEs and bigger companies do. In Pakistan, extremely poor business owners have to pay a bribe to run their businesses more than twice as often as richer business owners. In Pakistan's rural areas, the poor are five times more likely to have to bribe an official. And when poorer business owners turn to the courts to mediate and adjudicate their disputes, they have to pay more than the non-poor, and they are half as likely to be satisfied with the outcome.[19]

Enlarging Markets = Enlarging Opportunity

The leaders of poor countries have to work on four broad fronts if they are to increase the opportunities available to their poorest citizens: (1) reduce the costs and risks that unnecessarily shrink markets; (2) expand the rural sector; (3) make it easier for SMEs to expand; and (4) enhance the skills and flexibility of the workforce while making it cheaper for firms to hire those workers.

The overall goal should be to develop a private sector that is sufficiently dynamic to allow the poor to develop their own businesses or find stable jobs that will help them climb permanently out of poverty. The state's role should vary depending on its implementation capacity and the needs of the country. Wherever possible, however, the state should strive to enhance the functioning of markets and to enable companies to acquire technology and know-how (see the text box "*Bayam Sellam* in Cameroon").

Reducing the Costs and Risks of Doing Business

By far the most important step that the state can take is to reduce the unnecessary costs and risks that farmers and businesspeople face. If the state can make progress on this front, it will encourage all kinds of businesses not only to start, grow, and expand, but also to trade and cooperate with one another. But it must work on many fronts to be successful; the issues involved are much more complex than typically recognized by organizations such as the World Bank in publications such as its annual *Doing Business*, which concentrate mainly on formal regulations.[20]

Exactly how might a state do this? Let us imagine a well-led country in Africa, whose government has decided to launch an all-out effort to drive down the costs and risks of doing business. As a start, it takes steps to ensure macroeconomic stability. Its small but well-trained staff in the treasury ministry introduces measures to keep the rate of inflation consistently under 20 percent,[21] a step that provokes very little opposition.

Next, the government does everything possible to increase trade, competition, and business formation and expansion. It reduces the paperwork involved in running a company. It establishes two new ministries, one devoted to promoting and facilitating trade (domestically as well as internationally), the other focused on promoting competition to combat the tendency (which the president has noticed in countries as diverse as Mexico and Ethiopia) for one company to dominate important markets in developing countries. The new ministry of trade promotion sets up its own transport police, which is tasked with reducing unnecessary checkpoints that can slow down the movement of goods across the country and across borders. The president invites businesses, farmers, financiers, and governments to a conference to discuss how they can work together to tackle systemwide problems with markets.[22]

In order to reduce uncertainty about property rights and contracts and increase investor confidence, the government sets up streamlined commercial courts to settle disputes. The president gets advice on how to do this from officials in Ghana, Nigeria, and Peru, all of which have had success with streamlined judicial systems.

The government then invests what resources it can find in improving the infrastructure (especially the patchy and poorly maintained road network) used to move and trade goods. It invests, too, in boosting the supply, reliability, and cost-effectiveness of electricity supplies. And it tackles the difficult and labor-intensive process of clarifying property and water rights, thereby creating much greater certainty among businesses, farmers, and various social groups about who owns what. This may require working with local authorities in a creative manner (see chapter 8).

And what is the result of all this activity? Growth. Growth in the number of companies doing business in the country and in the size of their investments going forward. Growth in the number of people with steady jobs and growth in the size of the pay packets they bring home. Growth in trade not only within the country but also internationally. Growth in exports, tax receipts, and eventually public services.

This need not be just a fictional scenario. Some of these sorts of measures have been tried in the real world and have made a big difference in a short space of time. For instance, Rwanda's Doing Business National Task Force, a specialized reform unit, has slashed the forest of paperwork that used to confront the country's would-be entrepreneurs. Whereas the process of registering a business once involved 9 procedures, took 18 days, and cost more than twice the average annual income of a Rwandan, now it involves 2 procedures, takes 3 days, and costs less than one-tenth of the average annual income.[23] Rwanda has leapt in the rankings of the World Bank's annual Ease of Doing Business index, climbing from 158 in 2005 to 58 just five years later.

Where states are too enfeebled to undertake these measures, establishing special economic zones may prove an effective short-term remedy (see the box "Special Economic Zones: An Effective Way to Jumpstart Development"). Another approach may be for weak states to work together on a regional basis. A regional trade-facilitation agency, for instance, could tackle the myriad causes of high transaction costs, quickening the movement of goods by enacting unified, simplified, transparent procedures for customs clearance and payments and by dispatching its own people to ensure the removal of the many blockages. The agency could unify technical standards for goods conveyance, enforce reduced transit charges, and streamline export procedures. A regional infrastructure bank could link up markets currently underserved by road networks.

Special Economic Zones: An Effective Way to Jumpstart Development

Establishing one or more special economic zones (SEZs) may allow some countries to bypass the dysfunction, corruption, or dearth of capacity that make these areas so unappealing to investors.

By suspending national tax and legal regimes within a small, clearly defined area and setting up an independent organization to exclusively manage operations and marketing, many states have successfully used SEZs to lure companies that otherwise would not dare venture within their territories. High-quality infrastructure (including electricity, roads, and customs services) and high-quality management of operations combine with lower tax rates to reduce costs and risks markedly. Workers benefit by having access to both more and better-paying jobs. SEZs do have their drawbacks. For instance, they may reduce national tax revenue, and they may starve other regions of the country's limited financial and managerial resources. Governments may use the establishment of an SEZ as an excuse to grab land from farmers at unfairly low prices or to give away land or tax benefits to companies with corrupt ties to local officials.

But many countries have benefitted from the introduction of SEZs, including Bangladesh, the United Arab Emirates, Kenya, Mauritius, Honduras, and Costa Rica. Even China was forced to adopt this policy early in its reform era to overcome foreign investors' suspicion of a country with a history of expropriating foreign assets, a void in terms of legal protections (or any functioning legal system), and an army of officials who had been educated to see most foreigners as enemies of the state. Tax-exemption schemes—relatively easy to implement compared with almost any other government reform—were used to compensate for any deficiencies in the investment environment or for any perceived risk that might discourage the first foreign investors the country would see in decades. In time, the SEZ model would be copied by hundreds of municipalities around the country, and its lessons so absorbed by local governments that eventually the concept became somewhat superfluous.

China's experience with SEZs has been so positive that it has begun to export the idea. In 2006, the Chinese government announced that it would support the establishment of as many as 50 overseas "economic and trade cooperation zones," many in poor countries. Of the first 19 zones approved as of 2010, 5 are in Sub-Saharan Africa: in Ethiopia, Mauritius, Nigeria (2), and Zambia.[24]

Aggressive steps in all these areas can lead to dramatic results. By simply providing businesses what they usually cannot find in India—less onerous labor laws, passable roads, reliable electricity, and effective bureaucracy—and by working hard to promote growth (including by establishing special economic zones), Gujarat has become the country's economic powerhouse. Containing one-twentieth of India's population, Gujarat produces one-sixth of India's industrial output and over one-fifth of its exports. In most parts of India, factories are hard to find. In Gujarat, manufacturing flourishes, soaking up rural labor in the process.[25]

Energizing the Rural Sector

One out of two people in the world live in urban areas, but three out of four *poor* people live in the countryside.[26] In part, because of this rural concentration, growth originating in agriculture is at least twice as effective in reducing poverty as growth originating in other economic sectors. In China, by far the biggest source of poverty reduction worldwide in recent decades, it has been well over three times as effective.[27] As Kanayo Nwanze, the president of the International Fund for Agricultural Development, explains:

> Agriculture is the main employer, job creator, and export in most developing countries. Historically, agriculture has driven economic performance in many countries. . . . Indeed, the vast majority of today's developed countries grew from strong agricultural foundations, where surplus production generated wealth and prosperity. . . . Poverty is predominantly rural. . . . A vibrant rural sector generates local demand for locally produced goods and services. In turn, this can spur sustainable non-farm employment growth in services, agro-processing, and small-scale manufacturing. This is crucial for rural employment.[28]

But the rural sector has been systemically neglected for decades in many countries. Elites in many countries are wedded to the notion that agriculture is inherently backward and an inappropriate basis for national development.[29] International aid agencies have accentuated this abandonment. U.S. funding for agricultural development, for instance, declined from about 20 percent of official development assistance in 1980 to around 5 percent in 2007.[30]

Empowering smallholders is especially important, because growing the incomes of peasant farmers will in many countries be the best way not only to directly reduce poverty but also to spur a much broader economic transformation. Sub-Saharan Africa has 80 million small (and mostly poor) farms, and the agricultural sector is responsible for 30 percent of the region's GDP and at least 40 percent of its exports. Reducing poverty in Sub-Saharan Africa is inconceivable without vastly enhancing the rural sector.

Despite sharing many of the same governance problems experienced by other poor states, Southeast Asian countries have grown rapidly for decades—a success story that began when those countries started focusing on developing their rural sectors. As Tracking Development, a research project that compares the development trajectories of Southeast Asia and Sub-Saharan Africa, concluded:

> Southeast Asian planners saw that the obvious way to address the problem of mass poverty, given that most of the population lived in the countryside and depended on agriculture, was by raising farm incomes. . . . The single most important distinction between Southeast Asian and African development strategies is that in Southeast Asia, macroeconomic stabilization has been paired with a concern for "shared growth" through agricultural and rural development. Southeast Asian government spending tends to show a pronounced "rural bias". . . . Industrialization was more a result than a cause of the initial developmental turning point. The typical sequence of events, most clearly distinct in the Indonesian case, is that growth first takes place in the agricultural sector, followed by an initial reduction of poverty, and only then by the development of export-oriented manufacturing.[31]

This rural bias is clear from spending patterns. Malaysia, for instance, spent one quarter of its national development budget—almost ten times its expenditure on industrial development—on agriculture in the 1970s, despite already having made substantial progress in developing its industrial sector.

Southeast Asian governments sought to supplement, not replace the market. They built irrigation systems, developed and distributed improved rice varieties, subsidized fertilizers and insecticides, and subsidized credit. The result was a process that was initiated by the state, mediated by the market, and directed at the smallholder.[32]

One of the most underappreciated elements of the Chinese economic miracle is the important role rural areas have played in the country's remarkable development. Reform started in the countryside. Investment capital for the first stream of industrial enterprises came from farm profits. And many of the country's most successful private manufacturing firms are based in relatively backward, predominantly agricultural areas.

The Hope Group, one of China's most important private businesses, started as a breeding farm raising quail and chickens in rural Sichuan in the western part of the country. Four brothers, who sold their bicycles, watches, and other possessions to raise the RMB 1000 to get started (worth $528 in 1982), are now among the richest people in China.[33] Their animal-feed factories provide a good, steady income to tens of thousands of workers.[34] Huanyuan, China's largest air conditioner maker, is located in the agricultural province of Hunan. And China's most promising automobile exporter, Chery, comes not from Shanghai but from the agricultural hinterland of Anhui province.[35]

Zhejiang province, poor and deeply agrarian as recently as the 1970s, is now home to half of China's largest private-sector firms. It is also far richer, having seen its GDP per capita climb over 100 times since 1978, the highest rate in the country.[36] In contrast, the most important cities in China—Beijing, Shanghai, and Tianjin—have very few of the country's successful manufacturing corporate giants. Despite having more educated people, larger local markets, stronger linkages to export markets, and higher incomes, they have proven to be less successful at producing successful companies in the most competitive manufacturing sectors. Much of the Chinese miracle is thus based on these rural enterprises, which have spurred the country's incredible export prowess, producing tens of millions of jobs for the poor and raising incomes across China in the process.[37]

Although there are many reasons for this puzzling outcome, two stand out as highly relevant for all developing countries. First, China invested heavily in the health and education of its rural areas throughout the 1950, 1960s, and 1970s, putting its rural citizens into a position to take advantage of reforms when they were launched in the late 1970s. Second, regional and local governments were very supportive from early on, helping the more promising small enterprises gain access to funding when money was scarce and ensuring easy access to larger markets by providing contacts, infrastructure improvements, and resources such as land and training. Risks were limited. Costs were manageable. Both highly skilled specialists and a well-educated workforce were readily available. Over time, the more successful small companies blossomed into successful large companies.

Sadly, such far-sighted government intervention has been conspicuously absent from most parts of the developing world. For instance, while Suharto was devoting almost one-third of Indonesia's development budget to agriculture, Nigeria spent only 6 percent of its development funds on agriculture. Nigerian state planners instead chose to focus their oil windfall on ill-conceived heavy industrial projects. African and Latin American countries spend far less than Asian countries on both agriculture and transportation even today.[38] Farmers and other rural workers are greatly disadvantaged, as the example in the box shows.

As a rule of thumb, say the authors of Tracking Development, poor countries should allocate at least 10 percent of total public spending and 20 percent of the public capital investment to the agricultural sector. They should spend this money not only on tangible improvements to the land such as irrigation and drainage but also on research and credit and replanting subsidies.[39] (African governments have recognized—at least on paper—the need: they committed at the African Union Summit in 2003 to increase public spending on agriculture to at least 10 percent of budgets by 2008. But only six countries stand out as having achieved this figure.[40])

Giving agriculture a boost will be a shot in the arm for agro-based SMEs. Brazil, a food importer four decades ago, has evolved in recent years into an agro-business powerhouse, thanks in part to the country investing over many years in agricultural research, which helped several of Brazil's SMEs evolve into large corporations that employ many people.[41] Africa also has some notable SME successes in the agricultural sector: Ethiopia has developed cut flower exports; Uganda, organic produce; Kenya and Côte d'Ivoire, horticulture; and Mali, cotton.[42]

Bayam Sellam in Cameroon

Bayam Sellam (a locally produced phrase coined from the English "buy and sell") is the name given to poor people who buy foodstuff from markets and plantations to resell in nearby or distant urban centers. It is an important source of income for many underprivileged people in Cameroon, but especially for women, who have few options to overcome the discrimination they suffer at the hands of men. The women mainly operate individually and, because of their family responsibilities, social status, and limited capital, cannot stay away from home for long.

But getting to urban areas is difficult. Many of the roads connecting farms to markets are narrow and unpaved and very slippery in the rainy season. The vehicles that bounce along those roads—"Dynas" (pickups), "DX" (farm taxis), and motorcycles—are unregulated and can be dangerous for women traveling alone. Accidents are common. So are robberies. And the women run the all too real risk of being raped and contracting AIDS.[43]

Helping SMEs Expand

Helping entrepreneurs start and grow businesses is crucial for job creation and fostering a more balanced distribution of wealth. Although steps to help micro businesses and household enterprises are important to boosting the incomes of poor people, the potential of SMEs (which includes those microenterprises that have expanded to qualify as SMEs) to contribute to overall growth, productivity, innovation, stable employment, and the building of a resilient and diversified economy is much greater.

Micro enterprises face many of the same problems as poor individuals. SMEs, however, face a completely different set of challenges. Microfinance, for instance, may be very helpful for micro entrepreneurs, but it can rarely provide the type of capital SMEs need to expand. While a simple set of skills may be enough to run a company with just one or a handful of employees, managing dozens of people requires more sophisticated knowledge about accounting systems, human resource policies, and marketing strategies.

Entrepreneurs in developing countries would seem to have a vast array of business opportunities—from fisheries to food processing, jewelry to furniture, data entry to tourism. But all too often those entrepreneurs quickly discover that what African telecom magnate Mo Ibrahim says is true: governments restrict rather than encourage business.

> Our governments are obsessed with control. They love to control everything. Whatever stage of [business] you want to do, there is always red tape, papers and then you have to sign [documents]. . . . People try to find a way to stop you doing anything. Honestly. I am not joking. It is terrible. It is very difficult to hire or fire people. . . . That is why many businesses shun the formal economy.[44]

If SMEs are to prosper, their governments must embrace a completely different mind-set. Governments need to make it easier, not harder, to run a business. Tens of millions of people have started a company in China in the last three decades precisely because they believed the business environment would reward them for doing so.[45] Improving infrastructure and taking steps to reduce the risks and costs of operating a company, as discussed above, is vital. So, too, is removing whatever red tape slows down or limits the birth and growth of dynamic companies—or that delays the death of outmoded or inefficient companies. Reducing entry requirements into markets—such as land-use restrictions, start-up costs, and extra licenses—will encourage more companies to leave the shadow economy and enter the formal economy. Reducing barriers to cooperating with other companies—the all-important linkages mentioned above—allows firms to specialize, grow, and extend their reach, while encouraging the expansion of clusters of businesses that complement and support each other.

If companies are to grow, they also need a web of supporting institutions to reduce the costs and risks of expanding. More reliable information providers help determine which suppliers, customers, and employees are worth pursuing. Employment bureaus or apprentice programs help locate potential employees.

Professional accountants and lawyers reduce corruption, improve the validity of contracts, and enhance the quality of management. Business training—which need not be expensive—helps executives maintain or upgrade the quality of their operations.

Financial institutions are especially important if small-scale manufacturing, farming, and services firms are to get the capital needed to grow. But whereas micro enterprises and poor individuals may have microfinance options and large companies and wealthy individuals have large banks to turn to, SMEs are often left with no ready supplier of capital. The development of a series of small banks with deep roots in local communities could fill this crucial financing gap. "Small local banks," explains Justin Yifu Lin, chief economist of the World Bank as of 2011,

> are the best entities for providing financial services to the enterprises and households that are most important in terms of comparative advantage—be they asparagus farmers in Peru, cut-flower companies in Kenya or garment factories in Bangladesh. . . . To make sustained progress in lifting the weight of the extreme poverty that will remain after the crisis has subsided, low-income countries need to make their financial institutions small and simple.[46]

Instead of focusing on "modern" reforms that will yield stock exchanges and sophisticated financial products—as often advocated by governments, elites, and international donors—developing economies should get the fundamentals of finance right. Nurturing a series of small, efficient, well-managed, well-capitalized banks offers the best hope to get financing to where it is most needed. As companies expand or develop more sophisticated needs, these small banks will do so too, or the larger banks will supplement their services. Regulation is key, especially to ensure that underachieving banks, large or small, are rooted out and forced to liquidate or merge with a stronger player.[47] This depends on a robust finance ministry, which is much easier to create than most parts of government because it can depend on a relatively small number of people.

Taiwan, which developed the most robust SME sector among East Asian countries, has historically had a large number of relatively small banks. The country proved more resilient than its neighbors during the 1997 financial crisis because the structure of its economy and financial system created more flexibility to deal with rapid changes in the environment. Even the United States depended on local banks during the first few decades of its industrial development; important roles for stock exchanges and national banks came much later.

Increasing access to wealthy members of diasporas and to "angel" investment networks (where private individuals seek out or pool their money to invest in small companies with high potential) can also help. Establishing new associations of investors, new forums in which entrepreneurs can present their ideas, and new organizations for business owners can quicken the growth of promising companies. Kinship groups can also play an important financing role, as they have for many small Asian start-ups. Nine of ten people in Wenzhou—arguably China's most dynamic city—and almost six out of ten of its enterprises have borrowed money outside the banking system.[48]

Governments need to stop trying to control everything, but they also need to step in to ensure that these institutional gaps are filled and to facilitate the operation of markets (see the box "The Role of the State in Market Development"). Developing countries have many more institutional voids and market failures than rich countries and often require the state to play a stronger role until development is well under way.

The Role of the State in Market Development

The more robust a state apparatus is, the more likely it will be able to ensure sufficient security and the rule of law (and other public services) to attract investment. But government often has to do more than just provide an environment attractive to businesspeople to ensure a country can expand its agricultural sector, produce more sophisticated goods for export, and expand the proportion of its population that can contribute to growth.

Although there are some notable exceptions (such as Hong Kong, which has thrived with a laissez-faire government), in many of the more successful developing countries, the state played a crucial role as an enabler and catalyst of economic activity. As discussed above, intervention to encourage rural growth has been essential to expanding agriculture and integrating peasant farmers into the broader economy (and raising their incomes) across much of Asia. Many late-developing countries may face significant obstacles if they depend purely on the market to attract the investment and technology necessary to jumpstart their manufacturing sectors, given the advantages other countries already have.[49]

Justin Yifu Lin points out that governments have sometimes played an important role in identifying growth sectors and investing in the facilitating infrastructure, research, training, and tax changes necessary to attract investment or nurture local companies able to compete internationally.[50] In some cases, governments have also accelerated the transfer of resources from nonproductive to productive sectors and increased the incentives for the adoption of technology and other productivity enhancements, enhancing growth in the process.[51] Selecting emerging winners (both in terms of types of industry and individual companies) and helping them expand faster is easier than trying to create winners from scratch.[52]

A number of countries have achieved great success with some variation of this approach, including a number of Middle Eastern countries in the energy sector and a wide range of Asian countries in manufacturing. Chile has used this approach to diversify its economy and boost exports. Mauritius started off by targeting labor-intensive industries such as textiles and garments. States such as Singapore have even made such policies the dominant force behind their economies.

But not all countries are capable of implementing this approach. To be successful, states must have sufficient government capacity—usually in the form of a highly technocratic core group of officials backed by a decent amount of implementation capacity. And those officials must be shielded from interfering politicians. In the absence of such resources, funds targeted for some useful purpose are likely to be siphoned off to serve private interests. There is a long list of countries, especially in Africa and Latin America, that attempted to develop local industry in the 1960s and 1970s through strong government intervention and that instead produced a large number of uncompetitive companies and white elephant projects. If governments are unable to intervene competently and judiciously, they should limit their role to a few core elements (as discussed in chapter 8).

Increasing the Skills and Flexibility of Workers and Managers

Many developing countries—including many African states, India to some extent, and some Latin America states—have actually produced significant growth in recent years but have not seen this accompanied by a parallel increase in jobs.[53] Jobless growth has myriad causes, but the fact that workers are not worth hiring because, with poor education and few skills, they cost more than they can produce discourages companies from expanding their payrolls. Enhancing the skills and knowledge of workers is crucial to boosting their ability to find and to keep well-paying jobs.

Business owners and white-collar staff need better education, too, if they are to reduce business costs, target new markets, and expand their companies. Schools that teach sales, marketing, finance, accounting, exporting, the law, human resources, and management can improve productivity across an economy. Most developing countries, however, do not have quality education institutions that can teach these skills. According to the Africa Management Initiative, "Fewer than 10 African [business schools] measure up to international standards." Just two of these exist in Sub-Saharan Africa outside of South Africa.[54] The Middle East, Central Asia, and, to a lesser extent, South Asia are similarly deficient. Making the development of a skilled workforce and set of managers a high priority—as Singapore and South Korea have done—is essential to growth, job creation, and income increases.

Unfortunately, many developing countries have not prioritized business and technical education. While the global economy demands growing numbers of engineers, scientists, and technicians, 57 percent of Latin American college students are pursuing social science degrees; only 16 percent are studying engineering or technology. The Pulitzer Prize–winning author Andres Oppenheimer, who was born in Argentina, complains, "While Asians and Eastern Europeans are creating increasingly highly skilled labor forces, most Latin American countries have barely modified their outdated education systems."[55] And there are few opportunities for adults to upgrade their skills.

The poor, of course, are unlikely to be able to afford to go to college, but they certainly could benefit from apprenticeship programs and vocational schooling that includes work placement or small company start-up assistance.[56] These programs could teach useful trades such as carpentry or masonry, plumbing or tailoring, horticulture or draftsmanship; many would not require substantial funding. In most poor countries, however, few students get the chance to benefit from technical and vocational education and training. Few children go to secondary school in the developing world, and among that small group only 1 in every 40 receives vocational training. The comparable figure for the developed world is 1 in 5.[57]

The Malaysian government has strongly promoted human resource development for many decades, including vocational and technical training. The Ministry of Education oversees technical and vocational programs adapted to meet the needs of companies, especially manufacturers, and attended by tens of thousands of students. The Ministry of Human Resources provides pre-employment industrial skills training programs to new graduates, and advanced skills training programs to workers who need to upgrade their skills. The Ministry of Entrepreneur Development offers various programs on social advancement and commercial and industrial activities, especially in rural areas. The Ministry of Youth and Sports gives work and vocational training to young school leavers. Meanwhile, a national skills certification system certifies qualifications, making it easier for workers to find jobs and for companies to find qualified workers. Foreign companies, which make up a large share of the industrial base, are required to give their employees technical training.[58]

Simultaneously with boosting educational levels and skills, governments should do everything they can to reduce what it costs a company (in addition to its wage bill) to employ workers. Making it cheaper for companies to expand their workforces will create more jobs for those who need them. Taxes on firms that are meant to fund social benefits to employees drive many firms into the informal economy, where they can evade paying taxes at the same time as they ignore laws governing working conditions (if a government is going to increase social benefits, it should find other sources of revenue, such as taxes on consumption or energy). And where governments are weak (and known for their corruption), lots of regulations create perverse incentives for both officials and managers at firms. Many countries have dual labor markets: a formal market, which is often stagnant or shrinking, and an informal one, which often thrives. In Brazil, for instance, about half of the workforce is informally employed. In Africa, the proportion is typically far higher. Such conditions do not benefit the majority of populations, especially the great numbers of poor people not fortunate enough to have jobs in the first place.

The solution is not to stop protecting and insuring workers but to calibrate labor taxes and labor laws to the local environment. Workers need protection from discrimination and exploitation and, if a country can afford it, pensions and insurance against layoffs and long-term injury. But it is pointless to introduce labor laws and taxes that companies cannot afford to observe—because observing them would make a company uncompetitive—and governments are too weak to enforce competently. Such legislation and taxation discourages companies from expanding and often drives them into the informal economy, where they usually stay small and out of the reach of officials (thus making the laws useless). Two authors who have studied the impact of employment laws in developing countries have concluded:

> Developing countries with rigid labor regulation tend to have larger informal sectors and higher unemployment, especially among young workers. Some studies also find that rigid labor regulation results in an increase in urban poverty, fewer business start-ups, foregone benefits from other . . . reforms, and female unemployment.[59]

A sudden shift in a developing country from little or no regulation of workplace conditions to, say, the kind of level of regulation encountered in some Western European countries would do the workers in that developing country no favors. Their employers either would simply ignore the new slate of regulations, safe in the knowledge that the government lacks the capacity to enforce them, or would go out of business trying to respect regulations that their competitors ignore. Fundamental protections must be given to all workers—the kinds of protections embodied in the International Labor Organization's "core conventions," which outlaw child labor and forced labor, give workers the right to form trade unions, and call for employees doing the same work to be paid the same wage. More extensive regulations, however, should be introduced gradually and incrementally, at a pace that does not exceed the local capacity to respect and enforce them.

Labor market reform to boost employment has yielded marked reductions in unemployment in the past decade, even in wealthy countries such as Germany, the Netherlands, and Denmark. In recent years, developing countries as diverse as Colombia, Peru, Burkina Faso, Senegal, Azerbaijan, and Georgia have learned from this experience, shifting to a more flexible regime that, for instance, makes it easier to hire workers on a part-time basis. Colombia, which started reforming way back in 1990, has reduced unemployment and increased productivity as a result.[60]

*   *   *

Businesses can easily become a corrupting or exploiting force, especially when governments are too weak to stand up for their country's interests or to devise and enforce a set of regulations in their people's interests. Given the chance, many companies will rig markets, mistreat employees, pollute the environment, and evade taxes. In conflict zones, they may even play a role in promoting or prolonging violence (by, for instance, buying valuable minerals such as diamonds from rebel groups). But only businesses can create the jobs and wealth necessary to reduce poverty and empower the poor. And they can play a key role in importing know-how, strengthening economies, and holding politicians to account. The question for a leader seeking to develop his or her country's economy and society is not whether businesses have a role to play in achieving that goal, but how to maximize that role.

Governments Can't Do It Alone

Expanding markets is crucial to empowering the poor, as are reshaping all the macro and micro factors considered in the past several chapters: the attitudes of elites; the implementation capacity of states; the structure of governments; and the collection of livelihood factors each person has access to.

But we cannot expect the governments of the developing world, by themselves, to accomplish this formidable task. Why not? Because, apart from the fact that many in the elites don't want to empower the poor because they fear that doing so will strip them of some of their wealth, power, and status, even "enlightened" leaders have to contend with corrupt administrations, with corrupt and divided societies, with a dearth of resources and expertise, and with a host of other problems, large and small.

If the governments of the developing world are to empower the poor, they need help doing so. In particular, they need help from actors who possess what their own administrations usually lack: a commitment to change, an insight into how change can be created, and a capacity to deliver. In the next two chapters, we look at two sources of such help, individuals and organizations within poor societies, and foreign aid.

PART III

A Plan of Action

CHAPTER 12

Leading Change from Within

B RAC, the largest NGO in the world, shows what one person with a clear vision and keen mind can do to empower the poor and contribute to the transformation of a society. Established in 1972 to provide humanitarian relief to the tens of millions of Bangladeshis suffering in the aftermath of the war of independence (and thus originally called the Bangladesh Rehabilitation Assistance Committee), it has evolved into one of the largest promoters of development worldwide.

Founded by Fazle Hasan Abed, a British-educated former Shell accountant from a distinguished Bangladeshi family, BRAC is huge by any measure. And it is larger, more effective, and more transformational than any development organization based in the West, at least partly because it has been able to use its firsthand knowledge about the places where it operates to improve the quality of the programs it runs.

Focusing on the promotion of self-employment and human development among the poor, BRAC works in some 65,000 villages and over 4,300 urban slums in every district of Bangladesh. BRAC employs 37,000 full-time staff, over 53,000 part-time teachers, and tens of thousands of poultry and community health and nutrition workers and volunteers. Its microfinance operation disburses $1 billion a year. Its schools educate almost a million students (more than one-tenth of the country's children are enrolled in BRAC's primary schools). It also runs a university, feed mills, chicken farms, tea plantations, packaging factories, a bank, a printing company, an internet service provider, and the country's largest cold storage company. BRAC's organizational capacity rivals that of any private company in Bangladesh, and BRAC easily outperforms the government in many ways.

Two things separate BRAC from the great majority of other actors in the development field. First, as the *Economist* highlighted in a 2010 article, it is run like a business. From the beginning, it has tried hard to be self-funding, halting any activity that required continuous subsidies. Today, the organization earns about four-fifths of the money it disburses to the poor from its own operations, an exceptionally high amount. BRAC emphasizes research and learning far more than just about any other organization in the field and has never been afraid to admit a mistake, change direction, or try something new. It also has been unusually aware of the need to create scale to have a large impact. According to one of BRAC's unofficial mottoes, "Small may be beautiful, but big is necessary."

Second, it takes the "social context of poverty" seriously. Whereas most big donors see poverty as an economic problem that money can solve, BRAC has long recognized that structural factors also play an important role. In these circumstances, the rich are much more likely to benefit from growth than the poor. Efforts to help the poor must therefore take into account context and focus on well-targeted programming that can literally change society.

Women are a major focus of BRAC's initiatives because they have the lowest status in society and are most in need of help. Small companies receive a lot of loans and training, because they create jobs and wealth and help reshape society from the bottom up.

The organization has been so successful at home that it is now expanding across the developing world. BRAC is the largest NGO in Afghanistan, Tanzania, and Uganda and operates in places such as Haiti, Liberia, Pakistan, and South Sudan. Coming from a poor, Muslim country has helped BRAC better understand the problems of development, while making sure it is more adaptable to local environments, less expensive to operate (no one in BRAC drives an SUV), and less condescending than its rich-world counterparts.[1]

But BRAC is not alone. Companies, NGOs, and other types of organizations from developing countries are playing a larger and larger role in transforming lives and societies. The political leaders of countries are best placed to make the biggest impact, but anyone who belongs to a country's political and social elite or has good contacts with it can, if they are determined, help shape the futures of their fellow citizens.

Members of the elite who can leverage their knowledge, resources, and contacts (as Abed has) can make a substantial impact. Compared with most foreigners, they have a better understanding of the problems their countries face. Compared with most of their compatriots, they have more management know-how, more money, and more access to those in power. They may be able to take advantage of international assistance and use their personal relationships to press for change in a way others may not. But before we examine what individuals and groups can do, let's remind ourselves of the nature of the relationship between power and poverty, so we can judge what types of programs are likely to have the largest impact.

Power and Poverty

The use—and misuse—of power lies at the heart of a country's willingness and ability to empower its poor citizens. Who controls government, what interests prevail in the political arena, and what pressure society can exert on its leaders all strongly influence the policies that states adopt. If one wants to help the poor over the long term, one needs to reshape the power relationships that have left the poor structurally disadvantaged within their own societies.

As this book has made plain, the poor suffer from a combination of social exclusion and poor incorporation that limits their ability to fully participate in social, economic, and political life. A lack of education limits their ability to seek out the best jobs. A lack of access to savings and loan schemes limits their ability to take risks, embrace new technology, and expand their businesses. A lack of personal ties to well-placed officials limits their ability to receive government services, secure property rights, and fight discrimination.

Individual schemes that tackle these issues—such as those outlined in part II of this book—help the poor but cannot really empower them in the short term, given the multifaceted nature of the challenges they face. Only a sustained and comprehensive campaign that affects multiple areas of economic, political, and social life can reshape the power dynamics of a country sufficiently to enable the poor to compete on an equal footing with other members of their societies.

Creating better-integrated societies may take a very long time to accomplish, especially if the disadvantages the poor face are the product of not merely decades but centuries of social exclusion, as is the case in much of Latin America. Enlightened leaders can speed up the process, however. Brazil is a case in point. Since Fernando Henrique Cardoso's administration took office in the mid-1990s, Brazil has adopted the most inclusive policies in its history, substantially reducing poverty and inequity across the country in the process and giving many more poor people access to opportunity.

As the example of Brazil also shows, efforts will be most successful when they operate at both the macro and micro levels in ways that complement and reinforce change on both. At the macro level, this means finding ways to fundamentally reorient the relationship between those inside and outside the power structure, so that those on the inside feel either an obligation or a need to help those on the outside. The three tools discussed in chapter 7—social cohesion, an inclusive pro-development ideology, and incentives—are crucial to changing elite attitudes.

Research by the Institute of Development Studies (IDS) on social accountability and the role of public-private networks has shown the importance of developing linkages between reformers and power brokers. Such links give reformers the chance of persuading power brokers that reform will benefit them in some way. In contrast, civil society organizations and social movements that are completely disconnected from power structures are unlikely to be able to influence elites to change direction.[2]

Building broad alliances that cross the public-private divide and that bring together a wide range of actors with common interests in reform is critical to change at the macro level. In China in recent decades, local governments and businesses have consistently worked together to promote reform and growth. Such ties—often informal, and sometimes even covert—were crucial to jumpstarting reform in the 1980s, when Chinese law offered scant protection for property rights and profits.

At the micro level, the power necessary for communities, families, and individuals to participate fully in a society depends on their ability to accumulate a broad range of assets: human, social, financial, and physical assets (as discussed in chapter 10).[3] The more of these assets that the poor have, the more they will be able to build up their economic resources and political power, challenge existing social structures, and incorporate themselves into all aspects of economic, social, and political life. Self-interested elites have a much harder time dictating how communities, regions, and states are governed—and how equitable markets and governments will be—when everyone has a certain minimum collection of these assets.

The goal should be a society in which all individuals and all groups—regardless of ethnicity, religion, caste, clan, gender, or income level—participate on an even playing field. Equality of opportunity will always be elusive, but there are many steps that can reduce the deep inequalities that hold back the poor.

Linking up action at the micro and the macro levels means that the existing inequitable power structure will be pressured from below while it is also pushed from within (see figure 12.1). These impetuses will reinforce each other and gradually refashion the existing political structure. They will also feed into a virtuous cycle, with greater opportunity producing more equitable markets, which will generate more growth, which in turn will yield greater opportunity (as discussed in chapter 5). And changes in the economic sphere will feed into

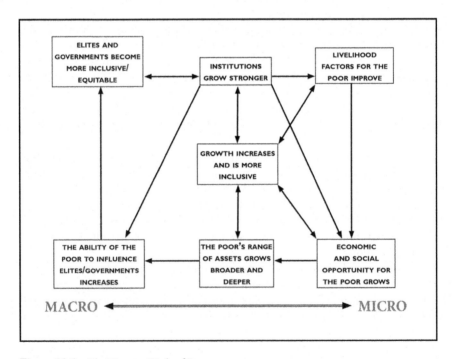

Figure 12.1 The Virtuous Circle of Empowerment

changes in the political and social spheres and vice versa. Greater wealth among the lower classes will promote social change, greater political and social integration, and greater empowerment. The whole process will, in turn, lead to better governance, stronger institutions, and a more equitable distribution of opportunity and eventually wealth.

Organizations that unite large groups of poor people can exert significant influence at both the micro and the macro levels. They can press for greater access to financial tools, housing, and education at the micro level. And, if they are sufficiently politically adroit, they can make institutions and powerful actors more responsive at the macro level.

Taxes and Accountability

Taxes can play an important role in shaping the power dynamics of a country when they make government officials more accountable to a country's citizens (or at least to its important economic actors). Indeed, taxes ought to be a powerful tool with which citizens can shape the behavior of their leaders.

Western Europe's history of state building shows how state-society bargaining over taxes strengthened government capacity, accountability, and responsiveness. The need to raise revenue to fight wars forced leaders to cede power to those who paid taxes and to provide more services (such as better public security, more equitable courts, and stronger property rights) to the societies they ruled.

Today, however, alternative sources of revenue—most notably, natural resources and foreign aid—interfere with this dynamic in most developing countries. Leaders do not need to bargain with their citizenry if they can export oil or extract money from a former colonizer. Nevertheless, even in relatively authoritarian regimes, governments are more likely to take into account the opinions of those they govern when those governments depend on tax revenue to support themselves. As *An Upside View of Governance* observes:

> The contemporary experience of Ghana, Kenya and Ethiopia provides clear evidence of a broad causal mechanism linking government reliance on taxation with pressures for increased responsiveness and accountability. Within this broad mechanism, three more specific causal processes were identified:
>
> i. direct tax bargaining with citizens, which led to particular episodes of political reform;
> ii. tax resistance by citizens in response to unpopular governments, which created more indirect pressures for change and subsequent reform;
> iii. taxation as a catalyst for strengthening civil society organisations, and encouraging mobilisation around broader common interests.[4]

Although some taxpayers may instinctively disagree, their interests (in terms of having an accountable government) are served by an efficient tax-collection apparatus, not by an incompetent or impotent one. Initiatives that enhance tax administration, improve tax compliance, broaden the tax base (for instance, by introducing property taxes), lessen dependence on foreign aid, and increase the transparency and consistency of tax collection actually make governments more dependent on their citizens. So, too, does the creation of forums (such as business associations) in which major tax-payers can work together to promote reforms.

Social, Business, and Political "Entrepreneurs" Lead the Way

Many individuals and organizations—some not even in the traditional development field—have played major roles in creating social and political change across the developing world. Like Abed and BRAC, they are deeply enmeshed within their societies, understand the value of good management, make wise use of people, take a very long-term perspective, are not afraid to innovate, and recognize the scale of the challenges they face.

Although the individuals who can make large impacts are not limited by age, gender, education, or location, most are well educated, relatively young, live in urban areas, and come from the elite. But there are plenty who just bring street smarts, an idea, and lots of energy, or are older, or who live in smaller villages and towns. What sets them apart are their *entrepreneurial* instincts and zeal—their determination to make a break with the past, their creativity, and their acute sense of what is possible given the many constraints they face.

In some cases, these individuals (often known as "social entrepreneurs" no matter what field they work in) are former members of a diaspora who chose to leave their adopted countries and bring their knowledge home to contribute directly to its political transformation. As Liberia's president Ellen Johnson Sirleaf—who returned home after her country's civil war—declared in her 2006 inaugural address, "We have hundreds of doctors, engineers, and economists, as well as thousands of teachers, nurses, professors, and other Liberians who possess specialized skills currently living abroad. I re-echo my appeal to all of you to please come home!! Please make the sacrifice, for your country needs you and needs you now!!!"[5]

How, exactly, can social, business, and political entrepreneurs reshape their societies? The rest of this chapter examines five of the most effective approaches.

Building Links and Coalitions That Can Promote Reform

As discussed in chapter 7, politics plays an extraordinarily important role in determining how inclusive and pro-poor governments are. Ideally, reform-minded leaders or coalitions will promote inclusive development at both the national and local levels. But when they do not, nonstate actors have many ways to persuade them to reconsider.

Bottom-up change typically occurs when groups representing the poor or middle classes can take advantage of—and work to expand—the opportunities for engagement with the existing political system to press for reform. Enhancing the ability of organizations working on behalf of the poor to talk to and work with state actors (government leaders, ministry officials, and so forth) is thus an important task for reform-minded entrepreneurs. So, too, is building ties between those organizations and powerful political, social, and economic interests (e.g., political parties, business leaders).

Working within existing social networks that rely chiefly on the power of relationships, mutual obligations, and persuasion has generally proven to be more successful in promoting change—especially in less developed countries—than any attempt to create entirely new mass social movements that are isolated from the sources of power and try to threaten or bludgeon elites to reform. As the 2010 IDS report *An Upside View of Governance* concluded:

> Collective action that benefits poor people does not arise automatically from strengthening civil society organizations—existing networks of actors will greatly influence whether (or how) strengthening particular organisations translates into greater capacity to shape policy, and on whose behalf. . . . Facilitating the formation of linkages between existing actors, and between them and agents of the state, may be particularly important.[6]

In countries with established democracies, this means working through political parties, unions, and well-established social groups that can leverage large numbers of people and have ready access to the corridors of power. But in countries with weak institutions and divided populations, would-be reformers often have to create or at least expand organizations that can bring together large and diverse groups of people—most of which are isolated from one another and excluded from political power—and then create mechanisms for them to strengthen ties with the powerful social networks that determine policy.

In Indonesia, the Kecamatan Development Project (KDP), which operates in 28,000 villages across the archipelago, helps the poor organize politically and press for a bigger share of public funding. By creating new institutions and new ways to work with politically influential groups and individuals, KDP has helped the poor develop enough political power to establish schools and medical clinics. In the process, the poor also build self-confidence and the means to permanently protect their interests.[7]

Indigenous groups in many South American countries (such as Bolivia and Ecuador) have substantially increased their political power by building strong political organizations—around existing social groups—that can win elections and influence elite policies. The Confederation of Indigenous Nationalities of Ecuador, for instance, has helped indigenous people win several county mayorships and gain a number of ministerial positions. More public money is now flowing to indigenous areas, and traditional identities and culture are playing a more prominent role in the public arena. Power relationships are far more equitable—and indigenous peoples are much more able to participate in the economic and political arena—than was the case just a generation ago.[8] In Bolivia, a similar process helped Evo Morales become Latin America's first indigenous national leader.

Well-organized groups that have close links to officials are—not surprisingly—particularly well placed to influence policy. In São Paulo, for instance, Sanitarista, a well-established health network, has been able to influence a succession of government health-care reforms because of its strength and access to decision makers at both the national and local levels. Medical professionals from Sanitarista are both well organized and have multiple links with policymakers at the national level, as well as those who implement policy at the local level.[9]

"Issue networks," which bring together a wide range of nongovernmental actors and policymakers around individual issues, can be especially potent. It is usually much easier to build enduring coalitions around a single common interest than to construct a movement with much broader goals. In India, a coalition that cut across class and caste and included laborers, farmers, journalists, bureaucrats, lawyers, and social activists created the Right to Information campaign that led to the passage of the Right to Information Act in 2004.[10] This legislation has helped actors outside government hold those in power accountable for their actions.

Even single-issue coalitions, however, are susceptible to factionalism, sectionalism, sectarianism, regionalism, localism, and all those other forms of parochialism that weaken the power of reformists. Factionalism is the enemy of reformers, not only because it undercuts their ability to unite diverse groups behind a common cause but also because it weakens the potency of their links with the people in power. The fragmented nature of many poor societies helps explain why the poor have such a hard time challenging those in power.

Harnessing the Power of Information

Establishing mechanisms that shed light on the performance of government complement these efforts to build coalitions. Greater awareness of how government actually functions gives everyone—from parents and workers to national leaders—a better chance of determining how it might function more effectively. Greater transparency in government also makes all officials (from chief ministers to judges, minor officials to police officers) more accountable and thus more likely to act fairly and efficiently.

One significant step in this direction is to give the public better access to information with which to judge the performance of those who govern them and who are supposed to serve them. After all, corruption and incompetence can easily be disguised as commendable public service under a thick veil of misinformation and can disappear from sight entirely in the absence of any information on government performance. The dearth of quantitative information in Africa has prompted the World Bank to talk of "Africa's statistical tragedy."[11]

The more the general public, watchdog groups, and top ministers (who often do not know how their subordinates actually behave) can monitor how budgets are spent, policies are determined and implemented, judges act, and public officials perform, the more likely they are to hold these officials accountable and demand better results. In Bangalore, for instance, citizen report cards have been used to tally public opinion of the providers of various services. Publishing the results in the local media has shamed or otherwise inspired those providers to do a much better job (as subsequent report cards have testified).[12]

Another way of improving how the state operates is to create and strengthen NGOs capable of analyzing relevant information. Such organizations (budget watchdogs, think tanks, academic research institutions, pressure groups, etc.) are most effective when they have both impressive internal resources, such as experienced staff and ample funding, and extensive external links with powerful political figures and groups. The Center for the Implementation of Public Policies Promoting Equity and Growth (CIPPEC) in Argentina, for instance, is so well respected and has such close ties with top officials that the latter often turn to it for analysis and recommendations on how to budget for social services. The Center for Democratic Development (CDD) in Ghana has such a strong reputation among important media that it was able to shape the public debate on how to make government education budgets more efficient during the 2008 presidential and parliamentary election campaigns. The Research Center of the University of the Pacific (CIUP) in Peru had the clout among politicians and experience working with the government to use the recommendations from a comprehensive study of national and regional education and health spending to improve the state's overall budgeting process.[13]

At their best, organizations such as these transform perceptions and upend debates about what governments should be doing. Pratham, an Indian organization started by Madhav Chavan, a chemical engineer who was educated in the United States, has transformed attitudes toward education among policymakers by simply providing much better information on what students are actually learning in schools. Pratham's Annual State of Education Report (ASER) evaluates learning outcomes in every one of the country's 600 districts—by testing 700,000 children. The results—much worse then anyone imagined—have generated so much news that the media, academia, government, and public all closely monitor their annual announcement. In fact, the methodology used—and Pratham's own efforts to fix the deficiencies exposed—have received so much attention that many school systems in India and from around the world (including from places such as Senegal and Mali) have sought to learn from them.[14]

Newspapers, radio, and television also have important roles to play in ensuring that information is disseminated to as wide an audience as possible and in checking that elites act according to the law and in the public interest. The media can, for instance, educate the public on their legal rights, on how they can make best use of government resources, and on how they can best seek equitable treatment from officials. In Brazil, auditing randomly selected municipalities (chosen in a television lottery) and making sure the results of the audit were widely disseminated through the Internet and other media made it harder for corrupt incumbents to get reelected and easier for honest incumbents to remain in office.[15]

Increasing the Ability of the Poor to Participate as Equals in Society

On a micro level, initiatives that help the poor gain a more complete collection of positive livelihood factors can help them participate in economic and political life as equals, and eventually challenge the status quo. (As explained in chapter 10, livelihood factors come in three types: opportunity enhancers, such as ownership of housing, savings, land, and other physical assets; risk reducers, such as access to affordable, reliable health-care providers; and connectors, such as access to transport links to dynamic economic centers. See table 10.1 for a more complete list.)

Although programs to help the poor that add individual ingredients (a vaccination program, for instance) to that collection are valuable, interventions that take a comprehensive approach to empowerment are especially effective. BRAC has developed an innovative program along these lines that takes advantage of its impressive administrative capacity, willingness to learn from experience, reputation (which helps attract funding), and deep understanding of local context. The Targeting the Ultra Poor (TUP) program starts from the premise that the extremely poor are unable to participate in normal economic and social activities because they either lack the necessary assets to engage or are socially excluded in some way. TUP then seeks to develop new and better livelihoods through a combination of promoting capabilities (e.g., by offering training in particular skills or grants to buy useful assets), reducing vulnerabilities (e.g., by providing monthly stipends or health programs), and addressing exclusionary forces that hold back people (e.g., by helping women become more autonomous).

TUP employs two broad strategies: it aims to "push down" development programs so that they reach the poorest people while seeking to "push out" programs so that they address dimensions of poverty that are typically ignored (such as low expectations). Selected households are targeted for a two-year investment program involving the transfer of an income-generating asset (such as chickens or a cow), training (to generate more income), social development (to build confidence and awareness of rights), and health services. Building links upward and fostering a supportive environment are crucial. The program recruits village-level elites to support the very poor rather than seeing them purely as obstacles. As the poor progress, a carefully sequenced set of programs helps them move farther out of poverty and institutionalizes their improved position within society so they are less likely to fall back in the future.[16]

India's SEWA (the Self-Employed Women's Association) was started by Ela Bhatt, a lawyer who has acquired the nickname "the mother of microfinance" and aims to empower women by increasing their incomes and self-reliance. Its one million members have organized over one hundred cooperatives to turn their collective efforts into enhanced economic security. Programs give members access to markets, create alternative employment opportunities, and establish institutions to provide services such as health care and insurance. A union helps members in over 70 trades fight for fair treatment, upgrade skills, and increase wages and benefits. SEWA Bank (the largest cooperative) gives members the ability to save and to borrow in small amounts and on reasonable terms, increasing their ability to build up assets. Various types of training and capacity-building develop leadership abilities, self-confidence, and life skills.[17]

The cumulative aim of all these programs is to empower women by giving them the financial independence, support networks, and skill sets to challenge existing social, political, and economic structures. Samuben Ujabhai, for example, participated in a SEWA program that trains women to grow seedlings and then finds them work. According to Samuben, "Now we do not have to beg to be taken as laborers on the fields of rich farmers of the village."[18]

Government officials can also play crucial roles by championing or personally introducing programs that take a comprehensive approach to empowerment. Santiago Levy, a former Boston University economics professor, transformed ideas about helping the poor worldwide when he introduced the first conditional cash transfer program (see chapter 10) as deputy minister in Mexico's Ministry of Finance between 1994 and 2000. Asked to restructure the country's complex system of distributing welfare to the poor, he looked for a way to link government pay outs to family commitments to enhancing human capital such that state assistance would both reduce poverty in the short term and create a healthier, better educated population that would no longer need help. This led to the creation of Progresa (later called Oportunidades), which was so successful that subsequent governments had no choice but to maintain and expand it. The concept has since spread all over the world.[19]

Highly cohesive social groups can combat discrimination by working together to develop their human and social capital. The Nadars, for example, are one of India's lower castes and have traditionally been consigned to making palm wine. Within two generations, however, many Nadars have become remarkably successful businesspeople by cooperating to build up the group's skills, financial resources, dignity, and self-reliance. They established business associations to pool their financial resources and fund their own entrepreneurs, created charities to help poor Nadar children go to school, and built their own temples to avoid religious discrimination. "We are supposed to be a backward community but we don't think of ourselves that way," says Nadar businessmen C. Manickavel, who went to one of the country's best engineering schools and now runs a million-dollar-a-year business designing e-books for big American publishers. "I make sure my daughter studies at the best school in Chennai. We are as good as anybody else."[20]

Promoting Social Change from the Corporate Sector

Businesses can promote social change in many ways. For example, by innovating, they can give the poor access to a much wider range of goods and services, and, by increasing the number or quality of jobs, they can help the poor build up their incomes and enter the middle class.

The private sector is especially well placed to help because it generates its own funding, can exert significant political influence, and often has the most robust organizational capacity in a country. It also can have a strong vested interest in promoting policies that enhance growth, stability, and incomes. This is not to say that all businesses promote positive change, as there are obviously many contrary examples. Many natural resource companies, for instance, have been only too happy to pay their royalties and operate in closed-off enclaves, with little regard for how their funds distort the political dynamics of the countries in which they operate. Many executives are all too happy to profit on the backs of the poor with little concern for how their factories treat their workers. But given the right leadership, businesses do have the tools, the resources, and sometimes the incentive to promote positive change in ways other actors do not.

Many executives in the developing world (as well as in the global headquarters of some multinationals) have recently rethought their attitudes toward the poor. Whereas business leaders previously tended to ignore those at the bottom of society, now companies realize that the billions of poor people around the world are an important, previously untapped market for their goods and services, as well as important drivers of growth and innovation. "Bottom of the pyramid" (BOP) oriented marketing, product innovation, and distribution has become a crucial component of many companies' strategies, immensely enhancing the well-being of many poor consumers around the world. The phrase "bottom of the pyramid" was coined by C. K. Prahalad in his widely esteemed book *The Fortune at the Bottom of the Pyramid*. The author, a professor at the University of Michigan's School of Business until his untimely death in 2010, explained in a 2005 interview:

> The development of markets and effective business models at the BOP can transform the poverty alleviation task from one of constant struggle with subsidies and aid to entrepreneurship and the generation of wealth. When the poor at the BOP are treated as consumers, they can reap the benefits of respect, choice, and self-esteem and have an opportunity to climb out of the poverty trap.[21]

The incredible spread of cellular phones across the developing world is probably the most prominent of the changes spawned by BOP thinking. Whereas technological innovation was once concentrated on products intended for the richest people, now it could be undertaken on behalf of the poor—and profitably. India alone is adding tens of millions of new users a month. Throughout Africa, cell phones are changing lives and expanding opportunities. For instance, Kenya's M-Pesa mobile cash system (see chapter 10) has revolutionized the kinds of services that phones can provide (such as greatly expanding access to financial services).

Various types of "frugal innovation" have created products and distribution systems to reach consumers previously left unserved. In India, for instance, entrepreneurs have developed a $200 portable bank branch, a $23 wood-burning stove that emits more heat and less smoke than alternatives, a $43 water-purification system, a $70 refrigerator that runs on batteries, and heart monitors and baby warmers one-tenth as expensive as those found in other countries. As Arindam

Bhattacharya, the managing director of the Boston Consulting Group in India, says, "These are not cheap knockoffs of Western products, they are in many cases very different products. Western companies have not often explored these segments so they are untapped markets."[22]

Companies can also play an important role lobbying for change or even stepping in to replace government in the provision of public services when states cannot do an adequate job. In Brazil, for instance, businesspeople created a partnership called Todos Pela Educação (Education for All) to push for improvements in schooling. They were dissatisfied with government performance in the education sector and saw its deficiencies as a major disadvantage for them compared to their Asian competitors. Founded by the presidents of the DPaschoal car parts chain; the steelmaker Gerdau Group; major banks Itaú, Bradesco, and Santander; and other business leaders, Todos Pela Educação established five goals for the country to attain by 2022 and set up a system to monitor progress. The group then convinced the owners of Brazil's biggest media groups as well as important journalists, academics, and artists to promote the importance of education. The twofold aim was to persuade parents that their children need a better education (less than half of Brazilian youngsters aged 19 have completed high school) and to lobby the government to enact change. The campaign resonated so strongly with the public that President Luiz Inácio Lula da Silva put together a similar initiative and presented it as his own government's creation. Lula set a completion date of 2021—one year ahead of Todos Pela Educação's target.[23]

Companies are also running schools, funding the development of new teaching methodologies, and improving school management. The Bradesco Foundation, the philanthropic arm of Brazil's second-largest bank, operates 40 schools with more than 51,000 students. These all have science labs, libraries, and well-furnished classrooms—none of which can be taken for granted within the country. There is no tuition, and students get books, supplies, meals, and uniforms for free. Teaching is highly valued, with constant training, research into teaching methods, and high salaries emphasized. Fernando Rossetti, the secretary general for the Group of Institutes, Foundations and Enterprises in Brazil, says that "thousands, maybe tens of thousands, of companies are involved. Brazil, as it globalizes and its economy becomes more sophisticated, needs a much more educated labor force."[24]

Businesses can have a major impact on poverty just by making investments that produce jobs for the poor and taxes for governments to spend on public services. And this impact can be intensified if companies can also form linkages with local suppliers, contribute to local infrastructure, and pressure governments to adopt better policies in the process.

Maquiladoras (export factories) in Mexico have traditionally been considered exploitative because they pay low salaries. But because the women who work there typically have not completed high school, the jobs on offer are much better than the alternatives in retail, restaurants, and the transportation sector. Work is more secure and pay is higher (albeit only because the hours are longer). And the stability the positions create can transform outlooks, with workers adopting a longer term perspective for their own lives and that of their families because they have more confidence in their futures and a greater sense of control over their lives. Children benefit immensely. One study showed that the mere presence of a maquiladora in the town where a mother lived when she was 16 years old substantially increased the heights of her children when compared to those born to similar mothers in places where no such factory existed.[25]

Companies run by individuals who are determined to make a difference in the lives of the poor can accomplish more than many not-for-profits, because while the latter have to fundraise to grow, companies can grow by reinvesting the profits they make. The Aga Khan Fund for Economic Development—an international organization with roots in the developing world and run by the Aga Khan—has self-consciously sought to acquire and use wealth ethically, promoting economic self-reliance among developing countries and their poorest people. It has avoided investing in booming China and instead concentrated on markets in Africa and Central Asia. In Uganda, the Aga Khan Fund owns the country's largest pharmaceutical company, a tannery, a bank, an insurance company, and a fish net factory. In Afghanistan, the fund started investing shortly after the Taliban was ejected from government, setting up the first five-star hotel in Kabul and a cellular phone company called Roshan. In total, the Aga Khan Fund owns 90 businesses across the developing world, which employ some 36,000 people.

The fund seeks to spur wider economic growth by its investments. The Ugandan net factory, for instance, is an attempt to seed a technology that did not exist locally in order to create an industry that did not previously exist. Mahmood Ahmed, the Aga Khan Fund's representative in Uganda, says, "We can take a decision like this because we think long term. We won't enter a business without the promise of profit, but we have more considerations than profit."[26]

Since the end of Mozambique's civil war in the early 1990s, the Mozambique Leaf Tobacco Company (MLTC) has extended its supply network to include 125,000 growers, transforming as many as 1 million lives in the process. Backed by 500 technicians on motorbikes (out of a workforce of over 5,000) who ride around the country advising on the use of fertilizer and other farming techniques, farmers who used to be operating on a subsistence basis now earn $400 each annually. The company exported $154 million worth of goods in 2008.

Conscious of its reputation and relationships with the farmers, MLTC has taken its responsibility to the communities in which it works seriously. The company is involved in malaria spraying programs and builds infrastructure such as schools, bridges, and clinics. These steps have spurred local people to invest more heavily in various agribusinesses and in transportation infrastructure, as the profitability of these have risen as a result.[27]

Enhancing Key Institutions

Another way in which entrepreneurs—not just business entrepreneurs but also the political and social varieties—can have a major impact is to improve the institutions that underpin vital nationwide systems, such as the health-care and legal systems. By upgrading the performance of just one or a few influential institutions, an entrepreneur can see the multiplier effects spread throughout a country.

Individuals—especially members of a diaspora—with excellent management skills can have an outsized influence when they bring those talents into government services. Of course, their skills will have to be applicable to local circumstances (working in a rich country may not prepare you for running a government department in a poor country), and they will need the backing of government leaders when some of their decisions encounter, as they inevitably will, resistance from people opposed to change.

After completing her medical training in Belgium and France, Dr. Agnes Binagwaho returned to Rwanda in 1996, shortly after the genocide, to treat HIV/AIDS. Starting work as a doctor in public hospitals, she eventually rose to become the head of the country's National Commission for the Fight against HIV/AIDS. In the process, she helped establish the standard of care for the treatment of patients, improve access to health care in places previously not well served, and develop the country's strategy to fight the disease. By the end of the 2000s, the number of annual deaths from HIV/AIDS had dropped by 70 percent compared with the late 1990s.

Binagwaho, who became minister of health in 2011, wants to transform Rwanda's health-care system so that it can play an important role in the country's economic development. She is leading a campaign to make wider use of information and communication technologies to overcome weak infrastructure and shortages of professionals and make the country's health-care system more effective and resilient.[28]

Nandan Nilekani earned billions as cofounder and later chief executive officer of Infosys, India's second-largest information technology firm, which has more than 130,000 employees worldwide. But in 2009 he joined the government as chairman of the new Unique Identification Authority of India, a cabinet post. He brought with him a very ambitious goal: to introduce a new identification system that will improve the quality of public services and reduce the opportunity for corruption. If he succeeds, he will revolutionize the implementation capacity of the state, giving the Indian government a much better chance of actually accomplishing what it sets out to achieve. He will also substantially improve the lives of his poor compatriots, because the new system will make it easier for them to access various services provided by the state, banks, and the private sector.[29]

Mo Ibrahim made billions as a mobile communications entrepreneur before trying to improve institutions across Africa from the outside. He established the Ibrahim Index of African Governance (which measures the quality of government) and the Mo Ibrahim Prize for Achievement in African Leadership (which rewards leaders of countries who democratically transfer power) in an attempt to transform how leaders act and states work.

C. V. Madhukar set up the Parliamentary Research Service (PRS) in New Delhi to improve how the country's legislature works. An independent research institute, it provides research on legislation and policies for members of Parliament from over 20 different political parties. It also seeks to increase public debate on important national issues and "devise platforms for their opinions to be expressed." PRS says that its aim is "to strengthen the legislative process in India by making it better informed, more transparent and participatory."[30]

People can also make a difference by building institutions *outside* of government that poor countries lack but sorely need to become better run and more inclusive. The writer and policymaker Benno Ndulu has made substantial contributions to development across Africa by establishing one of the continent's most effective research and training networks, the African Economic Research Consortium (AERC) and by expanding access to postgraduate education in economics. In 2008, he became governor of the Central Bank of Tanzania.[31]

Patrick Awuah set up a small liberal arts college, Ashesi University, in Ghana expressly to educate the continent's next generation of leaders. "Africa can only be transformed by enlightened leaders," Awuah argues. "Leaders have to be trained and educated right . . . and they are not. There is little emphasis on ethics [in education] and a stronger sense of entitlement than responsibility so I decided to engage this particular problem."[32]

What Outsiders Can Do to Help to Stimulate Change

This chapter has focused on what homegrown social entrepreneurs can do to reshape their societies, but it is important to recognize that foreign organizations can play a similar role in encouraging change. (The next chapter focuses on one particular type of foreign organization: foreign aid agencies such as bilateral donors and the World Bank, and more particularly on their overall philosophies and broad policies. In this text box, the focus is on specific programs run or funded by foreign organizations of all kinds.) Foreign actors can have a substantial impact, especially when they are deeply enmeshed in local societies and therefore know which initiatives are most likely to have a positive impact. Such local knowledge must be complemented, however, by, at the very least, a long-term perspective, a determination to empower (rather than merely aid) local peoples and organizations, and an ability to transfer knowledge in ways that build up local institutions.

Funding and building up the capacity of local organizations may be the most effective way for outsiders to help. After all, these local entities probably know the local terrain better than anyone. However, nourishing such organizations usually requires a delicate touch. Outsiders need to provide just enough money that the organizations can use in the near future and just enough training that they can assimilate at one time; too much of either resource may change the organization's incentives and redirect its activities, undercutting its reasons for success. Think tanks that come to depend too much on foreign donors, for instance, may focus only on projects that these donors find desirable. Universities that are funded exclusively by foreign donors may not work hard enough to adapt their curricula to produce students suited to the local job market.

Helping local organizations add personnel and money incrementally is more likely to build up their capacity than overwhelming them with resources that strain their internal management system. The Hewlett Foundation project to build up think tanks (discussed in chapter 13) has wrestled with many of these issues as it has rolled out its funding. The Acumen Fund, possibly the best exemplar of this approach, supports entrepreneurs in poor places with "small amounts of philanthropic capital" and "large doses of business acumen" in the expectation that they will create "thriving enterprises that serve vast numbers of the poor" in ways that help improve their lives.[33]

Foreign organizations that seek to establish themselves in poor countries would be wise to localize themselves as much as possible, without giving up their advantages in management and know-how. The Aga Khan Development Network (which includes the Aga Khan Fund for Economic Development)[34] has achieved much in Asia and Africa through its commitment to partnering with local communities, developing local human resources, working over long time horizons, and focusing on projects that can be locally managed. Akhtar Iqbal, Aga Khan's director in Badakhshan, Afghanistan, says that "people have to be mentally ready" for projects to succeed. If they are not ready, any school or health clinic built will end up being unused, something that occurs all too frequently in aid programs.[35] Although its programs (which promote better governance) have a very different focus, the Open Society Institute (OSI) has also been able to operate successfully in difficult environments by trying to embed its initiatives within local societies. By establishing a series of autonomous institutions backed by local boards of directors and led by local managers, the OSI has sought to ensure that its programs are customized to local circumstances and run in ways that best fit local environments. Interestingly, both the OIS and the Aga Khan Development Network have built universities to enhance the ability of local citizens to run their own affairs.

Multinationals have considerable potential to help promote reform in different parts of the developing world because they are world leaders in localizing their operations (they have a far better track record in this area than aid agencies) and bring advanced management systems. Like domestic companies, they can build roads (which they need to deliver their goods), provide education and health care (which the communities their workforces live in need), and protect natural resources (which they may need to tap later). American corporations alone contribute nearly half a billion dollars for education in developing countries.[36] Multinationals are also huge employers in many places. Hindustan Unilever, India's largest consumer products company (owned by the Anglo-Dutch Unilever), has helped turn 42,000 women from poor backgrounds into entrepreneurs who sell its products across more than 100,000 villages.[37]

One very effective way to help transfer skills and knowledge is to focus on education or training in some form and cooperate with local communities, partners, and government to build up local institutions in some way. Room to Read, which was started by a burned-out Microsoft executive in Nepal in 2000 and now operates in nine countries, aims to develop literacy skills and a habit of reading among primary school children by establishing libraries and schools, and publishing new content for children in local languages. It seeks to keep costs down while promoting the acceptance and sustainability of projects by delegating in-country operations to local staff, by enlisting local community involvement from an early stage, and by using "challenge grants" (which require local communities to fund a portion of projects).[38]

Doctors, teachers, accountants, and managers of various stripes who choose to relocate to poor countries for a lengthy period of time can also play important roles transferring skills to local peoples and organizations. Many young doctors from the United States, for instance, are playing important roles helping to fill gaps in health systems in poor countries, either by treating patients themselves or by training local pediatricians, surgeons, and other specialists.[39]

New Leaders, New Attitudes

Many individual initiatives may seem small when compared with the enormous challenges poor countries face. But change actors should not be discouraged. Any program that improves, for example, community oversight of public services or increases the ability of the poor to be self-reliant can build on and work with other programs, creating a considerable impact over time. Countries are rarely—if ever—transformed overnight. Real change takes a very long time. But every initiative can shorten the overall process.

Today, many more people in the developing world are hopeful of escaping poverty than was the case a generation ago. That surge in optimism has much to do with the contributions made by the kinds of people featured in this chapter. It also has much to do with the fact that a new generation of leaders—throughout society, from business to religion to politics—have worked hard to change their societies in recent decades. More educated and worldly than their predecessors and shaped by different ideas and circumstances, these new leaders look at problems and issues from a new perspective and are committed to building self-reliant, dynamic societies.

But these leaders cannot do it by themselves. They need the support of their elites and government and the hard work of their fellow citizens. They would also benefit if assistance from the outside world was focused on the issues that matter most to the leaders and people of the developing world. In the next chapter, the spotlight falls on foreign aid agencies, which are the most important international actors promoting development and poverty reduction across the developing world.

CHAPTER 13

What Role for Foreign Aid?

The role of foreign aid in reducing poverty has been at the center of a heated debate in recent years. On one side, there are those such as Jeffrey Sachs, adviser to the United Nations and director of the Earth Institute at Columbia University, who push for large increases in foreign assistance budgets in the belief that poor countries and individuals are unable to create wealth on their own given their current disadvantages. As he explains in his best selling book *The End of Poverty*:

> When people are . . . utterly destitute, they need their entire income, or more, just to survive. There is no margin of income above survival that can be invested for the future. This is the main reason why the poorest of the poor are most prone to becoming trapped with low or negative economic growth rates. They are too poor to save for the future and thereby accumulate the capital that could pull them out of their current misery. . . .[1]
>
> [Foreign aid can create] an economy with roads that work the year round, rather than roads that are washed out each rainy season; electrical power that is reliable twenty-four hours each day, rather than electric power that is sporadic and unpredictable; workers who are healthy and at their jobs, rather than workers who are chronically absent with disease. . . . [Foreign aid can] enable the economy to break out of the poverty trap and begin growing on its own.[2]

On the other side, there are those such as William Easterly, co-director of the Development Research Institute at New York University and publisher of two well-known books (*The Elusive Quest for Growth* and *The White Man's Burden*), who doubt that foreign assistance does much good. While accepting that aid has been helpful in some specific cases, they believe that aid agencies are unaccountable bureaucracies that fuel corruption while wasting vast sums trying to do what outsiders cannot do. As Easterly explains:

> It is a fallacy to think that overall poverty can be ended by a comprehensive package of "things," like malaria medicines and clean water. The complex poverty of low-income societies will slowly give way to prosperity the same way it happened

in rich countries, through the gradual homegrown rise of political and economic freedom. This is NOT an easy quick fix—"democracy" and "free markets" evolve from below with a lot of supporting social norms and institutions, they cannot be imposed from the top by the IMF [International Monetary Fund], World Bank, or U.S. Army.[3]

Most people who work for development agencies take the middle ground between Sachs and Easterly. They acknowledge that some money has been wasted, but they also believe that aid has brought real improvements in the lives of the world's poor and can do even more if we can iron out the kinks in how it is disbursed. As Steve Radelet, chief economist for the U.S. Agency for International Development (USAID), explains:

Most development practitioners and researchers don't fully buy either [Sachs' or Easterly's] argument. While there is some truth in each, the accumulated evidence suggests a much more nuanced picture in which overall aid has done a fair amount of good in many countries despite its failures in others, and that increased aid can do more if we improve how we give it. . . . Going forward we need to move beyond the bashing and the rah-rah and honestly learn from both aid's successes and its failures. The real challenges are to find hardheaded solutions to make aid more effective, and to get more of it to those that can use it well.[4]

Bill Gates, chairman of Microsoft and co-chair of the Bill & Melinda Gates Foundation, concurs:

Aid money can and does work. It improves people's lives and makes the world a better and safer place. . . . Wasteful and corrupt aid projects are probably inevitable, and they should never be tolerated. But overall, when you look at the big picture, quite a lot of good things are happening.[5]

All of these arguments have merit, and every side can find data to support its opinion. But the problem with all these attempts to understand the value of aid is that they focus on the givers, not on who really matters: the receivers. Understanding the value of aid means understanding the capacity of the receivers to make good use of it. Instead of looking at poverty from the outside in—from the perspective of the donors—we should be looking from the inside out—from the perspective of those who live in poor countries.

Some Countries Benefit, Some Do Not

As this book has shown, not all countries are equally capable of making use of foreign aid. Those that are more cohesive or inclusively minded (as discussed in chapter 7), have capable governments (chapter 8), take advantage of the spatial dimensions of development (chapter 9), enhance the ability of the poor to take advantage of opportunity (chapter 10), or have environments conductive to business development (chapter 11) are most likely to benefit and to promote a broad-based development model that will empower the poor (as explained in chapter 6).

The Marshall Plan—the massive U.S. aid program aimed at helping Western European countries recover after World War II—was a major success because it gave money to a set of countries that were already doing most of these things well. South Korea and Taiwan benefitted enormously from American largesse in the 1950s and 1960s—at one point, foreign aid financed more than two-thirds of South Korean imports and three-quarters of investment[6]—because both had the leadership, mind-set, and capacity to make good use of it. More recently, countries such as Botswana and Mauritius have also made excellent use of foreign aid, again because they had enough of the factors spotlighted in the preceding chapters, as well as elites committed to improving those areas in which their countries were deficient.

In all of these very different countries, governments introduced policies that could foster growth and spread its benefits widely—and, no less important, the states had the capacity to implement those policies. They managed outside money well, invested it in programs that nurtured self-reliance and knowledge, learned from interacting with outside technicians and specialists, and were determined to end dependence on foreigners as soon as possible.

In sharp contrast, the countries that have clearly *not* benefitted from foreign aid have few of the elements necessary for development discussed in preceding chapters, and their elites have little interest in creating them. Countries such as Haiti, the Central Africa Republic, the Philippines (under Ferdinand Marcos), the DRC, Guinea-Bissau, Somalia, Gambia, Nicaragua, Guyana, and Chad have little to show for the billions of dollars they have received in foreign aid. Their societies are divided, their governments weak, their elites selfish, and their business climates grim. In many cases, foreign aid has made things worse by propping up kleptocratic rulers. (Kleptocrats feasting on foreign aid were common in the Cold War, but sadly they are not yet an endangered species.) The leaders in these countries typically funnel money to their friends or to projects that earn short-term accolades abroad but do nothing to develop their states. Aid projects transfer little knowledge, build little capacity, and yield few advantages for the economy.

Some Sectors Gain, Some Do Not

Just as aid can make a difference to some countries but not others, so aid can make a big difference in some spheres but have little or no impact in others. Aid has played an important role in reducing hunger, improving health, and getting children into schools around the world. Even Easterly, the aid critic, admits that aid can be credited with contributing to the

> elimination of smallpox, the near-eradication of river blindness and Guinea worm, the spread of oral rehydration therapy for treating infant diarrheal diseases, DDT campaigns against malarial mosquitoes . . . and the success of WHO vaccination programs against measles and other childhood diseases. The aid campaign against diseases in Africa . . . is likely the single biggest success story in the history of aid to Africa.[7]

Virtually everywhere, infant mortality and malnutrition is down and life expectancy is up, partly because of foreign aid. Nearly 90 percent of the world's children are now enrolled in primary schools, compared with less than half in 1950, again partly due to foreign aid.[8]

But other sectors of national life seem impervious to the impact of foreign aid. Take the example of income. Outside a few Asian countries, the income levels of most poor people around the world have risen little over the past century. Even Charles Kenny, a former senior economist at the World Bank and author of the book *Getting Better: Why Global Development Is Succeeding—and How We Can Improve the World Even More*, admits that hundreds of billions of dollars of foreign aid have had a limited impact on income in poor countries. In fact, despite receiving all this money, the income gap between rich and poor countries has actually grown wider over the past few decades. People in many countries in Africa are worse off—in terms of per capita incomes—than the people of Britain were when they were part of the Roman Empire.[9] And many of the countries that have most dramatically boosted their incomes—such as China and Vietnam—have received little in outside assistance.

Some Organizations Work Well, Some Do Not

Some organizations have consistently shown a capacity to deliver aid efficiently and to generate good results. The United Kingdom's Department for International Development (DFID), for instance, is well managed and plays a leading role in a number of areas, such as research and development, on which it spent the equivalent of $300 million in 2010. Norway's development agency—the Norwegian Agency for Development Cooperation (NORAD)— has made significant differences to life in some parts of the developing world by concentrating its efforts on peace and reconciliation and on helping countries distribute what they earn from their natural resources fairly. NORAD's Oil for Development program, for example, encourages governments to be transparent about how they handle income from natural resources and to make arrangements to share the profits among all regions of the country and all sectors of society.[10]

Unfortunately, many other aid agencies contribute little toward development in poor countries. In fact, some of them probably make a bigger contribution toward development at home, given that much of their funding ends up in the pockets of their own contractors, consultants, and companies. Almost three-quarters of American official aid money, for instance, is "tied," meaning that a certain percentage of it must be spent on goods bought in the United States, where prices are usually a lot higher than in the developing world. Many organizations spend a lot of money on conferences and programming that has little to do with development—and may not even involve any people from poor countries! Many of the United Nations agencies are highly inefficient; the United Nations Development Programme, for instance, spends more on administration than disbursements. On average, an employee of the World Food Program or the United Nations High Commissioner for Refugees disburses less than one-hundredth as much as an employee of Norway's aid agency.[11]

Some donors use foreign assistance to reward friends or to promote broader interests rather than to promote development. U.S. funding for Egypt and Israel, for instance, is widely classified as "development aid," but the $4.5 billion that the United States gives these countries every year should really be called "foreign policy aid," because it is intended to encourage the recipients to keep the peace in the Middle East, and thereby serve U.S. interests in a stable Middle East.

The Contradiction That Hampers Aid Agencies

Aid agencies operate under the shadow of a huge contradiction that undermines their effectiveness as organizations and their ability to promote development in poor countries. Whether bilateral donors, NGOs, or multilateral institutions, Western aid organizations need to please their rich world patrons—political leaders, governments, taxpayers, and contributors. But the agencies' raison d'être is to help poor countries and people.

This becomes a problem when what benefactors want is not the same as what poor countries need. For example, benefactors are much more likely to support building a school than putting money into improving how well the education ministry works, even if the latter is more important. Moreover, benefactors tend to want to see concrete results immediately, even though the kinds of changes that poor countries most need take a long time to make and progress may be hard to measure.

Figure 13.1, which is based on a diagram presented by development expert Alan Hudson, captures the essence of this contradiction.[12] Short-term, measurable achievements ("quick wins") and projects that advertise the source of their funding ("planting the flag") win applause within the donor countries, whereas long-term programs with uncertain and hard-to-measure outcomes (such as building up the capacity of an education ministry) are far more likely to foster development within the recipient countries.

Governments have handled this contradiction in a number of ways. They have handed a large portion of the money earmarked for foreign aid to companies, NGOs, and consultants from their own countries, creating a domestic constituency that directly benefits from the foreign aid budget. They have funded activities (such as health care), organizations (such as humanitarian NGOs), and campaigns (such as the antislavery crusade) that are most likely to appeal to domestic public opinion, while avoiding supporting activities that could prompt opposition from powerful domestic political actors (such as agricultural and environmental lobbies). They have emphasized results at every turn, which has meant funding only programs that are easy to measure and can produce a positive outcome quickly. They have often shunned transparency in their own operations, even though this is what they often call for within developing countries.

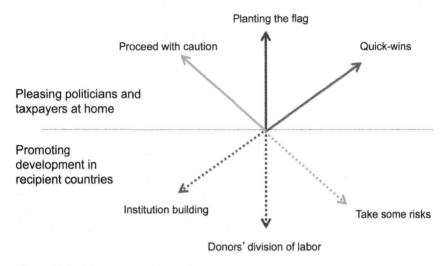

Figure 13.1 The Foreign Aid Contradiction

Source: Alan Hudson, "Impossible Geometries?" (presentation at Overseas Development Institute event "A Results Take-over of Aid Effectiveness? How to Balance Multiple or Competing Calls for More Accountability," London, July 25, 2011), slide 2.

An Overemphasis on Quantifiable Social Programs

The consequences of this contradiction are manifold. Most obviously, there is an enormous overemphasis on programming that is politically appealing domestically, is easy to assess, and yields an immediate result. Andrew Natsios, who ran the U.S. Agency for International Development (USAID) from 2001 until 2006, delivered a cutting critique of his old organization in a report entitled *The Clash of the Counter-Bureaucracy and Development*:

> The counter-bureaucracy [the compliance side of government] ignores a central principle of development theory—that those development programs that are most precisely and easily measured are the least transformational, and those programs that are most transformational are the least measurable. . . . The regulatory pressures in Washington created a force of auditors, accountants, lawyers, procurement, and contracts officers. . . . In practice, this means compromising good development practices such as local ownership, a focus on institution building, decentralized decision-making and long-term program planning horizons. . . . The building of local self-sustaining institutions—government, private sector, and non-profit—through the training of staff, the construction of business systems, and the development of regular organizational procedures and institutional cultures; and policy dialogue and reform, which means an ongoing discussion and debate about reform and policy changes. . . . [These] are neither easily measured nor very visible, and often require a long time horizon to achieve success, and more importantly they require the cooperation and consent of the power structure and leadership in the

developing countries. . . . For that reason, those latter two functions are increasingly underfunded and neglected. And yet, it is those latter two missions that are most important in the long run, as they are more transformational and more central to what development—and state building—is all about.[13]

In recent decades, there has been a large shift in resources away from programs that produce results in the long term—such as building colleges, improving rural economies, investing in infrastructure, and conducting research—even though all of these are crucial to alleviating poverty, promoting development, and ending dependency on foreign aid.

In Haiti, for instance, as of mid-2011, $2.4 billion had been committed in aid after the devastating earthquake of January 2010. Of that money, roughly one-third went to civil and military organizations of donor countries, one-third to UN agencies and international NGOs, and one-third to other NGOs and private contractors. Just 1 percent went to the Haitian government. In other words, virtually nothing was expended on enhancing the country's most important institution—the one that will matter most for the state's long-term development prospects.[14]

Donors in North America and Europe have ramped up funding for health programs—making it the largest sector of most bilateral aid agencies—at the expense of other sectors precisely because such programs are the easiest to justify to their constituencies at home, to measure, and to generate quick results with. In the case of the United States, for instance, spending on health increased from 6 percent of the foreign aid budget in 1995 to nearly 30 percent in 2008. Only 4 percent of USAID spending (excluding money spent on Iraq and Afghanistan) went toward rule of law and governance programming, which are typically hard to quantify and verify, even though these are key to state building and helping the poor.[15] The biggest new American aid initiative over the past decade—the Bush administration's President's Emergency Plan for AIDS Relief (PEPFAR)—was focused on a few narrow health-care outcomes at least partly because only something with such appealing and measurable objectives could get through Congress.

Similarly, many of the largest NGOs that work in poor countries, such as the California-based World Vision (one of the largest international aid organizations in the world with a total revenue of $2.6 billion),[16] focus their resources on humanitarian or health activities, because sponsors and the media respond most readily to them.

It might seem heartless to criticize efforts that have helped eliminate particular diseases, provided drugs to combat AIDS, or reduced child mortality, but those efforts do little to improve the ability of poor societies to take care of themselves. Governments are not improved, knowledge centers are not built, and economies are not energized. If anything, local institutions are avoided—because they are unpredictable, mistake-prone, poor record-keepers, and corrupt. In this respect, many aid programs are not development programs at all; they are humanitarian programs in disguise.[17]

Even the Gates Foundation, by far the largest private donor in the development field and with no need to satisfy any constituency beyond its few benefactors, has targeted health as its primary focus in poor countries, seeing this sector as the one in which it can best achieve measurable results. But, by focusing on very specific goals—such as eliminating polio—instead of on trying to improve health-care systems, the Gates Foundation often ends up limiting its ability to create self-sustaining institutions that could outlast its presence.[18] Without robust health-care systems—including competent regulators, medical schools, and private providers—will countries ever be able to take care of themselves?

The same logic drives programming in other areas too. Ending hunger is near the top of the agenda; building robust agricultural sectors is low down. The United Nations' Millennium Development Goals (MDGs) project, the single largest development initiative in the world, emphasizes the achievement of a series of quantifiable objectives but says little about building up local institutions. Aid has contributed to the fact that, compared with one or two decades ago, the poor in the developing world tend to be better fed, to receive more vaccinations, and to attend school more often. But, while some individuals and places are better off thanks to aid, in general developing countries are no richer and no more independent because of aid. And despite some prominent successes at the micro level, the development community is surprisingly unable to fix macro-level problems. As a result, the poor are anything but empowered in most of the developing world.

"In the current framework, such as it is," writes Laurie Garrett of the Council on Foreign Relations:

> improving global health means putting nations on the dole—a $20 billion annual charity program. But that must change. Donors and those working on the ground must figure out how to build not only effective local health infrastructures but also local industries, franchises, and other profit centers that can sustain and thrive from increased health-related spending. For the day will come in every country when the charity eases off and programs collapse, and unless workable local institutions have already been established, little will remain to show for all of the current frenzied activity.[19]

Too Little Attention to Wealth Creation

Meanwhile, sectors essential to creating wealth—such as agriculture, infrastructure, and local businesses—are deemphasized or even ignored. A report issued by the leading Danish development research institute—and appropriately titled *Reframing the Aid Debate: Why Aid Isn't Working and How It Should Be Changed*, observes:

> The key to long-term poverty reduction and higher standards of living in Africa is to spur on the twin processes of agricultural transformation and increasing the share of manufacturing. Why is it that we do not talk about this any more in international debates of ending world poverty? Instead, we only talk about providing

potable water, health care and primary education. Sure these things are important for increasing people's standards of living. But if they had more income they could pay for these things and government could provide them itself, instead of relying on aid to subsidize the provision in a short-term, unsustainable way.[20]

Less Pretension, More Ambition, a report produced by The Netherlands' Scientific Council for Government Policy, strikes the same note:

> Direct poverty alleviation is relatively simple to visualise and is high on the agenda for moral reasons, but the development aid sector's attention has acquired a very strong focus on this facet. Almost eighty percent of the budget is currently spent on social sectors—productive sectors such as agriculture and infrastructure which are less likely to lead to visible results, but which—in the long term—can structurally alleviate poverty, each receive no more than ten percent. Entrepreneurship should be given more attention and . . . the provision of credit, in particular to small and medium-sized companies, should be supported in developing companies. Moreover, the question as to whether job opportunities should be created, should become an important parameter for development policy. . . . Not the quantity, but the quality of our contribution to a world in which people and countries are self-sufficient and in which international public goods are adequately safeguarded, should be the point of departure for what we now still refer to as development aid.[21]

This inattention to wealth creation is not helped by the fact that very few people in the development field have any practical experience in creating wealth. Despite the fact that enriching countries and families ought to be the starting point for strengthening states and reducing poverty, it is rare to find a person working in an aid agency or multilateral institution who does not come out of academia, government, or the nonprofit world. Indeed, the foreign aid community tends to look down on businesspeople (as I have personally experienced) and considers many businesses to be troublemakers that should be avoided rather than welcomed as potential partners.

Looking from the Outside In

These programming emphases have combined with a natural inclination among development professionals to project the experiences of their own countries onto the countries they are trying to help. The net result has been to produce generic policy and programming, precluding the types of learning and customization to local conditions that are essential if foreign aid is to be effective in very different places.

"Western policymakers," explains a British report that synthesizes years of research into the governance of developing countries and the role of outside actors,

> find it very hard to discard developed country models. They mostly come from or live in OECD states; they are driven by normative values (rights, democracy, poverty reduction); they work for organisations that are supply-driven and have short time horizons; and many have hard-won professional knowledge. Such

knowledge—about the law, or private investment, or public expenditure management, or delivery of water, health and education services—is entirely valid and indeed essential in certain contexts. But it can get in the way of attempts to understand what is really driving behaviour and development outcomes in poor countries and fragile states. . . . Implicit in much Western policy relating to developing countries is still that West is best, that developed countries have the answers, that they need to take the lead in finding solutions, and that aid is a primary engine of development.[22]

These "mental models of development"[23] are not challenged partly because aid agencies offer neither the resources nor the time for employees to properly understand local societies. The dearth of investment in the type of local knowledge-producing institutions—such as think tanks, statistics bureaus, governance institutes, and universities—that could provide better understanding also does not help.

Yet, of course, there are enormous differences between developed and developing countries in in terms of the capacities of governments, sociopolitical dynamics, the rule of law, financial resources, and so on. Furthermore, each country—and in many cases, different areas within each country—has its own needs, which can be quite different from those of its neighbors. Pakistan, for instance, faces distinctly different challenges than those confronting Afghanistan, Iran, China, and India, its four neighbors. Ghana is next door to Côte d'Ivoire, but they are light years apart in terms of the problems they face.

On the macro level, aid agencies prescribe the same governance remedies—elections, economic reforms, improvements to central ministries—without really attempting to understand how individual countries and societies work. The agencies aim to reproduce what has worked elsewhere ("best practice") instead of developing an approach appropriate to the local circumstances ("best fit").[24]

Little effort is devoted to understanding where a country lies on the state-building continuum and how best to customize policy accordingly, especially when such customization might depart substantially from the standard governance model or infringe rich world sensibilities. The result is often the willful blindness of the whole donor herd; all agencies see only what they want to see.

Little effort is spent discovering what local people are capable of achieving on their own, creatively harnessing the implementation capacity that already exists in poor countries. Indeed, instead of seeking to make best use of the organizations and institutions that poor people are familiar with, aid agencies typically try to simply install the type of government models they are most familiar with—even though such an approach is likely to increase governance problems and reduce self-reliance.

Aid agencies want to work with "safe" partner organizations—ones with experience in handling donors' paperwork and that have already established professional relationships with Western experts and institutions. Local organizations in poor countries are often the least likely to be able to navigate the maze of regulations and relationships necessary to get funding—even though these should be central to the knowledge transfer that ought to be the core ingredient in aid programs.

The net effect of this Western-centrism can be the pursuit of catastrophically ill-judged policies. In Somalia, for instance, the international community has launched at least 14 peace initiatives and spent more than $8 billion on efforts to create a strong central state since 1991, even though each attempt has failed and the country's sociopolitical dynamics call for a much more decentralized approach. Similarly, in the Democratic Republic of Congo (DRC), aid agencies spent over $500 million on a national election in 2006 but have invested relatively little in trying to find a way for the country to put in place a looser, more horizontal governing structure, in which power and responsibility would be distributed among those most likely to wield it effectively. In Afghanistan, as Dennis de Tray, an adviser to the American 173rd Airborne Brigade Combat Team deployed in Logar and Wardak provinces in 2010, explains:

> Nearly 80 per cent of Afghan assistance since 2001 has been delivered through channels that bypass the country's government . . . at almost every turn, the coalition (with the US in the lead) has signaled to the Afghan people that their government is incompetent, incapable of providing even the most basic services. . . . But . . . when stability is the goal, even modest programmes delivered through the Afghan state trump blockbuster programmes delivered through donor's own organisations. . . . Rebuilding faith in the state has to start at the provincial and district levels, since local government is the only government most Afghans know . . . . Afghan sub-national governments in Logar and Wardak provinces . . . show that Afghans can manage resources and respond to local needs . . . with the right combination of money, support, transparency and trust, local governments can and will serve their people.[25]

Few aid programs address the social exclusion and social inequities that hurt the poor.[26] World Bank and International Monetary Fund loans may actually increase inequality in many cases by advocating changes that the poor are ill placed to take advantage of, leaving the upper classes to benefit.[27] Even the Poverty Reduction Strategy Papers that governments are required to prepare before receiving World Bank loans and that are supposed to be the centerpiece of international aid efforts to help the poor, generally ignore the role of politics (see the box "A Glut of Economists").[28]

None of this means that aid has not produced some demonstrable successes (such as in case of expanding girls' access to education in Afghanistan), just that it falls far short of achieving some of its most important goals.

How to Do a Better Job

Remedying the shortcomings of the foreign aid apparatus calls for changes not only in how institutions work but also in how their staff think. Transforming the institutional culture of aid agencies and the mind-set of development specialists is no less important than clarifying their missions. Many organizations may discover, however, that they are not in the development promotion field and that they should focus on humanitarian objectives.

Understand and Respect Local Capacities

Aid agencies need much greater knowledge about local sociopolitical dynamics, much greater respect for local institutions and practices, and much greater humility.[29] Major aid agencies have to take a much more sophisticated approach to promoting better governance and stop assuming that all good things—democracy, empowerment, and better governance—go together and that civil society can make a large difference in these areas in anything but the long term.[30] They have to be much more open minded about local, informal institutions—including those based on faith, ethnicity, and clans—than they are now. Greater political awareness would allow agencies to partner with enlightened elites and invest in programs likely to promote an inclusive state-building agenda instead of promoting a generic program of state building, which typically reinforces the prevailing status quo.

Agencies also have to accept more realistic timeframes. Portugal took ten years to transition to an elected civilian presidency after its 1975 revolution; South Korea took decades to democratize. Forcing developing countries to move faster can be counterproductive.[31] External interventions typically run on unrealistic timeframes that leave important issues unresolved and important local institutions unprepared for the changes wrought.

Realism needs to be complemented by humility—a quality for which the foreign aid community is not famous. Greater humility means recognizing that domestic actors must play the leading role and that the primary role of outside actors should be to build on what already works and facilitate an organic, domestically driven process of state building and policymaking. It also means creating an enabling environment in which local populations can solve their own problems instead of the foreign aid community trying to solve those problems for them. Local communities are bound to make mistakes, but the job of outside actors should be to help local people learn from those mistakes.[32] Refocusing the involvement of foreign actors in this way will allow a more collaborative aid system to take the place of the current externally driven process (see table 13.1).

An infusion of humility would allow agencies to learn much more from developing countries than they do now. The two most successful "aid innovations" in recent decades—conditional cash transfers and microfinance (discussed in chapter 10)—have been invented in poor countries, where governments and NGOs have a much better understanding of their own needs and a much greater incentive to create pragmatic solutions for them than anyone from the rich world. As was discussed in the last chapter, many organizations and companies in developing countries play prominent roles in development at home and abroad. The more resources—especially human capital—developing countries can apply to their own problems, the more likely they are to produce more such innovations.

This points to a new role for aid agencies as facilitators and conveners, bringing together local actors and gently nudging them toward more inclusive policies and perspectives. Substantial and sustainable change takes a long time to accomplish.

Table 13.1 Comparison of Two Aid Paradigms

Externally Driven Aid Delivery System	Collaborative Aid System
Local people seen as beneficiaries and aid recipients	Local people seen as colleagues and drivers of their own development
Focus on identifying needs	Focus on identifying local priorities, supporting/reinforcing capacities, and increasing self-reliance
Preplanned/predetermined programs	Context-relevant programs developed jointly by recipient communities and aid providers
Provider-driven decision making	Collaborative decision making
Focus on spending on a predetermined schedule	Fit money and timing to strategy and realities on the ground
Staff evaluated and rewarded for managing projects on time and on budget	Staff evaluated and rewarded for enhancement of local institutions and transfer of knowledge
Monitoring and evaluation by providers on project spending and delivery of planned assistance	Monitoring, evaluation, and follow-up by providers and recipients on the long-term effects of assistance
Focus on growth	Planned and mutually agreed exit/end of assistance strategy

Source: This is a modestly revised version of a table in Mary Anderson, Dayna Brown, and Isabella Jean, *Time to Listen: Hearing People on the Receiving End of International Aid* (Cambridge, MA: CDA Collaborative Learning Projects, 2012), 138.

It should be an evolutionary process, with incremental improvements building on what already works, and windows of opportunity exploited to the fullest. As a report published in 2011 by three distinguished development academics concluded, "In general, aid is most likely to be effective if it essentially organic, in the sense of (a) supporting existing domestic initiatives and pressures for change, and (b) in ways that are consistent with the initial state of the polity."[33]

Aid agencies would have to make many institutional changes to make this agenda work. Political scientists and country specialists would play a greater role while economists would play a smaller part (see the box "A Glut of Economists"); employees would spend much more time in individual countries and in the poorest places; local staff would be more involved in formulating and implementing policy; local organizations would receive more funding and skills training; entire agencies would focus on building specialized knowledge about countries and sectors.

Agencies would also have to make much greater efforts to not undermine local governance by how they "invade" the poorest countries. Many working practices—such as outrageously high salaries for local staff—can actually reduce the capacity of the very governments they are meant to strengthen. In Afghanistan, for instance, foreign aid organizations may have undermined attempts to reconstruct the country's government in the aftermath of the 2001 U.S. invasion by luring away many of the new government's best staff. "Within six months of starting my job as finance minister, my best people had been stolen by international aid organizations who could offer them forty to a hundred times the salary we could," complained the country's first postwar finance minister.[34]

The proliferation of development actors—globally, there are now over 50 bilateral donors, more than 200 special funds, and over 1,000 different organizations offering various forms of development-related financing[35]—has too often overburdened local leaders. Budgets are divided into many small pieces; one survey found that donors averaged 38 different activities per country, with each project getting on average just $1.1 million. Such relatively meager funding means that individual programs have little impact except bureaucratically, distracting governments from important priorities.[36] Former British prime minister Tony Blair, who currently works as an adviser to numerous African governments, complains that

> it is the international community itself which often places some of the biggest demands on leaders' time. . . . I've met senior officials in finance ministries who spend 60 percent of their time servicing donor missions. We should be asking ourselves: is this really the best way to get the effective leadership we talk about and which Africa needs?[37]

A Glut of Economists

One of the biggest reasons why international efforts to help poor countries have so often come up short is that the development field is full of economists but the development process is really rooted in politics. Aid policies tend to be are based on a narrow economic reading of circumstances, with little thought given to the political, social, and institutional context.

Academia trains and major agencies employ thousands of "development economists," but there are no "development political scientists"—the discipline simply doesn't exist. Many academics work in the political science field, and a subset of these work on developing countries. But more often than not they use a quantitative approach to analyzing local dynamics, and do not delve into difficult-to-measure issues related to power, incentives, and leadership. The leading think tank dedicated to development in the United States, the Center for Global Development in Washington, has far more economists than people from other specialties. Understanding how local politics work has never been a strong suit of the development field; as a consequence, the best studies of some local societies were those done in the nineteenth century by colonial anthropologists (and a lot has changed since then!).

Economists alone do have the tools to understand the dynamics affecting local politics and the development process. In 2011, when he was president of the World Bank, Robert Zoellick, who is not an economist, said, "Too often research economists seem not to start with the key knowledge gaps facing development practitioners, but rather search for questions they can answer with the industry's currently favorite tools. . . . We need to know what works: we need a research agenda that focuses on results." He has also expressed frustration that economists have yet to figure out the most important issues related to development, including what makes countries grow rapidly over a long period of time.[38]

Universities and development think tanks should take the lead (possibly assisted by organizations such the World Bank) in creating a new type of specialist, one specifically trained to deal with the challenges of political development. "Development political science" would be a multidisciplinary affair, combining knowledge from the fields of history, political economy, economics, sociology, and anthropology. Those trained in this new discipline should play a role equal in prominence to development economists in interpreting and recommending policy for developing countries.

Above All, Create Self-Reliance

"Create self-reliance!" should be the rallying cry for aid agencies. After all, the best help anyone can give other people is to free them from the need to ask for more help. The goal of development assistance should be to enable a country to look after itself: protecting its people at home, defending its interests abroad, exporting what other countries need and importing what it needs, cooperating with other countries to promote shared values—an equal partner within the international community. As the report by the Dutch Scientific Council for Government Policy concluded, "Aid must make a more targeted contribution to the development and self-sufficiency of countries, and should therefore place less emphasis on immediate poverty alleviation."[39]

Forward-looking leaders of poor countries certainly agree. Paul Kagame, the president of Rwanda, says: "Any aid, any support will have a meaning if it builds capacity of the people so that they can stand on their own two feet. Aid should be accepted and invested in a way that ensures that tomorrow you don't need more aid. That way, recipients can reap from the benefits that aid provides."[40]

Creating self-reliance will require aid agencies to devote far more attention to building self-sustaining systems—including education systems, health systems, legal systems, and governing systems. "One cannot improve human beings," observes Ram Sevak Sharma, the director general of India's national ID project. "But one can certainly improve systems. And the same flawed human beings with a better system will be able to produce better results."[41]

Better systems, however, need well-qualified people to run them. Aid agencies will thus have to spend a much larger portion of their money on developing the knowledge institutions that can feed these self-sustaining systems—teacher-training colleges, think tanks, governance academies, rule of law institutes, agricultural research centers, and business schools. If poor countries are to manage their own affairs and enrich themselves, they need a much broader and deeper reservoir of people knowledgeable about business, governance, agriculture, and other vital elements of local economies and societies.

Enlightened leaders have known this for decades. Muhammad Ali Jinnah, the founder of Pakistan, declared as far back as 1947 that "there is an immediate and urgent need for training our people in scientific and technical education in order to build up our future economic life . . . do not forget that we have to compete with the world which is moving very fast in this direction."[42] Julius Nyerere, the "Father of Tanzania," lamented after he had left office that "most African countries still lack the necessary physical infrastructure and the education and training in skills needed for rapid economic and social development."[43]

Clarify Budgets, Roles, and Priorities

Moving in this direction would require aid agencies to adopt new strategies and measures of performance, with a commitment to investing substantially greater proportions of aid money in transformative development-oriented activities.

As a start, aid spending should be better labeled to make clear the different goals it encompasses. Those goals can be remarkably varied, ranging from the defense of a country's strategic and security interests to the provision of humanitarian and emergency aid, the promotion of a nation's business and industry overseas, support for global public goods (such as climate change and the issues discussed in the text box "Global Problems"), the promotion of economic development, and the reduction of poverty. These different objectives should be evaluated differently.[44] Money given to Egypt for strategic purposes should not be confused with spending on hunger relief in parts of Africa or promoting local industry in Pakistan when projects are evaluated. Of course, some projects will have more than one label, as goals and missions overlap. In Afghanistan and other conflict or post-conflict situations, for instance, intertwined security and development needs may require funds that serve dual purposes.

Labeling budgets in this way would allow different criteria to be used to evaluate projects that focus on different goals. It would also create greater clarity about what proportion of budgets are being used to promote long-term structurally transformative activities (which require new evaluation criteria—see the text box "New Criteria to Evaluate Countries and Aid Agencies"). At present, most donors and agencies say they promote development but rarely if ever provide information on their budgets in a way that allows an independent evaluation of how they contribute to structural transformation and self-reliance.

New Criteria to Evaluate Countries and Aid Agencies

Too often, developing countries and aid programs are evaluated on a very narrow set of indicators, leading to an overemphasis on certain programs and to a preoccupation with "results" that have little to do with the promotion of development and self-reliance. These indicators may be adequate for some types of foreign assistance, but they are not suitable for development aid.

Evaluating the latter requires a more sophisticated and extensive range of measurements that assess such things as sociopolitical dynamics, political development, the rule of law, and the capacity of societies to create wealth and train capable leaders. The new evaluation criteria could include the following:

- Extent of economic, political, and cultural inequities (known by people working in the development field as "horizontal inequities") by ethnicity, religion, caste, region, and other group identities
- Level of diversification of exports
- Level of violence and security of individuals and property
- Ability to promote investment in labor-intensive industries such as manufacturing
- Percentage of government revenue earned from local sources (especially local non-natural resource sources)
- Expansion of the institutional capacity of the state (and the various systems that governments operate)
- The quality and inclusiveness of education systems
- The ability of the judicial systems to work effectively and equitably (including protecting the poor)
- Number and quality of knowledge-producing institutions (universities, think tanks, research organizations, teacher-training colleges, business schools, rule of law academies, and so on)

These should also be included in some form in whatever goals the development community as a whole sets to measure its progress after 2015, when the existing set of goals (the MDGs) expires.

Every country is different; some criteria will matter more in one place than another. Wherever possible, local researchers and organizations should play a role in crafting criteria that are pertinent to local circumstances. Indeed, the g7+ group of fragile and post-conflict states is developing a set of indicators similar to the above with the understanding that they will have to be customized for each individual country.

Such changes would help aid agencies better articulate their missions and devote more of their resources to the longer term investments that poor countries need. Those organizations that dedicate themselves to development promotion need to make significant changes if they are to be more effective in that role. They need to commit themselves to long-term objectives, narrow their geographic and sectoral focus, strive to operate independently of political influence (from politicians in the rich world), build relationships with local actors, and devote more attention to transferring knowledge to receiving countries.

DFID has many of the attributes of an effective development-focused agency. Separated from the British Foreign Office in 1997 and operating as an independent government department with its own minister ever since, the organization has a longer term perspective than most other bilateral donors. It is widely recognized for its professionalism, clear program focus, and research initiatives. In the 2000s, it spearheaded efforts to better understand the political dynamics of poor countries and how poverty could be tackled. DFID is by no means perfect. For instance, it is often criticized for not doing enough to integrate what it learns from research on politics and social dynamics into its programming or to transition to a more development-oriented paradigm. And it (like a lot of other agencies) is moving—under pressure from Parliament—more toward the kind of quantification of outcomes/outputs that is commonplace at USAID.[45] Even so, it, like a few other Western European government aid agencies, does a fairly good job of helping poor countries to develop.

Many other government agencies, however, are far less effective. USAID, for instance, certainly has the resources and the influence (given its huge budget and the global role of the United States) to make an impact, but it is shackled by the bureaucratic procedures and controls imposed by an army of "auditors, accountants, lawyers, procurement, and contracts officers."[46] The organization has seen a marked degrading of its capabilities in recent decades due to an exodus of capable people. It lacks the independence enjoyed by DFID.

This decline is unfortunate, as USAID used to be one of the better agencies doing development programming. In the 1980s, USAID granted more than 17,000 scholarships to people in government and civil society in developing countries to help build up their institutions. Many people regard this program as the most powerful and transformational that USAID has ever run. But since the 1990s, USAID has cut back its funding for scholarships (it now awards fewer than 1,000 per year) because it does not produce results that are easily measured within the shorter time horizon now required for USAID projects.[47] Rajiv Shah, who took charge of USAID in early 2010, has recognized the need for change and is working hard to cooperate with more local partners, increase transparency, reduce waste, and focus on more transformative programs, but he still faces many institutional constraints.[48]

The U.S. Millennium Challenge Corporation (MCC), which distributes money directly to governments based on how they perform (in terms of promoting civil liberties, political rights, and government effectiveness), offers a different model of an aid agency. By limiting aid to good performers, it does a better job than other agencies in nurturing good policies and self-reliance. But it does not offer a model for laggards, who do not qualify for MCC assistance even though they are in most need of such help.

The World Bank plays a unique role as a funder and is the best information-producing agency in the aid business, but it is hampered by its own internal culture, operating structure, and bureaucratic controls. It does not have the flexibility or the funding mechanisms to work with nonstate actors; it shies away from issues that are politicized; and its dependence on economists and technical analyses reduces its ability to tackle the problems of development. Given its size and central role, it is hard to see development aid being transformed without it working differently.

Whereas most government-funded organizations are constrained by political sensitivities and bureaucratic red tape from playing a more effective role in promoting development, private foundations have a freer hand. Those foundations with large endowments can afford to have long-term outlooks and to safeguard their independence from political interference. Some, such as the Rockefeller Foundation, have considerable experience in developing countries.

In recent years, a number of private foundations have launched some creative initiatives to strengthen institutions and nourish self-reliance in developing countries. The Partnership to Strengthen African Universities, established in April 2000 by four U.S. foundations (the Carnegie Corporation of New York, the Ford Foundation, the Rockefeller Foundation, and the MacArthur Foundation—three other foundations have since come on board), has contributed hundreds of millions of dollars to higher education on the continent.[49] The Hewlett Foundation launched a ten-year, $100 million initiative in 2007 to strengthen independent research centers in the developing world in cooperation with the International Development Research Centre. The goal is to support high-quality research that developing countries can use to formulate better national policies.[50] The Gates Foundation has played a crucial role over the past decade in promoting the development of medicines needed by the developing world. It has started to play a similar role in promoting agricultural research.

Much more could be done along these lines. The Gates Foundation, for instance, could redirect some of its funding away from technical programming and toward efforts to build self-sustaining systems (such as health-care systems). Besides working to improve government ministries and key local organizations (such as hospitals, medical schools, and insurance companies), it could also work to build political support for better health-care systems or for more inclusive development. Such a shift would mirror what the foundation has done within the United States in recent years, as it has learned that technical improvements in education can accomplish only so much without broader changes to political dynamics and education policy.[51]

Global Problems

Given how much difficulty aid agencies have experienced in trying to enhance the performance of individual countries, they should devote more effort to tackling issues that affect *all* countries but are particularly damaging to developing countries. Among other potential advantages, this approach would enable the agencies to make a difference in the lives of the poor in developing countries without first having to solve intractable governance problems in those places.

For instance, aid agencies could work toward the following:

- Reducing the international incentives to act criminally or corruptly within developing countries with weak governments by making it harder to launder corrupt money, by legalizing some drugs, and by better monitoring natural resource revenue.
- Enhancing international cooperation and regulation to combat tax avoidance, international fraud, hazardous waste dumping, and illicit arms trafficking.
- Investing in steps that reduce insecurity (such as better monitoring of conflict zones and more funding and training for regional peacekeepers).
- Investing more in technology specifically aimed at poor countries, such as ways to make cell phones more useful in financial transactions and consumer goods more affordable by the poor.
- Supporting agricultural research into ways to increase yields, and supporting medical research into drugs targeted at diseases that mainly afflict poor countries (such as the Gates Foundation is doing with malaria and tuberculosis).
- Investing more in regional organization (see chapter 9).

Some progress has been made on these issues over the past decade or so, but much more is possible.

Specialize

Specialization is the key to success in the foreign aid world, as it is in the private sector. Aid agencies should do less but do it better, in the same manner that developing country governments should aim to do less better (as discussed in chapter 8). A sharper focus in terms of what countries and sectors a particular agency serves will allow that agency to develop a clearer idea of what works in specific places.

One of the smaller agencies, for instance, could focus solely on building roads (not just on developing plans and funding construction but also on improving the capacity of the government agencies and industries involved in road building). A good road network can stimulate jobs, entrepreneurship, growth, local governance capacity, strategic urbanization, social cohesion, and broad-based development. For instance, the development of a nationwide network of freeways will not only provide jobs for tens of thousands of people but also provide or create a market for locally manufactured construction materials.

Aid agencies, however, tend to be generalists and are preoccupied with achieving measurable results (such as how many miles of road are built) without regard for how these aims influence self-reliance. In Afghanistan, for instance, foreign aid agencies have spent billions on infrastructure and other construction projects, but they have contracted only with foreign companies, which have imported materials and hired foreign laborers to do much of the work, even unskilled and semiskilled tasks that Afghans could easily have shouldered. Little of the money earmarked for creating infrastructure has reached local companies, which must operate at the end of a long chain of contracts.[52]

Another agency could focus exclusively on agriculture and rural development, which has countless linkages with other sectors (finance, manufacturing, transportation, storage and distribution, and so forth). A third could focus solely on education, working to build up a government ministry capable of managing a countrywide educational system, developing a network of teacher-training colleges, creating early-intervention programs to reach the poorest people, and introducing a financing scheme that will allow the local government to raise a greater share of the education budget locally. A fourth could devote itself to enhancing government capacity through customized training, mentoring by foreign experts, partnering between foreign and domestic institutions, the funding of think tanks, and so on. A fifth could focus on regionalism.

Many of the most valuable contributions aid agencies can make to promote development are nonfinancial. Transferring knowledge, strengthening institutions, developing close partnerships with local actors (such as think tanks, universities, and government ministries) to improve how they work, encouraging the creation of reform-minded coalitions: such activities do not require vast sums of money, but they do require close attention and specific kinds of expertise and knowledge. As long as donors try to be jacks of all trades, they will fail to become masters in specific fields.

There should also be a sharp reduction in the number of countries and sectors each agency focuses on. No organization that wants to be consistently productive should try to operate in 146 countries, as USAID does now.[53] DFID reduced the number of countries it serves from 49 to 27 in a 2011 review.[54] In the same year, the Dutch government's aid agency reduced the number of its recipients from 33 to 15 and cut the number of its target sectors to four.[55]

Such concentration increases efficiency and spurs creativity. Focusing on education alone, for instance, would allow an agency to develop a much keener sense of how education might be reformed to better reach minorities not fluent in the national language, how incentives could be changed to encourage better teaching, how subjects can be made more relevant for labor markets, and how media such as a radio and television could be used to teach skills to a large number of students.

Having each donor specialize on just a few countries would create the opportunity for each agency to have a greater impact on a country's development prospects. DFID, for instance, has prioritized aid to Ethiopia, Pakistan, Nigeria, Somalia, the Democratic Republic of Congo, and Yemen, giving it an opportunity to make a particularly large contribution to those countries' futures.[56]

As part of this approach, one country or major international organization (such as one of the development banks) should take the lead in coordinating donor efforts for each recipient country. This approach has often been used successfully in the mediation of international disputes or in cases of multilateral intervention into intrastate conflicts, with one state or a small group of states (known as "groups of friends" or "core groups") or a single individual (such as a special representative of the UN secretary-general) orchestrating the involvement of multiple international actors. And it has been mentioned in international efforts to make aid more effective (such as the Paris Declaration on Aid Effectiveness, which was signed by over one hundred governments and international agencies in 2005). When performed ably, this coordinating role ensures that funds, political support, military forces, technical expertise, and other resources complement one another rather than undercutting, duplicating, or negating one another.[57]

USAID, for instance, could play the lead role in the Caribbean, a region in which the United States has significant interests and ties and of which it has substantial knowledge. DFID could play a leading role in Pakistan, with which the United Kingdom has strong cultural ties and a long history.

As well as reducing overlap and duplication of efforts, a central coordinator could target efforts more precisely while limiting the burdens placed on a recipient government (such as attending meetings and reporting to numerous partners). The coordinator could also package funds from different agencies, enabling more comprehensive and longer term initiatives to be supported.

In a number of countries, multidonor trust funds have been established, but such an approach has at times led to confusion because no single agency is in charge, and coordination is organized horizontally, between the various donors. A better approach would be for a single major donor or multilateral agency to assume a commanding role, coordinating efforts vertically. Specialization would make such coordination much easier to achieve.

As part of this shift toward specialization and closer collaboration with local partners, agencies should also learn to expect and accept some failures and to learn from them. In the same way that businesses try many new ideas in the anticipation that only a few will work well and many will be written off as necessary expenses, agencies seeking to promote development should allow enough space for creativity to flourish. As Aleem Walji, who joined the World Bank from Google, explains, "The private sector talks about failure freely and candidly," while the nonprofit world "has to worry about donors who don't want to be associated with failure and beneficiaries who may not benefit from admissions of failure."[58]

Conclusion

Implementing what this chapter has just outlined will make Western aid not only more effective but also more cost efficient. Thus, without harming the developing world, budgets can be reduced—as many in the West have urged and as these economically tough times demand.

In fact, if development aid is to be more effective, the amount of aid must decrease, not increase. At present, the West warps incentives by how it deploys its money. Leaders become more accountable to outsiders than to their own people, more likely to act in ways that satisfy international interests instead of building up the capacities of their own countries. Large budgets—in 2011, the United States gave $31 billion in overseas development aid, and the rich world as a whole gave $133 billion—[59]also make donors more likely to throw money at a problem rather than to work with what local societies have to offer. Donors focus on short-term goals to justify their budgets instead of concentrating on empowering local societies with strategic, targeted investments designed to build up the ability of those societies to build wealth and govern themselves. An emphasis on the amount of aid earmarked for the developing world also distracts from the many other useful things that can be done to help developing countries, such as transferring technology, opening up Western markets to goods from the developing world, and reducing the demand in the global North for the illicit drugs produced in the global South (legalizing at least some of these drugs would do more for the countries ravaged by drug gangs than aid).

"In general," write a trio of development specialists,

> aid should not be focused on "money". This can be counter-productive. . . . Rather, external partners can provide technical assistance in designing locally-grown interventions; they can play a role in financing information-gathering by local NGOs; and can finance experimental interventions (and their learning). Most valuable is likely to be support for a domestic process of innovation and learning involving a generalized approach of experimentation.[60]

Western aid agencies are no longer the only source of funds for poor countries. Whereas until the mid-1990s, the UN system, the multilateral banks, and a few key donors played a dominant role in the economies of most developing countries, recent years have seen an astounding number of new actors enter the scene in various guises. Rapidly developing states (including China, Brazil, India, and Turkey), OPEC members (such as Saudi Arabia and Qatar), private philanthropists (such as Gates), private investors (including hedge funds, sovereign wealth funds, and multinationals), and even developing country NGOs (such as BRAC, mentioned in chapter 12) are all playing increasingly important roles promoting development in poor countries, whether as business partners, financers, suppliers, or donors.

And these new actors know a thing or two that the Western aid agencies don't know about how to get things done in the developing world. As a result, they are, for the most part, a boon to developing countries. New approaches, often backed by a more practical focus on activities that foster growth and create wealth, are proving successful. New demand for goods, new investors, new trading patterns, new opportunities to migrate abroad, and new chances to learn new skills are all helping to empower the poor.

Among the new actors, the non-Western ones are bringing experiences and knowledge that are at times more pertinent than Western norms and expertise to tackling the problems of development. Companies in other developing countries have relevant technology to sell, individuals have relevant knowledge to transfer, and NGOs have relevant organizational models to teach. And the governments in at least some developing countries have practical solutions to weak government, social exclusion, and a largely barren corporate sector.

Of course, these new non-Western actors have their flaws and self-interested agendas. And they have sometimes hurt, rather than helped, developing countries. But, on the whole, their growth and expansion overseas has brought many benefits to Africa and elsewhere.

Western aid agencies should form partnerships with these new actors and create powerful synergies that take advantage of each other's resources and know-how. The preceding chapter already explained the advantages of working with NGOs from the developing world, but opportunities for productive partnerships extend far beyond the NGO community. Working more closely with institutions and companies in Brazil, for instance, would give donors access to agricultural technology and know-how that could help them vitalize African agriculture. Teaming up with private investors in public-private partnerships could create stronger incentives for investors to pump their money into infrastructure, special export zones, and job-generating industries in the developing world. Such partnerships would also allow the aid agencies to encourage these new actors to pay more heed to issues that matter to them, such as the environment, workers' rights, and poverty reduction.

The development landscape is changing rapidly. But, as the book's last chapter underscores, the fundamental challenges of development remain the same in most places: How to boost growth? How to make it more inclusive? How to improve how governments work? How can the poor become better integrated into the societies and economies of the developing world?

Meeting these challenges is going to require significant support from a wide variety of international actors and strong and determined leadership by the elites of the developing world. And sometimes the best way to lend support and to lead is to empower others to help themselves.

CHAPTER 14

Putting It All Together

Whereas once the Third World was seen as nothing more than an economic disaster zone in need of humanitarian assistance, today the emerging world grabs headlines as the new engine of global growth. Yet, for all the progress being made in places such as China, Brazil, Indonesia, and parts of India and Africa, billions remain poor because their states and societies are unwilling—or unable—to act inclusively. Their public services reach only part of the population, their institutions are weak, and their investment climate is at best stormy—at worst wintry.

There are far more Nigerias and Pakistans than there are Chinas. And even where progress is being made, many are being left behind—including in China, which has increasingly stark income inequities. India, for all its success over the past generation, now contains more poor people than any other country. Hundreds of millions within the country remain mired in poverty.

As one Indian villager asked, "When will India's high rate of growth remove poverty in this village? There are many poor people here. How will their poverty be removed? Will they get jobs? Will their agricultural fields begin to yield more? Will something happen to make their earnings greater and their expenses fewer than before?"[1]

John Githongo, who has fought corruption in Kenya as both a journalist and a government official, points an accusing finger at "structural inequality" that excludes millions from the benefits of growth. "We have a model of economic management across the world in which entire sections of the population are being left behind. The proportion living in poverty in Kenya is increasing despite a growing economy."[2]

While the proportion of people in absolute destitution may be dropping, the number of excluded or disadvantaged may not be. The outward face of poverty has changed over the past decade or so. Impoverished people today often have access to vaccines, schools, and cell phones, yet most are still confined to the margins of the economic growth that is occurring. Instead of empowering them, their political and social systems are still shackling them, still denying them the chance to profit from their hard work, talents, and ambition. They may be a little better-off in some ways, but they are still destitute in terms of opportunity and have meager stores of self-efficacy (see chapter 6).

Combating Poverty: Four Key Questions

Anyone, whether in the Global South or North, who wants to help the poor in the developing world must answer four questions.[3] Together, they form a catechism of empowerment.

1. What Can Improve the Quantity, Quality, and Sustainability of Growth?

Growth must be the starting point for any effort to develop a country's infrastructure, increase the incomes of its workers, and reduce the poverty of its citizens. Growth is the only mechanism that can create more jobs and produce more government revenue to spend on public services. Yu Yongding, a prominent Chinese economist, makes no bones about the value of growth to his country's success: "Growth has been the single-most-important objective of Chinese policies for decades. Without growth, there are not enough jobs, and there is instability."[4]

The good news is that much of the developing world has experienced brisk growth in recent years, generating optimism about the futures of Asia, Africa, and Latin America. The bad news, unfortunately, comes in three parts.

The first bit of bad news is that the growth may not be brisk enough. Despite the recent spurts in growth rates, most developing countries' economies are expanding more slowly than they could and should. Few are expanding as fast as East Asian states such as South Korea, China, and Malaysia did during their initial takeoff phase—and they maintained that pace for decades.

The second part of the bad news is that the recent growth is in many cases relatively low-quality growth. Most developing countries are growing thanks to exports of just a few commodities to just a few markets. This recent spurt, however, is highly susceptible to an economic downturn in those markets. Despite being one of the poster children for emerging economies, Brazil's growth rate is far below its potential—closer to the slower rates found in much richer countries, such as the United States, than to speedy pace of a dynamic, emerging market such as China. Furthermore, commodities and commodity-related manufactured goods—as opposed to more sophisticated products based on robust supply chains and a highly skilled workforce—make up three-fifths of Brazil's total exports, up from one-half a generation ago.[5]

The third bit of bad news is that most countries are doing far too little to ensure that the benefits of growth are widely shared and that growth itself becomes sustainable. Few developing countries are taking advantage of their current growth to invest in infrastructure, education, and innovation, which would create a foundation on which they could diversify their exports, create higher paying jobs, and lessen their dependence on growth being generated elsewhere.

Osvaldo Rosales, who works for the United Nations Economic Commission for Latin America and the Caribbean, observes:

> It's worrisome. While economic history shows there are no cases of successful development without diversification of exports, we're seeing that the region's exports tend to be increasingly concentrated in commodities. . . . The key question is whether South American countries, especially, are taking advantage of this commodity export boom to invest in key areas, such as infrastructure and education. My impression is that we are not doing it.[6]

Many other parts of the developing world are facing similar challenges. South Africa, Egypt, and Pakistan, for instance, struggle with low growth and high unemployment. Africa as a whole is growing faster but is too dependent on commodities. Almost all of Africa's exports in 2011 were either fuel and mining products (which accounted for two-thirds of exports), iron and steel (which totaled over one-tenth and which reflected the continent's rich iron ore deposits), or agricultural products (which added up to one-tenth).[7] The continent's savings rate was less than half of Asia's, holding down investment and future growth prospects.[8]

Enhancing the quantity, quality, and sustainability of growth requires structural changes in economies that most developing countries outside of East Asia have found hard to make. Diversifying and expanding the sources of economic growth in a way that increases productivity while expanding opportunity requires both greater success in manufacturing and a more dynamic rural sector, such that an ever greater share of an economy and population can contribute to and gain from growth. This, in turn, requires a business environment that dramatically reduces the costs for farmers, microenterprises, and SMEs to trade and form linkages with one another, especially across distance and time (where personal relationships matter much less).

Linkages are especially important if an economy is to be structurally transformed because of the need for businesses to specialize to increase productivity—which requires individual firms to depend on other firms to do more and more of the tasks they previously did themselves. Where linkages can be established easily, growth in one firm more easily leads to growth in others, and expansion in one sector (such as agriculture) more easily leads into expansion in others (such as packaged or canned foods). When economic activity grows like a vine in this manner, climbing beyond its narrow starting point and reaching ever more areas, industries, and groups of people, it transforms the capabilities of populations and companies, generating many jobs and much investment.

2. What Can Make Growth More Inclusive?

Growth is essential but, by itself, is not enough to help the poor. To do that, growth must be inclusive. Some growth trajectories can end up helping no one outside of a small circle; they can even end up increasing poverty. Such trajectories are most commonly found in countries such as Nigeria, Angola, and the

Democratic Republic of Congo (DRC), where growth is being generated by one or two commodities harvested by foreign investors in small enclaves cut off from the rest of the economy. In such places, a narrow elite can control all the royalties and taxes paid by the foreign investors while doing nothing to help the rest of the population.

Despite enjoying one of the fastest growth rates in the world over the past 15 years and becoming the first ever "high-income country" in Africa in the 2000s (a "high-income country" is one in which per capita income is higher than $12,500 per year),[9] Equatorial Guinea has one of highest poverty rates in the world. The wealth from its oil revenues (it is the third-biggest exporter on the continent) benefits very few people. The son of the president has a $35 million California home, complete with 16 acres, a golf course, a tennis court, and a swimming pool, but over two-thirds of the population of Equatorial Guinea live in poverty, and two-fifths are mired in extreme poverty.[10]

For growth to be inclusive it has to produce ever greater stability and a continuing increase in the number and quality of jobs, skills, public services, and infrastructure. Less developed countries that have ample mineral wealth must find ways to translate their relatively strong tax revenue into broader based growth. The gains from assets below ground (such as oil) must be reinvested in assets above ground (such as roads and schools) that enable more people to contribute to and gain from economic activity.

The better the collection of livelihood factors and the greater the physical, financial, human, and social capital that the poor possess (as discussed in chapter 10), the more likely it is that they will gain from positive changes in their economies. As Amartya Sen points out, if more people are to benefit from the market economy, they first need access to a variety of other kinds of "enabling conditions," including health care, education, and legal protection.

> The benefits of the market economy can indeed be momentous, as the champions of the market system argue (on the whole rightly). But then the non-market arrangements for the sharing of education, epidemiology, land reform, microcredit facilities, appropriate legal protections, women's rights and other means of empowerment must be seen to be important even as ways of spreading access to the market economy (issues in which many market advocates take astonishingly little interest). Indeed, many advocates of the market economy don't seem to take the market sufficiently seriously, because if they did, they would pay more attention to spreading the virtues of market-based opportunities to all. In the absence of advancing these enabling conditions for widespread participation in the market economy, the advocacy of the market system end up being mere conservatism, rather than supporting the promotion of market opportunities as widely as possible. The institutional requirements of an equitable use of market efficiency go well beyond the confined limited of simply "freeing the markets."[11]

Employment is the main conduit that translates growth into rising incomes for a population. As more people get jobs, and as the wages for those jobs rise, the benefits of growth increase and are more widely shared.

Dynamic, job-producing economies—backed by governments able to invest in their populations' education, health, and job preparedness—will do more to reduce poverty (and enhance self-efficacy) than any series of anti-poverty programs. As a report from the United Nations Development Programme on poverty reduction in China concluded:

> The poverty incidence fell most rapidly before there were specific poverty alleviation programs in existence. When these programs were flourishing, on the other hand, poverty reduction at times stagnated and even suffered reversal. This is not because China's poverty reduction policies and programs have been useless or counter-productive; on the contrary, there is reason to believe they have made a difference in the localities where they were carried out. Rather, it is because much larger forces have determined the shape and speed of poverty reduction, namely, macroeconomic and other general economic policies and trends. These include, inter alia, policies concerning farm prices, factor prices, state investments, fiscal structure, financial reform and the social safety net and social insurance regimes. When the constellation of such policies was strongly pro-poor, poverty reduction occurred at a breathtaking speed, despite the absence of explicit poverty-reduction institutions.[12] [Emphasis in original]

This does not mean that governments should neglect efforts to directly help the poor. Programs designed to boost household incomes, for instance, will remain extremely valuable—and, thanks to greater growth, can be more generously funded by a government with growing tax revenues. But such efforts will always play a secondary role to efforts to create an environment in which people have the opportunity to better their own lives.

3. What Role Can the State Play?

The state has a number of critical contributions to make both in promoting growth and in making sure that it is inclusive in nature. But more often than not, governments in the developing world are not up to the challenge. Although most debates about the state revolve around how large or proactive it ought to be, the biggest question is how effective it can be. Few states in the developing world are able to provide even the most basic public services in a reliable, equitable fashion.

Such deficiencies have much greater consequences for the poor than for the rich. In the first place, the rich have the resources to compensate for the shortcomings of the state; the poor do not. In the second place, the poor lack the education, experience, and social networks to benefit as much as the rich from whatever opportunities an economy does produce.

Only strong, effective, and inclusive governments can give the poor the legal protections, higher quality education, more reliable transportation, and all those other prerequisites of participation in the market economy described by Amartya Sen. Such a state is also necessary to ensure that gains in one area (growth) are translated into gains across a broad range of areas (better and more equitable public services). Those who do not benefit directly (through, say, jobs) should be able to benefit indirectly (through, say, better schools).

An effective state is also crucial to devising and implementing the policies necessary to nurture and attract the types of companies and investment that can help transform economies in a way that generates broad-based sustainable, job-rich growth. Although informal relationships can yield important short-term gains—indeed, as discussed in chapter 7, such relationships may be essential to jumpstarting the development process at the beginning—they cannot by themselves ensure that entrepreneurs and businesses act in ways beneficial to a country and its poor over the long term. Firms only establish big factories that employ hundreds of people, create extensive networks of local suppliers, and transfer advanced skills to a wide range of people when they are confident in the quality and integrity of local institutions.

While inadequate state capacity is the biggest problem, inappropriate government policies and priorities are also a barrier to inclusive growth. This may be true even when governments are adopting the types of ostensibly market-enhancing reforms advocated by many Western development agencies. Steps that look as though they will open markets to competition may in fact serve only the elites who already have the skills and connections to compete under the new rules or who have the power to manipulate the new rules to their own advantage (as happened in places such as Tunisia and Egypt before the Arab Spring). Governments in developing countries typically focus on maximizing short-term gains for elites (or, at least, government officials), and if that means ignoring or even encouraging corruption and injustice, then so be it. Policies and priorities need to reflect local conditions to really help populations.

The sequence in which these reforms are introduced is also important. Ill-timed reforms can weaken already fragile institutions and disrupt already fragile lives. When reforms are introduced in ways that maintain a minimum level of economic stability and hold down unemployment—especially long-term unemployment— the poor are more likely to gain. In contrast, economic volatility or a sudden loss of a large number of jobs can destroy human capital, deplete savings, and ruin the health of those must vulnerable. Creating jobs is much harder than destroying them.[13]

4. What Can Be Done to Encourage the State to Promote Inclusive Growth?

States are run (usually) by governments, and governments in the developing world are dominated (usually) by elites. Whether states take steps that promote inclusive development thus depends above all else on elite behavior, especially in poor places with weak governments. Elites who are too self-interested to work toward the greater good, too greedy to take a long-term perspective, and too secure in their positions are unlikely to take steps that empower the poor. Selfish elites tend not to invest in public services, to stimulate growth in industries they don't profit from, or to widen participation in the economy. Any extra revenue that growth does generate is spent in ways that bolster the elite's power and wealth, not in ways that strengthen the state or enrich its lower classes.

In the absence of strong, enlightened political leaders—such as Ghana's Jerry Rawlings, Liberia's Ellen Johnson Sirleaf, and India's Nitish Kumar—elite-centered political cultures can be changed only gradually. Elections are rarely a quick fix. Too often, they change the personnel in government but not the nature of government in the countries where the poor are concentrated. For example, despite its significant progress economically and socially, Bangladesh continues to be plagued by the weak governance perpetuated by its winner-takes-all politics. The country's democracy looks more like a family vendetta between two political parties and their leaders than a give-and-take two-party system. Similarly, elections have done little to change the clan-based patronage system that dominates the political system in Pakistan.

Change in such circumstances does not come easily (especially in the absence of an economic or political crisis), but it is possible, especially if it begins away from the center of power and does not seem to threaten (or, at least, directly threaten) the interests of dominant elites. In such places, leadership can be exercised by people in all sorts of positions: heads of government departments, judges, business executives, heads of NGOs, local chiefs, and so on (see the box "The Need for Leadership at All Levels").

Similarly, a series of modest initiatives can, over time, create a critical mass of empowering reforms, especially if they are calibrated with the three tools discussed in chapter 7—social cohesion, an inclusive pro-development ideology, and incentives—to change elite behavior. Long journeys consist of many small steps. And a series of steps to enhance public services, increase the ability of the poor to participate in economic activity, stimulate investment in new industry, and strengthen linkages between various ethnic, religious, and interest groups (thus building social cohesion and a more powerful collective to promote change) can move a country a long way. Over time, a political culture can shift far enough to permit the introduction of substantial institutional and cultural change.

Building a strong judiciary, for example, may first require developing a relatively active and diverse private-business sector (which will want the courts to be able to protect property rights) and civil society (which will want to see the rights of citizens better protected), establishing a number of law schools (which can supply the personnel to staff the courts), and accumulating significant financial resources (to pay the salaries of the court staff).

Nudging the overall system forward in this way encourages a self-reinforcing, dynamic process of change. Even so, truly transformative change will typically take at least a generation or two to occur.[14] Reform-minded central leadership can quicken the pace, but the process will still take years or decades, not weeks or months. Other factors can also accelerate the process: for instance, reform will be quicker to take root in a country whose neighbors are also reforming or have already done so.

Pressure from below will also add to the momentum for change. Indeed, it makes perfect sense for a move toward accountable government to be pushed by the same people to whom the government should be accountable. Popular support for measures to strengthen national-level institutions that hold leaders to account—including legislatures, the judiciary, auditing agencies, ombudsmen, and the media—is thus important. Nonetheless, popular pressure is unlikely to force change by itself. Selfish elites can and will resist such pressure unless other changes in society have already set a process of change in motion.

The Need for Leadership at All Levels

Leadership is crucial to spurring both development and empowerment. It is especially important in overcoming elite resistance to reforms, in promoting national cohesion, in enhancing hard-to-improve public services, and in facilitating innovation in how government (and private industry) operates.[15] The more conducive an environment is for change agents, the more any individual or group can accomplish. Leadership should ideally start at the top. Examples set by the most senior officials, businesspeople, and members of society are most likely to be emulated.

But even if top people don't set a good example (and they usually won't unless they are sure that their own position is secure), less important people can still accomplish a lot. Leaders at all levels of society and in all sectors of society can enable and accelerate progress toward a more inclusive economic and social system:

Political leadership can play an important role in communicating a vision of inclusiveness, mobilizing support through coalition building, and inducing change in how government operates. As discussed in chapter 7, Jerry Rawlings and Paul Kagame have transformed their countries. President Lula led the way in Brazil in social security reform and in consolidating a national consensus on economic policy.

Government leadership within ministries and other public bodies can have a powerful influence on the design and implementation of policies and programs and on the state's ability to make the rule of law a reality. Dr. Agnes Binagwaho has transformed the standard of care for patients and improved access to health-care across Rwanda since returning to the country in 1996. Claudia Paz y Paz Bailey, Guatemala's first woman attorney general, has significantly increased the number of prosecutions and convictions since taking office in 2010. In a country long known for its weak judicial system and inability to prosecute powerful figures, she has brought to justice criminal gang leaders, drug traffickers, and war criminals.

Civic leadership can push improvements in public services, challenge politicians and officials to perform efficiently and accountably, and build cooperation across ethnic and religious divides. People such as Fazle Hasan Abed, the founder of BRAC, have started NGOs and private firms that have played a significant role in improving access to public services in Bangladesh. In India, a wide range of people, including academics, social movement activists, and trade unionists have advocated for legislation that benefits the rural poor, improves government transparency, and reduces corruption. Madhav Chavan established Pratham, which is working to transform the education sector in India by providing much better information on learning outcomes.

Moral leadership can heal wounds caused by conflict, set new standards of behavior that benefit wider society, and inspire people to make difficult decisions that may not be in their best interests, at least in the short term. South Africa's Bishop Desmond Tutu fought apartheid for decades, yet worked tirelessly after its fall to forge a "rainbow coalition" (a term he coined) of diverse ethnic groups. He headed the country's Truth and Reconciliation Commission in order to help the country overcome its difficult past.

Business leadership can expand opportunity, create products that meet unsatisfied needs, encourage government and society to be more inclusive, and invest in environments desperately in need of an infusion of opportunity, confidence, and hope. Business leaders are playing a major part in the reform of education in Brazil. Inventers in India and elsewhere have created inexpensive products that raise living standards even when incomes do not grow. Companies can weaken prejudice and promote social reform by giving equal opportunity to people who are accustomed to encountering discrimination. In many countries, businesses are at the forefront of empowering women, giving them opportunities that others in society do not (and giving themselves advantages over companies that do not).

Successful leaders do not depend on charisma (though it can help) but on their ability to win support and cooperation for their goals and to delegate responsibility. Their effectiveness is tied to their capacity to be pragmatic, to respond to changing needs, and to build institutions to harness their vision and to outlast them.

Surprising Success Stories

Substantial progress in improving lives can occur almost anywhere if the right leadership and ideas are in place.

Despite still being one of world's poorest countries, Ethiopia shows how much a cohesive elite ideologically committed to inclusive state building can accomplish in a relatively short period. In less than a generation, Ethiopia has made remarkable social and economic progress.

It recorded the third-best improvement worldwide in the Human Development Index (a measure of the health, education, and standard of living of a population) between 2000 and 2010.[16] Access to education has skyrocketed, with enrollment in primary schools jumping from about 3 million in 1994–1995 to over 15 million by 2008–2009.[17] The Ethiopian economy has grown by an average of over 10 percent since 2004[18] and was predicted by the International Monetary Fund to be the world's third-fastest-growing economy in 2011–2015, trailing only China and India.[19]

All of this marks a sharp change in a country long equated with famine and conflict. Ethiopia suffered from over two decades of instability, bad governance, and war until the mid-1990s. But its current leadership, in power since then, has been committed to inclusive development (albeit with a tendency toward authoritarian rule and sometimes ham-fisted intervention in markets).

This commitment comes from a mixture of ideology and practical politics. As the 2008–2009 Chronic Poverty Report explains, in Ethiopia, "the ideology and rural power base of the ruling party means that the preferences of the rural political elite are joined with those of the poor in rural areas. . . . Throughout its history, the [ruling party] has seen the rural poor as its primary political constituency, and key government policies and programmes have often had a strong rural bias."[20]

Bangladesh has also made impressive strides in improving the lives of its poor, despite having a weak government and a dysfunctional political system. NGOs such as BRAC, Grameen Bank, and Proshika Manobik Unnayan Kendra (Proshika Human Development Centre) have given individuals and communities the tools and support they need to develop. The government, for its part, has recognized the importance of these organizations, encouraging their involvement in policymaking and service delivery.[21]

Despite its reputation for corruption, Cambodia has enjoyed strong growth for over a decade while expanding public services that were decimated during the genocidal regime of the Khmer Rouge. Three out of 4 teachers, 19 out of 20 university students, and 2 out of 3 primary and secondary school pupils were killed or died of overwork under the Khmer Rouge. Today, however, the country is moving toward universal enrollment at the primary school level and has made substantial gains in access to secondary school and in the quality of education at all levels. The late minister of education, Tol Lah, provided the leadership to move toward a more pro-poor, sector-wide planning framework—drawing in part on the pioneering work of a number of NGOs in the sector.[22]

The Importance of Political Development

These four questions highlight the importance of effective government in any country that wants to empower its poor. Effective government, of course, can be hard to find in the developing world—not least because it depends on a country's political development, which is intertwined with but separate from its economic development.

Defined almost half a century ago by Samuel Huntington as "the institutionalization of political organizations and procedures," political development depends on "the extent to which the political organizations and procedures encompass activity in the society" and are able by their "adaptability, complexity, autonomy, and coherence" to resiliently respond to the ever growing needs of rapidly evolving societies.[23] More recently, Francis Fukuyama has explained that political development is a product of three processes: the building of a strong and capable state; the establishment of a strong rule of law; and the creation of an accountable government. Countries can proceed at different speeds in each area but need all three to fully develop.[24]

The importance of political development is illustrated by the crucial role that long-standing institutions have played in the economic success stories of many countries, especially in East Asia. China, Vietnam, and Korea have been able to leverage the public governance knowledge, systems, and cultures built up over millennia to advance development. Turkey was able to make use of its Ottoman (and, looking further back, Byzantine) heritage to build up new institutions in its formative years.

Political development is especially important in the early stages of growth, when leaders have few institutional incentives to act for the common good. As Tony Blair writes:

> In these highly resource-constrained environments, leaders face a daily dilemma: do they try to govern responsibly, and drive a weak and cash-strapped bureaucracy to deliver the services that will persuade people that government is on their side; or do they take the easy way out, and secure the loyalty of their citizens through patronage, favours and intimidation? The rationale for encouraging contested elections, supporting powerful anti-corruption authorities and other accountability mechanisms is to sharpen leaders' incentives to choose the first path. But this assumes that the capacity of the state to respond to what leaders ask it to do is not in question. While this might hold true in developed countries (and it's easier said than done even there, in my experience), it is certainly not the case in many African countries.[25]

Unlike economic development—which has been the focus of research and debate for decades—political development has received little attention, especially in Western countries. Capitalism is too often assumed to work without sufficient attention to its institutional prerequisites. As a result, the processes that produce or advance political development (and the institutionalization of the state) are not well understood, are misunderstood, or are considered unimportant. Few governments or members of the international community make the promotion of political development an explicit policy objective, despite its glaring importance across the developing world.

When international actors seek to improve how less developed countries work, they almost always focus on either the government (for instance, by providing training directly to public servants) or civil society (for instance, by promoting elections and NGOs that can pressure officials). Yet there is little evidence that either of these two approaches—one focused on the supply of good government, the other on the demand for it—can improve governance in the least developed places. Great social divisions and the weak institutionalization of political organizations limit the effectiveness of either approach in such countries.[26]

Promoting "good governance" (or, as discussed in chapter 9, "just-enough governance") is a high priority for donors—but it is different from promoting political development. The former attempts to achieve a set of specific outcomes, typically based on Western norms of how governments are supposed to work, such as regular elections and transparent governmental procedures. The latter is concerned with the degree of institutionalization of the state and the ability of various institutions within it to manage complex, multifaceted tasks in a flexible and resilient manner. Important political and economic institutions have to be able to effectively coordinate large numbers of people and departments, manage interactions with many other entities, and perform across many locations and over long periods of time.

Greater institutionalization is a prerequisite to establishing effective, large government ministries (such as the agricultural and education ministries) and sophisticated regulatory regimes (such as those overseeing business). Institutionalization is equally important to the establishment of large political parties, NGOs, and companies. Implementing an inclusive development agenda requires the organizational capacities that come with high levels of political development—yet developing those capacities is not one of the key goals of the "good governance" agenda. Many of the more successful developing countries—such as the long-established East Asian nations—are highly developed in terms of their political institutions, even though their governance has been deemed poor by Western standards.

Advancing or catalyzing political development is never easy and always takes a long time. In today's poor countries, it is often particularly challenging because of how social divisions and weak governments interact in a vicious cycle that holds back efforts at reform. But enlightened members of a poor country's elite can facilitate and accelerate the process of political development if they follow the kinds of steps suggested throughout this book for how to make their countries better.

How does one turn a rudimentary or ramshackle state into one with a high degree of political development? A complete answer would fill several shelves in a political science library, but the key steps are as follows.[27]

First, establish a predictable political environment. How? By building a stable, durable ruling coalition committed to promoting progress and prepared to make the difficult decisions necessary to achieve it. The more predictable and stable an environment is, the easier it will be for institutions—both inside and outside of the state itself—to develop organizationally. In the least developed places, such stability needs to last at least a generation to have the desired impact on organizational development. The three tools discussed in chapter 7—social cohesion, an inclusive pro-development ideology, and incentives—can play important roles here.

Second, create a rules-based system of governance such that institutions depend less on patronage and relationships. How? Depersonalize government bodies, political parties, companies, and civil society. Institutions that make rules and oversee compliance in a complex environment featuring many different actors have to be apolitical and technocratic if they are to be effective.

Strengthening the ability of the state—or, in some very difficult environments, a third party such as an international organization—to set and enforce rules and arbitrate between different individuals, organizations, and interests is essential to spurring the depersonalizing process.

Third, develop a reservoir of competent personnel. How? By investing in institutions that train managers and other personnel crucial to strengthening large-scale organizations, whether public or private. The biggest institutional shortfall in the developing world as a whole exists at the middle-management level, where millions of people lack any formal training and have never seen a well-managed organization in action up close. Thus, developing countries must make it a high priority to establish and upgrade not only business schools but also universities, accounting schools, public administration academies, law colleges, and a host of other institutions that can accelerate the upgrading of organizations.

Fourth, as the first three steps advance the institutionalization process, make sure that a wide range of institutions develop outside the state. Entities such as companies, political parties, NGOs, trades unions, professional associations, and media must be allowed and encouraged to grow in number, variety, size, and strength. There is a delicate balance here: if organizations independent of key powerbrokers develop too fast when a state is weakly institutionalized, they will either provoke a backlash (because the state is not institutionalized enough to protect them) or destabilize the institutionalization process (because they will undermine stability). But a state cannot develop politically and economically without these independent organizations. They are crucial to nurturing a dynamic economy, improving the rule of law, increasing the accountability of government, and enlarging the opportunities available to a population.

As institutions both within and outside the state mature, they will become more resilient, adaptable, coherent, and capable, especially of managing large tasks that require the participation of hundreds or even thousands of people across many departments and large distances. They will increasingly be able to function independently of any particular person or set of people. Their procedures and methods will become increasingly standardized. And they will be able to manage large numbers of relationships with outside actors on an impersonal, professional basis.

Developing a country politically does not guarantee that it will turn toward an inclusive development agenda that ensures a high level of self-efficacy for everyone, rich and poor. There are certainly examples to the contrary. But the lack of political development markedly increases the chances that a state will be captured by narrow interests in a way that works against the interests of most citizens, and especially the poor.

Building Confidence in Reform

Enlightened leaders who seek to jumpstart a program of reform need to find mechanisms that "lock-in" their efforts if they hope to gain the confidence of powerful political, economic, and social actors. Given that trust between such actors is low in many developing countries, leaders have to make their reform commitments as clear and credible as possible.[28]

Change works best when it is part of a process that reinforces itself over time and enlists the support of an ever larger group of stakeholders and powerbrokers. Creating a virtuous cycle of reform, whereby success in one area nourishes reform in another area, can eventually transform institutions, norms, and capacities. Windows of opportunity produced by a breakdown in existing political and economic arrangements—often caused by some sort of shock—are usually the best time to launch such efforts.

But few will believe in reform efforts initially. Most politicians, investors, and community leaders will be highly skeptical, because long experience with political instability and economic volatility has conditioned them to avoid anything that smacks of risk. Even if leaders are well intentioned, their past records—or at least perceptions of how they behaved in the past—may deter people from believing that this time will be different. When Rawlings introduced economic reforms in Ghana, it took many years before the middle classes risked their capital on new investment, because the country had a long history of instability and the new regime had attacked wealthy interests when it first came to power.[29]

To convince skeptics that one wants to make a real break with the past—that this time is indeed different—requires putting one's own interests on the line and creating mechanisms to prevent reforms being easily reversed. If successful, one will persuade other actors to commit themselves to the process of change, which in turn will convince yet more people to join the effort.

When Colombia sought to build confidence in its restoration of security after years of kidnapping and attacks by guerillas, paramilitaries, and drug traffickers, it devised a program called "Live Colombia, Travel across It" (*"Vive Colombia, Viaja por Ella"*). The program promoted the use of roads and highways and was preceded by a major military, police, and intelligence operation to ensure the security of the road network. By showing people that they could drive across the country without fear, the government restored hope, increased investment, and reactivated tourism and trade.

Both Liberia and Guatemala have sought to bolster confidence in reform by establishing new institutions in partnership with international agencies. Liberia's Governance and Economic Management Assistance Program, which is jointly managed by the government and the international community, oversees state budgets, reducing corruption and mismanagement in the process. The confidence it brings encourages donors and investors to make larger commitments than they would otherwise risk. The International Commission against Impunity in Guatemala (CICIG), created through an agreement with the United Nations in 2007, improves the state's ability to combat gang-related violence and police and judicial corruption by establishing a Special Prosecutor's Office, able to mount its own judicial proceedings. Greater confidence in the country's security and rule of law will change the expectations—and actions—of leaders, businesses, and the average citizen.

There are many ways in which reform-minded leaders can demonstrate a break from the past that will build confidence and encourage others to embrace the cause of reform. For instance, a leader might accomplish the following:

- Establish a realistic agenda and timeline for introducing a specific set of measures to reform the economy, decentralize government, fight corruption, and build a more robust judiciary.
- Appoint people with a reputation for integrity and pro-reformist views to senior ministerial positions.
- Remove discriminatory policies that disadvantage sections of the population.
- Introduce transparency in government expenditures.
- Create new independent agencies to fight corruption, reduce monopolies, oversee elections, monitor budgets, oversee courts, or implement contentious reforms.
- Empower an international organization—such as a regional grouping—to oversee important business agreements, elections, government expenditures, and so on; the same international organization could also help implement reforms (as in the above discussion of Guatemala and Liberia).
- Reallocate resources to enhance the security of ordinary citizens and to make the justice systems more accessible.
- Create mechanisms within the political system to ensure excluded groups have better representation in government (such as introducing quotas or giving minority groups vetoes over certain legislation).

Partnerships That Strengthen Institutions

As emphasized in chapter 13, all international efforts should seek to promote self-reliance. An important aspect of this process is helping countries enhance the workings of their institutions. The international community needs to build upon what local people already know and do and construct bridges to where they might want to go instead of trying to insist that local communities learn entirely new skills and adopt entirely new goals. This calls for a greater appreciation of local knowledge and ways of working and more attention to developing the ability of local people to find their own ways forward.

Foreign donors should try their hand at "accompaniment," whereby a foreign organization partners with governments, local authorities, businesses, or community leaders to improve their implementation capacity—which is typically the biggest challenge for any large organization in developing countries. Accompaniment helps local people build the systems of their organizations such that they gradually become more robust and self-reliant. But it requires real cooperation, as well as openness and humility on the part of the foreign workers.

The American Red Cross helped Haiti's General Hospital build stronger human resource systems by adopting an accompaniment approach. Instead of simply paying for performance-based salary support as it originally intended, the Red Cross decided to work with the General Hospital to set up the systems necessary for it to conduct staff evaluations on its own once it discovered the lack of infrastructure for this purpose. Employees are now better paid, and the hospital is better equipped to manage on its own in the future.[30]

The opportunities for accompaniment are numerous and varied. For instance, well-run NGOs, businesses, and universities (from either the developed or developing world) could cooperate with their counterparts elsewhere in the world to improve the latter's systems and management. The Global Business School Network strengthens management education capacity around the world by matching its network of top business schools with colleagues in the developing world. More ambitiously, countries (or international organizations) could partner with a less developed country (or regional organization) to jointly manage some state functions, in the process transferring knowledge so that the latter builds its own capacity to govern itself. This already happens in Liberia, with its Governance and Economic Management Assistance Program (see main text). Other areas where such partnerships could be effective include the judiciary, education ministries, export-promotion zones, cities, and environmental protection agencies.

Each Country Must Find Its Own Path

The countries that have taken the biggest bite out of poverty (and countries such as Vietnam, Indonesia, and China have taken a very big bite indeed) have at least three things in common. They have political regimes committed to promoting inclusive development. They have the institutional capacity to realize that goal. And they have a development model that fits both their own cultural and social dynamics and their institutional and financial capacities. As a report issued by the Brenthurst Foundation, one of Africa's most prominent think tanks, concludes:

> The Asian model was extremely successful in lifting a large proportion of the global population out of poverty. . . . While lessons can be learned directly from the Asian experience, it is more important to learn some more basic truths from Asia: alternative pathways to development outside the dominant paradigm are possible, and the most effective development strategies are those that harness local institutions, social systems and political realities. . . . Development policy is not just a technical matter, but is a profoundly political process that involves intense contestation. A strong and effective state is needed to oversee and co-ordinate these processes and to ensure that serious destabilization does not take place. . . . A clear sense of vision is needed, but one that is compatible with local resources and institutional capacities. Such visions of the future need to reflect an appreciation of the past and a willingness to accept that the past did have value and should be celebrated.[31]

Given that each country and situation is different, the first step toward reproducing such success is to realize that there are no infallible prescriptions for poor countries, only a process that encourages incremental change. Deng Xiaoping, who as the initiator of China's reforms has arguably been responsible for bringing more people out of poverty than any other person in history, understood this far better than most leaders. He sought to better the lives of the Chinese people by following two principles embodied in two famous quotes of his. "It doesn't matter whether it is a yellow cat or a black cat, a cat that catches mice is a good cat," was one of his mottoes. The other was "Cross the river by feeling for the stones at the bottom of the ford with your feet."

Deng's exhortations to be pragmatic and to proceed cautiously, coupled with the freedom he gave China's citizens to stretch their entrepreneurial muscles, worked wonders. He rarely dictated specific policies; instead, he offered a general direction ("To get rich is glorious!") and then allowed people to try different approaches in different places.

Providing the tools, knowledge, and space for local problem solving enables people to come up with their own solutions—solutions that they will own, understand, can manage, and can grow with. This is what the wisest leaders demand. When he was prime minister of Ethiopia, Meles Zenawi called for a more open-minded approach by the international donor community:

> There has to be more political space for experimentation in development policy than has been the case so far in Africa. . . . The international community has a role in creating such a space by tolerating development paradigms that are different from the orthodoxy preached by it. Africans have to demand and create such a space.[32]

It is not just the international community that should listen to such sage advice. Africans—indeed, people throughout the developing world—should also heed the call for experimentation. Every country, and every region within a country, is different. Those differences are sometimes glaring, but also sometimes subtle, so subtle that they are hard to see close up and impossible to discern from afar. Solutions to local problems must thus be designed, implemented, and adjusted locally.

This book has highlighted some general principles of inclusiveness and empowerment that hold true throughout the developing world. But each part of that world must apply those principles flexibly and imaginatively, crafting unique answers to unique problems.

Notes

Chapter 1

1. Chinua Achebe, *The Trouble with Nigeria* (Oxford: Heinemann, 1985), 1 and 3.
2. Lydia Polgreen, "Change Unlikely from Angolan Election, but Discontent Simmers," *New York Times,* August 31, 2012, http://www.nytimes.com/2012/09/01/world/africa/change-unlikely-from-angola-election-but-discontent-simmers.html.
3. Deepa Narayan, Lant Pritchett, and Soumya Kapoor, "Moving out of Poverty: Success from the Bottom Up" (presentation at Overseas Development Institute, London, May 21, 2009), slide 24.
4. William Easterly, *The White Man's Burden: Why the West's Efforts to Aid the Rest Have Done So Much Ill and So Little Good* (New York: Penguin Press, 2006); Paul Collier, *The Bottom Billion: Why the Poorest Countries Are Failing and What Can Be Done About It* (Oxford: Oxford University Press, 2007); Jeffrey Sachs, *The End of Poverty: Economic Possibilities for Our Time* (New York: Penguin Press, 2005).
5. Dambisa Moyo, *Dead Aid: Why Aid Is Not Working and How There Is a Better Way for Africa* (New York: Farrar, Straus and Giroux, 2009).
6. Hernando de Soto, *The Other Path: The Invisible Revolution in the Third World* (New York: Harper & Row Publishers, 1989); Hernando de Soto, *The Mystery of Capital: Why Capitalism Triumphs in the West and Fails Everywhere Else* (New York: Basic Books, 2000).
7. Daron Acemoglu and James Robinson, *Why Nations Fail: The Origins of Power, Prosperity, and Poverty* (New York: Crown Business, 2012).
8. Jared Diamond, *Guns, Germs, and Steel: The Fates of Human Societies* (New York: W. W. Norton, 1997); Max Weber, *The Protestant Ethic and the Spirit of Capitalism* (New York: Scribner, 1958; originally published in 1905 in German); Niall Ferguson, *Civilization: The West and the Rest* (New York: Penguin Press, 2011); and David Landes, *The Wealth and Poverty of Nations: Why Some Are So Rich and Some So Poor* (New York: W. W. Norton, 1998).
9. Deepa Narayan, Lant Pritchett, and Soumya Kapoor, "Moving out of Poverty: Success from the Bottom Up" (presentation at Overseas Development Institute, London, May 21, 2009), slide 30.
10. See, among others, David Booth, "Development as a Collective Action Problem: Addressing the Real Challenges of African Governance," Synthesis Report of the Africa Power and Politics Programme (London: Overseas Development Institute, 2012), http://www.institutions-africa.org/page/appp+synthesis; Institute of

Development Studies (IDS), *An Upside-Down View of Governance* (Brighton, UK: IDS, 2010), http://www2.ids.ac.uk/gdr/cfs/pdfs/AnUpside-downViewofGovernance.pdf; Lindsay Whitfield, "Reframing the Aid Debate: Why Aid Isn't Working and How It Should Be Changed," DIIS Working Paper 2009:34 (Copenhagen: Danish Institute for International Studies, 2009), http://www.diis.dk/sw87889.asp. An Australian think tank has also contributed to this work; see Adrian Leftwich, "Thinking and Working Politically: What Does It Mean, Why Is It Important and How Do You Do It?" in *Politics, Leadership, and Coalitions in Development: Policy Implications of the DLP Research Evidence*, Developmental Leadership Program Research and Policy Workshop Background Papers, Frankfurt, Germany, March 2011, http://www.dlprog.org/ftp/info/Public%20Folder/Politics,%20Leadership%20and%20Coalitions%20in%20Development%20-%20Policy%20Implications%20of%20the%20DLP%20Research%20Evidence.pdf.html.

11. Douglass North, John Wallis, Steven Webb, and Barry Weingast, eds., *In the Shadow of Violence: Politics, Economics, and the Problems of Development* (Cambridge: Cambridge University Press, 2012). North, Wallis, and Weingast are also the authors of *Violence and Social Orders: A Conceptual Framework for Interpreting Recorded Human History* (Cambridge: Cambridge University Press, 2009).

Chapter 2

1. The first quotation is from 1833, the second from 1828. Both are quoted in Arnoldo De León, *They Called Them Greasers: Anglo Attitudes toward Mexicans in Texas, 1821–1900* (Austin: University of Texas Press, 1983). See http://utpress.utexas.edu/index.php/books/delgre.

2. C. R. L. Fletcher and Rudyard Kipling, *A School History of England* (Oxford: Clarendon Press, 1911), 240.

3. John Cobin, *The Andean Altiplano: Lessons for the Mises-Tullock View of Development*. See *http://www.policyofliberty.net/AndeanAltiplano.html*.

4. Lawrence Harrison, *Underdevelopment Is a State of Mind: The Latin American Case*, updated edition, (Lanham, Maryland: Madison Books, 1995).

5. Oscar Lewis, "The Culture of Poverty," *Society* 35 no. 2 (January, 1998): 7.

6. Samuel Huntington, "Cultures Count," foreword in *Culture Matters*, ed. Lawrence Harrison and Samuel Huntington (New York: Basic Books, 2000), xiii.

7. Mariano Grondona, "A Cultural Typology of Economic Development," in *Culture Matters*, ed. Harrison and Huntington, 50–51.

8. Proverbs 6:9–11.

9. Bill O'Reilly, *The Radio Factor* (a nationally syndicated radio program), June 11, 2004. See http://mediamatters.org/research/200406160005. A similar diagnosis is offered by Myron Magnet, long-time editor of *City Journal*, the flagship magazine of a free market think tank in Manhattan. Magnet argues that poverty among his fellow citizens comes from "a destitution of the soul, a failure to develop the habits of education, reasoning, judgment, sacrifice, and hard work required to succeed in the world." Quoted in H. R. Rodgers, *American Poverty in a New Era of Reform* (New York: M. E. Sharpe, 2000), 69. George Will, the Pulitzer Prize–winning newspaper columnist, attributes poverty to "a scarcity of certain habits and mores—punctuality, hygiene, industriousness, deferral of gratification, etc.—that are not developed in disorganized homes." George F. Will, "Looking Back (and Ahead) with Edwards," *Washington Post*, March 5, 2006.

10. Pew Research Center, *Americans Struggle with Religion's Role at Home and Abroad*, March 20, 2002. See http://www.people-press.org/2002/03/20/part-3-religion-politics-and-policy/.

11. Howard White and Tony Killick, *African Poverty at the Millennium: Causes, Complexities, and Challenges* (Washington: World Bank, 2001), 72.

12. V. I. Lenin, *Imperialism: The Highest Stage of Capitalism* in Selected Works Vol. 1 (Moscow: Foreign Languages Publishing House, 1975, 699–700. [originally published in 1917]

13. I. John Mohan Razu, "The Symbiosis between Poverty and Globalization: A Need for a Critique from Political Ethics National," *Council of Churches of India Review* 120 no. 10 (November 2000): 875–89; online at http://www.religion-online.org/showarticle.asp?title=1108.

14. David Korten, *When Corporations Rule the World* (London: Earthscan, 1995), 229.

15. Deepa Narayan, Lant Pritchett, and Soumya Kapoor, *Moving Out of Poverty: Success from the Bottom Up* (Washington DC: World Bank and Palgrave Macmillan, 2009), 19 and 26.

16. Other especially useful reports include the World Bank's *African Poverty at the Millennium: Causes, Complexities, and Challenges* (Washington DC: World Bank, 2001) and *Poverty Reduction and Growth: Virtuous and Vicious Circles* (Washington DC: World Bank, 2006).

17. See Chronic Poverty Research Centre, *The Chronic Poverty Report 2008–09: Escaping Poverty Traps*, Brooks World Poverty Institute, University of Manchester (Manchester: CPRC, 2008), appendix L, http://www.chronicpoverty.org/publications/details/the-chronic-poverty-report-2008-09.

18. Soumya Kapoor, Deepa Narayan, Saumik Paul, and Nina Badgaiyan, "Caste Dynamics and Mobility in Uttar Pradesh," in ed. Narayan, *Moving Out of Poverty: The Promise of Empowerment and Democracy in India* (Washington DC: World Bank and Palgrave Macmillan, 2009), 167–68, 185–86.

19. Deepa Narayan, Robert Chambers, Meera Shah, and Patti Petesch, *Global Synthesis Consultations with the Poor*, Draft for Discussion (Washington: World Bank Poverty Group, September 20, 1999), 38.

20. Narayan, Pritchett, and Kapoor, *Moving Out of Poverty: Success from the Bottom Up*, 57 and 126.

21. Flora Kessy, Oswald Mashindano, Dennis Rweyemamu, and Prosper Charle, *Moving Out of Poverty: Understanding Growth and Democracy from the Bottom Up*, Regional Synthesis Report (Dar es Salaam: Economic and Social Research Foundation, 2006), 23.

22. Panos London, "Nasreen: Just Surviving," (part of Panos London's *Living with Poverty* series of oral testimonies), http://panos.org.uk/resources/nasreen-just-surviving/.

23. Kessy et al., *Moving Out of Poverty: Understanding Growth and Democracy from the Bottom Up*, 79.

Chapter 3

1. Childhood Poverty Research and Policy Centre (CHIP), *Case Study—Bakyt: Missing Out on School and Play Because of Poverty*, http://www.childhoodpoverty.org/?action=casestudy&id=137.

2. From World Food Programme, "Blog: A Day in the Life of Four African Women," March 8, 2007, http://www.wfp.org/stories/blog-day-life-four-african-women.

3. Quoted in "Economics Focus: A Wealth of Data," *Economist*, July 31, 2010, 62. Researchers at the Oxford Poverty and Human Development Initiative at the University of Oxford have produced the Multidimensional Poverty Index (MPI), which the United Nations Development Programme (UNDP) has included in its "Human Development Report." See http://www.ophi.org.uk/.

4. World Bank, *World Development Report 2010* (Washington: World Bank, 2010), 392.

5. Laurence Chandy and Geoffrey Gertz, *Poverty in Numbers: The Changing State of Global Poverty from 2005 to 2015*, (Washington DC: Brookings Institution, 2011), 3.

6. Shaohua Chen and Martin Ravallion, *Measuring Global Poverty*, Knowledge in Development Notes, World Bank Development Research Group, October 19, 2009, 3. See http://go.worldbank.org/NODTCVO0M0.

7. Rebecca Rolfes, "A Stamp on the World," *Chicago Booth Magazine*, Fall 2012, https://www.chicagobooth.edu/magazine/34/3/Karlan.aspx; Frances Moore Lappe, "Poverty Down! Inequality & Hunger Up . . . Huh?" *Huffington Post*, September 13, 2012, http://www.huffingtonpost.com/frances-moore-lappe/poverty-down-inequality-up_b_1878850.html; and World Bank's PovcalNet, http://iresearch.worldbank.org/PovcalNet/index.htm?1, with $76 per month (the equivalent of $2.50 per day) inserted into its workbook.

8. See Abhijit Banerjee and Esther Duflo. "The Economic Lives of the Poor" (unpublished paper, MIT: Cambridge, MA, 2006), 8 and 32–33; online at http://econ-www.mit.edu/files/530. The authors use $2.16 a day as their cut-off mark, which was the equivalent of the current $2.50 World Bank poverty line at the time they did their research. (The WB poverty lines have grown from $1 and $2 to $1.25 and $2.50 over the past two decades due to inflation.)

9. These statistics date from between 1993 and 2001. Banerjee and Duflo. "The Economic Lives of the Poor," 34 (table 5).

10. United Nations Department of Economic and Social Affairs (UNDESA), *Rethinking Poverty: Report on the World Social Situation 2010* (New York: United Nations, 2009), 57–59.

11. Childhood Poverty Research and Policy Centre, "Case Study—Bakyt: Missing out on School and Play Because of Poverty," (part of CHIP's series of case studies), http://www.childhoodpoverty.org/?action=casestudy&id=137.

12. World Bank, "How We Classify Countries," http://data.worldbank.org/about/country-classifications. Note that "gross national income (GNI) per capita" does not refer to the average wage or salary. GNI per capita is calculated by dividing all the income a country earns from whatever sources by the number of people in that country.

13. Interpretations of the West's recent record in tackling poverty vary widely. Some analysts point to significant improvements in levels of consumption among the poor; see, for example, Nicholas Eberstadt, "Poor Statistics," *Forbes*, March 2, 2009, http://www.forbes.com/forbes/2009/0302/026_on_my_mind.html. Others points to widening gaps in income levels; see, for example, West Coast Poverty Center, "Social and Economic Inequality in the United States" (West Coast Poverty Center, University of Washington, n.d., [2009?]), http://depts.washington.edu/wcpc/Inequality.

14. Laurence Chandy and Geoffrey Gertz, *Poverty in Numbers: The Changing State of Global Poverty from 2005 to 2015*, (Washington DC: Brookings Institution, 2011), 8–10.

15. Andy Sumner, *The New Bottom Billion and the MDGs—A Plan of Action*, IDS in Focus Policy Briefing (Brighton, UK: Institute of Development Studies, 2010).

16. Shaohua Chen and Martin Ravallion, "An Update to the World Bank's Estimates of Consumption Poverty in the Developing World," February 29, 2012, http://siteresources.worldbank.org/INTPOVCALNET/Resources/Global_Poverty_Update_2012_02-29-12.pdf.

17. World Bank, "World Development Indicators 2012" (Washington DC: World Bank, 2012), [Accessed April 2012], http://data.worldbank.org/data-catalog/world-development-indicators.

18. Shaohua Chen and Martin Ravallion, "An Update to the World Bank's Estimates of Consumption Poverty in the Developing World."

19. Shaohua Chen and Martin Ravallion, "An Update to the World Bank's Estimates of Consumption Poverty in the Developing World."

20. UNDP, *Human Development Report 2009*, 176–79.

21. Narayan, Pritchett, and Kapoor, *Moving Out of Poverty: Success from the Bottom Up*, 25.

22. United Nations Development Programme, *Human Development Report 2007* (New York: UNDP, 2007), 26.

23. Guillermo Perry, Omar Arias, J. Humberto López, William Maloney, and Luis Servén, *Poverty Reduction and Growth: Virtuous and Vicious Cycles* (Washington DC: World Bank, 2006), 90.

24. Howard White and Tony Killick, *African Poverty at the Millennium: Causes, Complexities, and Challenges* (Washington DC: World Bank, 2001), 17.

25. Panos London, "Palmira: Great Suffering" (part of Panos London's *Living with Poverty* series of oral testimonies), http://panos.org.uk/resources/pamira-great-suffering/.

26. Panos London, "Deborah: Widows Have Rights," http://panos.org.uk/resources/deborah-widows-have-rights/.

27. Paul Vallely, "From Dawn to Dusk, the Daily Struggle of Africa's Women," *Independent*, September 21, 2006.

28. UNDESA, *Rethinking Poverty*, 124.

29. Panos London, "Basran: Desperate Times," http://www.panos.org.uk/?lid=3798.

30. Kate Bird, David Hulme, Karen Moore, and Andrew Shepherd, *Chronic Poverty and Remote Rural Areas*, Chronic Poverty Research Centre (CPRC) Working Paper no. 13 (Birmingham, UK: CPRC, 2002), 12–13.

31. Seth Kaplan, *Fixing Fragile States: A New Paradigm for Development* (Westport, CT: Praeger Security International, 2008), 89.

32. Howard Husock, "Slums of Hope," *City Journal* 19 no. 1 (New York: Manhattan Institute, Winter 2009), http://www.city-journal.org/2009/19_1_slums.html.

33. White and Killick, *African Poverty at the Millennium*, 86.

34. Panos London, "Warren: The HIV Burden," http://panos.org.uk/resources/warren-the-hiv-burden/.

35. United Nations Children's Fund (UNICEF), *The State of the World's Children 2005* (New York: UNICEF, 2004), 20.

36. John Iliffe, *The African Poor: A History* (Cambridge, UK: Cambridge University Press, 1987), 57.

37. UNICEF, *The State of the World's Children 2005*, table 2, Nutrition, 110–113.

38. See, for instance, Marie Besançon, "Inequality in Ethnic Wars, Revolutions, and Genocides," *Journal of Peace Research* 42 no. 4 (July 2005): 393–415.

39. See Frances Stewart (ed.), *Horizontal Inequalities and Conflict: Understanding Group Violence in Multiethnic Societies* (London: Palgrave, 2010). Also see Ploughshares, *Human Development and Armed Conflict* (Waterloo: Project Ploughshares, 2007).

40. World Bank, *World Development Report 2011: Conflict, Security, and Development* (Washington: World Bank, 2011), 63.

41. Martin Wolf, "Remove the Scourge of Conflict," *Financial Times*, April 26, 2011, http://www.ft.com/cms/s/0/837e25ba-7035-11e0-bea7-00144feabdc0.html#axzz1L3ceDaqe.

42. Geoff Handley, Kate Higgins, and Bhavna Sharma, *Poverty and Poverty Reduction in Sub-Saharan Africa: An Overview of the Issues*, Working Paper 299 (London, UK: Overseas Development Institute, January 2009), 3.

43. United Nations Children's Fund (Unicef), "Adult Wars, Child Soldiers: Voices of Children Involved in Armed Conflict in the East Asia and Pacific Region" (Bangkok: Unicef, October 2002), 17.

44. UN Refugee Agency, *UNHCR Annual Report Shows 42 Million People Uprooted World-wide*, press release, June 16, 2009. See http://www.unhcr.org/4a2fd52412d.html.

45. Anil Aggrawal, "Refugee Medicine," in *Encyclopedia of Forensic and Legal Medicine*, vol. 3, ed. Roger Byard, Jason Payne-James, Tracey Corey, and Carol Henderson (London: Elsevier Academic Press, 2005), 514–525.

46. From "Blog: A Day in the Life of Four African Women," World Food Programme, March 8, 2007, http://www.wfp.org/stories/blog-day-life-four-african-women.

Chapter 4

1. Panos London, "Kishore: Living Prudently" (part of Panos London's *Living with Poverty* series of oral testimonies), http://panos.org.uk/resources/kishore-living-prudently/.

2. This account in based on David Hulme, *Thinking "Small" and the Understanding of Poverty: Maymana and Mofizul's Story*, Institute for Development Policy and Management Working Paper no. 22 (Manchester, UK: University of Manchester, February 2003).

3. See Seth Kaplan, *Fixing Fragile States: A New Paradigm for Development* (Westport, CT: Praeger Security International, 2008), 35–45, and Francis Deng, *Identity, Diversity, and Constitutionalism in Africa* (Washington: United States Institute of Peace Press, 2008), 4.

4. This phrase was used in Kenya in the 2000s by opposition ethnic groups eager to gain power because they believed the government unfairly favored certain ethnic groups and regions. Michela Wrong used it as the title of a book, *It's Our Turn to Eat: The Story of a Kenyan Whistle-Blower* (New York: HarperCollins, 2009).

5. Some of the ideas in this section parallel those put forth in Douglass North, John Wallis, Steven Webb, and Barry Weingast, *In the Shadow of Violence: Politics, Economics, and the Problems of Development* (Cambridge: Cambridge University Press, 2012).

6. Department for International Development (DFID), *Reducing Poverty by Tackling Social Exclusion*, DFID Policy Paper (London: DFID, September 2005), 6–7. Similar problems, of course, afflict the poor in more developed countries. For instance, the report notes that, in Serbia and Montenegro, 30 percent of Roma children have never attended primary school.

7. Deepa Narayan, Patti Petesch, and Saumik Paul, "Communities Where Poor People Prosper," in ed. Narayan, *Moving Out of Poverty: The Promise of Empowerment and Democracy in India* (Washington DC: World Bank and Palgrave Macmillan, 2009), 141.

8. Deng, *Identity, Diversity, and Constitutionalism in Africa*, 7.

9. Panos London, "Lemaron: Challenging Discrimination," http://panos.org.uk/resources/lemaron-challenging-discrimination/.

10. Deepa Narayan, Lant Pritchett, and Soumya Kapoor, *Moving Out of Poverty: Success from the Bottom Up* (Washington: World Bank and Palgrave Macmillan, 2009), 141.

11. Geoff Handley, Kate Higgins, and Bhavna Sharma, *Poverty and Poverty Reduction in Sub-Saharan Africa: An Overview of the Issues*, Working Paper 299 (London, UK: Overseas Development Institute, January 2009), 4–5.

12. Soumya Kapoor, Deepa Narayan, Saumik Paul, and Nina Badgaiyan, "Caste Dynamics and Mobility in Uttar Pradesh," in ed. Narayan, *Moving Out of Poverty: The Promise of Empowerment and Democracy in India* (Washington DC: World Bank and Palgrave Macmillan, 2009), 166.

13. Anand Giridharadas, *India Calling: An Intimate Portrait of a Nation's Remaking* (New York: Times Books, 2011), 39.

14. Flora Kessy, Oswald Mashindano, Dennis Rweyemamu, Prosper Charle, *Moving Out of Poverty: Understanding Growth and Democracy from the Bottom Up*, Regional Synthesis Report (Dar es Salaam: Economic and Social Research Foundation, 2006), 80.

15. DFID, *Reducing Poverty by Tackling Social Exclusion*, 6–7.

16. Bert Koenders, *Engagement in Fragile States: A Balancing Act*, speech at Johns Hopkins University, Washington DC, October 19, 2007.

17. This box borrows heavily from "The Worldwide War on Baby Girls: Technology, Declining Fertility, and Ancient Prejudice Are Combining to Unbalance Societies," *Economist*, May 4, 2010, http://www.economist.com/node/15636231. Also see Amartya Sen, "More Than 100 Million Women Are Missing," *New York Review of Books*, December 20, 1990, http://www.nybooks.com/articles/archives/1990/dec/20/more-than-100-million-women-are-missing/?pagination=false.

18. DFID, *Reducing Poverty by Tackling Social Exclusion*, 6–7.

19. Douglass North, John Wallis, Steven Webb, and Barry Weingast, *In the Shadow of Violence: Politics, Economics, and the Problems of Development* (Cambridge: Cambridge University Press, 2012).

20. Sheila Coronel, Yvonne Chua, Luz Rimban, and Booma Cruz, *The Rulemakers: How the Wealthy and the Well-Born Dominate Congress* (Quezon City, Philippines: Philippine Center for Investigative Journalism, 2007), 49.

21. Panos London, "Karim Bux: Lacking Support," http://panos.org.uk/resources/karim-bux-lacking-support/.

22. Deepa Narayan, Lant Pritchett, and Soumya Kapoor, *Moving Out of Poverty: Success from the Bottom Up* (Washington: World Bank and Palgrave Macmillan, 2009), 140.

23. These surveys include the World Values Survey, a worldwide survey conducted by social scientists every five years. See Omar Azfar, *Institutions and Poverty Reduction*, draft, February 2005, p. 22, http://siteresources.worldbank.org/INTPGI/Resources/342674-1115051862644/Institutions8.pdf.

24. Quoted from community timeline focus group, Dang Kdar, in Ingrid FitzGerald and So Sovannarith, *Moving Out of Poverty? Trends in Community Well-being and Household Mobility in Nine Cambodian Villages* (Cambodia Development Resource Institute, August 2007), 116–8.

25. Deepa Narayan, Lant Pritchett, and Soumya Kapoor, *Moving Out of Poverty: Success from the Bottom Up* (Washington: World Bank and Palgrave Macmillan, 2009), 245–46.

26. Panos London, "Mircho: Losing Dignity," http://panos.org.uk/resources/mircho-losing-dignity/.
27. Onyebuchi Ezigbo, "Nigeria: MDGs–Poverty Rate Rises to 76 Percent–UN," allAfrica.com, February 27, 2009, http://allafrica.com/stories/200902270161.html.
28. Peter Ekeh, "Colonialism and the Two Publics in Africa: A Theoretical Statement," *Comparative Studies in Society and History* 17 no. 1 (January 1975): 108 and 111.
29. William Easterly, *Can Institutions Resolve Ethnic Conflict?* Policy Research Working Paper Series 2482, (World Bank, February 2000), 12.
30. Gary Haugen and Victor Boutros, "And Justice for All: Enforcing Human Rights for the World's Poor," *Foreign Affairs* 89 no. 3 (May/June 2010), 51–62.
31. Stephen Philip Cohen, *The Idea of Pakistan* (Washington DC: Brookings Institution Press, 2005), 69.
32. U.S. Department of State, "Background Note: China," October 2009, http://www.state.gov/r/pa/ei/bgn/18902.htm.
33. Wayne M. Morrison, *China's Economic Conditions*, CRS Report for Congress (Washington: Congressional Research Service, December 11, 2009), 10, http://www.dtic.mil/cgi-bin/GetTRDoc?AD=ADA511980.
34. UNICEF, State of the World's Children 2007 (New York: UNICEF, 2006), http://www.unicef.org/sowc07/docs/sowc07.pdf.
35. Asian Development Bank Statistical Database System Online, https://sdbs.adb.org/sdbs/index.jsp.
36. Kareem Fahim, Michael Slackman, and David Rohde, "Egypt's Ire Turns to Confidant of Mubarak's Son," *New York Times*, February 7, 2011, A1.
37. Deepa Narayan, Lant Pritchett, and Soumya Kapoor, *Moving Out of Poverty: Success from the Bottom Up* (Washington: World Bank and Palgrave Macmillan, 2009), 180.
38. See, for instance, Naomi Mapstone, "Bolivia's President Keeps Faith with Populism," *FinancialTimes*, December 4, 2009. http://www.ft.com/cms/s/0/f48c1118-e0fd-11de-af7a-00144feab49a.html.

Chapter 5

1. A number of other authors have discussed traps that poor countries fall into. For instance, see the discussion of "capability traps" in Lant Pritchett and Frauke de Weijer, "Fragile States: Stuck in a Capability Trap?" *World Development Report 2011* Background Paper, October 2010, http://siteresources.worldbank.org/EXTWDR2011/Resources/6406082-1283882418764/WDR_Background_Paper_Pritchett.pdf; and the discussion of "conflict traps," "natural resource traps," "landlocked with bad neighbors traps," and "bad governance in a small country traps" in Paul Collier, *The Bottom Billion: Why the Poorest Countries Are Failing and What Can Be Done About It* (Oxford: Oxford University Press, 2007).
2. United Nations Development Programme, *Human Development Report 2009*, table H, Human Development Index 2007 and Its Components (New York: UNDP, 2009), 171–75.
3. International Finance Corporation (*IFC), "Starting a Business," in *Doing Business: Measuring Business Regulation* (Washington: IFC, 2010), http://www.doingbusiness.org/ExploreTopics/StartingBusiness/?direction=Desc&sort=4.
4. IFC, "Getting Credit," *Doing Business: Measuring Business Regulation* (Washington: IFC, 2010), http://www.doingbusiness.org/ExploreTopics/GettingCredit/?direction=Asc&sort=5.

5. Guillermo Perry, Omar Arias, J. Humberto López, William Maloney, and Luis Servén, *Poverty Reduction and Growth: Virtuous and Vicious Cycles* (Washington DC: World Bank, 2006), 104.

6. Seid Hassan, "To Invest or Not to Invest in Ethiopia," *Ethiopian Review,* July 28, 2008, http://www.ethiopianreview.com/content/3010.

7. María Teresa Matijasevic (Report Director), *Moving Out of Poverty: Understanding Freedom, Growth and Democracy from the Bottom Up,* National Synthesis Report (Manizales, Colombia: Centro de Estudios Regionales Cafeteros y Empresariales, May 2007), 105.

8. Philibert de Mercey, Alejandra Val Cubero, and Najibullah Ziar, *Moving Out of Poverty: Understanding Freedom, Democracy and Growth from the Bottom Up,* Afghanistan National Synthesis Report (Kabul, Afghanistan: Altai Consulting, 2006), 43.

9. Flora Kessy, Oswald Mashindano, Dennis Rweyemamu, and Prosper Charle, *Moving Out of Poverty: Understanding Growth and Democracy from the Bottom Up,* Tanzania Regional Synthesis Report (Dar es Salaam, Tanzania: Economic and Social Research Foundation, 2006), 43.

10. Andrés Oppenheimer, "Education Too Important to Be Left in Government Hands," *Miami Herald,* October 3, 2010.

11. Perry, Arias, López, Maloney, and Servén, *Poverty Reduction and Growth,* 129.

12. Jayshree Bajoria, "Stabilizing Pakistan: Boosting Its Private Sector" (New York: Council on Foreign Relations, April 30, 2009). See http://www.cfr.org/publication/19260/stabilizing_pakistan.html.

13. Andres Oppenheimer, "Quake May Delay Chile's First World Goal," *Miami Herald,* March 4, 2010.

14. Sri Kusumastuti Rahayu and Vita Febriany, *Moving Out of Poverty: Understanding Freedom, Democracy, Governance, and Growth from the Bottom Up,* Indonesia Country Synthesis Report (Jakarta, Indonesia: SMERU Research Institute, 2007), 83.

15. Centre for Poverty Analysis (CEPA), *Moving Out of Poverty in the Estate Sector in Sri Lanka: Understanding Growth and Freedom from the Bottom Up* (Colombo, Sri Lanka: CEPA, 2005), 55.

16. Philibert de Mercey, Alejandra Val Cubero, and Najibullah Ziar, *Moving Out of Poverty: Understanding Freedom, Democracy, and Growth from the Bottom Up,* Afghanistan National Synthesis Report (Kabul, Afghanistan: Altai Consulting, 2006), 36.

17. Aart Kraay, "When Is Growth Pro-Poor? Evidence from a Panel of Countries," *Journal of Development Economics* 80 no. 1 (June 2006): 198–227.

Chapter 6

1. Reinhard Bendix. *Max Weber: An Intellectual Portrait* (Berkeley, CA: University of California Press, 1977), 124–25 and 135–41. The original source of these observations is Max Weber, *The Religion of China: Confucianism and Taoism,* which was first published in 1915 in German. An English-language version was published in 1951.

2. Arvind Subramanian, "India's Weak State Will Not Overhaul China," *Financial Times,* August 16, 2010.

3. The phrase "Hindu rate of growth" has been widely used. See, for instance, Montek Singh Ahluwalia, "First Raj Krishna Memorial Lecture, 1995: Economic Reforms for the Nineties" (University of Rajasthan, Jaipur, India).

4. Albert Bandura, "Personal and Collective Efficacy in Human Adaptation and Change," in *Advances in Psychological Science,* vol. 1, *Social, Personal, and Cultural Aspects,* ed. J. G. Adair and D. Belanger (Hove, England: Psychology Press/Erlbaum [UK] Taylor & Francis, 1998), 51–71, http://jamiesmithportfolio.com/EDTE800/wp-content/PrimarySources/Bandura2.pdf.

5. Deepa Narayan, Lant Pritchett, and Soumya Kapoor, *Moving Out of Poverty: Success from the Bottom Up* (Washington: World Bank and Palgrave Macmillan, 2009), 127–28.

6. Frances Tay McHugh, *Empowerment Social Development* (http://www.scribd.com/doc/2296028/Empowerment-Social-Development, 2008), 3.

7. The other two were security and opportunities. World Bank Group, *Attacking Poverty: World Development Report 2000/2001* (Oxford: Oxford University Press, 2000).

8. See, for instance, James Wolfensohn, "Securing the 21st Century" (address to the Board of Governors of the World Bank Group at the Joint Annual Discussion during the 2004 Annual Meetings, Washington DC, October 3, 2004).

9. See, among others, Amartya Sen, *Development as Freedom* (New York: Knopf, 1999).

10. Narayan, Pritchett, and Kapoor, *Moving Out of Poverty*, 132.

11. Ibid., 126.

12. Ibid., 126.

13. Ibid., 171.

14. Panos London, "Lemaron: Challenging Discrimination," http://panos.org.uk/resources/lemaron-challenging-discrimination/.

15. Oscar Lewis, *La Vida: A Puerto Rican Family in the Culture of Poverty* (New York: Random House, 1965), xl–xli.

16. Khaled Diab, "Out of Egypt," *Guardian,* January 15, 2008, http://www.guardian.co.uk/commentisfree/2008/jan/15/outofegypt.

17. David Martin, "The Evangelical Upsurge and Its Political Implications," in *The Descularization of the World*, ed. Peter L. Berger (Washington DC: Ethics and Public Policy Center, 1999), 39, 41.

18. This point and the resulting sociopolitical dynamics are at the center of my book on fragile states. See Seth Kaplan, *Fixing Fragile States: A New Paradigm for Development* (Westport, CT: Praeger Security International, 2008), 35–45. It is also discussed in Gareth Williams, Alex Duncan, Pierre Landell-Mills, and Sue Unsworth, "Politics and Growth," *Development Policy Review* 29 no. S1 (January 2011): S41.

19. Raphaël Franck and Ilia Rainer, "Does the Leader's Ethnicity Matter? Ethnic Favoritism, Education, and Health in Sub-Saharan Africa," *American Political Science Review* 106 no. 2 (May 2012): 294–325.

20. Giorgio Blundo and Jean-Pierre Olivier de Sardan , "The Popular Semiology of Corruption," in Blundo and de Sardan (eds.), *Everyday Corruption and the State (*2006), 112.

21. Mahaman Tidjani Alou, "Corruption in the Legal System," in Blundo and de Sardan (eds.), *Everyday Corruption and the State (*2006), 145–46.

22. Robert Wade, "The Market for Public Office: Why the Indian State Is Not Better at Development," *World Development* 13 no. 4 (1985): 477.

23. Blundo and Olivier de Sardan, "The Popular Semiology of Corruption," 116.

24. Natalie J. Kitroeff, "Castresana Resigns, the Fight against Corruption in Guatemala Intensifies," *www.freedomhouse.org,* June 17, 2010, http://blog.freedomhouse.org/weblog/2010/06/castresana-resigns-the-fight-against-corruption-in-guatemala-intensifies.html.

Chapter 7

1. Kwesi Ahwoi, "Government's Role in Attracting Viable Agricultural Investment: Experiences from Ghana" (presentation at the World Bank Annual Conference on Land Policy and Administration, Washington DC, April 26–27, 2010), 11.

2. Steven Radelet, *Emerging Africa: How 17 Countries Are Leading the Way* (Washington DC: Center for Global Development, 2010), 9 and 71–72.

3. Rawlings was not the first Ghanaian leader to focus on inclusiveness. The founder of Ghana, Kwame Nkrumah, both made national unity a major objective and took an ethnically blind approach to policymaking. Arnim Langer, "When Do Horizontal Inequities Lead to Conflict? Lessons from a Comparative Study of Ghana and Côte d'Ivoire," in Frances Stewart, ed., *Horizontal Inequities: Understanding Group Violence in Multiethnic Societies* (New York: Palgrave Macmillan, 2008), 176–86.

4. Nuhu Ribadu, *Challenging Corruption in Africa: Beyond the Bleak Projections* (Washington DC: Center for Global Development, August 2010), 2.

5. "Africa's Year of Elections: The Democracy Bug Is Fitfully Catching On," *Economist*, July 22, 2010, http://www.economist.com/node/16640325.

6. Deepa Narayan, Lant Pritchett, and Soumya Kapoor, *Moving Out of Poverty: Success from the Bottom Up* (Washington DC: World Bank and Palgrave Macmillan, 2009), 253.

7. Ibid., 249.

8. Lydia Polgreen, "Turnaround of India State Could Serve as a Model," *New York Times*, April 11, 2010, A6, http://www.nytimes.com/2010/04/11/world/asia/11bihar.html; and Jim Yardley, "Turning Around an Indian State," *New York Times*, November 24, 2010, A6, http://www.nytimes.com/2010/11/24/world/asia/24bihar.html.

9. Pew Research Center, "Pew Globale Attitudes Project: Key Indicators Database," 2010 results, http://pewglobal.org/database/?indicator=3.

10. When demonstrators in Cairo filled the streets demanding regime change, those in Muscat came out in fewer numbers and actually expressed support for their leader (while also demanding some reforms). Robert Kaplan, "Why the World Needs Virtuous Autocrats," *Financial Times*, March 2, 2011, http://www.ft.com/cms/s/0/403b2920-450a-11e0-80e7-00144feab49a.html#axzz1KxN7o64q.

11. This definition of *social cohesion* is broader than that used by some activists and scholars who equate it with the redistribution of money via progressive taxation and income-support programs for the poor. See, for instance, the many reports published on social cohesion by the European Union and the Council of Europe.

12. "Social cohesion determines the quality of institutions, which in turn has important impacts on whether and how pro-growth policies are devised and implemented . . . key development outcomes (the most widely available being 'economic growth') should be more likely to be associated with countries governed by effective public institutions, and that those institutions, in turn, should be more likely to be found in socially cohesive societies." William Easterly, Jozef Ritzan, and Michael Woolcock, "Social Cohesion, Institutions, and Growth," Working Paper no. 94 (Washington DC: Center for Global Development, August 2006), 1–2.

13. Charles Tilly has argued that war makes the state and the state makes war. See Tilly, *Coercion, Capital, and the European States, AD 990–1990* (Cambridge, MA: Basil Blackwell, 1990).

14. "A country's social cohesion is essential for generating the confidence and patience needed to implement reforms: citizens have to trust the government that the short-term losses inevitably arising from reform will be more than offset by long-term gains . . . countries strongly divided along class and ethnic lines will place severe constraints on the attempts . . . to bring about policy reform." Easterly, Ritzan, and Woolcock, *Social Cohesion, Institutions, and Growth*, 1–2.

15. For a lengthier discussion, see Seth Kaplan, *Fixing Fragile States: A New Paradigm for Development* (Westport, CT: Praeger Security International, 2008), chapter 2.

16. Lee Kuan Yew, *From Third World to First: The Singapore Story: 1965–2000* (New York: HarperCollins, 2000), 691.

17. United Nations Economic Commission for Latin America (ECLA), *Social Cohesion: Inclusion and a Sense of Belonging in Latin America and the Caribbean* (Santiago, Chile: United Nations, 2007), 9–10.

18. Paul Kagame, "Oppenheimer Lecture 2010," delivered at The International Institute For Strategic Studies, London, September 16, 2010, http://www.iiss.org/conferences/oppenheimer-lecture/oppenheimer-lecture-2010-paul-kagame/.

19. Many of these same themes appear in the Peacebuilding and Statebuilding Goals (PSGs) formulated by the International Dialogue on Peacebuilding and Statebuilding, reflecting the important role fragile and conflict-affected countries play in this process. See http://www.newdeal4peace.org/peacebuilding-and-statebuilding-goals/.

20. "Ethiopian PM Prescribes Developmental State Paradigm for African States," *Ethiopian News (ethiopian-news.com)*, March 29, 2011, http://www.ethiopian-news.com/ethiopian-pm-prescribes-developmental-state-paradigm-for-african-states/.

21. Tim Kelsall and David Booth, *Developmental Patrimonialism? Questioning the Orthodoxy on Political Governance and Economic Progress in Africa*, Working Paper No. 9 (London: Africa Power and Politics Programme, July 2010), 11–24; Paul Collier, "The Case for Investing in Africa," *McKinsey Quarterly*, July 2010, https://www.mckinseyquarterly.com/Africa/The_case_for_investing_in_Africa_2611; and Annie Chikwanha, "Governing on a Pressure Cooker," www.the-african.org, August 2010, 12, http://www.issafrica.org/publication/The-African/Archive/Issue8%20August-September % 202010.pdf.

22. Benjamin Leo and Julia Barmeier, *Who Are the MDG Trailblazers? A New MDG Progress Index*, Working Paper 222 (Washington DC: Center for Global Development, August 2010), 16.

23. Mahathir Mohamad, Vision 2020: The Way Forward," speech given to the Malaysian Business Council, http://www.pmo.gov.my/?menu=page&page=1904.

24. Séverine Deneulin and Masooda Bano, *Religion in Development: Rewriting the Secular Script* (London: Zed Books, 2009), 88–98.

25. The Arab septet includes Syria, Egypt, Libya, Jordan, Oman, Morocco, and Tunisia, all of which score exceedingly well on indicators that measure "the level of, and change in, average welfare/deprivation, using data covering at least 20 years between 1970 and 2003." CPRC, *Chronic Poverty Report 2008–09*, 14–15.

26. Among the 21 "Partial Consistent Improvers," the second-highest CPR categorization, 6 are Middle Eastern states with a majority (60 percent or above) Muslim population: Iran, Lebanon, Turkey, Algeria, Kuwait, and the United Arab Emirates.

27. Only Iraq, Yemen, and Saudi Arabia are in the bottom two categories (the West Bank and Gaza has insufficient data to be categorized), and two of these have been plagued by violence.

28. Deneulin and Bano, *Religion in Development*, 138.

29. Interview with the author, September 2010.
30. Rachel Naylor, *Ghana: An Oxfam Country Profile* (Oxford, UK: 2000), 22.
31. Alex de Waal, "The Price of Peace," *Prospect*, November 17, 2009, http://www.prospectmagazine.co.uk/2009/11/the-price-of-peace/; and Kelsall and Booth, *Developmental Patrimonialism?*
32. De Waal, "The Price of Peace"; Adrian Leftwich, "Developmental States, Effective States and Poverty Reduction: The Primacy of Politics," UNRISD Project on Poverty Reduction and Policy Regimes (Geneva: United Nations Research Institute for Social Development, 2008), 21.
33. Leslie Elliott Armijo and Philippe Faucher, "We Have a Consensus: Explaining Political Support for Market Reforms in Latin America," *Latin American Politics and Society* 44 no. 2 (July 2002): 1–40.
34. Kelsall and Booth, *Developmental Patrimonialism?* 4–5.
35. World Bank, *World Development Report 2006* (Washington: World Bank, 2006), 126–27.
36. Kelsall and Booth, *Developmental Patrimonialism?* 4–5.
37. Department for International Development (DFID), *The Politics of Poverty: Elites, Citizens, and States* (London: DFID, 2010), 88–89.
38. Gareth Williams, Alex Duncan, Pierre Landell-Mills, and Sue Unsworth, "Politics and Growth," *Development Policy Review* 29 (January 2011): S43.
39. Some of these ideas come from Adrian Leftwich, "Developmental States, Effective States and Poverty Reduction: The Primacy of Politics," UNRISD Project on Poverty Reduction and Policy Regimes (Geneva: United Nations Research Institute for Social Development, 2008), 22.
40. Seth Kaplan, "The Remarkable Story of Somaliland," *Journal of Democracy* 19 no. 3 (July 2008), 148.
41. Institute of Development Studies (IDS), *An Upside-Down View of Governance* (Brighton, UK: IDS, 2010), 13, and DFID, *The Politics of Poverty*, 8.

Chapter 8

1. Human Rights Watch (HRW) interview with 20-year-old commercial minibus passenger, Lagos, November 27, 2008. HRW, *"Everyone's in on the Game": Corruption and Human Rights Abuses by the Nigeria Police Force* (New York: HRW, August 2010), 29.
2. HRW, *"Everyone's in on the Game,"* 2–4 and 62.
3. Anatol Lieven, *Pakistan: A Hard Country* (New York: Public Affairs, 2011), 105 and 108.
4. Charles Kenny, *Learning about Schools in Development*, Working Paper 236 (Washington DC: Center for Global Development, 2010), 5.
5. Jim Yardley, "India Asks, Should Food Be a Right?" *New York Times*, August 9, 2010, A1.
6. Jim Yardley, "In India, Dynamism Wrestles with Dysfunction," *New York Times*, June 9, 2011, A1.
7. Tony Blair, *Not Just Aid: How Making Government Work Can Transform Africa*, public address at the Center for Global Development, Washington DC, December 16, 2010, 2.
8. This happens everywhere, even in rich countries, but is much more likely where governments work badly.

9. Knowledge@Wharton, *Punj Lloyd's Atul Punj: Why Fixing Rural Infrastructure Is India's Top Priority*, India Knowledge@Wharton (August 15, 2010), http://knowledge.wharton.upenn.edu/india/article.cfm?articleid=4513.

10. Ogaga Ifowodo, "Yes Opinion in 'Debate: Is Nigeria a Failed State?'" *BBC*, July 7, 2009, http://news.bbc.co.uk/2/hi/africa/8112800.stm.

11. Transparency International, *Corruptions Perceptions Index 2010 Results* (Berlin: Transparency International, 2010), http://www.transparency.org/policy_research/surveys_indices/cpi/2010/results.

12. International Monetary Fund, *2010 World Economic Outlook* (Washington DC: IMF, 2010), http://www.indexmundi.com/cambodia/gdp_real_growth_rate.html.

13. Lieven, *Pakistan*, 27.

14. Some scholars have argued that some countries may take centuries to create a robust government apparatus or may never create one. See, for instance, Lant Pritchett and Frauke de Weijer, "Fragile States: Stuck in a Capability Trap?" *World Development Report 2011*, Background Paper, October 2010, http://siteresources.worldbank.org/EXTWDR2011/Resources/6406082-1283882418764/WDR_Background_Paper_Pritchett.pdf.

15. Steven Radelet, *Emerging Africa: How 17 Countries Are Leading the Way* (Washington DC: Center for Global Development, 2010), 87–88.

16. In some places, states do such a miserable job of enforcing the law, delivering public services, and securing property that people seek out alternatives. Faith-based organizations, for instance, provide half of the health care and schooling in Sub-Saharan Africa, partly because the states are unable to. James Wolfensohn, "Millennium Challenges for Faith and Development: New Partnerships to Reduce Poverty and Strengthen Conservation" (speech to the Interfaith Conference of Metropolitan Washington, Trinity College, Washington DC, March 30, 2004).

17. See, for instance, Dennis de Tray, "Only an Aid Rethink Can Save Afghanistan," *Financial Times*, June 16, 2011, http://www.ft.com/intl/cms/s/0/9590300e-979f-11e0-9c37-00144feab49a.html#axzz1Qr2yvxka.

18. Some of these ideas come from Merilee Grindle, "Good Enough Governance Revisited," *Development Policy Review* 29, issue supplement (January 2011): S208–09.

19. Many of the ideas in this section come from the Africa Power and Politics Programme, a consortium (led by the Overseas Development Institute) of research organizations and policy think tanks in France, Ghana, Niger, Uganda, the United Kingdom, and the United States. For more information, see http://www.institutions-africa.org/.

20. See Tim Kelsall, "Going with the Grain in African Development?" *Development Policy Review* 26 no. 6 (November 2008): 627–55, and David Booth, "Aid, Institutions and Governance: What Have We Learned?" *Development Policy Review* 29, issue supplement (January 2011): s5–s26.

21. The 85 percent figure was recorded in 2003. World Bank, *World Development Report 2006: Equity and Development* (Washington DC: World Bank, 2006), 159.

22. Department for International Development (DFID), *The Politics of Poverty: Elites, Citizens, and States* (London: DFID, 2010), 46–47.

23. Blair, *Not Just Aid*, 11–12.

24. Levy, "Development Trajectories," 6.

25. Caroline Sage and Michael Woolcock, "Breaking Legal Inequality Traps: New Approaches to Building Justice Systems for the Poor in Developing Countries" (paper presented at the World Bank conference New Frontiers of Social Policy: Development in a Globalizing World, Arusha, Tanzania, December 12–15, 2005), 20.

26. Janine Ubink and Benjamin van Rooij, *Towards Customary Legal Empowerment: An Introduction* (Rome: International Development Law Organization, 2011), 17.

27. Sage and Woolcock, "Breaking Legal Inequality Traps," 26.

28. Ha-Joon Chang, "Institutional Development in Developing Countries in a Historical Perspective: Lessons from Developed Countries in Earlier Times" (paper presented at the European Association of Evolutionary Political Economy Annual Meeting, Siena, Italy, November 8–11, 2001), 1–2.

29. Ricardo Hausmann, Dani Rodrik, and Andrés Velasco, "Growth Diagnostics," John F. Kennedy School of Government, Harvard University (Cambridge, MA: Harvard, 2005).

30. Brian Levy, "Development Trajectories: An Evolutionary Approach to Integrating Governance and Growth," *Economic Premise* 15 (Washington DC: World Bank, May 2010).

31. Ibid.

32. Among other things, increasing trade and business links between regions promotes common interests in stability, growth, and a stronger central government.

33. See UNICEF, *Enquete Nationale sur la Situation des Enfants et des Femmes*, MICS2/2001 (Kinshasa, DRC: UNICEF, July 2002), 31, 43, and 69.

34. Ministry of Education, Science, and Sports, *The Development and State of the Art of Adult Learning and Education* (Accra, Ghana: Ministry of Education, Science, and Sports, March 2008), 27.

35. Jean-Paul Rodrigue and Cesar Ducruet, *The Geography of Transport Systems* (New York: Routledge, 2009), http://people.hofstra.edu/geotrans/eng/ch1en/conc1en/ch1c3en.html.

36. Wendell Cox, "China Expressway System to Exceed U.S. Interstates," *NewGeography.com*, January 11, 2011, http://www.newgeography.com/content/002003-china-expressway-system-exceed-us-interstates.

37. World Bank, *World Development Report 2006*, 169–70.

38. Lee Kuan Yew, *From Third World to First: The Singapore Story, 1965–*2000 (New York: HarperCollins, 2000), 664–65.

39. This section combines information from two sources: Knowledge@Wharton Network, *Change of State: Bihar Gains, Bengal Wanes*, India Knowledge@Wharton, January 28, 2010, http://knowledge.wharton.upenn.edu/india/article.cfm?articleid=4446; and Lydia Polgreen, "Turnaround of India State Could Serve as a Model," *New York Times*, April 11, 2010, 6.

Chapter 9

1. Lydia Polgreen, "15 and Broke in a Cut-Throat Congo Mining Town," *New York Times*, November 16, 2008, http://www.nytimes.com/2008/11/16/world/africa/16imani.html.

2. Lydia Polgreen, "Congo's Riches, Looted by Renegade Troops," *New York Times*, November 16, 2008, A1, http://www.nytimes.com/2008/11/16/world/africa/16congo.html?ref=africa.

3. It was once the leading source for industrial diamonds worldwide, and it has one of the world's greatest concentrations of copper, cobalt, and coltan (10 percent, 33 percent, and 85 percent, respectively, of global reserves). Uranium for the first U.S. atomic bomb was mined in the territory. See http://www.cyberwonders.com/law/index.php/intl/2005/12/21/dr_congo_new_constitution.

4. Melanie Stiassny, "The Challenge of Traveling the Congo River," Scientist at Work Blog, *New York Times*, August 10, 2010, http://scientistatwork.blogs.nytimes.com/2010/08/10/the-challenge-of-traveling-the-congo-river/.

5. In 2003, GDP per capita had fallen to only 28 percent of its level at independence. USAID/DRC, *USAID/DRC Integrated Strategic Plan FY 2004–2008*, 6.

6. Nicholas Kristof, "Orphaned, Raped, and Ignored," *New York Times*, January 31, 2010.

7. Some of the ideas in this paragraph are borrowed from Jeffrey Herbst, *State and Power in Africa: Comparative Lessons in Authority and Control* (Princeton, NJ: Princeton University Press, 2000).

8. Robert Picciotto, "Conflict Prevention and Development Co-operation in Africa: An Introduction," *Conflict, Security & Development* 10 no. 1 (March 2010), 19–20.

9. Panos London, "Pedro: Importance of Agriculture," (part of Panos London's *Living with Poverty* series of oral testimonies), http://panos.org.uk/resources/pedro-importance-of-agriculture/.

10. Overseas Development Institute (ODI), *Mapping Progress: Evidence for a New Development Outlook*, Progress in Development: A Library of Stories project (London: ODI, 2011), 42 and 46, www.developmentprogress.org.

11. ODI, *Mapping Progress*, 40; and Jakob Engel, *Ethiopia's Progress in Education: A Rapid and Equitable Expansion of Access* (London: ODI, 2010).

12. ODI, *Mapping Progress*, 40.

13. Stephen Biddle, Fotini Christia, and J. Alexander Thier, "Defining Success in Afghanistan: What Can the United States Accept?" *Foreign Affairs* 89 no. 4 (July–August 2010): 52.

14. Alfred Stepan, Juan J. Linz, and Yogendra Yadav, "The Rise of 'State-Nations,'" *Journal of Democracy* 21 no. 3 (July 2010), 50–68.

15. Biddle, Christia, and Their, "Defining Success in Afghanistan," 52–54.

16. Anatol Lieven, *A Hard Country* (New York: Public Affairs, 2011), 260.

17. Many of the top-down ideas, including these two examples, come from David Booth, "Towards a Theory of Local Governance and Public Goods Provision in Sub-Saharan Africa," Draft, June 2010.

18. Paul Collier, *The Bottom Billion: Why the Poorest Countries Are Failing and What Can Be Done About It* (Oxford: Oxford University Press, 2007), 150.

19. Tim Kelsall, "Going with the Grain in African Development?" Discussion Paper No. 1 (London: Africa Power and Politics Programme, 2008), 12–14.

20. For West African figures, see Nwakego Linda Eyisi, "Potential of ECOWAS Economic Community in Africa," Afribiz.info, March 23, 2010, http://www.afribiz.info/?p=3804. For Norway's, see World Bank, World Development Indicators database, http://data.worldbank.org/indicator.

21. United Nations Development Programme, *Human Development Report*. See http://hdr.undp.org.

22. As measured by the Human Development Index in United Nations Development Programme (UNDP), *Human Development Report 2010*.

23. World Bank, *Memorandum of the President of the International Development Association to the Executive Directors on a Regional Integration Assistance Strategy for West Africa* (Washington DC: World Bank, July 11, 2001), 3.

24. See http://www.doingbusiness.org/data/exploretopics/getting-electricity for the information on electricity. There are numerous studies of the problems of transporting

goods across the region. See, for instance, the USAID–funded http://www
.watradehub.com/activities/tradewinds/jan11/2011-leaders-expect-west-africas-
continued-business-success.

25. World Bank, *Doing Business in 2011: Making a Difference for Entrepreneurs*
(Washington DC: World Bank, 2010), 184.

26. United Nations Economic Commission for Africa (UNECA) and World Bank,
*Africa Transport Technical Note: Improving Management and Financing of Roads
in Sub-Saharan Africa* for the Sub-Saharan Africa Transport Policy Program
(SSATP), December 1999 (See the SSATP website http://web.worldbank.org/
WBSITE/EXTERNAL/COUNTRIES/AFRICAEXT/EXTAFRREGTOPTRA/
EXTAFRSUBSAHTRA/0,,menuPK:1513942~pagePK:64168427~piPK:6416
8435~theSitePK:1513930,00.html); UNECA, *Economic Report on Africa 2004:
Unlocking Africa's Trade Potential* (Addis Ababa: Economic Commission for
Africa, 2004), 163.

27. Commission for Africa, *Our Common Interest: Report of the Commission for Africa*
(London: Commission for Africa, 2005), box 8.3, 258.

28. New America Foundation, "Potential India-Pakistan Trade at Least 10 Times Current Amount: Stakeholders in Both Countries Recognize Vast Benefits of Normal-
izing Trade Relations," January 30, 2013, http://newamerica.net/pressroom/2013/
new_report_potential_india_pakistan_trade_at_least_10_times_current_amount.

29. He goes on to say that it is "unacceptable" that the cost of shipping a truckload of
goods across an African country's border often exceeds the cost of the goods themselves. Africa urgently needs good roads and transportation links (see chapter 10).
Charles W. Corey, "'Mo' Ibrahim: Governments Need to Foster, not Frustrate, Business," U.S. Department of State website www.america.gov, May 3, 2010, http://
www.america.gov/st/business-english/2010/May/20100430155029WCyeroC9.975
833e-02.html.

30. David Smith, "Change Beckons for Billionth African," *The Guardian*, December 28,
2009, http://www.guardian.co.uk/world/2009/dec/28/billionth-african-future.

31. UNECA, *Assessing Regional Integration for Africa*, (Addis Ababa: Economic Commission for Africa, 2004), 24.

32. Ernest Harsch, "Making African Integration a Reality," *Africa Recovery* 16 no. 2–3
(September 2002): 10.

33. Paul Masson and Catherine Pattillo, *Monetary Union in West Africa: An Agency of
Restraint for Fiscal Policies?* (Washington DC: International Monetary Fund, December 21, 2001), 12.

34. Although the role of France in this North-South partnership is controversial at times,
the CFA has undoubtedly delivered currency stability, lower inflation rates, reduced
administrative costs, budgetary discipline, and a less risky business environment for
investors over the years.

35. "Regional Integration in Latin America: The Pacific Players Go to Market," *Economist*, April 7, 2011, http://www.economist.com/node/18529807.

36. Many of the ideas for this section are taken from or inspired by Chronic Poverty
Research Centre (CPRC), *The Chronic Poverty Report, 2008–09: Escaping Poverty
Traps*, Brooks World Poverty Institute, University of Manchester (Manchester:
CPRC, 2008), 67–68.

37. Jack A. Goldstone, "What If China's Economic Expansion Is about to Slow?"
Washington Post, April 14, 2011, http://www.washingtonpost.com/opinions/what-
if-chinas-economic-expansion-is-about-to-slow/2011/04/12/AF8BN6eD_story.html.

38. United Nations Population Division, *World Urbanization Prospects: The 2007 Revision Population Database*, http://esa.un.org/unup/.
39. George Packer, "The Megacity," *New Yorker*, November 13, 2006, http://www.newyorker.com/archive/2006/11/13/061113fa_fact_packer.
40. "A Rare Good Man: The Governor of Lagos Does His Job Well," *Economist*, May 5, 2011, http://www.economist.com/node/18652563.
41. Lieven, *Pakistan,* 319–20.
42. Duncan Green, "Can Cities Build Local 'Developmental States'? Some Surprising Good News from Colombia," *From Poverty to Power Blog*, August 26, 2011, http://www.oxfamblogs.org/fp2p/?p=6593.
43. CPRC, *The Chronic Poverty Report 2008–09*, 67.
44. Shahid Yusuf, "China Urbanizes: Consequences, Strategies, and Policies," *China Urban Development Quarterly*, Issue 5 (July–September, 2008), 8–10.
45. Rama Lakshmi, "India Unprepared for Urban Boom," *Washington Post*, July 8, 2011, http://www.washingtonpost.com/world/asia-pacific/india-unprepared-for-urban-boom/2011/07/03/gIQA9K3q3H_story.html.
46. "Brazil's North-East: Catching Up in a Hurry," *Economist*, May 19, 2011, http://www.economist.com/node/18712379.
47. Li Shi, "Rural Migrant Workers in China: Scenario, Challenges and Public Policy," Working Paper no. 89 (Geneva: International Labour Organization, 2008), 1.
48. Priya Deshingkar, Rajiv Khandelwal, and John Farrington, *Support for Migrant Workers: The Missing Link in India's Development*, Natural Resource Perspectives 117 (London: ODI, 2008), 3.

Chapter 10

1. Deepa Narayan, Lant Pritchett, and Soumya Kapoor, *Moving Out of Poverty: Success from the Bottom Up* (Washington DC: World Bank and Palgrave Macmillan, 2009), 187–88.
2. Ibid.
3. Narayan, Pritchett, and Kapoor, *Moving Out of Poverty*, 99–101.
4. Guillermo Perry, Omar Arias, J. Humberto López, William Maloney, and Luis Servén, *Poverty Reduction and Growth: Virtuous and Vicious Cycles* (Washington DC: World Bank, 2006), 150.
5. Amartya Sen, "Inequality and Institutions," *Pakistan's Daily Times*, July 14, 2008, http://www.dailytimes.com.pk/default.asp?page=2008%5C07%5C14%5Cstory_14-7-2008_pg3_4.
6. Anirudh Krishna, *One Illness Away: Why People Become Poor and How They Escape Poverty* (Oxford: Oxford University Press, 2010), 70.
7. World Bank, *World Development Report 2006* (Washington: World Bank, 2006), 148.
8. David Hulme and David Lawson, "What Works for the Poorest?" in David Lawson, David Hulme, Imran Matin, and Karen Moore, eds., *What Works for the Poorest? Poverty Reduction Programmes for the World's Extreme Poor* (Warwickshire, UK: Practical Action Publishing, 2010), 11–12.
9. Armando Barrientos, "Eradicating Extreme Poverty: The Child Solidario Programme," in Lawson, Hulme, Matin, and Moore, eds., *What Works for the Poorest?* table 8.1, 143.
10. Raj M. Desai and Shareen Joshi, "Can the Poor Be Organized? Evidence from Rural India," Brookings Global Economy and Development Working Paper 61, March 2013,

2–3, http://www.brookings.edu/~/media/Research/Files/Papers/2013/3/rural%20india%20poor%20desai/rural%20india%20poor%20desai.pdf.

11. Narayan, Pritchett, and Kapoor, *Moving Out of Poverty*, 280 and 282.

12. Narayan, Pritchett, and Kapoor, *Moving Out of Poverty*, 293.

13. David Brown, "Study: Mom's Education Level Is Connected to Child Mortality," *Washington Post*, September 17, 2010, A6.

14. Gary Haugen and Victor Boutros, "And Justice for All: Enforcing Human Rights for the World's Poor," *Foreign Affairs* 89 no. 3 (May/June 2010), 51–62.

15. Caroline Moser, *Ordinary Families, Extraordinary Lives: Assets and Poverty Reduction in Guayaquil, 1978–2004* (Washington DC: Brookings Institution, 2009), 44–45.

16. Andrew Shepherd, *Tackling Chronic Poverty: The Policy Implications of Research on Chronic Poverty and Poverty Dynamics* (Manchester, UK: Chronic Poverty Research Centre, 2011), 24.

17. Abhijit Banerjee and Esther Duflo, *Poor Economics: A Radical Rethinking of the Way to Fight Global Poverty* (New York: Public Affairs, 2011), 1.

18. Charles Kenny, *Learning about Schools in Development*, Working Paper 236 (Washington DC: Center for Global Development, 2010), 5.

19. Geeta Anand, "India Graduates Millions, But Too Few Are Fit to Hire," *Wall Street Journal*, April 5, 2011.

20. Banerjee and Duflo, *Poor Economics*, 91.

21. Ibid., 118.

22. "Music Videos Expand Literacy," *New York Times*, October 31, 2010, WK 2.

23. Banerjee and Duflo, *Poor Economics*, 96.

24. India Knowledge@Wharton, *Punj Lloyd's Atul Punj: Why Fixing Rural Infrastructure Is India's Top Priority*, August 15, 2010, http://knowledge.wharton.upenn.edu/india/article.cfm?articleid=4513.

25. Chronic Poverty Research Centre (CPRC), *The Chronic Poverty Report, 2008–09: Escaping Poverty Traps*, Brooks World Poverty Institute, University of Manchester (Manchester, UK: CPRC, 2008), 28. Also see, "Rural Development in Peru—The Andean Connection: Diminishing Distance, Falling Poverty," *Economist*, April 13, 2013, 40.

26. World Bank, *World Development Report 2006*, 169–70.

27. Ibid., 169.

28. World Bank Group, *Attacking Poverty: World Development Report 2000/2001* (Oxford: Oxford University Press, 2000), 3.

29. Krishna, *One Illness Away*, 89–90.

30. Ibid., 87 and 158.

31. "A Special Report on Latin America," *Economist*, September 11, 2010, 12.

32. Department for International Development (DFID) Policy Division, *Cash Transfers: Evidence Paper* (London: DFID, 2011).

33. Juan Forero, "Fast-Growing Brazil Tries to Lift Its Poorest," *Washington Post*, May 11, 2011.

34. Duncan Green, "'Just Give Money to the Poor: The Development Revolution from the Global South,' an Excellent Overview of Cash Transfers," May 24, 2010, http://www.oxfamblogs.org/fp2p/?p=2547.

35. "Record 128 Million of World's Poorest Received a Micro-Loan in 2009," *Microcredit Summit Campaign*, March 7, 2011, http://www.microcreditsummit.org/news/record_128_million_of_worlds_poorest_received_a_micro-loan_in_2009/.

36. Daniel Clarke, "What Have We Learned from All the Agricultural Microinsurance Pilots?" Centre for the Study of African Economies Blog, November 16, 2012, http://blogs.csae.ox.ac.uk/2012/11/what-have-we-learned-from-all-the-agricultural-microinsurance-pilots/.

37. See, for instance, http://www.microensure.com/.

38. Steven Radelet, *Emerging Africa: How 17 Countries Are Leading the Way* (Washington DC: Center for Global Development, 2010), 117–19.

39. "Revving Up the Pace: Petri-Dish Economies: Kenya," *Economist*, May 21, 2011, 80–81.

40. Banerjee and Duflo, *Poor Economics*, 66–68 and 268.

41. Krishna, *One Illness Away*, 139.

42. Ibid., 125–43, 161–62.

43. Charles Kenny, "Revolution in a Box," *Foreign Policy* (November/December 2009), http://www.foreignpolicy.com/articles/2009/10/19/revolution_in_a_box.

44. Inspired by Moser, *Ordinary Families, Extraordinary Lives*, table 2.1, 29.

45. Moser, *Ordinary Families, Extraordinary Lives*, xviii.

46. Ibid., 252–258.

Chapter 11

1. Panos London, "Hodat: Diversifying Business" (part of Panos London's *Living with Poverty* series of oral testimonies), http://panos.org.uk/resources/hodat-diversifying-business/.

2. Abhijit Banerjee and Esther Duflo, *Poor Economics: A Radical Rethinking of the Way to Fight Global Poverty* (New York: Public Affairs, 2011), 141–42.

3. Ibid, 135.

4. Claire Melamed, "After 2015: New Challenges for Development—Jobs and Growth," Overseas Development Institute event report, May 11, 2011, http://www.odi.org.uk/events/details.asp?id=2638&title=after-2015-new-challenges-development-jobs-growth#report.

5. As Adam Smith explained in *The Wealth of Nations*, "the division of labour" (in other words, specialization) is always limited "by the extent of the market. When the market is very small, no person can have any encouragement to dedicate himself entirely to one employment." Where specialization is possible, productivity rises, reducing the cost of goods and services for consumers and eventually creating the scale that can lead to large numbers of stable jobs. Adam Smith, *The Wealth of Nations* (New York: The Modern Library, 2000), 19–23. Also, see: http://geolib.com/smith.adam/won1-03.html.

6. Nassirou Bako Arifari, "'We Don't Eat the Papers': Corruption in Transport, Customs and the Civil Forces," in Giorgio Blundo and Jean-Pierre Olivier de Sardan (eds.), *Everyday Corruption and the State* (2006), 192.

7. Deepa Narayan, Lant Pritchett, and Soumya Kapoor, *Moving Out of Poverty: Success from the Bottom Up* (Washington DC: World Bank and Palgrave Macmillan, 2009), 214.

8. Deepa Narayan, Binayak Sen, and Katy Hull, "Moving Out of Poverty in India: An Overview," in ed. Narayan, *Moving Out of Poverty: The Promise of Empowerment and Democracy in India* (Washington DC: World Bank and Palgrave Macmillan, 2009), 46.

9. Arifari, "'We Don't Eat the Papers': Corruption in Transport, Customs and the Civil Forces," 192.

10. Daniel Yohannes and Mo Ibrahim, "Africa Is Awakening, Helped by Free Trade," *Wall Street Journal,* June 27, 2011, http://online.wsj.com/article/SB1000142405270 2304070104576398081888183032.html.

11. World Bank, *World Development Report 2011: Conflict, Security and Development* (Washington DC: World Bank, 2011), 5.

12. Economist Intelligence Unit (EIU), "Sub-Saharan Africa Economy: Closing the Infrastructure Gap," EIU Viewswire, June 28, 2011, http://viewswire.eiu.com/ index.asp?layout=VWPrintVW3&article_id=888249073&printer=printer.

13. World Bank, *World Development Report 2011,* 160.

14. "The Service Elevator: Can Poor Countries Leapfrog Manufacturing and Grow Rich on Services?," *Economist*, May 19, 2011, http://www.economist.com/node/ 18712351.

15. John Sfakianakis, "The Arab Spring Risks Economic Malaise," *Financial Times*, April 5, 2011, http://www.ft.com/cms/s/0/83410a60-5fb7-11e0-a718-00144feab49a. html#axzz1IlS7MIj6.

16. Rama Lakshmi, "India Tries to Boost Manufacturing," *Washington Post*, July 2, 2011, http://www.washingtonpost.com/world/india-tries-to-boost-manufacturing/ 2011/06/18/AGB7MQvH_story.html.

17. Alan Beattie, "US Plan Fails to End Africa's Trade Isolation," *Financial Times*, August 8, 2010, http://www.ft.com/cms/s/0/0fbe7cec-a321-11df-8cf4-00144feabdc0.html# axzz1Q0Ol6qoj.

18. World Bank, *World Development Report 2013* (Washington: World Bank, 2012), 105.

19. World Bank, *World Development Report 2006* (Washington: World Bank, 2005), 48.

20. See http://www.doingbusiness.org/ for more information.

21. This is the highest level typically associated with macroeconomic stability. It is also the figure used in the Tracking Development report noted later in the chapter.

22. Department for International Development (DFID), *The Engine of Development: The Private Sector and Prosperity for Poor People* (London: DFID, 2011), 12.

23. World Bank, "Doing Business: Rwanda in Top 20 Reformers Globally," September 25, 2008, http://web.worldbank.org/WBSITE/EXTERNAL/COUNTRIES/AFRI-CAEXT/RWANDAEXTN/0,,contentMDK:21916643~menuPK:368660~pagePK: 2865066~piPK:2865079~theSitePK:368651,00.htmlandhttp://www.doingbusiness .org/Custom-Query/rwanda.

24. Deborah Brautigam, Thomas Farole, and Tang Xiaoyang, "China's Investment in African Special Economic Zones: Prospects, Challenges, and Opportunities," *Economic Premise* 5 (Washington: World Bank, March 2010), http://www.worldbank. org/research/2010/03/11999239/chinas-investment-african-special-economic-zones-prospects-challenges-opportunities.

25. "Gujarat's Economy: India's Guangdong," *Economist*, July 7, 2011, http://www .economist.com/node/18929279.

26. Four-fifths of all extremely poor people in South Asia live in rural areas. http://www .un.org/apps/news/story.asp?NewsID=38149&Cr=asia-pacific&Cr1.

27. World Bank, *World Development Report 2008* (Washington: World Bank, 2008), 6.

28. Kanayo F. Nwanze, "Change Africa from Within," *Project Syndicate*, April 29, 2010, http://www.project-syndicate.org/commentary/nwanze2/English.

29. Booth, "Aid, Institutions and Governance: What Have We Learned?" DPR, S9.

30. CRS, *The Obama Administration's Feed the Future Initiative*, (January 10, 2011), 1.

31. Jan Kees van Donge, David Henley, and Peter Lewis, "Tracking Development in Southeast Asia and Sub-Saharan Africa: The Primacy of Policy," Draft Version, 9–12, http://www.institutions-africa.org/trackingdevelopment_archived/resources/docs/TD%20in%20SA%20and%20SSA_The%20primacy%20of%20policy.pdf.

32. van Donge, Henley, and Lewis, "Tracking Development in Southeast Asia and Sub-Saharan Africa," 9–11.

33. Wenge Fu, "China's Feed Industry in Transition: The Case of New Hope Group—An Industry Perspective," *Journal of Agribusiness in Developing and Emerging Economies* 1 no. 2 (2011), 162–78.

34. New Hope Group company website, http://www.newhopegroup.com/EN/AboutUs.aspx?CategoryID=23.

35. Yasheng Huang, "China"s True Economic Miracle," *The Globalist*, January 6, 2009, http://www.theglobalist.com/storyid.aspx?StoryId=7400.

36. China National Statistical Bureau, *China Statistical Yearbook 2010* (Beijing: China Statistical Press, 2010), http://www.enotes.com/topic/List_of_Chinese_administrative_divisions_by_GDP.

37. Yasheng Huang, "China's True Economic Miracle," *The Globalist*, January 6, 2009, http://www.theglobalist.com/storyid.aspx?StoryId=7400.

38. Shenggen Fan, Bingxin Yu, and Anuja Saurkar, "Public Spending in Developing Countries: Trends, Determination, and Impact," in Shenggen Fan (ed.), *Public Expenditures, Growth, and Poverty: Lessons from Developing Countries* (Baltimore: Johns Hopkins University Press, 2008).

39. van Donge, Henley, and Lewis, "Tracking Development in Southeast Asia and Sub-Saharan Africa," 9–10.

40. Samuel Benin, Adam Kennedy, Melissa Lambert, and Linden McBride, "Monitoring African Agricultural Development Processes and Performance: A Comparative Analysis," *Regional Strategic Analysis and Knowledge Support System (ReSAKSS) Annual Trends and Outlook Report 2010* (Washington DC: ReSAKSS, 2010), 22, www.resakss.org/index.php?pdf=50920.

41. "Brazil's Agricultural Miracle: How to Feed the World," *Economist*, August 26, 2010, http://www.economist.com/node/16889019.

42. Steven Haggblade and Peter Hazell (ed.), *Successes in African Agriculture: Lessons for the Future* (Baltimore: Johns Hopkins University Press, 2010).

43. Vivien Meli, "Bayam Sellam: Market Women and Rural Highway Insecurity in Cameroon," (London: International Forum for Rural Transport and Development, 2007), http://www.ifrtd.org/new/proj/safety/Cameroon.doc.

44. Charles Corey, "'Mo' Ibrahim: Governments Need to Foster, Not Frustrate, Business," Bureau of International Information Programs, U.S. Department of State, May 3, 2010, http://www.america.gov/st/business-english/2010/May/20100430155029WCyeroC9.975833e-02.html?CP.rss=true.

45. "Entrepreneurship in China: Let a Million Flowers Bloom," *Economist*, March 10, 2011, http://www.economist.com/node/18330120.

46. Justin Lin, "Economics Focus: Walk, Don't Run," *Economist*, July 9, 2009, http://www.economist.com/node/13986299.

47. Ibid.

48. "Entrepreneurship in China: Let a Million Flowers Bloom."

49. Mushtaq H. Khan, "Governance, Economic Growth, and Development Since the 1960s," United Nations Department of Economics and Social Affairs, Working Paper 54, August 2007, 4–5.

50. See, for instance, Justin Yifu Lin, "Choosing Countries as Models for Industrial Growth," February 1, 2001, http://blogs.worldbank.org/developmenttalk/choosing-countries-as-models-for-industrial-growth, and Justin Yifu Lin, "Why 'Securing Transformation' Matters in Development Economics," October 4, 2010, http://blogs.worldbank.org/developmenttalk/why-securing-transformation-matters-in-development-economics.
51. Khan, "Governance, Economic Growth, and Development Since the 1960s," 4.
52. Duncan Green, "A Surprising World Bank Recipe for Industrial Policy: New Proposal from Justin Lin," *From Poverty to Power* blog, http://www.oxfamblogs.org/fp2p/?p=2910.
53. Claire Melamed, Renate Hartwig, and Ursula Grant, "Jobs, Growth, and Poverty: What Do We Know, What Don't We Know, What Should We Know?" Background Note (London: Overseas Development Institute, May 2011), 3.
54. African Management Initiative, "Catalyzing Management Development in Africa: Identifying Areas for Impact," Johannesburg, 2011, executive summary, 3, and interview with Rebecca Harrison, who manages the African Management Initiative, January 2013.
55. Andres Oppenheimer, "Latin America in Denial about the Quality of Its Schools," *Miami Herald*, September 26, 2010, http://www.cleveland.com/opinion/index.ssf/2010/10/latin_america_in_denial_about.html.
56. World Bank, *World Development Report 2011*, 161.
57. "Technical and Vocational Education and Training," Canadian International Development Agency Background Paper, Ottawa, August 2, 2011, http://www.acdi-cida.gc.ca/acdi-cida/ACDI-CIDA.nsf/eng/NAT-824104736-KCT#al35.
58. "Human Resource Development Policy for Youth in Asia: Malaysia," Report of *Symposium on Globalization and the Future of Youth in Asia*, http://www.mhlw.go.jp/english/topics/globalization/report.html.
59. Simeon Djankov and Rita Ramalho, "Employment Laws in Developing Countries," *Journal of Comparative Economics* 37 no. 1 (March 2009), 12.
60. Ibid., 3–13.

Chapter 12

1. Most of this information comes from "BRAC in Business," *Economist*, February 18, 2010, http://www.economist.com/node/15546464. See also, David Hulme and Karen Moore, "Assisting the Poorest in Bangladesh: Learning from BRAC's 'Targeting the Ultra Poor' Programme," in David Lawson, David Hulme, Imran Matin, and Karen Moore, eds., *What Works for the Poorest? Poverty Reduction Programmes for the World's Extreme Poor* (Warwickshire, UK: Practical Action Publishing, 2010), 151; and Naomi Hossain, "Thinking Big, Going Global: A Southern NGO Takes on the World" (Institute of Development Studies, February 25, 2010), http://www.ids.ac.uk/go/news/thinking-big-going-global-a-southern-ngo-takes-on-the-world.
2. Institute of Development Studies (IDS), *An Upside-Down View of Governance* (Brighton, UK: IDS, 2010), 35–47; and David Booth, "Turning Governance Upside Down," *Development Policy Review* 29 no. 1 (January 2011): 118–20.
3. Caroline Moser, *Ordinary Families, Extraordinary Lives: Assets and Poverty Reduction in Guayaquil, 1978–2004* (Washington DC: Brookings Institution, 2009), xviii.
4. IDS, *An Upside View of Governance*, 60.

5. H. E. Ellen Johnson Sirleaf, "Inaugural Address," January 16, 2006, http://www .liberianliteracyfoundation.org/history/presidentellenjohnsonsirleafsinaugaraladdress .html.
6. IDS, *An Upside View of Governance*, 45.
7. World Bank, *World Development Report 2006* (Washington: World Bank, 2006), 50 and 71.
8. World Bank, *World Development Report 2006*, 50–51.
9. IDS, *An Upside View of Governance*, 38–43.
10. IDS, *An Upside View of Governance*, 35–47.
11. Shantayanan Devarajan, "Africa's Statistical Tragedy," *Africa Can . . . End Poverty* blog (hosted by the World Bank), October 6, 2011, http://blogs.worldbank.org/africacan/africa-s-statistical-tragedy.
12. Shantayanan Devarajan, Stuti Khemani, and Michael Walton, "Civil Society, Public Action, and Accountability in Africa," HKS Faculty Research Working Paper Series RWP11-036, John F. Kennedy School of Government, Harvard University, 2011, 26.
13. Charles Griffin, et al. [six authors], *Lives in the Balance: Improving Accountability for Public Spending in Developing Countries* (Washington: Results for Development Institute and Brookings Institutions Press, 2010), 15 and 98–102.
14. Abhijit Banerjee and Esther Duflo, *Poor Economics: A Radical Rethinking of the Way to Fight Global Poverty* (New York: Public Affairs, 2011), 75, 84–86, and 90–98.
15. Abhijit Banerjee and Esther Duflo, *Poor Economics*, 253.
16. David Hulme and Karen Moore, "Assisting the Poorest in Bangladesh: Learning from BRAC's 'Targeting the Ultra Poor' Programme,'" 149–63.
17. John Blaxall, "India's Self-Employed Women's Association (SEWA)—Empowerment through Mobilization of Poor Women on a Large Scale," a case study presented at Scaling Up Poverty Reduction: A Global Learning Process and Conference, Shanghai, May 25–27, 2004.
18. Gita Sen, "Empowerment as an Approach to Poverty," Background Paper to the *Human Development Report 1997* (December 1997), 10–11.
19. Abhijit Banerjee and Esther Duflo, *Poor Economics*, 78–79.
20. Lydia Polgreen, "Business Class Rises in Ashes of Caste System," *New York Times*, September 11, 2010, http://www.nytimes.com/2010/09/11/world/asia/11caste.html.
21. Rhett Butler, "A Long-Term Approach to Helping the Poor in Africa through Private Enterprise," www. mongabay.com, May 24, 2005, http://news.mongabay .com/2005/0705-poverty.html.
22. Eric Bellman, "Indian Firms Shift Focus to the Poor," *Wall Street Journal*, October 21, 2009, http://online.wsj.com/article/SB125598988906795035.html.
23. Andres Oppenheimer, "Improving Brazil's Education System Shouldn't Be Left to Government," *Miami Herald*, October 2, 2010, http://www.mcclatchydc .com/2010/10/09/101619/commentary-improving-brazils-education.html.
24. Juan Forero, "Firms Open Alternatives to Weak Brazilian Schools," *Washington Post*, April 16, 2011, http://www.washingtonpost.com/world/firms-open-alternatives-to-weak-brazilian-schools/2011/04/16/AFHjbeKE_story.html.
25. Abhijit Banerjee and Esther Duflo, *Poor Economics*, 228–29.
26. G. Pascal Zachary, "Do Business and Islam Mix? Ask Him," *New York Times,* July 8, 2007, http://www.nytimes.com/2007/07/08/business/yourmoney/08khan.html?pagewanted=all.

27. Greg Mills, *Why Africa Is Poor,* (Johannesburg: Penguin Books, 2010), 370–71.
28. Steven Radelet, *Emerging Africa: How 17 Countries Are Leading the Way* (Washington DC: Center for Global Development, 2010), 128–29.
29. Lydia Polgreen, "Scanning 2.4 Billion Eyes, India Tries to Connect Poor to Growth," *New York Times*, September 2, 2011, http://www.nytimes.com/2011/09/02/world/asia/02india.html?pagewanted=all.
30. See http://www.prsindia.org/aboutus/objectives/.
31. Radelet, *Emerging Africa*, 132–33.
32. Patrick Awuah, "Patrick Awuah on Educating Leaders," *Ted Talks*, June 2007, www.ted.com/talks/patrick_awuah_on_educating_leaders.html.
33. See company introduction on http://www.linkedin.com/company/acumen-fund.
34. See http://www.akdn.org/about.asp.
35. Sabrina Tavernise, "Afghan Enclave Seen as Model for Development," *New York Times,* November 13, 2009, http://www.nytimes.com/2009/11/13/world/asia/13jurm.html?pagewanted=all.
36. Justin van Fleet and Rebecca Winthrop, "Corporate Philanthropy and Social Responsibility: Enhancing Global Education," Brookings Institution Up Front Blog, March 31, 2011, http://www.brookings.edu/blogs/up-front/posts/2011/03/31-corporate-philanthropy-fleet-winthrop.
37. "MNCs in Rural India: At a Turning Point," India Knowledge@Wharton, May 6, 2010, http://knowledge.wharton.upenn.edu/india/article.cfm?articleid=4472.
38. For more information, see http://www.roomtoread.org/page.aspx?pid=183.
39. Celia Dugger, "Doctors Go Far Afield to Battle Epidemics," *New York Times*, April 3, 2011, http://www.nytimes.com/2011/04/03/world/africa/03aids.html?pagewanted=all.

Chapter 13

1. Jeffrey Sachs, *The End of Poverty: Economic Possibilities for Our Time* (London: Penguin Press, 2005), 56–57.
2. Sachs, *The End of Poverty*, 250.
3. William Easterly, "The Effectiveness of Foreign Aid," *Council on Foreign Relations Online Debate*, December 1, 2006, http://www.cfr.org/foreign-aid/effectiveness-foreign-aid/p12077.
4. Steve Radelet, "The Effectiveness of Foreign Aid," *Council on Foreign Relations Online Debate*, December 1, 2006, http://www.cfr.org/foreign-aid/effectiveness-foreign-aid/p12077.
5. Bill Gates, "The Real Successes of Foreign Aid," *Wall Street Journal*, May 21, 2011, http://online.wsj.com/article/SB10001424052748703509104576331251275217720.html.
6. Charles Frank Jr., Kwang Suk Kim, Larry Westphal, *Foreign Trade Regimes and Economic Development: South Korea* (Cambridge, MA: National Bureau of Economic Research, 1975), 12.
7. Wiliam Easterly, "Can the West Save Africa?" *Journal of Economic Literature* 47 no. 2 (June 2009): 406–07.
8. Gates, "The Real Successes of Foreign Aid."
9. Gates, "The Real Successes of Foreign Aid."
10. See http://www.norad.no/en/thematic-areas/energy/oil-for-development.
11. William Easterly and Tobias Pfutze, "Where Does the Money Go? Best and Worst Practices in Foreign Aid," *Journal of Economic Perspectives* 22 no. 2 (Spring 2008): 15–23.

12. Figure 6.2 in the 2011 *World Development Report* portrays the same problem in a different way. World Bank, *World Development Report, 2011: Conflict, Security and Development* (Washington DC: World Bank, 2011), 201.

13. Andrew Natsios, "The Clash of the Counter-Bureaucracy and Development," *Center for Global Development Essay* (Washington: CGD, July 2010), i, 3, 5, http://www.cgdev.org/content/publications/detail/1424271.

14. Paul Farmer, "Partners in Help: Assisting the Poor over the Long Term," *Foreign Affair*, July 29, 2011, http://www.foreignaffairs.com/articles/68002/paul-farmer/partners-in-help.

15. Natsios, "The Clash of the Counter-Bureaucracy and Development," 11.

16. See http://www.worldvision.org/.

17. Natsios, "The Clash of the Counter-Bureaucracy and Development," 48–49 and 60–61.

18. Robert Guth, "Gates Rethinks His War on Polio," *Wall Street Journal*, April 23, 2010, http://online.wsj.com/article/SB1000142405270230334850457518409323 9615022.html.

19. Laurie Garrett, "The Challenge of Global Health," *Foreign Affairs* 86 no. 1 (January/February 2007), http://www.foreignaffairs.com/articles/62268/laurie-garrett/the-challenge-of-global-health.

20. Lindsay Whitfield, "Reframing the Aid Debate: Why Aid Isn't Working and How It Should Be Changed," DIIS Working Paper 2009:34 (Copenhagen: Danish Institute for International Studies, 2009), 9.

21. Peter van Lieshout, Robert Went, and Monique Kremer, *Less Pretension, More Ambition. Development Aid That Makes a Difference* [Dutch] (Scientific Council for Government Policy, January 22, 2010), http://www.thebrokeronline.eu/en/layout/set/print/Articles/WRR-report-Less-pretension-more-ambition.-Development-aid-that-makes-a-difference, conclusion and summary translated online, http://www.thebrokeronline.eu/en/Magazine/articles/Conclusion-Less-pretension-more-ambition and http://www.thebrokeronline.eu/en/Magazine/articles/WRR-report-Less-pretension-more-ambition.-Development-aid-that-makes-a-difference (accessed January 2012). The full report is at http://www.wrr.nl/en/publicaties/publicatie/article/minder-pretentie-meer-ambitie/.

22. Centre for the Future State, *An Upside Down View of Governance* (Brighton, UK: IDS, 2010), 1–2.

23. Centre for the Future State, *An Upside Down View of Governance,* 69.

24. David Booth, "Governance for Development in Africa: Building on What Works," Policy Brief 1 (London: Africa Power and Politics Programme Policy, April 2011), 1.

25. Dennis de Tray, "Only an Aid Rethink Can Save Afghanistan," *Financial Times*, June 15, 2011, http://www.ft.com/intl/cms/s/0/9590300e-979f-11e0-9c37-00144feab49a.html#axzz1Qr2yvxka.

26. Frances Stewart, Graham K. Brown, and Arnim Langer, "Major Findings and Conclusions on the Relationship between Horizontal Inequities and Conflict," in *Horizontal Inequities and Conflict,* ed. Frances Stewart (New York: Palgrave Macmillan, 2008), 299–300.

27. I am referring here to the "Structural Adjustment Loans" that insist on policy changes in return for cash. William Easterly, "The Effect of IMF and World Bank Programs on Poverty," WIDER Discussion Paper no. 2001/102, http://papers.ssrn.com/sol3/papers.cfm?abstract_id=256883.

28. Chronic Poverty Research Centre, "The Chronic Poverty Report, 2008–09" (Manchester: CPRC, 2009), 22–36, http://www.chronicpoverty.org/publications/details/the-chronic-poverty-report-2008-09.

29. See, among others, Adrian Leftwich, "Developmental States, Effective States and Poverty Reduction: The Primacy of Politics," United Nations Research Institute for Social Development Project on Poverty Reduction and Policy Regimes (Geneva: UNRISD, 2008).

30. Booth, "Governance for Development in Africa," 2.

31. Sarah Cliffe, presentation at the Overseas Development Institute's event "Towards a Responsible State: Building Legitimate and Accountable Institutions" held in London, November 12, 2009, http://www.odi.org.uk/events/details. asp?id=2060&title=towards-responsible-state-building-legitimate-accountable-institutions#report.

32. Duncan Green, "Can States Empower Poor People? Your Thoughts Please," *From Poverty to Power Blog*, June 26, 2013, http://www.oxfamblogs.org/fp2p/?p=15041.

33. Shantayanan Devarajan, Stuti Khemani, and Michael Walton, "Civil Society, Public Action, and Accountability in Africa," HKS Faculty Research Working Paper Series RWP11-036, John F. Kennedy School of Government, Harvard University, 2011, 32.

34. Toby Poston, "The Battle to Rebuild Afghanistan," *BBC News*, February 26, 2006, http://news.bbc.co.uk/2/hi/business/4714116.stm.

35. The figures include nonprofits, investment funds, and stand-alone arrangements within larger legal entities. See Geoff Handley, Kate Higgins, and Bhavna Sharma, *Poverty and Poverty Reduction in Sub-Saharan Africa: An Overview of the Issues*, Working Paper 299 (London: Overseas Development Institute, January 2009), 28–29.

36. World Bank, *World Development Report, 2011: Conflict, Security and Development* (Washington DC: World Bank, 2011), 25.

37. Tony Blair, *Not Just Aid: How Making Government Work Can Transform Africa* (public address at the Center for Global Development, Washington DC, December 16, 2010), 13.

38. Bob Davis, "World Bank Chief Ignites a Debate," *Wall Street Journal*, September 30, 2010, http://online.wsj.com/article/SB10001424052748703431604575521940492730342.html.

39. Van Lieshout, Went, and Kremer, *Less Pretension, More Ambition*.

40. Edmund Kagire, "Rwanda: Trade and Investment Key to Development—Kagame," *New Times* (Rwanda), June 9, 2011, http://allafrica.com/stories/201106090377.html.

41. Lydia Polgreen, "Scanning 2.4 Billion Eyes, India Tries to Connect Poor to Growth," *New York Times*, September 1, 2011, http://www.nytimes.com/2011/09/02/world/asia/02india.html?pagewanted=all.

42. Canadian International Development Agency, "Background Paper: Technical and Vocational Education and Training," (n.d.) http://www.acdi-cida.gc.ca/acdi-cida/acdi-cida.nsf/eng/NAT-824104736-KCT.

43. George Ayittey, "Julius Nyerere: A Saint or a Knave?" *Wall Street Journal* (European edition), October 20, 1999, 12.

44. Yash Tandon suggested something similar in *Ending Aid Dependence* (Cape Town: Fahamu Books, 2008).

45. Comments by Andrew Natsios, April 2013.

46. Natsios, "The Clash of the Counter-Bureaucracy and Development," 3.

47. Ibid., 15 and 64.

48. Sarah Jane Staats, "Not Your Father's USAID," Rethinking US Foreign Assistance Blog, Center for Global Development, March 25, 2013, http://www.cgdev.org/blog/not-your-fathers-usaid?utm_&&&.

49. See http://www.foundation-partnership.org/about.php.

50. See http://www.hewlett.org/programs/global-development-and-population-program/research-policy-analysis-advocacy/think-tanks.

51. Sam Dillon, "Behind Grass-Roots School Advocacy, Bill Gates," *New York Times*, May 21, 2011, http://www.nytimes.com/2011/05/22/education/22gates.html.

52. Nathaniel Fick, "The Economic Imperative: Stabilizing Afghanistan through Economic Growth," Center for a New American Security Policy Brief (Washington DC: CNAS, April 2010), 4, http://www.cnas.org/node/4335.

53. Connie Veillette, "DFID Rocks: A New UK AID Report Promises More Focus— Will the United States Follow?" *Center for Global Development Rethinking US Foreign Assistance Blog*, March 4, 2011, http://blogs.cgdev.org/mca-monitor/2011/03/dfid-rocks-a-new-uk-aid-report-promises-more-focus-will-the-united-states-follow.php.

54. Annie Kelly, "Winners and Losers in the UK Aid Review," *The Guardian Poverty Matters Blog*, March 1, 2011, http://www.guardian.co.uk/global-development/poverty-matters/2011/mar/01/winners-losers-uk-aid-review-reaction.

55. Rizza Leonzon, "Netherlands Plans More Focused Aid Sector Priorities," *Devex Development Newswire*, March 22, 2011, http://www.devex.com/en/blogs/the-development-newswire/netherlands-plans-to-narrow-aid-sector-priorities.

56. Kelly, "Winners and Losers in the UK Aid Review."

57. For an overview, with many concrete examples of the work of "groups of friends," see Teresa Whitfield, *Working with Groups of Friends*, Peacemaker's Toolkit (Washington DC: United States Institute of Peace, 2010).

58. Stephanie Strom, "Nonprofits Review Technology Failures," *New York Times*, August 16, 2010, http://www.nytimes.com/2010/08/17/technology/17fail.html.

59. See Organisation for Economic Co-operation and Development (OECD), "Development: Aid to Developing Countries Falls Because of Global Recession," http://www.oecd.org/newsroom/developmentaidtodevelopingcountriesfallsbecauseofglobalrecession.htm.

60. Devarajan, Khemani, and Walton, "Civil Society, Public Action, and Accountability in Africa," 33.

Chapter 14

1. Anirudh Krishna, *One Illness Away: Why People Become Poor and How They Escape Poverty* (Oxford: Oxford University Press, 2010), 9–11.

2. Madeleine Bunting, "Corruption Has to Be Confronted from the Grassroots," *Guardian*, May 6, 2011, http://www.guardian.co.uk/global-development/poverty-matters/2011/may/06/corruption-confronted-grassroots-john-githongo-kenya.

3. These four questions have their roots in a 2011 discussion I had with Simon Maxwell, the former director of the Overseas Development Institute in London.

4. David Leonhardt, "In China, Cultivating the Urge to Splurge," *New York Times*, November 24, 2010, http://www.nytimes.com/2010/11/28/magazine/28China-t.html?pagewanted=all.

5. Andres Oppenheimer, "Latin America's Bonanza May Be Short-Lived," *Miami Herald*, January 6, 2011, http://www.cleveland.com/opinion/index.ssf/2011/01/latin_americas_bonanza_may_be.html.

6. Ibid.

7. World Trade Organization, World and Regional Export Profiles 2011, October 2012, http://www.wto.org/english/res_e/statis_e/world_region_export_11_e.pdf.

8. Africa Partnership Forum and the NEPAD Secretariat, "Investment: Unlocking Africa's Potential," Briefing Paper no. 2, based on a paper presented to the Eighth Meeting of the Africa Partnership Forum in Berlin, Germany, May 22–23, 2007.

9. Rebecca Holmes and Eliana Villar, "Social Protection to Tackle Child Poverty in Equatorial Guinea," ODI Project Briefings Issue 24 (London: Overseas Development Institute, 2009), 1.

10. Ibid., 1; and "Equatorial Guinea's Corruption Scandal: African Poverty, Mansions, and the California Sun?" *Global Development: Views from the Center* blog, November 16, 2006, http://blogs.cgdev.org/globaldevelopment/2006/11/equatorial-guineas-corruption.php.

11. Amartya Sen, "Inequality and Institutions," *Daily Times* (Pakistan), July 14, 2008, http://www.microcapital.org/new-wire-pakistan-harvards-amartya-sen-discusses-inequality-and-institutions/.

12. Nathalie Bouché, Carl Riskin, et al., "The Macroeconomics of Poverty Reduction: The Case of China," United Nations Development Programme Asia-Pacific Regional Programme on Macroeconomics of Poverty Reduction, Beijing, 2004, 12.

13. Joseph Stiglitz, "Reducing Poverty: Some Lessons from the Last Quarter Century," (presentation at the Chronic Poverty Research Centre International Conference 2010, Manchester, UK, September 8, 2010).

14. Brian Levy, "The Case for Principled Agnosticism," *Journal of Democracy* 21 no. 4 (October 2010): 30–31.

15. This box draws heavily on Overseas Development Institute (ODI), *Mapping Progress: Evidence for a New Development Outlook*, Progress in Development: A Library of Stories project (London: ODI, 2011), 42 and 46, www.developmentprogress.org.

16. Daniel Berhane, "Ethiopia: 3rd Fastest HDI Growth Rate in the World [Human Development Report 2010]," *Danielberhane's Blog*, November 6, 2010, http://danielberhane.wordpress.com/2010/11/06/ethiopia-3rd-fastest-hdi-growth-rate-in-the-world-human-development-report-2010/.

17. Jakob Engel, "Ethiopia's Progress in Education: A Rapid and Equitable Expansion of Access," Development Progress (London: ODI, 2011), 7.

18. IndexMundi, "Ethiopia GDP: Real Growth Rate," http://www.indexmundi.com/ethiopia/gdp_real_growth_rate.html.

19. "The Lion Kings?" *Economist*, January 6, 2011, http://www.economist.com/node/17853324.

20. Chronic Poverty Research Centre, *The Chronic Poverty Report, 2008–09: Escaping Poverty Traps* (Manchester, UK: CPRC, 2008), 30–31.

21. ODI, *Mapping Progress*, 26.

22. Ibid., 16 and 25.

23. Samuel P. Huntington, "Political Development and Political Decay," *World Politics* 17 no. 3 (April 1965): 393–94.

24. Francis Fukuyama, *The Origins of Political Order: From Prehuman Times to the French Revolution* (New York: Farrar, Straus and Giroux, 2011), 250.

25. Tony Blair, *Not Just Aid: How Making Government Work Can Transform Africa* (public address at the Center for Global Development, Washington DC, December 16, 2010), 10.

26. David Booth, "Development as a Collective Action Problem: Addressing the Real Challenges of African Governance," Synthesis Report of the Africa Power and Politics Programme (London: Overseas Development Institute, 2012), www.institutions-africa.org.

27. Many of these ideas come from Douglass North, John Wallis, Steven Webb, and Barry Weingast, *In the Shadow of Violence: Politics, Economics, and the Problems of Development* (Cambridge, MA: Cambridge University Press, 2012).
28. This section borrows from World Bank, *World Development Report 2011: Conflict, Security and Development* (Washington DC: World Bank, 2011), 12–16, 21, 115, 190, and 206.
29. John L. Adedeji, "The Legacy of J. J. Rawlings in Ghanaian Politics, 1979–2000," *African Studies Quarterly* 5 no. 2 (2001): 1, http://www.africa.ufl.edu/asq/v5/v5i2a1.htm.
30. Paul Farmer, "Partners in Help: Assisting the Poor over the Long Term," *Foreign Affairs*, July 29, 2011, http://www.foreignaffairs.com/articles/68002/paul-farmer/partners-in-help.
31. John McKay, "The Asian 'Miracle' after the Global Financial Crisis: Some Lessons for Africa: A Retrospective Analysis & Critical Evaluation of the Asian Model of Development," Discussion Paper 2010/7 (Marshalltown, South Africa: Brenthurst Foundation, 2010), 21–22.
32. Meles Zenawi, "African Development: Dead Ends and New Beginnings," (unpublished MA diss., Erasmus University, Rotterdam, no date), 39. Quoted in Alex de Waal, "The Theory and Practice of Meles Zenawi," *African Affairs*, December 5, 2012, http://afraf.oxfordjournals.org/content/early/2012/12/04/afraf.ads081.full?keytype=ref&ijkey=NBplmdUjEpY2AIv.

Index

280 • Index